EXPLOITATION

Key Concepts in Critical Theory
Series Editor
Roger S. Gottlieb

JUSTICE
Edited by Milton Fisk

DEMOCRACY
Edited by Philip Green

ALIENATION AND SOCIAL CRITICISM
Edited by Richard Schmitt and Thomas E. Moody

GENDER
Edited by Carol C. Gould

ECOLOGY
Edited by Carolyn Merchant

EXPLOITATION
Edited by Kai Nielsen and Robert Ware

Key Concepts in Critical Theory

EXPLOITATION

EDITED BY

Kai Nielsen and Robert Ware

HUMANITIES PRESS

NEW JERSEY

First published in 1997 by
Humanities Press International, Inc.,
165 First Avenue, Atlantic Highlands, New Jersey 07716.

Library of Congress Cataloging-in-Publication Data

Exploitation / edited by Kai Nielsen and Robert Ware.
    p.   cm. — (Key concepts in critical theory)
    Includes bibliographical references and index.
    ISBN 0–391–04000–6 (paper)
    1. Marxian economics.   I. Nielsen, Kai, 1926–
II. Ware, Robert.   III. Series.
HB97.5.E889   1997
335.4—dc20   96–19782
                                       CIP

Printed in the United States of America

10 9 8 7 6 5 4 3 2 1

CONTENTS

Series Editor's Preface   vii

Introduction: What Exploitation Comes To
    Kai Nielsen and Robert Ware   ix

PART I: THE GENERAL IDEA OF EXPLOITATION

1   Exploitation
        Allen W. Wood   2

2   Exploitation, Freedom, and Justice
        Jon Elster   27

3   A Democratic Theory of Economic Exploitation
    Dialectically Developed
        David Schweickart   49

PART II: MARXIAN EXPLOITATION

4   Exploitation
        Anwar Shaikh   70

5   Exploitation
        Nancy Holmstrom   76

PART III: MARXIAN EXPLOITATION UNDER DEBATE

6   The Labor Theory of Value and the Concept of
    Exploitation
        G. A. Cohen   94

7   Should Marxists Be Interested in Exploitation?
        John E. Roemer   122

8   Exploitation, Force, and the Moral Assessment of
    Capitalism: Thoughts on Roemer and Cohen
        Jeffrey Reiman   154

9   What Is Exploitation? Reply to Jeffrey Reiman
        John E. Roemer   189

10   Roemer versus Marx: Alternative Perspectives on
      Exploitation
             Gary A. Dymski and John E. Elliott   197

11   *Ne Hic Saltaveris*: The Marxian Theory of
      Exploitation after Roemer
             Gilbert L. Skillman   208

      PART IV: EXPLOITATION AND FEMINISM

12   The One-Sidedness of Wage Labor
             Michael A. Lebowitz   232

13   Exploitation Comes Home: A Critique of the Marxian
      Theory of Family Labor
             Nancy Folbre   246

14   Social Origins of the Sexual Division of Labor
             Maria Mies   264

15   Sex and Work
             Ann Ferguson   272

16   Feeding Egos and Tending Wounds
             Sandra Lee Bartky   281

      PART V: EXPLOITATION EXTENDED

17   Capitalism, Nature, Peasants, and Women:
      Contemporary Problems of Marxism
             Gail Omvedt   294

18   Exploitation in the Periphery
             Samir Amin   305

19   International Oligopoly Capitalism and
      Superexploitation
             Guglielmo Carchedi   315

20   Marxism and Ecology
             Juan Martinez-Alier   326

21   Racial Inequality and Capitalist Exploitation
             Gary A. Dymski   335

      Bibliography   348
      Index   355

SERIES EDITOR'S PREFACE

THE VISION OF A rational, just, and fulfilling social life, present in Western thought from the time of the Judaic prophets and Plato's *Republic*, has since the French Revolution been embodied in systematic *critical theories* whose adherents seek a fundamental political, economic, and cultural transformation of society.

These critical theories—varieties of Marxism, socialism, anarchism, feminism, gay/lesbian liberation, ecological perspectives, discourses by antiracist, anti-imperialist, and national liberation movements, and utopian/critical strains of religious communities—have a common bond that separates them from liberal and conservative thought. They are joined by the goal of sweeping social change; the rejection of existing patterns of authority, power, and privilege; and a desire to include within the realms of recognition and respect the previously marginalized and oppressed.

Yet each tradition of critical theory also has its distinct features: specific concerns, programs, and locations within a geometry of difference and critique. Because of their intellectual specificity and the conflicts among the different social groups they represent, these theories have often been at odds with one another, differing over basic questions concerning the ultimate cause and best response to injustice, the dynamics of social change, the optimum structure of a liberated society, the identity of the social agent who will direct the revolutionary change, and in whose interests the revolutionary change will be made.

In struggling against what is to some extent a common enemy, in overlapping and (at times) allying in the pursuit of radical social change, critical theories to a great extent share a common conceptual vocabulary. It is the purpose of this series to explore that vocabulary, revealing what is common and what is distinct, in the broad spectrum of radical perspectives.

For instance, although both Marxists and feminists may use the word "exploitation," it is not clear that they really are describing the same phenomenon. In the Marxist paradigm the concept identifies the surplus labor appropriated by the capitalist as a result of the wage-labor relation. Feminists have used the same term to refer as well to the unequal amounts of housework, emotional nurturance, and child raising performed by women in the nuclear family. We see some similarity in the notion of group inequality (capitalists/workers, husbands/wives) and of unequal exchange. But we also see critical differences: a previously "public" concept extended to the private realm; one first centered in the economy of goods now moved into the life of emotional relations. Or, for another example, when deep ecologists speak of "alienation" they may be exposing the contradictory and destructive relations of humans to nature. For socialists and anarchists, by contrast, "alienation" basically refers only to relations among human beings. Here we find a profound contrast between what is and is not included in the basic arena of politically significant relationships.

What can we learn from exploring the various ways different radical perspectives utilize the same terminology?

Most important, we see that these key concepts have histories and that the theories of which they are a part and the social movements whose spirit they embody take shape through a process of political struggle as well as of intellectual reflection. As a corollary, we can note that the creative tension and dissonance among the different uses of these concepts stem not only from the endless play of textual interpretation (the different understandings of classic texts, attempts to refute counterexamples or remove inconsistencies, rereadings of history, reactions to new theories), but also from the continual movement of social groups. Oppression, domination, resistance, passion, and hope are crystallized here. The feminist expansion of the concept of exploitation could only grow out of the women's movement. The rejection of a purely anthropocentric (human-centered, solely humanistic) interpretation of alienation is a fruit of people's resistance to civilization's lethal treatment of the biosphere.

Finally, in my own view at least, surveys of the differing applications of these key concepts of critical theory provide compelling reasons to see how complementary, rather than exclusive, the many radical perspectives are. Shaped by history and embodying the spirit of the radical movements that created them, these varying applications each have in them some of the truth we need in order to face the darkness of the current social world and the ominous threats to the earth.

ROGER S. GOTTLIEB

INTRODUCTION

What Exploitation Comes To

KAI NIELSEN AND ROBERT WARE

WHEN PEOPLE ARE EXPLOITED they are used, typically in a coercive and unjust way. The concept of exploitation is generally applied pejoratively to relations between people. Bosses exploit workers. Domineering people exploit the dominated. Adults exploit children. In common discourse, the concept is used, often vaguely, to make a variety of moral charges. It has also been used in more technical and theoretical ways, usually in a condemnatory way. Critical social theory requires careful attention to the different ways in which the concept of exploitation has been used and to the contribution it makes to our understanding of society and especially political economies. There is a renewed and vigorous debate about the concept, and as the essays in this anthology show there are important extensions of the concept that have broad implications for critical theory in general.

The word "exploitation" comes from the early nineteenth century.[1] It arose in the interstices of the battles between the owners of the means of production and workers. Karl Marx was the premier theorist of the capitalist exploitation of workers, who, he said, became wage slaves alienated by the productive process. The concept of exploitation continued to be important throughout the century following Marx's publication of *Capital*, volume 1, in 1867.[2]

The late twentieth century has seen interesting and challenging debates about exploitation with the flowering of Marxist writings and with new developments in Marxian scholarship over the last couple of decades. These recent debates have deepened our understanding of exploitation in the economy, but they have also reached out to aspects of exploitation about which Marx had very little to say, such as exploitation in the home, in international trade, of the environment, of race, and in socialist societies.

This anthology draws largely on the lively debates of the last decade about the nature and extension of exploitation. We have had to make difficult compromises in order to present a reasonably comprehensive selection of topics and positions. The reader will see there are a number of criss-crossing debates about the concept of exploitation and about how to theorize about its extension. Especially in the section on "Marxian Exploitation under Debate," there is a continuing debate, much of which is focused on the seminal work of John Roemer. This debate will not finish with the work reprinted here. As our bibliography reveals, there is a growing literature on the subject. Much of the work on exploitation is cumulative, as progressively more adequate accounts of exploitation are developed.

Unfortunately, we have had to give less attention to some issues than we would have liked and none at all to some important ones, for example, that of exploitation under socialism. More generally, it should be noted that there is much debate relevant to the issue of exploitation that we cannot begin to explore here. Thinking only of economic exploitation, there is important literature on the nature of value and its relations to prices. There is also much in the literature on feminism and on imperialism that is relevant to the material reprinted here. We hope that the bibliography will provide some guidance where we have had to neglect areas of important discussion.

It is appropriate for a volume like this, and indicative of the complexity of the topic and the richness of the contemporary debate, that the coeditors are themselves undecided and ambivalent about many central issues in the debate. Moreover, we differ with each other in our own views, but we are in agreement about the importance and interest of the essays collected here. We hope that readers will agree that this collection contains rich debate that will prompt new developments and speculations.

Often, but not invariably, the words "exploit" and "exploitation" are used in a morally charged way. In many linguistic environments these words imply or at least suggest that some mistreatment has occurred. However, the terms "exploit" and "exploitation" do not have a negative emotive force in sentences such as "A mine is exploited for its minerals" or "The chess player exploited her opponent's opening." Dictionaries give these normatively neutral uses as well as the morally charged ones—the pejorative uses.[3]

The contrast between the normatively neutral and the normatively non-neutral uses of "exploit" comes out distinctly in the following Oxford English Dictionary entries for "exploitation": (1) "the action of turning to account" and (2) "the action of utilizing for selfish purposes." It is even more tersely expressed in the Gage Dictionary where "exploitation" is (1) "use" and (2) "selfish or unfair use."

If the dictionaries and our common intuitions (linguistic and otherwise) are right about there being these two concepts of exploitation, or at least uses of the term, we will want to know what the moral force of the normative use of the term is and what the unfair use of something is where there is exploitation. We also want to know whether exploitation (in the negative moral sense) is a necessary part of capitalism, even in societies such as Sweden, where capitalism has a more "human face." Marxists have usually claimed that it is a necessary part of capitalism, whether it be a matter of definition or a matter of fact. And most classical Marxists have gone on to claim, however problematically, that socialist societies will be free of exploitation. Those claims introduce considerations about exploitation that go far beyond conceptual intuitions, which in any case, according to Marxists, could be ideologically distorted.

Marx himself had a technical conception of exploitation which was based on his labor theory of value and his corollary account of surplus value. According to Marx, exploitation in capitalism is the appropriation of the surplus value (and surplus product) of the class of workers by a class of nonworkers who are also the principal owners of the means of production. (See the essays by Anwar Shaikh and Nancy Holmstrom in this volume.) There is also the nontechnical normative use of "exploitation" employed by many Marxists (following a common usage by Marx). On this use, exploitation involves an exercise of power by some over others to the disadvantage, including extensive harm, domination, and oppression, of the less powerful. All of these things are at least prima facie wrong.

Before considering the normative concept of exploitation, we will comment on the technical concept of exploitation that classically was based on the labor theory of value, which many in the contemporary debate, including some leading Marxists, reject. In this collection, the rejection of the labor theory of value is made most explicitly by G. A. Cohen, John Roemer, and Jon Elster. Though they take different positions among themselves about the nature and relevance of exploitation, they agree that capitalist societies are exploitative and unjust. Indeed all the authors in this volume who discuss economic exploitation condemn capitalism in one way or another for being exploitative. Still there is much dispute about what is to be condemned in the exploitation. Some of the dispute centers on the question of whether capitalism is *unjust* (see Elster's essay). There are also conceptual differences about whether or not exploitation necessarily involves force or coercion (see Jeffrey Reiman and Roemer's reply).

Another important debate represented in this collection revolves around rather more general theoretical and methodological differences. Gary Dymski and John Elliott are critical of Roemer's property relations account of exploitation, which focuses on unequal distribution of property. They regard it a mistake to treat the concept of exploitation as redundant, which, in their judgment, eliminates much of the critical social relevance from Marx's theory. They agree with Roemer that the question of the distribution of productive assets is important, but, according to Dymski and Elliott, it should only be understood in the context of a social theory about exploitation, domination, and class struggle. They argue for a theory with a wide and dynamic framework and with clear ethical implications. (The debate is pursued in Devine and Dymski 1991 and 1992 and Roemer 1992.)

An astute defense and careful development of Roemer's work is found in Gilbert Skillman's contribution. In his account, questions of domination arise but are set aside in order to gain, as Skillman believes, a clearer understanding of what exploitation is. For Skillman it is crucial to distinguish between what makes a situation exploitative and what intensifies exploitation. For Roemer, as for Skillman, it is the having and controlling of differential assets, and not noneconomic forms of domination, that are essential to capitalism and capitalist exploitation and that need to be brought to an end to achieve socialism. As Roemer says in reply to James Devine and Dymski, "by far the more important power that capitalists have over workers is their political power, which flows directly from their ownership of productive assets" (Roemer 1992). The debate opened up important and interesting questions about what concepts are to be used and how best to formulate the theory about control and exploitation under capitalism. The development of theory goes far beyond linguistic intuitions about the term "exploitation" and points to theoretical extensions of exploitation to issues of gender and race and to global issues of trade and the environment.

Consider now the normative use of the term "exploitation," as found in some of the standard debates about exploitation in capitalist societies. A crucial feature of capitalist societies is that there are different classes of strikingly unequal power. In contemporary capitalist market economies— the economies of present-day constitutional democracies—these inequalities in power assume the form of great disparities in bargaining power between capitalists and workers, systemic disparities that have led to what some have called systemic exploitation.

Many would say that capitalist societies are exploitative because (a) capitalists, those who own and control the means of production, have vastly more social power than the producers (the workers), (b) they use that power to gain advantage, indeed mastery, over workers, and (c) the thoroughly unequal distribution of economic advantages and disadvantages that result from this is undeserved. Hence, exploitation has commonly been thought to be unfair and unjust. It may be, however, that even extensive exploitation is, everything considered, still the lesser of a number of very considerable evils. Exploitation is bad, so it is often claimed, but escaping it may very well lead to something still worse.

Some argue, alternatively, that even a complex society would be non-exploitative if it had a cooperative economy owned and controlled by its producers in a world where all able-bodied people were producers (in a broad sense) and where the economy meets everyone's basic needs while striving to satisfy people's compatible desires even at the cost of a certain amount of drudgery. How much drudgery for how many resources would be decided democratically by the society of cooperative producers.[4] There would be a shift in such a society from production for profit to production for human needs. Many Marxists now argue for some form of market socialism in which the markets are *purely instrumental* to the end of meeting human needs equitably. It was Marx's view that once the workers gain control of social production the "wealth is no longer measured by labour time but by DISPOSABLE TIME."[5] Decisions would be made about the disposable time for meeting human needs, and for many through the medium of markets.

In a properly working socialist society, each person would have a fair share of economic goods in exchange for a willingness to contribute (during the appropriate periods of life) a fair share of the work, which *sometimes* will require drudgery to produce needed goods and in some instances even goods that are simply desired. "A fair share of goods" and "a fair share of drudgery" come to roughly an equal share, once allowances are made for differences in basic needs, capacities, the time and extent of drudgery in producing different goods, the need to compensate people for taking on especially onerous or dangerous jobs, and the like.[6]

A society so ordered, it has been argued, would be just. To the extent that a modern society deviates from these ideal standards, as certainly modern capitalist democracies extensively do, that society will be exploitative and, particularly where its conditions are those of productive abundance, unjust. "To be exploited," Richard Arneson puts it, "is roughly to be forced to perform drudgery to an unfairly great extent, and to receive in return an unfairly small share of goods, where this forcing is brought about via an inequality of power favoring some economic agents over others" (1981, 213). Whether some such characterization of exploitation is adequate, whether it captures something intrinsic to exploitation, is one of the issues argued in this volume.

A central element in the various dictionary definitions of "exploitation," in its pejorative sense, is that exploitation is the taking of unfair advantage of someone. Taking unfair advantage of someone else, in its more extreme forms, comes to treating people as "mere workable material" (as the Oxford English Dictionary puts it). What (among other things) is so deeply wrong about exploitation is that it is a treating of people as *means only*, means to one's own satisfaction or profit, and not as ends and as members of a common kingdom of ends. People are simply used rather than being treated with respect as ends in themselves. Slave societies and feudal societies are such societies where people's autonomy is severely restricted and typically undermined. Capitalist societies, state socialist societies, and sexist or racist societies are also societies in which autonomy is undermined. Powerful elements in such societies dominate and oppress people in certain social positions in a number of very vital areas in their lives. Marx and Engels thought that capitalism unavoidably did just that. Consequently, they deeply hated capitalism, and rightly so *if* their empirical account of the world was close to the mark.

Debate about the moral character of capitalism has been carried out by the distinguished economists Peter Bauer and Amartya Sen. Most economists, including those in most think tanks, agree with Bauer's conservative position that most economic differences within our Western capitalist societies and between rich and poor countries are the result of differences in people's capacities and motivations.[7] Bauer maintains that if we actually look at the process of production, rich people normally produce more than poor people, and thus, he reasons, they deserve higher incomes. This "personal production view," as he calls it, argues that the incomes of those who are prosperous or own property typically accrue to people who have achieved these things by their own production *and* with the use of the resources they own. Bauer believes this is the vital fact that justifies much of the inequality within capitalist countries and between the North and the South.

Amartya Sen begins a trenchant criticism of Bauer by rightly conceding some plausibility to the personal production view. As Sen says:

> It is quite plausible to think that the personal production view, if correct, can lead to a moral case for inequality. If, say, person A has produced—quite unaided—some food or some medicine, and persons A and B need that food or that medicine equally, then the case for A rather than B having the food or the medicine might well be seen to be strong. Of course, even with such a simple case of unaided production, this judgement may not have irresistible force, and it is quite plausible to entertain this value without giving it invariable priority over other objectives. If, for instance, person A has produced the food or the medicine (as in the previous example), but has little need for it, while B who is hungry or C who is ill needs them desperately, then—consistent with the earlier judgement—A's relative claim on the food or the medicine can be seen as morally weakened. But it is difficult to deny that if the personal production view were correct in a particular case, it can be the basis of a *prima facie* argument for Bauer's approach.[8]

However, the personal production view is, as Sen argues, very problematical. Much of our production is *interdependent*. In the vast majority of cases, production is, as Sen points out, "based on the joint use of different resources, possibly provided by different people, and it is not in general possible to separate out who—or which—resource produced how much of the total output." If we use the conventional economic device of the marginal product to try to determine this, we still face considerable difficulties in ascertaining how much each resource contributed to the total output. It is, as Sen contends, arbitrary "to assert that each resource's earnings reflect the overall contribution made by that resource to the total output."

Bauer, like most defenders of capitalism, neglects, in setting forth the personal production view, to place any moral relevance on the distinction between what is produced by *a person* and what is produced by the use of the *resources* the person happens to *own*. There is a prima facie moral appeal, in some circumstances, to giving more to those who through their conscientious productive activity have contributed more. But that appeal hardly carries over, as Sen puts it, "to giving more to those who own more productive resources which contribute more to output." It is a very considerable mistake to equate "being more productive" with "owning more productive resources." It is a further mistake, one commonly made, to think that just the *owning* of assets or resources is itself a productive activity. After all, the owner, qua owner, merely *lets* the workers, managers, and entrepreneurs (who are also capitalists if they own a significant amount of capital) use the resources or the money in question in production. *But permission to use or the right to use is certainly not a productive activity.*

What other responses are there to the charge that capitalist societies are invariably exploitive and unjust?[9] Familiar capitalist defenses of their profits and unequal power relations are the following: (1) The capitalist's capital—the resources he owns and puts to work in production—is capital created by his past labor. He has the right to the fruits of his past exertions. It is only fair that because of this he should have a large share of the pie. (2) The profit of the capitalist is a wage equivalent for her skill in entrepreneurial management and organization. Because of this, the capitalist deserves this profit. In addition to any considerations of desert, her getting that profit has *a pragmatic rationale* in that such profits are essential, or at least important, *incentives* for the capitalist to engage in her entrepreneurial management, which in turn is essential for the development of the productive forces. (3) The capitalist takes a risk in investing. He may lose his shirt. He deserves a reward for the risks he willingly takes. (4) The profit the capitalist takes is her reward for waiting. She defers gratification to build up capital—something generally useful to society—and she deserves her reward for her socially useful abstinence. These four defenses of capitalism have a prima facie plausibility, but they are sharply criticized in readings that follow and in their most sophisticated forms are subjected to a withering critique by David Schweickart in chapter 1 of *Against Capitalism*.

Behind these four familiar defenses of capitalism stands the fundamental question of whether capitalists do or do not exercise vital and indispensable functions that any complex society with developed productive forces and a complex economy would be the worse off for being without. If capitalists do not have such functions, then it would appear that workers are unfairly exploited by capitalists who appropriate unearned wealth.

Even if it were acknowledged that workers under capitalism are exploited, it could still be maintained that exploitation is an evil with which we must live since the feasible alternatives to capitalism are still worse. This claim, along with the nature, intensity, extent, kinds, causes, and effects of exploitation, is examined in the readings that follow. The possibility of attaining an exploitation-free society is also discussed, along with the question of whether that is, everything considered, something that we ought to try to achieve.

It should be borne in mind that on classical Marxist accounts *by definition* a communist society and perhaps even a socialist society could not be exploitative. But many consider the actually (and formerly) existing socialisms to have been in fact exploitative. From such historical and sociological considerations, as well as some theoretical considerations such as some of those deployed in this volume, the question emerges whether any feasible society, socialist, communist, or otherwise, could actually be without at least some exploitation. This is an important issue that we regret not being able to pursue in this volume. The issue is, however, being actively pursued in the current literature on exploitation. In particular, we draw attention to the key work of Robert J. van der Veen and Philippe Van Parijs. Their work provides excellent models of how such investigations should proceed.[10]

The concept of exploitation was first and primarily applied to exploitation of wage laborers at the point of production, typically industrial workers. Most obviously, that does not take into account the oppression of women who are outside the labor force. In the last couple of decades, there has been important work on the political economy of reproduction and on the household in general. (See the collections by Fox and Malos, among others.) In this volume, Nancy Folbre applies the concept of socially necessary labor time to the household in order to understand exploitation outside wage labor. Ann Ferguson describes the nature of sex/affective production that is normally the work of women. Sandra Bartky shows how this leads to a better understanding of the disempowerment of women under patriarchy and the subjective aspects of exploitation in caregiving that results. These essays, by discussing the micropolitics of the personal, lead to a clearer understanding of the extension of the concept of exploitation and to a better understanding of the concept itself.

Capitalism invades the home, but it also reaches out to new continents. Marx recognized the drive of capitalism to extend to the globe as a whole through world markets,[11] but at the end of the twentieth century there has been a globalization of production far beyond what he could have imagined. Such globalization introduces many other issues widely discussed in the Marxist and non-Marxist literature: imperialism, international exchange, modernization, the creation of a world system, and forced underdevelopment. These issues provide the background for any discussion of exploitation, which is made international with the extensions of capitalism throughout the world. New groups of workers are exploited within new social and state structures. Investigations of the international economy take us beyond the point of production to a debate about unequal exchange and international finance, backed up by centers of military power.[12]

In different ways, Maria Mies, Samir Amin, and Guglielmo Carchedi point to forms of super-exploitation in the peripheries of international capitalism. In important ways, Gail Omvedt calls for a rethinking of exploitation as a globalized and systemic phenomenon and shows that exploitation extends far beyond wage labor and points of production. A new debate opens up here about the related issues of the exploitation of peasants and the class structure of peasant societies. More still needs to be done on the concrete basis for the super-exploitation of people in international oligopoly capitalism, to use Carchedi's term.

In such extensions of exploitation, one can say that whole countries are exploited and underdeveloped, but there are also other extensions of exploitation. An extension that is most widely recognized at the end of the twentieth century is to the environment. The environment is exploited locally and in especially vicious and unrestained ways in Third World countries, with clear global effects. It is more than simply economic exploitation, at least in the sense that has been discussed according to which only people are exploited.

We noted above the morally neutral sense of "exploitation" in talking about exploiting a mine, but it is now common knowledge that any such exploitation is itself rarely neutral, even if the concept itself is neutral. Large countries and ecosystems—Brazil, for example—are thrown into turmoil by the exploitation of fields, forests, and resources. This extension introduces a new concept of exploitation or at least a new way of looking at exploitation. Although "deep ecologists" talk about the moral offenses to the environment and its parts, thus going beyond both economic exploitation and the notion that only people are subject to exploitation, the important considerations (vis-à-vis such matters) explored in this volume are the relations between environmental exploitation and international exploitation on a world scale.[13] The political economy of international oligopoly capitalism is a system of intertwining forces adversely affecting particular peoples, humankind as a whole, the environment, and their diverse relations, local, regional and global. Exploitation enters deeply and pervasively here, although perhaps in ways that require some reconceptualization of exploitation.

The anthology ends with a new essay on racism by Gary Dymski. Dymski challenges contemporary Marxian accounts of exploitation and race and suggests some new directions in understanding racial dimensions of capitalist injustice. Like others who are exploring the dynamics of how exploitation is extended, Dymski considers aspects of how the development of Marxian theory will challenge contemporary social relations in all their complexity. The essays on feminism, imperialism, ecology, and race show how new areas of theoretical investigation are being opened up, thus extending the theory of exploitation beyond the classical focus on the point of production. Such extensions of critical theory point to new directions for political change.

Frederick Engels said that capitalist "exploitation is the basic evil which the social revolution wants to abolish by abolishing the capitalist mode of production."[14] Is it *the*, or at least *a*, basic evil of our societies? Can it be got rid of instead of just being ameliorated to some extent? Indeed, viewed globally, can it even be significantly ameliorated? Can we put an end to it, by bringing an end to the capitalist mode of production and constructing and sustaining a socialist world under conditions of reasonable abundance? And if so, can the resulting socialist society at least eventually end exploitation, given a full consideration of all the moral and otherwise human issues awash in contemporary life? It is these matters that, directly or indirectly, are centrally at issue here. The abstractness of some of these readings should not be allowed to obscure that. Economics, philosophy, and social inquiry more generally are demanding disciplines, but the question "What is to be done?" is in the background of most of what is discussed in this volume.

Notes

We thank Ona Stonkus for research and editorial assistance and Kathryn Gillis for editorial assistance and the preparation of the index.
1. See the Oxford English Dictionary and Webster's Collegiate Dictionary.
2. See Marx, *Capital*, vol. 1, and Mandel 1976. For Marx's views about exploitation in a popular form, see his "Value, Price, and Profit," in Marx and Engels, *Collected Works*, vol. 20, 103–49. For a useful selection of works by Marx on exploitation, see Jon Elster, ed., *Karl Marx: A Reader* ch. 4 ("Exploitation"),

121–67. The essays in this anthology on Marxian exploitation and the debate also present (contested) interpretations of Marx's own views.

3. Making this distinction is by now rather standard in writings on exploitation. For a dissenting voice, however, see Allen Wood, "Exploitation," in this volume.

4. Against libertarian objections that no one can rightly be required, even by democratic decision, to work for others, see Kai Nielsen 1985, part 4 and 1989.

5. Karl Marx, *Grundrisse*, in *Collected Works* 29:94.

6. Many considerations could be added, but they would all be of the type mentioned explicitly. For an acute examination of the issues involved, see Nell and Nell 1976 and Ware 1992.

7. See Bauer 1981.

8. Sen 1982. The quotations in the following two paragraphs of the text come from the same source.

9. Some may acknowledge that actual capitalist societies emerged through conquest and appropriation, while maintaining that *in principle* there could be a "clean road" to a capitalist society that is nonexploitative and just. (See Levine 1984 and Schweickart 1993.) The use of extreme hypothetical ("in principle") examples and the underlying methodology of it is defended by Roemer (1989). See also Gilbert Skillman in this volume. Christie 1989 and Dymski and Elliott 1989 raise skeptical questions about what they consider to be a one-sided methodology used by Roemer and others.

10. See the work cited in the bibliography by Scott, van der Veen, Van Parijs, and others.

11. See, for example, Marx and Engels, "Manifesto of the Communist Party," in *Collected Works* 6:487 f.

12. See the seminal work on unequal exchange by Emmanuel (1972). For discussion of Emmanuel and other contributors to the debate, see Shaikh and Carchedi (in the bibliography). For an important study of these issues in a particular case, see Bunker 1988.

13. For a good discussion of the conceptual and moral issues, see Drydyk 1993. There are important and closely related issues that a broader study would have to pursue. On entropic limits, there is the important work of Nicholas Georgescu-Roegen 1971. Also closely related are the issues of a Marxist theory about the environment, humankind, and domination. For a selection of Marx's writings on the topic, see Parsons 1977. For some interesting debate and contemporary work, see Grundmann 1991; Benton 1992; Merchant 1994; O'Connor 1994; and work in the journal *Capitalism, Nature, Socialism*.

14. Frederick Engels, "The Housing Question," in *Collected Works* 23:318.

References

Arneson, Richard J. 1981. "What's Wrong with Exploitation?" *Ethics* 91, no. 2: 202–27.

Arnold, N. Scott. 1992. "Equality and Exploitation in the Market Socialist Community." *Social Philosophy & Policy* 9, no. 1: 1–28.

Arnold, N. Scott. 1994. *The Philosophy and Economics of Market Socialism: A Critical Study.* Oxford: Oxford University Press.

Bauer, Peter. 1981. *Equality, the Third World, and Economic Delusion.* Cambridge: Harvard University Press.

Benton, Ted. 1992. *Natural Relations? Animal Rights, Human Rights, and the Environment*. London: Verso.

Bunker, Stephen G. 1988. *Underdeveloping the Amazon: Extraction, Unequal Exchange, and the Failure of the Modern State*. Chicago: University of Chicago Press; originally published by the University of Illinois Press, 1985.

Carchedi, Guglielmo. 1991. "Technological Innovation, International Production, and Exchange Rates." *Cambridge Journal of Economics* 15:45–60.

Carchedi, Guglielmo. 1991. *Frontiers of Political Economy*. London: Verso.

Carolyn Merchant, ed. 1994. *Ecology*. Atlantic Highlands, NJ: Humanities Press.

Christie, Drew. 1989. "John Roemer's Economic Philosophy and the Perils of Formalism." In Robert Ware and Kai Nielsen, eds., *Analyzing Marxism*. Calgary: University of Calgary Press, 267–79.

Devine, James, and Gary Dymski. 1991. "Roemer's 'General' Theory of Exploitation Is a Special Case." *Economics and Philosophy* 7:235–75.

Devine, James, and Gary Dymski. 1992. "Walrasian Marxism Once Again." *Economics and Philosophy* 8:157–62.

Drydyk, Jay. 1993. "Exploiting Nature." In Jesse Vorst, Ross Dobson, and Ron Fletcher, eds., *Green on Red: Evolving Ecological Socialism*. Winnipeg: Society for Socialist Studies and Halifax: Fernwood, 119–31.

Dymski, Gary, 1992. "Towards a New Model of Exploitation: The Case of Racial Domination." *International Journal of Social Economics* 19, nos. 7–8–9: 292–313.

Dymski, Gary, and John Elliott. 1989. "Should *Anyone* Be Interested in Exploitation?" In Robert Ware and Kai Nielsen, eds., *Analyzing Marxism*. Calgary: University of Calgary Press, 333–74.

Elster, Jon, ed. 1986. *Karl Marx: A Reader*, ch. 4 ("Exploitation"), Cambridge: Cambridge University Press, 121–67.

Emmanuel, Arghiri. 1972. *Unequal Exchange: A Study of the Imperialism of Trade* (with comments by C. Bettelheim). New York: Monthly Review Press.

Fox, Bonnie, ed. 1980. *Hidden in the Household: Women's Domestic Labour under Capitalism*. Toronto: The Women's Press.

Georgescu-Roegen, Nicholas. 1971. *The Entropy Law and the Economic Process*. Cambridge, MA: Harvard University Press.

Grundmann, Reiner. 1991. *Marxism and Ecology*. Oxford: Oxford University Press.

Levine, Andrew. 1984. *Arguing for Socialism*. Boston: Routledge & Kegan Paul.

Malos, Ellen, ed. 1980. *The Politics of Housework*. London: Allison & Busby.

Mandel, Ernest. 1976. Introduction to *Capital*, vol. I, 11–86. Harmondsworth: Penguin Books.

Marx, Karl. 1976. *Capital*, vol. I. Harmondsworth: Penguin Books.

Marx, Karl and Engels, Frederick. 1975–present. *Collected Works*. New York: International.

Miller, David. 1989. "Exploitation [in the market]." In his *Market, State, and Community* Oxford: Clarendon Press, 175–199.

Nell, Edward, and Onora Nell. 1976. "On Justice under Socialism." In Karsten J. Struhl and Paul Rothenberg Struhl, eds., *Ethics in Perspective*. New York: Random House, 434–46.

Nielsen, Kai. 1985. *Equality and Liberty: A Defense of Radical Egalitarianism*. Totowa, NJ: Rowman and Allanheld.

Nielsen, Kai. 1989. "Equality of Condition and Self-Ownership" in Guy Lafrance, ed., *Ethics and Basic Rights*. Ottawa: University of Ottawa Press, 81–99.

O'Connor, Martin, ed. 1994. *Is Capitalism Sustainable? Political Economy and the Politics of Ecology*. New York: Guilford, chs. 1–8.

Parsons, Howard, ed. 1977. *Marx and Engels on Ecology*. Westport, CT: Greenwood Press.

Roemer, John. 1983. "Are Socialist Economics Consistent with Efficiency?" *The Philosophical Forum* 14, nos. 3–4: 369–88.

Roemer, John. 1989. "Marxism and Contemporary Social Science." *Review of Social Economy* 47, no. 4: 377–91.

Roemer, John. 1992. "What Walrasian Marxism Can and Cannot Do." *Economics and Philosophy* 8:149–156.

Schweickart, David. 1991. "The Politics and Morality of Unequal Exchange: Emmanuel and Roemer, Analysis and Synthesis." *Economics and Philosophy* 7:13–36.

Schweickart, David. 1993. *Against Capitalism*. New York: Cambridge University Press.

Sen, Amartya. 1982. "The Case for the Rich." *New York Review of Books* 29, no. 3: 4.

Shaikh, Anwar. 1979–80. "Foreign Trade and the Law of Value: Part I." *Science and Society* 43: 281–302.

Shaikh, Anwar. 1980–81. "Foreign Trade and the Law of Value: Part II." *Science and Society* 44: 27–57.

Van Parijs, Philippe. 1987. "Exploitation and the Libertarian Challenge." In Andrew Reeve, ed., *Modern Theories of Exploitation*. London: Sage, 111–31.

van der Veen, Robert. 1987. "Can Socialism Be Non-Exploitative?" In Andrew Reeve, ed., *Modern Theories of Exploitation*. London: Sage, 80–110.

Ware, Robert. 1992. "Marx on Some Phases of Communism." In Rodger Beehler, David Copp, and Béla Szabados, eds., *On the Track of Reason: Essays in Honor of Kai Nielsen* Boulder: Westview Press, 135–53.

PART I

The General Idea
of Exploitation

Exploitation

ALLEN W. WOOD

IT IS COMMONLY THOUGHT that exploitation is unjust; some think it is part of the very meaning of the word "exploitation" that it is unjust. Those who think this will suppose that the just society has to be one in which people do not exploit one another, at least on a large scale. I will argue that exploitation is not unjust by definition, and that a society (such as our own) might be fundamentally just while nevertheless being pervasively exploitative. I do think that exploitation is nearly always a bad thing, and will try to identify the moral belief which makes most of us think it is. But I will argue that its badness does not always consist in its being unjust.

1. IS EXPLOITATION A MORAL CONCEPT?

Worries about exploitation. The concept of exploitation has probably been most closely associated with the Marxian charge that wage labor is exploitative, but recently it has also figured in controversies about whether surrogacy contracts are exploitative of the birth mother.[1] In most of these uses, the concept of exploitation is left unanalyzed, and this has sometimes provoked the suspicion that we may need a more precise, technical conception of exploitation if claims using it are to be properly evaluated. Alan Wertheimer, for example, has noted with regret that there is no canonical (non-Marxist) account of exploitation, suggesting that this fact casts doubt on the claim that surrogacy involves any objectionable form of exploitation.[2] Yet Marxists themselves, when they have set about providing such a technical analy-

From Allen W. Wood, "Exploitation," *Social Philosophy and Policy* 12, no. 2 (Summer 1995): 135–58, reprinted with the permission of Cambridge University Press and the consent of the author.

sis, have sometimes been led to raise questions about whether "exploita-tion" (in their technical and allegedly "Marxian" sense) really identifies anything which should be of interest to social critics.[3] This is apt to render all charges of exploitation suspect, and make us wonder whether the notion itself may be too diffuse to be taken seriously.

In my view, however, social critics who have used the notion of exploi-tation naively, without explicating it, have generally been less guilty of obfuscation than the philosophers and economists who have been worried about providing more reflective accounts. In particular, I think most of these accounts have proceeded on assumptions which already distort the concept and tend to undermine its critical use. Accordingly, my aim will be to clarify the concept not by providing a technical analysis but by exploring what I think people mean when they object to behavior or social arrangements as exploitative, and identifying the moral convictions which give such objec-tions their force.

Moral and nonmoral concepts. Most philosophers who reflect on the con-cept of exploitation tend to follow the practice of dictionaries, distinguish-ing a "nonmoral" sense of "exploitation" from a "moral" sense, and taking the latter sense to involve the idea of making use of someone or something unjustly or unethically.[4] Since they suppose that it is only the latter, "pejo-rative" meaning of the term which interests social critics, they provide what I will call a "moralized" account of exploitation. That is, they suppose that the term "exploitation" (in the "pejorative" sense) already has wrongfulness or moral badness built into its very meaning.

"Murder", for example, is taken to be a moral concept in this sense when it is taken to mean "wrongful homicide." On such a moralized account of the concept of murder, to justify the claim that a homicide is an act of murder one must show it to be wrongful. Further, if I claimed that a certain homicide was an act of murder, but insisted nevertheless that it was not wrongful, I would be taken to be misusing the term, or at least using it with some new and nonstandard meaning. By contrast, terms like "homicide" or "abortion" are not normally taken to be moral terms in that to call an act by these names leaves open the question of whether it is wrong or justifiable.

Of course, it is true that some people believe, for example, that all acts of abortion, simply as such, are wrong; but they do not take this to be part of the very *meaning* of the word "abortion." They do not think that those who defend abortion are misusing the word or using it in a different sense, but take them instead to be expressing opposed moral convictions using the very same term in the very same sense. Analogously, if someone proposed a nonmoralized account of exploitation, that would not necessarily preclude saying that all acts of exploitation, simply as such, are morally wrong. Hence it would not preclude using the term pejoratively, as the term "abortion" may be used pejoratively by someone who thinks abortion is always wrong. It would merely deny that the moral wrongness was built into the very meaning of the term "exploitation."

Innocent and noninnocent exploitation. There clearly do seem to be cases of exploitation which we regard as innocent or even admirable. Nobody thinks it is wrong or unethical for a chess player to exploit her opponent's inattention in order to win the game. We may even compliment a lawyer for exploiting the weaknesses in her adversary's case in order to win a just verdict, or congratulate a resourceful person for exploiting her opportunities to the full. Realizing this, philosophers think that in such cases "exploit" is being used in a neutral, innocent, or positive sense, quite distinct from the pejorative sense which interests us in cases of "wrongful exploitation."[5]

But why should we suppose that "exploitation" has a special *meaning* when applied to cases of injustice or wrongdoing? Terms like "appropriation", "transaction", "seizure", or "agreement" apply sometimes to acts which are wrongful and sometimes to acts which are not, but we do not suppose that the word "transaction" has a different meaning in the case of wrongful or unethical transactions from the one it has in the case of rightful and proper transactions. If instances of exploitation are thought to be more often or more typically wrongful than instances of appropriation or transaction, perhaps that might be explained by the nature of exploitation as such, as it appears in both just and unjust cases, or by our substantive moral convictions about the kind of thing an act of exploitation itself is.

Michael Gorr writes that "[i]t is difficult even to conceive of a case in which we would describe someone's behavior as the *justified* exploitation of another person."[6] That is right, but it does not follow that "exploitation" is a moral term or that we must provide a moralized account of it. The "difficulty in conceiving" here is not a difficulty in understanding what someone might *mean* in holding that the exploitation of a person is morally justified. Rather, it is that we cannot imagine ourselves *agreeing* with a moral belief on this subject which is so deeply opposed to the one we hold.

Exploitation defended. In Plato's *Gorgias*, Callicles maintains that by nature some people are stronger than others, hence better and superior, and that it is only natural justice that the superior should use their strength to rule over the inferior and "to remove by force what belongs to the inferior."[7] Callicles does not directly use any word which should be translated as "exploit", but it seems quite a fair rendering of his view to say that he regards it as only natural justice that the strong should *exploit* the weak. Callicles clearly wants to argue that exploitation is right and just in those very cases where most of us take it to be wrong and unjust.

Or consider the similar views of Friedrich Nietzsche, which *are* sometimes explicitly couched in terms of exploitation. Nietzsche says that the economic life of modern society "represents a maximum in the exploitation (*Ausbeutung*) of humanity." Yet Nietzsche does not call for the abolition of this exploitation, as he knows the decadent moralists will do. Instead, he insists that it would be best for the exploitation even to be heightened, if only it could be given a new meaning through the emergence of a higher type of human being, who "stands upon and lives off" the masses. If the exploiters were strong, spiritual *Übermenschen*—rather than the philistine capitalists who presently exploit the masses—then as far as Nietzsche is concerned, the exploitation of humanity would be entirely welcome.[8]

The difference between Callicles or Nietzsche and ourselves is not plausibly regarded as a merely semantic difference, as though we are using "exploit" in a "pejorative" sense and they are using it in some neutral or nonpejorative sense. On the contrary, they are taking a stand in direct opposition to conventional moral opinions about exploitation, and this is something they can do only if they assert that exploitation is good or just while using the word in the same sense as we do when we more conventionally hold that it is bad or wrong. It may be correct to say that Nietzsche is using the word "exploitation" in order to shock us, but it is incorrect to say that he is using it in a different (nonstandard or nonpejorative) *sense* in order to shock us. On the contrary, what really shocks us about Callicles or Nietzsche is their *moral opinions*. Nietzsche heightens the shock by not mincing words or employing euphemisms, but asserting directly that he approves of something we regard as objectionable and referring to this thing using the very same word we would use in objecting to it. If Nietzsche used that word, but in a different and less pejorative sense, that would diminish rather than enhance the shock value. If, however, the word we use already had wrongness or badness built into its meaning, then in saying that the maximum exploitation of humanity by a superior race would be a good thing, Nietzsche would be contradicting only himself and not conventional moral opinion.

Wrong because exploitative. Another problem with moralized accounts of exploitation is that they make it more difficult to understand many arguments in which the concept of exploitation is used. Some people argue that commodified surrogacy is wrongful or bad *because* it is exploitative. In such an argument it is natural to take the premise that surrogacy involves exploitation as claiming that surrogacy has some property such that, in light of certain moral principles, the fact that surrogacy has that property is, under the given circumstances, a ground for regarding surrogacy as wrongful or bad. But following a moralized account of exploitation, if I say that a practice is exploitative (using the word, of course, in the "pejorative" sense), then my statement already *means* that the practice is wrongful or bad, and thus that before using the term (in that sense) I should already have shown that surrogacy is wrongful or bad. In that case, I cannot be justified in asserting the premise of my argument until I have already independently established its conclusion. If that is so, however, then the whole argument form which says that a practice is wrongful *because* it is exploitative looks merely rhetorical, if not downright confused. At most, such a statement could be understood as *categorizing* the wrongfulness of the act (where this wrongfulness has already been admitted), or as rhetorically emphasizing this wrongfulness to someone who already believes the act is wrong but is suspected of giving this belief insufficient deliberative weight. The statement cannot be understood as providing a substantive argument for considering the act wrongful, which might convince someone not antecedently persuaded of its wrongfulness—just as saying that an act is "wrong because it is murder" (where "murder" is understood to mean "wrongful homicide") cannot provide anyone with a new reason for thinking the act is wrong, but can at most serve to categorize the wrong (as a case of "murder", i.e., "wrongful *homicide*") or rhetorically drive home its wrongfulness through the use of the vivid term of condemnation (whose appropriateness would be accepted only by someone already persuaded that the act is wrong).

Analogously, a moralized account of exploitation will not permit us to understand the inference "wrongful because exploitative" as providing a genuine argument for considering some practice wrongful by invoking a contentful moral belief to the effect that exploitativeness is a substantively wrong-making feature of acts. For on a moralized account, "exploitation is wrong," like "murder is wrong," would be morally vacuous, true merely in virtue of the meaning of "exploitation". If "murder" means "wrongful homicide", then no one who did not already accept the judgment that a particular homicide is wrongful could have any reason to accept the judgment that it is a case of murder. Likewise, whatever substantive moral beliefs lie behind the claim that the practice in question is wrong must have established this conclusion before we could be justified in saying that this practice is exploitative.

No wonder, then, that those who want to provide more precise or technical accounts of exploitation, beginning from the standpoint that these must be moralized accounts, should have begun to doubt whether there is any moral interest at all in social criticisms which employ the concept of exploitation. But here the fault does not lie with the social critics; it is the philosophers, with their attempts at analytical clarity, who are guilty of introducing, conceptual confusion.

Suppose for a moment that there is substantive disagreement over the question of whether certain kinds of exploitation are good or bad, just or unjust. In that case, moralized accounts of the concept of exploitation will have the effect of disguising substantive moral commitments, and thereby enabling people less honest than Callicles and Nietzsche to conceal the extent to which they share similar views. Thus, a Callicles who accepted a moralized account of exploitation may (and not only may, but must) say that since it (in his opinion) is always naturally just for the strong to take by force whatever they want from the weak, the strong are not in the least guilty of *exploiting* the weak (not, at any rate, in any "pejorative" sense of the term).

It is no good merely to say here that we may still challenge Callicles' controversial claims about what is naturally just. For this observation completely misses the main point, which is that the contemptibly mealy-mouthed reformulation of his position forced on poor Callicles by the moralized account would entirely divest his strong character of that robust moral candor which Plato portrays as its one redeeming virtue. It also totally overlooks the additional point that whether or not an instance of exploitation is held to be wrongful or unjust, it may still be important, for both moral and nonmoral reasons, to recognize it as a case of *exploitation*. But that merely returns us to the main question: What is exploitation?

2. WHAT EXPLOITATION IS

Exploitation as use. The fundamental synonym for the verb "exploit" is "use." The exploiter must be a person or group of people, a human or humanlike subject, with the capacity for setting ends and using means; the object of exploitation is one such means. This object can be virtually anything that can be used: nonhuman things, such as natural resources, and even abstractions, such as occasions and opportunities.

Not every use counts as exploitation, however. A hiker in the woods who takes a drink from a stream is not exploiting it, though a miller who builds a mill on it is. The difference, I suggest, is that the exploitation of a resource is a use implying its availability to the exploiter in a plannable and manipulable way, especially some degree of control over the resource. We do exploit unpredictable opportunities or fortunate circumstances, but in those cases the opportunity or circumstance fits into some preexisting plan of the exploiter's, and the exploiter must do something, involving a degree of planning and manipulation, to *take advantage* of the fortunate circumstance, bringing it into the exploiter's control or within the purview of the exploiter's plans or machinations. When some unpredictable event suddenly drops success into my lap, I make use of the good luck, but I do not exploit it.

Exploiting things about people: advantage-exploitation and benefit-exploitation. There are many things about human beings that can be exploited: their talents, traits, habits, capacities, activities, desires, and circumstances. We exploit people's strengths and their weaknesses, but usually not in quite the same sense. We exploit some attribute of the person from which we derive benefit or use to achieve our end. Let us call this "benefit-exploitation" or, for short, "b-exploitation." It is in a different sense that we exploit someone's weakness or vulnerability, which gives us a hold or advantage over the person and puts at our disposal the attribute which we b-exploit. I shall call our exploitative relation to this weakness or vulnerability "advantage-exploitation" or "a-exploitation." The charming spy enchants a governmental official, playing on the victim's need for affection in order to obtain a state secret. Here the spy a-exploits the victim's need for affection (regarded as a vulnerability) and b-exploits the victim's official position or access to state secrets (regarded as an attribute from which the spy may reap some benefit).

As their names are meant to imply, a-exploitation and b-exploitation constitute a complementary pair, and a-exploitation is the foundation of b-exploitation.[9] Without b-exploitation there would be no *use* of the object of exploitation, while without a-exploitation there would be no control or manipulation of the object of exploitation, which is the element distinguishing exploitation (of nonhuman as well as human objects) from simple use. People and their abilities, activities, and so on may be nonexploitatively at our disposal, as through generosity or a mutual exchange of services where neither side is taking advantage of the other. The use of another through generosity or exchange may also be exploitative, but only when there is some element of vulnerability (a-exploitation) in the situation, such as when the exchange of benefits results from one person's having some decisive bargaining advantage over the other, or when the generosity is viewed as a weakness to be played upon. For this reason, we may also look upon a-exploitation as that which makes b-exploitation possible. The vulnerability exploited in a-exploitation is what puts at our disposal the benefit exploited in b-exploitation.

Human vulnerability. We might wish to clarify the notion of *vulnerability* here. But I am skeptical about the extent to which such clarification is achievable through any devices used by such technicians as philosophers, economists, or decision theorists. (Perhaps one reason these people are perplexed by exploitation is that their technical resources are as yet not up to handling it.) It has been suggested to me that you are made vulnerable to me in the required sense by something that enables me to control you, or that you are made vulnerable to me in a transaction by anything that makes us unequal with respect to the transaction (with my enjoying the superiority in that respect).[10] Suppose, however, that I am a cringing servant and you are my master. If I regularly pilfer from you, a-exploiting your naive trustfulness so as to b-exploit your wealth, I have not gained any control over you, nor have I acquired any superiority over you; if it may be said that I have become unequal to (superior to) you *with respect to that transaction* (that is, the pilfering), I am not sure that describing it in this way is any clearer than simply speaking of you as being vulnerable to my pilfering.

Clearly needs and desires can sometimes constitute vulnerabilities. An addict's need or desire for drugs, for example, is clearly a vulnerability which pushers may a-exploit. The emotional needs of lovers obviously make them vulnerable to those they love, and hence create opportunities for a-exploitation by the latter. Many human needs and desires can be viewed as vulnerabilities, and accordingly many dealings between human beings can be put in an exploitative light. As we become more sensitive to this unattractive side of human social life generally, we may very well begin to perceive a great deal more exploitation in it than we thought there was. I think that such a change in sensitivity might very well be a positive result of becoming clearer about what exploitation is and about its importance in human life.

Sensitivity and perceptiveness, however, are attributes of common sense. The changes in perception and sensitivity I am recommending are to be driven by common sense and not by inflexible philosophical conceptions or dogmas. Surely it would be implausible to the point of absurdity if someone were to suggest that *any* need or desire constitutes a vulnerability. To suppose this would be to make exploitation virtually ubiquitous in human social life and as much a factor in quite a number of innocent human relations as it is in many very nasty ones. If the account I am proposing is right, then those who have an interest in denying or disguising exploitation will also have an interest in making us insensitive to the difference between human interactions which play on genuine vulnerabilities and those which do not. We should therefore be suspicious of those who question whether such a distinction can be drawn.

The need for love may make us vulnerable, but a healthy personality is one that loves, and chooses its objects of love, in such a way that it will not be easily victimized or exploited. Thus, although greater sensitivity may make us aware of much more exploitation in love relationships than we thought was there, nothing in the concept of exploitation I am proposing makes it reasonable to suggest that all love relationships are inherently exploitative. Likewise, if someone claimed that *every* market exchange is exploitative simply on the ground that in such exchanges people use the needs of others to achieve their ends, then I think that claim would have exactly as much plausibility as the claim that every need or desire motivating market behavior is a vulnerability open to exploitation (the plausibility of both claims would, in my opinion, be very small).[11]

On the other hand, if one party to an exchange has a significantly stronger bargaining position than the other (as capitalists have in relation to workers, or prospective adoptive couples typically have in relation to the women they hire to be surrogate mothers), then that difference constitutes a clear case of vulnerability on the part of the weaker party; the weaker party is therefore a-exploited whenever the difference is used by the stronger party to obtain more favorable terms in the bargain. To the extent that market exchanges really do systematically involve this sort of differential advantage, they certainly may be considered systematically exploitative.

The notion of vulnerability needs clarification in other ways too. Joel Feinberg thinks there are three-person cases in which A exploits B but A receives a benefit not from B but from another person, C.[12] For example, a tabloid may exploit the unhappy situation of a celebrity, while neither helping nor harming the celebrity, but receiving a benefit from the public which pays to read about the celebrity. By "vulnerability", however, we do not necessarily mean vulnerability to being *harmed*, but only vulnerability to being *used*. The celebrity's misfortune or misconduct, which led to the unhappy situation, is clearly what makes the celebrity's life vulnerable to use by the tabloids; hence (in my terminology), the celebrity's situation is an object of a-exploitation, even if we suppose that the celebrity is neither helped nor harmed by the publicity. On the other hand, the sensational or heartrending character of the celebrity's situation (as the feature which sells papers) is an object of b-exploitation. In this case the exploitation may also be seen as directed at the public: Its prurient or sentimental tastes (regarded as a weakness) can be seen as the object of a-exploitation.

I do not mean to say that in any case of exploitation there must always be a neat pair of distinguishable objects of a- and b-exploitation. The point of pairing a-exploitation and b-exploitation is merely that where human beings and their attributes are the objects, exploitation usually involves some element of vulnerability on the part of what is exploited, and also some use of the attribute benefiting some project of the exploiter.[13] But there are exceptions. We sometimes exploit not only the qualities of others, but also our own qualities. This appears to be a case of b-exploitation, but it does not correspond to any a-exploitation, unless of someone else's vulnerability. We can exploit our own talents, however, without a-exploiting anything. Exploiting our own talents can be like exploiting natural resources, where the place of vulnerability is supplied by our having control over what we b-exploit or deploying it as part of some plan of ours. Sometimes there also seems to be a-exploitation without any clear object of b-exploitation distinct from the object of a-exploitation: The chess player a-exploits her opponent's lapse of attention, but there is nothing else of the opponent's besides this inattention which she needs to use (or b-exploit) in order to win the game. There can also be b-exploitation of *other* people's talents or capacities without a-exploitation, as when a manager exploits the base-stealing ability of his leadoff man in order to grab a quick first-inning lead. Here there is no vulnerability on the part of the leadoff man which is a-exploited by the manager, but there may be a control over the leadoff man (who will steal second when the manager gives the sign), and there is certainly the use of the leadoff man's ability as part of the manager's plan for victory.

Exploiting people themselves. We may well wonder what it means to exploit a *person*, as opposed to exploiting the person's capacities or activities or weaknesses. Generally speaking, what we are talking about here is b-exploitation, but as before, b-exploitation presupposes a-exploitation. In order for a person to be exploited, he or she has to be vulnerable to the exploiter, and it is this advantage over the exploited person that the exploiter plays upon in order to make use of the exploitee. But in which cases where I b-exploit your talents, capacities, activities, and so forth am I also exploiting *you*?

Pretty clearly not in every case. When Dusty Baker exploits Darren Lewis's speed, he does not thereby exploit Darren Lewis himself. If in the course of a casual conversation I ask you for a couple of small favors, slyly insinuating that if you refuse I may divulge some nasty secrets about your sexual or financial indiscretions, then I am a-exploiting your indiscretions and b-exploiting your ability to do the favors, but I do not seem to be exploiting *you yourself*. On the other hand, If I begin to use the same information to blackmail you out of considerable sums of money, then we might very well say that I am exploiting *you*; but this could depend on how regular and how large the payments turned out to be.

It seems to me there is no sharp dividing line here. We say that a *person* is exploited whenever we think the b-exploitation encompasses a sufficiently wide range of what the person does or is; and if I am sufficiently sensitive about the humiliation involved in having my weakness a-exploited, we may say that I "feel exploited" or "don't like being used" (thereby implying that it is *me*, and not merely something about me, that is being b-exploited). The exploitation of a person's labor—when this means the person's chief life-activity—clearly counts as exploitation of the person. When it is said that surrogacy exploits the mother, however, the idea is not *only* that surrogacy exploits her labor (whether in the birthing sense or in the more general working sense); the point is rather that it exploits her ability to carry and give birth to a child, which is taken to be such an intimate part of what she is that it could not be exploited without also exploiting *her*. Or it may be that having this ability put at someone else's disposal through her vulnerability is felt to be sufficiently humiliating to her that she is justified in regarding *herself* as exploited.[14]

To sum up: When people, or something about them, are its objects, exploitation consists in the exploiter's using something about the person for the exploiter's ends by playing on some weakness or vulnerability in that person. This is the basic idea behind all exploitation involving human objects. It applies equally to cases where exploitation is commonly considered unfair, wrongful, or unethical and to cases where it is not. There is no semantic distinction between "pejorative" and "nonpejorative" *senses* of "exploitation", any more than the words "seizure" and "payment" mean something different when the seizure is wrongful or the payment involves a breach of ethics. What there may be is a distinction between some cases in which exploitation is (or is taken to be) morally innocent, and other cases in which, on the basis of substantive moral principles, exploitation is taken to be morally objectionable and in which the use of the term "exploitation" calls attention to precisely those features of the situation in virtue of which it is found to be objectionable.

3. What Is Wrong with Exploitation

Not the distribution of benefits and harms. Many people seem to think that exploitation (at least in the "pejorative" sense) has to be unfair or unjust, and that the injustice consists in a redistribution of harms and benefits, with benefits flowing from the exploited to the exploiter. This is suggested by Marx's depiction of capitalist exploitation as the appropriation by capital of the worker's surplus labor, and it is quite explicitly involved in some Marxist accounts of exploitation, such as John Roemer's idea that being an exploiter consists in being able to command more labor embodied in goods than you have performed, or Jeffrey Reiman's insistence that exploitation involves unpaid labor.[15] In the same vein, Feinberg says that it is the element of "wrongfulness" which "distinguishes [exploitation] from non-exploitative utilization," and that "[one] element in exploitation is some redistribution of benefits and harms." According to Alan Wertheimer, "we typically say that A wrongfully exploits B when A takes unfair advantage of B. A must benefit from the transaction. . . . In addition, A exploits B only when the transaction is harmful or unfair to B."[16]

The drift of these remarks, however, seems to me in an important sense exactly wrong. Moreover, some of the writers on this topic appear to be aware of this. Gorr is struck by the fact that an exploitative offer typically expands the offeree's freedom of choice and that accepting it will normally net the offeree an increase in utility.[17]

Nor involuntariness, since exploitation is often voluntary. Feinberg too, in apparent contrast to the drift of the remarks just quoted, realizes that exploitation may benefit the exploited, and may occur "with the exploitee's fully voluntary consent"; exploitation may also be mutual, with each party acting in turn as exploiter and exploited, both benefiting from the arrangement.[18] Wertheimer, showing that he knows better as well, even realizes that exploited parties typically benefit *more* from an exploitative arrangement than exploiters do, and rightly points out that this should not surprise us. "It is precisely because the exploitee stands to gain so much from the transaction (relative to the exploiter) that his bargaining position is comparatively weak."[19] This also explains why exploitation should often be voluntary on the part of the exploitee, since it is only to be expected that you will voluntarily consent to an arrangement by which you benefit.

Marx's view of capitalist exploitation is not undermined but, on the contrary, confirmed by these observations. Back when the American press still thought it necessary to combat Marxist ideas, journalists simultaneously exercised their wit and proved their loyalty by noting satirically how eager unemployed workers are to subject themselves to (what Marxists regard as) "exploitation." More earnest defenders of the capitalist system have often represented capitalists as the benefactors of those they employ, and infer from this that it must be mistaken (indeed, a sign of cruel ingratitude) for wage laborers to think of their bosses as exploiters. But the mirth is misplaced and the inference invalid. Since being benefited and being exploited are often merely two sides of the same coin, and people may often be in dire need of the benefits in question, they can often be eager to be exploited.

The point is that it goes along with being vulnerable, or in a weak bargaining position, that you should have a lot to gain from being taken advantage of, and a lot to lose if you cannot find someone able and willing to take advantage of your vulnerability. Someone who is propertyless and starving has a lot to gain by striking a deal with an employer who is willing to offer bare subsistence in exchange for long, hard labor under dangerous conditions—and a lot to lose (namely, life itself) if no such exploitative bargain is in the offing. We can make the same point with a less controversial example. A gambler who owes a large amount of money to ruthless and violent characters will be in desperate need of the loan shark who offers the needed funds at a usurious rate of interest; such a person will be more than willing under these conditions to consent to virtually any terms of payment.

Not coercion either. Perhaps it will be said that people in such desperate straits are *forced* or *coerced* into making such deals. Certainly it is often said by Marxists that exploited workers are forced or coerced. This is often true in the sense that the exploited have no acceptable alternative to the arrangement under which they are exploited. But it does not follow that the exploiters themselves are coercing the exploited. (This is true only if the exploiters themselves are the ones who put the exploited in their vulnerable situation; Marx portrays things in this light when he represents the capitalist class as a whole as dispossessing the working class as a whole.)

Yet even if an exploitee has other *acceptable* alternatives to a given exploitative arrangement, and thus is not *forced* to accept the arrangement
even in that sense, these alternatives may be either equally exploitative or
far less desirable. For example, suppose that going on public assistance is an
alternative to taking employment under exploitative conditions, but when
the welfare system is administered by people with a rugged individualist
mentality, it may turn out—and quite intentionally—that the poor should
always choose to be exploited, when they are lucky enough to find an exploiter, rather than to live in misery and humiliation on the dole, even if
by doing so they would escape being exploited. For this reason, it seems to
me quite mistaken of Reiman to make it part of his concept of exploitation
that an exploited class must be *forced* to yield up unpaid labor.[20]

Certainly not "free-floating" evils. Exploitation, then, is not necessarily harmful
to the interests of the exploited; on the contrary, it will typically benefit
them to be exploited. Nor is it always correct to say that the exploited are
forced or coerced into accepting an exploitative arrangement. So what is
bad about exploitation? Those who operate with a moralized account of
exploitation must hold that even where exploitation is beneficial to the
exploited and fully voluntary on their part, there must be something bad
about it or the term could not be used at all (at least in the "pejorative"
sense). Feinberg's view of such cases is that they must involve some wrong
or badness other than harm to or involuntariness on the part of the exploited: either a harm to someone else, or some "free-floating" evil. Where
he cannot find any harm or evil of either sort, Feinberg thinks that one
person's use of another via the latter's vulnerability is "not exploitative at
all," or at any rate not "blamable exploitation." Feinberg is admirably sensitive to the wide range of evils which (in his view) can turn the harmless
(or even voluntary and beneficial) use of a person or features of a person
into exploitation, and also to the variety of controversial cases (commercial
fortune-telling, ticket scalping, various kinds of wrongful gain, threat, extortion, and blackmail) in which we can wonder whether exploitation should
be legally prohibited, or whether it is wrong though it should not be illegal,
or whether it is completely justified and hence (in his view) not a case of
exploitation "in the pejorative sense."[21]

Obligations to help others? Not quite. I should now explain why I find this
entire approach wrongheaded. In order to do so, I need to start being more
explicit about why I think most of us are disposed to see exploitation in
general as something bad. Most of us believe that when people are weak or
vulnerable, others should not use their weakness or seek to benefit from it,
but instead should seek to help them and rescue them from their bad situation. This is closely related to our reason for objecting to exploitation, but
I do not think Gorr is correct in saying that exploitation occurs only when

there is some *moral obligation* to help which the exploiter is failing to fulfill.[22]

This is clearly not so in cases where exploitation is not morally objectionable (a fact which is only concealed from Gorr by his adoption of a moralized account of exploitation). Even where exploitation is morally objectionable, it need not involve the violation of an "obligation to help." If I am a private detective hired by your wife to spy on you, I owe you no "obligation to help" making it incumbent on me not to tell her about your cheating—on the contrary, I owe her the obligation to inform on you. But I clearly do exploit you in a morally objectionable manner if I blackmail you by threatening to tell her.

The real reason. I suggest that the moral belief that makes exploitation objectionable is the following: Proper respect for others is violated when we treat their vulnerabilities as opportunities to advance our own interests or projects. It is degrading to have your weaknesses taken advantage of, and dishonorable to use the weaknesses of others for your ends. This moral belief, I submit, is widely shared, and it is why the term "exploitation" seems to us to refer to something bad, unfair, or unethical. This has nothing to do with the meaning of the word itself, but reflects a positive moral conviction which most of us hold.

Even when exploitation is both beneficial and voluntary on the part of the exploitee, it still involves the exploiter's a-exploitation of the exploitee's vulnerability, on the basis of which the exploiter furthers (through b-exploitation) some end of the exploiter's own. If we hold the moral belief I have just mentioned, then we must see something bad about this.[23] We think that in a wide range of cases it is degrading to human beings that they should be so treated, even if the exploitative arrangement is voluntary on both sides and no matter what the resulting distribution of benefits and harms.[24]

Confirmation of this account. One point in favor of this diagnosis is that those who reject this moral belief are precisely the people who see nothing bad about exploitation. Callicles and Nietzsche, for instance, see the world as divided by nature into the strong and the weak, and think that it is both natural and right that the world should contain these two types, and that the vulnerabilities of the weak should be taken advantage of by the strong. (Indeed, both think that this is what these vulnerabilities are naturally there *for.*) If my account is correct, then we should expect people with such views to approve of exploitation, as in fact they do.

Another point in favor of this account is that in cases where we do not regard exploitation as morally objectionable, there is normally some reason for thinking that our use of another's vulnerability will not be degrading to that other, or to the extent that it is, that the degradation is deserved or at any rate morally acceptable. Some instances of exploitation (exploiting the weaknesses of one's opponent in a game) can be regarded as innocent. One would not enter into the game with good sportsmanship if one did not expect (or even want) one's opponent to use one's weaknesses wherever possible, and competitive play remains morally innocent only as long as this sort of exploitation does not take a form which degrades the competitors.[25] Sometimes (e.g., the lawyer exploiting weaknesses in her opponent's case) we think people's vulnerabilities *ought* to be taken advantage of (for the sake of a just outcome).

Some disputed cases. Even in cases which are not innocent in these ways, we may think that exploitation is good (or morally acceptable, or at least satisfying on the whole), as when a person receives poetic justice through the a-exploitation of some morally bad quality—especially, as Feinberg points out, when the exploitee is "hoist with his own petard"—that is, a-exploited on the basis of a quality associated with a propensity to be an exploiter. Probably because he is disposed to a moralized conception of exploitation, Feinberg thinks it is even unclear whether, for example, the character Doyle Lonnegan (played by Robert Shaw in the movie *The Sting*) is exploited at all.[26] (Lonnegan, a powerful, wealthy, and utterly villainous mobster, is taken for half a million dollars by a gang of grifters, one of whom was killed on his orders early in the film.) However, I think nothing could be more obvious than that the elaborate con game portrayed in the film was an example of exploitation in exactly the same sense in which the term would apply if the same grifters had perpetrated one of their scams on a perfectly innocent victim.[27]

Another kind of case mentioned by Feinberg is that in which someone "cashes in" on the weaknesses of others precisely by helping them—as a business does when it supplies householders with protective devices during a crime wave, or as doctors do when they treat patients. Because Feinberg holds that exploitation requires that there be some sort of wrongness, unfairness, or unethical conduct on the part of the exploiter, he thinks that we cannot speak of exploitation at all in these cases unless those who help charge unfair prices for their services or gain disproportionately in comparison to those they help.[28] I disagree. Those who help people in a position of weakness typically exploit them as well, and they do so whether they make just profits, unjust profits, or even no profits at all, as long as they also use the vulnerability of the recipients to further some end of their own other than the helping itself. This they typically do, even if the end is an entirely innocent and noble one, such as developing or exercising their own moral virtues. No doubt in such a case we are disinclined to dwell on the exploitative aspect of the situation, not least because the helpers' further end may be in itself perfectly legitimate or even laudable, and because they are, after all, providing help to those who need it.

It is essential to keep in mind here, however, that when people are vulnerable and in need of help, it is not only the *helping* itself which they need. If one accepts the moral belief I have ascribed to most of us, then they are also beings with dignity, with whom not all is well as long as they lack the conditions under which a human being can be respected. Those who fulfill all their "obligations to help," or even display supererogatory virtue in helping, may (just by helping, and thereby exhibiting the terrible vulnerability of those they help) bring mercilessly to light the absence of these conditions.

Helping those in need therefore often has a profound moral ambivalence about it, making *solidarity* with them a far more vital achievement than any positive contribution to their welfare. (This is a point which radicals have generally gotten right, while liberals have often gotten it wrong.) For this reason, it seems to me extremely important for would-be benefactors of the weak and vulnerable to be fully (and even painfully) aware of the inevitably exploitative side of their beneficence. This is needed both to preserve the dignity of those they help and to protect the helpers themselves from a certain blind arrogance which sometimes afflicts those who have been fortunate enough to parley the doing of good into a successful career or life-defining activity.[29]

4. EXPLOITATION AND JUSTICE

Can exploitation be just? It is often thought that exploitation is bad because the exploiter takes *unfair* advantage of the exploitee. But if I am right about the source of our obligation to exploitation, then we have reason to consider exploitation bad even when it involves no unfairness or injustice. For if the badness of exploitation lies in the fact that it is base and dishonorable of the exploiter, and insulting and degrading to the exploited, for the former to make use of the latter's vulnerability, then this badness seems to be present even where the exploitation involves no unfairness, injustice, or violation of rights. This means that even if issues about exploitation are chiefly issues of distribution (the distribution of power), they still cannot be reduced to issues about distributive *justice*. In other words, a just distribution of power may still be highly objectionable if it leads to just, but still highly objectionable, forms of exploitation.

But in what cases should exploitation be considered unjust or a violation of rights? If we use Mill's admirably clarifying and theoretically neutral definition of justice or right—that a person's right is a valid claim on society to be protected in the possession of something[30]—then it follows that exploitation is unjust or violates a person's right if and only if the exploited person has a valid claim on society's protection against the exploitation.

If the account of exploitation described above is correct, there is also a distinction to be drawn between two ways in which society might go about protecting people against exploitation. Either society could make it more difficult for the powerful to use their power to exploit the vulnerable, or it could redistribute power so that people are less vulnerable to use by others, and hence less susceptible to exploitation. Let us call the first way of protecting people "interference"[31] and the second way "redistribution." Exploitation is unjust, then, whenever the weakness exploited is one which society should either prevent others from taking advantage of (by means of interference) or else prevent from occurring altogether (by means of redistribution).

Prima facie it might be reasonable to expect society to protect people from forms of exploitation which degrade them or violate their humanity, or which involve exploiters using their advantage in order to gain a very good mode of life for themselves while the exploited are condemned to a very bad or impoverished kind of life. Before we accept even such principles as these, however, we need to know what society is capable of accomplishing along these lines, and what costs it would incur in trying. These are large questions, but perhaps I can usefully make a couple of observations about how the approach I have been taking might impact on the issues of wage labor and surrogacy.

Capitalist exploitation. Regarding the first issue, people have usually thought that the controversial question is whether wage labor is exploitative. But if what I have said about the concept of exploitation is accepted, then it should be obvious—not a matter worthy of any dispute at all—that Marx was right: Capital virtually always exploits wage labor. At least this is self-evident if it is granted that those who own the means of production enjoy a decisive bargaining advantage over those who own little besides their capacity to labor, and that this fundamental vulnerability on the part of labor decisively influences the terms of wage contracts. Collective bargaining and governmental regulation of the labor market can sometimes strengthen the bargaining position of workers (though the role of the state has more often been to weaken it), but the fundamental bargaining advantage of capital over labor is an ineradicable structural feature of the modern capitalist (or so-called free market) economy. More generally, it is obvious that markets are bound to involve exploitative transactions whenever there are significant inequalities in the holdings of those who trade with one another, and whenever these inequalities significantly affect the terms of the transactions.[32]

It is another question whether capital's pervasive exploitation of labor is just or unjust. Using his own highly reductive account of justice (according to which the justice of a transaction is no defense of it), Marx thought that capitalist exploitation was generally just.[33] Those more favorably disposed toward capitalism argue for the same conclusion on various grounds: that it would be a violation of people's natural property rights either to interfere with capitalist transactions or to redistribute wealth in such a way as to forestall exploitation; or that the attempt to prevent capitalist exploitation either by interference or redistribution will necessarily involve excessive costs in individual liberty or the economic productivity of society. I will not comment on such arguments here, except to characterize, a bit later, the sort of position they support.

Surrogacy and exploitation. On the issue of surrogacy, it seems to me once again self-evident that it involves exploitation of the birth mother whenever she is in a position of significant economic disadvantage compared to the adopting parents. This is a simple consequence of the fact, just noted, that exploitation is endemic to all market transactions whose terms are significantly affected by the fact that the participants are in unequal bargaining positions. Some argue that surrogacy is exploitative because it involves the commodification of childbearing. I agree with this, but I do not agree with the reason often given for it, that there is something special about childbearing that ought to exempt it from commodification. For even if this is true it would not show why there is anything *exploitative* about commodifying what should not be commodified. The commodification of childbearing is apt to be exploitative simply because in a market to which people bring unequal assets, the commodification of *anything* is apt to be exploitative.

Once again, it is a separate question whether surrogacy contracts are unjust or violate anyone's rights. When the issue is posed entirely in terms of the enforceability of such contracts, it is assumed that interference (in the form of rendering the contracts unenforceable) is society's only means of preventing exploitation. This may be because, for various reasons, redistribution is not seen as a viable way of avoiding exploitation. The economic vulnerability typical of surrogate mothers is not generally regarded as avoidable within a modern market economy, and the psychological vulnerabilities involved here do not seem preventable by any means within society's power. But there is always a dilemma when we must consider interference alone as a remedy for exploitation. As we have noted, an exploitative arrangement may benefit both parties, and is even likely to benefit the exploitee more than it benefits the exploiter. By interfering with exploitative arrangements, we may prevent one person from taking advantage of another's weakness, but we thereby also risk consigning the vulnerable person to an even worse fate than being exploited. If we decide that interference is too cruel to those in a position of weakness, we may decide that the exploitation, however bad it may be in various respects, violates no one's rights and has to be considered just. Radical remedies for exploitation, where they exist, are therefore always redistributive.

Can exploitation be abolished? People are encumbered with weaknesses or vulnerabilities of many kinds—physical, psychological, emotional, economic, political. They are also mutually dependent and competitively motivated, so that they have strong incentives to exploit the weaknesses of others. Exploitation is therefore a pervasive fact of the social life of human beings, and yet (for those who share the moral belief I have ascribed to most of us) it is also a profound evil which tends to infect nearly all their relationships with one another. Those who see the extent of exploitation cannot realistically hope that it will ever be wholly abolished, yet they ought to hope (as Marx did) that the largest and most systematic forms of it can someday be abolished.

Radical remedies for exploitation are always redistributive. They involve transfers of power (political, economic, institutional, emotional) from the strong to the weak. But powerful individuals and groups seldom abandon their advantages willingly, and by the nature of the case they have great resources with which to protect their position. Therefore, redistributive remedies to exploitation are inevitably difficult, costly, and potentially explosive in their social effects, and they always face prospects of success which are uncertain at best. This entails that there will always be strong arguments in favor of saying that society either cannot or should not be expected to do what is necessary to protect people against exploitation. Following the Millian analysis of rights and justice, this directly entails that there will be strong arguments for saying that exploitation is just.[34]

In other words, there will inevitably be strong arguments for a position not too far from that of Callicles and Nietzsche. Such a position need not hold, with them, that exploitation itself is just or a good thing, but it will hold that exploitation is something we must learn to live with. For the present, I am not concerned to dispute this position. Nor am I concerned for the moment to deny what many of its supporters also believe, that capitalism is the freest, most just, and most productive economic order the world has ever known, that it is the social order which best accords with what we know of human nature, that no one has found a better or more workable system, or that every attempt to refound society on a radically less exploitative basis has not only been unsuccessful but had an utterly disastrous outcome.

Instead, I wish only to insist that people who think this way should recognize a simple truth which is entirely consistent with everything just conceded: that since under capitalism there are vast differences in economic power and ample opportunity in the market system for the strong to use these differences to their advantage, capitalism is also a highly exploitative social order, perhaps the most exploitative the world has ever known.

If you agree with Callicles and Nietzsche that this is all quite as it should be, then this admission need not disturb you. But if you agree with the moral belief I have ascribed to most of us—that it is an affront to people's human dignity to have their weaknesses used, and shameful to use the weaknesses of others—then you should find yourself in a troubling position. You should be ready to acknowledge that despite capitalism's long list of alleged virtues, we have strong grounds not to show any great loyalty to it. You should be willing to admit that even if we have yet to find a social system better than capitalism, we nevertheless have good and sufficient reasons to keep on looking for one, and reason too to put some of the cherished advantages of capitalism at risk in trying to achieve a better form of society. Finally, if the analysis of exploitation presented earlier in this essay is accurate, then you must also face the fact that you cannot honestly escape your ambivalent feelings about the society in which you live by the shallow ruse of arguing that since capitalism is just and "exploitation" (in the "pejorative" sense) is by definition wrongful or unjust, capitalism cannot be exploitative.

Notes

I am grateful for written comments on earlier drafts of this essay by G. A. Cohen, David Lyons, Julie Maybee, and Alan Wertheimer, and for oral comments and discussion by Elizabeth Anderson, Neera Kapur Badhwar, Dan Brock, Daniel Farrell, Michael Gorr, Terence Irwin, Loren Lomasky, Roderick Long, Fred Miller, Ellen Frankel Paul, Thomas Pogge, Larry Temkin, and Steve Wall.

1. The claim that surrogacy contracts are exploitative can be found in Peter Singer and Deane Wells, *The Reproductive Revolution* (New York: Oxford University Press, 1984), 125; Mary Warnock, *A Question of Life: The Warnock Report on Human Fertilisation and Embryology* (Oxford: Blackwell, 1985), 46; Heidi Malm, "Paid Surrogacy: Arguments and Responses," *Public Affairs Quarterly* 3 (1989): 61; Martha Field, *Surrogate Motherhood* (Cambridge: Harvard University Press, 1989), 25; George J. Annas, "Fairy Tales Surrogate Mothers Tell," in Larry Gostin, ed., *Surrogate Motherhood* (Bloomington: Indiana University Press, 1990), 43; Rosemarie Tong, "Overdue Death," in *ibid.*, 45; Alexander Capron and Margaret Radin, "Choosing Family Law over Contract Law as a Paradigm for Surrogate Motherhood" in *ibid.*, 62; Elizabeth S. Anderson, "Is Women's Labor a Commodity?" *Philosophy and Public Affairs* 19 (1990): 84; and Debra Satz, "Markets in Women's Reproductive Labor," *Philosophy and Public Affairs* 21 (1992): 123–24. Thoughtful replies to these claims have been made by Richard J. Arneson, "Commodification and Commercial Surrogacy," *Philosophy and Public Affairs* 21 (1992): 132–64; and Alan Wertheimer, "Two Questions about Surrogacy and Exploitation," *Philosophy and Public Affairs* 21 (1992): 211–39.
2. Wertheimer, "Two Questions," 212.
3. For instance, see John Roemer, "Should Marxists Be Interested in Exploitation?" in Roemer, ed., *Analytical Marxism* (Cambridge: Cambridge University Press, 1986), 260–82.

4. Under the verb "exploit", Webster's (1966) distinguishes "to turn a natural resource to economic account: to utilize" from "to make use of meanly or unjustly for one's own advantage or profit"; American Heritage (1985) distinguishes "to employ to the greatest possible advantage" from "to make use of selfishly or unethically."

5. See Joel Feinberg, *Harmless Wrongdoing* (New York: Oxford University Press, 1988), 178; Wertheimer, "Two Questions," 212.

6. Michael J. Gorr, *Coercion, Freedom, and Exploitation* (New York: Peter Lang, 1989), 147.

7. Plato, *Gorgias*, tr. Terence Irwin (Oxford: Clarendon Press, 1979), 488b5.

8. "Morally speaking, [modern society] represents a maximum in the exploitation of humanity; but it presupposes those on whose account this exploitation has meaning. . . . My concept, my metaphor for this type is, as one knows, the word *Übermensch*" (Friedrich Nietzsche, *Werke* [Leipzig: Naumann, 1901], 15:421; see Nietzsche, *The Will to Power*, ed. Walter Kaufmann [New York: Random House, 1967], sec. 866, 463–64).

9. John Kleinig describes various cases of exploitation, then writes that they all "involve one party's playing on some character trait of the other for the purpose of securing some advantage" (Kleinig, "The Ethics of Consent," *Canadian Journal of Philosophy* 11 [1981]). In my terms the "playing on" is a-exploitation, while the "securing some advantage" is b-exploitation.

10. These suggestions were made to me in conversation by Elizabeth Anderson and Dan Brock, respectively. But the formulations are my own, based on my memory of informal exchanges, and they may not do justice to what these individuals had in mind.

11. Michael Gorr reminds me of a passage in Marx's early notebooks where it is said that under the system of private property each person regards the other's needs only as sources of dependence and power, with the result that "mutual pillaging" is the basic social relationship between people (see Allen W. Wood, ed., *Marx: Selections* [New York: Macmillan, 1988], 37–38). Though Marx does not use the term "exploitation" here, I think it would be quite accurate to say that it was Marx's intent in these passages to put all market exchanges in an exploitative light. But the claim that all market exchanges are necessarily exploitative, if taken literally, seems to me simply wrong (and not something the mature Marx ever said or would have been inclined to say). However, there are a couple of points the young Marx is making in this passage that seem to me very insightful and on target. Marx is portraying the standpoint of the political economists, who (then as today) do tend to represent people's interest in one another as exclusively *exploitative* in a fairly straightforward sense, since they interpret the needs and desires of others as merely so many opportunities for me to satisfy my utility function. Marx wants to contrast production under such a system with a society in which we might "produce things as human beings," looking upon the needs of the other instead as opportunities to affirm our human potentialities and our commonality with other human beings, which is surely a more attractive picture of what human life might be like than what we see portrayed either in the theories of the economists or in the actual capitalist social order they intend to depict.

12. Feinberg, *Harmless Wrongdoing*, 184–92.

13. This can be illustrated by the example of the tabloid mentioned above. The tabloid a-exploits the public's tastes, and these tastes do enable the tabloid to

reap benefits. But various things suggest themselves as the means it uses: for example, these tastes themselves, or the public's purchasing power, or the market system through which the papers are sold; and none of these is readily identifiable as a distinct object of b-exploitation neatly correlated with the tabloid's a-exploitation of the public's tastes.

14. On the other hand, I think it would be hyperbole to say of an exploitation film, which exploits the public's bad taste or morbid curiosity, that it also exploits *the public*. Pornography is sometimes alleged to exploit *women*—not just the women who pose for pornographic pictures, but all women (see, e.g., Andrea Dworkin, *Intercourse* [New York: Free Press, 1987], and Catharine MacKinnon, *Only Words* [Cambridge: Harvard University Press, 1993]). The idea appears to be that pornography encourages a one-sided image of all women as sexual playthings, as objects of domination and humiliation, and this is seen as creating for all women a wide range of vulnerabilities which make possible various forms of a-exploitation with women as their victims. The claim that pornography exploits all women strikes me as hyperbole; but if the issue of whether a person is exploited turns on "how much of the person" is included in the exploitation, then we might expect that there will be a tendency to hyperbole on the part of those whose aim is to persuade us of the seriousness of a given kind of exploitation.

15. Roemer, "Should Marxists Be Interested in Exploitation?" 260; Jeffrey Reiman, "Exploitation, Force, and the Moral Assessment of Capitalism: Thoughts on Roemer and Cohen," *Philosophy and Public Affairs* 16 (1987): 3–41. I call these "Marxist" accounts only because that is the way their authors advertise them. There is no reason to ascribe any of them to Marx himself, since he has no technical concept of exploitation. Marx's economic theory does have a technical concept of the "rate of exploitation" (s/v, the ratio of surplus value to variable capital). But Marx gives it this name only because he already believes, on perfectly reasonable grounds that do not depend on his theory of value or any other technical notions, that capitalism involves the exploitation of wage labor; s/v is merely a technical device for *measuring* this exploitation. Marx need not think that every conceivable instance in which these technical concepts might be employed would be an instance of exploitation, only that the economic relations to which they apply in actual capitalism are in fact exploitative economic relations. Thus, it is beside the point that Roemer can construct examples of "exploitation" in his technical "Marxist" sense which do not intuitively strike us as unjust. For instance, Karl has fewer assets than Adam, but because Karl prefers low work and low consumption, he loans some of his assets to Adam, who prefers more work and more consumption, and who pays Karl "interest" on what he borrows. Here Adam is "exploited"—in the technical "Marxist" sense— by Karl, even though Adam has greater initial assets and becomes progressively richer over time than Karl is (Roemer, "Should Marxists Be Interested in Exploitation?" 272–74). But as Roemer presents it this is not really an example of exploitation at all (except in the technical "Marxist" sense he has defined), because neither Karl nor Adam is depicted as being in any way vulnerable to the other; they simply have different preferences and find a mutually satisfactory arrangement for satisfying them. Such examples, needless to say, bear no resemblance to the extraction of unpaid labor from workers by capital under real-life capitalism, where the weakness of the worker's bargaining position and its systematic exploitation by capital is *the* fundamental structural feature defining the entire economy.

16. Feinberg, *Harmless Wrongdoing*, 199, 192; Wertheimer, "Two Questions," 213.
17. Gorr, *Coercion, Freedom, and Exploitation*, 162.
18. Feinberg, *Harmless Wrongdoing*, 176, 191, 195–96; Wertheimer, "Two Questions," 213, 222–23.
19. Wertheimer, "Two Questions," 223.
20. Reiman, "Exploitation, Force, and the Moral Assessment of Capitalism," 3. Coercion is also made a requirement for exploitation in other interpretations of Marxist claims; see, e.g., Richard Arneson, "What's Wrong with Exploitation?" *Ethics* 91 (1981): 202–27.
21. See Feinberg, *Harmless Wrongdoing*, 184, 191; see also ibid., ch. 32, in which Feinberg tries to resolve many controversial issues surrounding wrongful gain.
22. Gorr, *Coercion, Freedom, and Exploitation*, 163–65.
23. Compare John Kleinig's view that the exploitation of another's weakness is wrong even when it does not violate another's right, does not wrong the other, and does not treat the other unfairly (Kleinig, "The Ethics of Consent").
24. Do these objections to exploitation rest on Kant's principle that we must not treat others merely as means, but always at the same time as ends in themselves? Both Kant and the moral belief I have ascribed to us permit us sometimes to use others as means. Kant permits this when we treat them at the same time as ends, and the belief I ascribe to us permits it when our use does not involve taking advantage of another's vulnerability. But Kant's principle is sometimes interpreted in such a way that it is a sufficient condition for treating another as an end that the other consent (or even *be able* to consent) to this treatment. For example: "If we treat other agents as mere means, . . . it is not merely that we act in ways to which they *do not* consent; we act on maxims to which they *could not* consent" (Onora O'Neill, *Constructions of Reason* [Cambridge: Cambridge University Press, 1989], 138). If this is a correct interpretation of Kant's principle, then it is much weaker than the belief I am ascribing to most of us. For on this belief we find exploitation objectionable even when people can and do consent to it. On the other hand, perhaps treating others as ends in themselves demands far more than that they be able to consent, or even than that they actually consent, to the way we treat them. Perhaps in order to treat others as ends in themselves we must also refrain, at least in a great many situations, from making use of their vulnerabilities for our ends, whether they consent to it or not. In that case, Kant's principle might turn out to be equivalent to the belief I am ascribing to most of us, which accounts for our moral objection to exploitation.
25. The difference between innocent and noninnocent exploitation is quite comparable, I think, to Richard Miller's distinction between innocent and noninnocent competition between people (see Miller, "From Responsibility to Justice," unpublished manuscript). Exploitation, as playing on others' weaknesses, is a typically competitive type of behavior; thus, generally speaking, it will be innocent only where human competition is innocent. I take Miller to agree with my view that noninnocent competition, which is pervasive in many social forms, including our own, constitutes the essence of some of the largest and worst social evils.
26. Feinberg, *Harmless Wrongdoing*, 203, 207.
27. It seems to me a misinterpretation of the film, moreover, for Feinberg to suggest that what the grifters do to Lonnegan is supposed to be morally acceptable,

all things considered. For the movie is not supposed to leave us righteously rejoicing in the triumph of virtue; on the contrary, we smile *wickedly* along with the story's low-life heroes, who—liars and con men though they are— have at least the honesty not to seek any moral justification for their crooked schemes. If we take satisfaction in Lonnegan's being exploited, this is simply because the evil of that exploitation is more than offset by the fact that this character receives a particularly delicious kind of poetic justice: for the scam brings low a powerful man who has lived by exploiting others, and the very weaknesses in Lonnegan which the grifters a-exploit—his greed, arrogance, vengefulness, cruelty—are precisely the vicious qualities which have made him an especially odious exploiter.

28. Feinberg, *Harmless Wrongdoing*, 184, 193–94.

29. Such examples also occasion the observation that, contrary to many dictionaries, there is nothing necessarily *selfish* about exploitation. It is true that those who use the weakness of others for their own ends typically do so for selfish ends, but there is nothing requiring that the ends be selfish. Imagine a nation struggling to free itself from the dominion of a foreign power which has set up a puppet government. A patriot learns that a collaborationist official is hiding some scandalous secret, and blackmails the official to cooperate in a resistance plot to overthrow the puppet government. Here the patriot clearly exploits the official: He a-exploits his vulnerability to blackmail and b-exploits his governmental position. The patriot's ends are not in the least selfish, however; the patriot may reap no personal gain from the overthrow of the puppet government, and we may even imagine that he knows all along that he will have to sacrifice his life in the course of carrying out the revolutionary plot.

30. John Stuart Mill, *Utilitarianism*, ed. George Sher (Indianapolis: Hackett, 1979), 52.

31. "Interference" includes the prohibition of acts through which exploiters might make use of their power, but perhaps it more often involves the refusal of the state to recognize and support exploitative arrangements; consider, for example, the law's refusal to support the collection of interest on loans at usurious rates, or the proposal that surrogate motherhood be permitted but that surrogacy contracts be legally unenforceable against the birth mother.

32. In this way, I wholeheartedly agree with John Roemer that the basic issue involved in capitalist exploitation is one of the initial distribution of assets (Roemer, "Should Marxists Be Interested in Exploitation?" 262–63, 274, 281–82). I fault Roemer only for employing a technical definition of "exploitation" which makes exploitation a matter entirely independent of initial distribution. For that obscures the fact that this has always been the main issue about capitalist exploitation.

33. This is an exegetical thesis I have explained and defended in many places and over a long period of time. See M. Cohen, T. Nagel, and T. Scanlon, eds., *Marx, Justice, and History* (Princeton: Princeton University Press, 1980), 3–41, 106–34, and Allen Wood, *Karl Marx* (London: Routledge, 1981), ch. 9.

34. Some might prefer to speak here of injustices whose rectification is prohibitively costly. That would require a modification of the Millian analysis of rights and justice which we have been using. From this analysis it follows that if it would be prohibitively costly for society to protect me in the possession of X, then society should not protect me in the possession of X, and so I do not have a right to X, and my being deprived of X is no injustice. Perhaps this is a basis

for objection to Mill's analysis of rights, but it does not seem to me a serious objection in practice. For it seems to me not to make a great deal of difference in practice whether we say of wage laborers or surrogate mothers that they have no right to be protected from exploitation, or that they have such a right but it is prohibitively costly for society to enforce it.

Exploitation, Freedom, and Justice

JON ELSTER

EXPLOITATION IS THE GENERATION of economic injustice through free market transactions. This is the thesis I want to discuss, and to a large degree to defend, in the present paper. The thesis will provoke disagreement along two different lines. First, Marxists might want to say that the worker is forced to sell his labor power; hence the wage agreement is not a free transaction. Conversely, libertarians might want to argue that if the transactions are free, the outcome cannot be unjust. Each of the objections has some merit; hence my defense of the thesis is not unconditional. I shall proceed by discussing in turn each of the three notions appearing in the title, exploitation, freedom, and justice. Since I am also concerned to elucidate what I take to be a major strand in Marx's thought, I shall often refer to his writings, but the exegetical issue is secondary to the substantive ones.

1. THE STRUCTURE OF CAPITALIST EXPLOITATION

I shall define Marxian exploitation as the intersection of two more general categories. On the one hand it is a special case of the more general Marxian notion of extraction of surplus labor, on the other hand it is a special case of a more general notion of exploitation that also encompasses non-Marxist varieties.

From Jon Elster, "Exploitation, Freedom, and Justice," in J. Roland Pennock and John W. Chapman, eds., *Marxism* (Nomos 26) (New York: New York University Press, 1983), 277–304, with the permission of New York University Press.

Surplus labor, according to Marx, may be extracted by "direct coercion"[1] or "extraeconomic compulsion"[2] on the one hand, by "the force of circumstances"[3] or "the dull compulsion of economic relations"[4] on the other. The former is the mode of surplus labor extraction characteristic of slavery and feudalism, or at least of the nonmarket sectors of these systems. The latter is found in capitalism, and more generally in market economies. I shall reserve the term "exploitation" for the latter, referring to the former as "forcible extraction of surplus labor." This terminology, while contrary to that of Marx,[5] is supported by the more general usage as well as by certain substantive considerations.

From consultation of the *OED*, Littré, Duden, and Harrap's German-English Dictionary, it would appear that "exploit," "exploiter," and "*ausbeuten*" have three central meanings that are relevant for our purposes. First, there is the morally neutral sense of "making use of," as in the exploitation of natural resources. In German this is rather rendered by "*ausnützen*," hence Marx's suggestion in *The German Ideology* of a link between utilitarianism and exploitation.[6] Second, there is a morally negative sense of "turning to account for selfish purposes" (*OED*) or "*/skrupellos/ für sich ausnützen*" (Duden). When applied to persons considered as "mere workable material" (*OED*), exploitation means treating another not as an end in itself, only as a means to one's own satisfaction or profit. Exploitation in this sense can be mutual, as in the act of exchange. In *The German Ideology* Marx does in fact speak of "mutual exploitation," when referring to the general tendency in capitalism to evaluate other people according to their utility.[7] Marx certainly believed this to be a morally deplorable phenomenon, but it is more akin to alienation than to what in the later economic writings he was to call exploitation.[8] Third, there is the asymmetrical notion of "taking unfair advantage of someone" (Harrap) or "*tirer un peu profit illicite ou peu honorable de quelque chose*" (Littré). This, I believe, best captures the notion of capitalist exploitation found in *Capital*.

As I understand it, the phrase "taking unfair advantage of someone" not only does not imply but actually excludes the idea of physically forcing someone to work for one's own profit. As I shall argue in section 2 below, this does not exclude that the person being taken advantage of is in some sense "forced" or "coerced," but this sense cannot be the one that implies an infringement of his physical liberty. Such infringement, on the other hand, was at the heart of surplus labor extraction from slave or serf. In an important special case, that of perfectly competitive markets, exploitation also differs from other forms of surplus labor extraction in that it is to the benefit of both parties.[9] There cannot be mutual exploitation, but there can be mutually beneficial exploitation. These differences between capitalist exploitation and precapitalist modes of surplus labor extraction provide the substantive reason behind the terminology I am using.

The starting point for my discussion of Marxian exploitation will be one of the models developed by John Roemer, in his recent, pathbreaking analysis of exploitation and class.[10] Roemer's work offers a series of models of exploitation. The most general approach (briefly explained in note 15 below) enables him to characterize exploitation in socialist no less than in capitalist economies. Here, however, I shall only draw on the models in part 2 of his book. These try to explain how exploitation and class division can arise endogenously through market exchange, thus breaking with the usual Marxist practice of taking these phenomena as given. More specifically, imagine a set of individuals all equipped with the same amount of labor power (or the same skill), but differentially endowed with other factors of production. In addition to the individuals, we must assume the presence of a state that guarantees their property rights and enforces contracts. There are well-defined techniques for producing all goods except labor power, which is the only scarce resource. Given the existence of a labor market, "an agent can engage in three types of economic activity: he can sell his labor power, he can hire the labor power of others, or he can work for himself. His constraint is that he must be able to lay out the operating costs, in advance, for the activities he chooses to operate, either with his own labor or hired labor, funded by the value of his endowments."[11]

Here the endowments and the labor power are evaluated at the prices and wage rate that obtain at the competitive equilibrium.[12] In addition to the capital constraint, Roemer assumes that there is a constraint on the length of the working day. Within these constraints, agents are supposed to maximize their net revenue. We can then ask three questions with respect to the economic agents:

1. What is their revenue?
2. Do they work for themselves, sell their labor power, or hire labor?
3. Do they work longer hours than are embodied in the commodities they can buy with their net revenue?

The first question concerns the *wealth* of the economic agents, the second their *class* membership, and the third their *exploitation* status. In a series of important theorems, Roemer proves that these are highly correlated.[13] Exploiters are rich people that hire others to work for them. This may not come as a surprise, yet earlier Marxists have tended to assume this to be true by definition, not seeing that a proof is required.

Roemer's model is admirably clear and instructive. Although highly abstract, it brings out very well many of the central features of the Marxian theory of exploitation and class. On the other hand, because of the high level of abstraction, it tends to obscure other important aspects of exploitation. To be specific, I shall argue that the model brings out very well the *modal* and *structural* nature of exploitation, while unduly restricting it by the *static* and *competitive* setting.

Class membership is a *modal* notion in the following sense. A worker is not defined as any agent who actually sells his labor power, but as an agent who *must* sell his labor power in order to optimize. Some agents have the option of optimizing by selling their labor power, but they may do equally well by working for themselves; hence they are petty bourgeois rather than workers. The workers are "forced to sell their labor power." Similarly, a capitalist is an agent who must hire labor to optimize, as distinct from the petty bourgeois who may have this as one optimal solution among others. We cannot look at actual behavior to define class membership; rather we must look at constraints, necessities, and possibilities. The class-exploitation correspondence principle holds only for classes thus modally defined: A person who must sell his labor power in order to optimize is always an exploited agent, while a petty bourgeois who chooses to do so may or may not be exploited.[14] I should add that there is another reason as well why behavior is an inadequate indicator of class: Some agents may choose not to optimize. A well-endowed person does not become a worker if he chooses to sell his labor power if this is not among his optimizing solutions. He remains a capitalist as long as his endowments would make him a compulsory hirer of labor were he to optimize. To leave the capitalist class he would have to give away his endowments, rather than using them inefficiently. This, I believe, makes good sociological sense. The analogous possibility for the worker is less interesting, since the worker is not only forced to sell his labor power in order to optimize, but also forced to optimize. I discuss this issue further in section 2 below.

The idea of *structural* exploitation can be taken in a variety of ways. In a wide sense, for instance, one might say that the unemployed are structurally exploited, even though they expend no labor, since they would be better off were they given their share of society's capital goods.[15] This is not the sense I have in mind here. Rather I use it to bring out the fact that exploitation is not a face-to-face phenomenon, but a general-equilibrium one—the net effect of all the various transactions an agent undertakes in different markets. In Roemer's models it is not possible, in fact, to define the relation "A exploits B," only the predicates "A is an exploiter" and "B is an exploited." Although it may be possible to identify a specific transaction between two individuals by virtue of which one is an exploiting and the other an exploited agent, this need not always be so. Marx, for instance, observes that a landlord who leases his land to a capitalist tenant is an exploiter, although he does not directly exploit labor.[16] On this structural understanding of exploitation, it is the capitalist class as a whole that takes unfair advantage of the working class as a whole, but it may prove impossible to define similarly clear-cut confrontations between individuals. I believe that for normative purposes, this structural sense of exploitation is indeed the proper one, but for explanatory purposes it may be less relevant. Managers rather than shareholders may be the target of collective action by the working class.[17]

The *static* character of Roemer's model is a serious drawback, for two reasons. First, part of the surplus accruing to the exploiter may be used for investment in future production, and part of that future production may benefit the workers. Marx writes in *Capital I* that "the greater part of the yearly accruing surplus-product [is] embezzled because abstracted without return of an equivalent."[18] If this is what constitutes the moral wrongness of exploitation, the return later of part of the surplus would make it less wrong.[19] Hence the injustice of exploitation would depend on the size and distribution of unearned capitalist consumption, not on the size of the surplus.[20] Second, workers no less than capitalists may save and invest, if wages are above subsistence. If workers save differentially, an equal initial distribution of resources might over time change into an unequal one that could in turn be the basis for exploitation of workers by ex-workers. It is not obvious that this is subject to the same moral condemnation as exploitation due to endowments that are not in this sense "deserved." Summing up, the static or one-period approach to exploitation is misleading because both the future use of profits and the past origin of capital are morally relevant. I return to these issues in section 3 below.

The *competitive* nature of the model makes it inapplicable to capitalist economies with collective bargaining or other modes of interaction involving coalitions, such as "divide and conquer" tactics by the capitalists.[21] To determine the rate of exploitation in a one-period model of collective bargaining, one will have to invoke some theory of bilateral monopoly, e.g., the Zeuthen-Nash-Harsanyi theory that makes the outcome dependent in a precise way on the relative bargaining strength of the parties.[22] It may then be true in a literal sense that the capitalist class is taking unfair advantage of the working class, as distinct from the more indirect sense in which that phrase was used above. In the more interesting case of multiperiod bargaining, both the working class and the capitalist class will have to take account of the impact of the present wage settlement on the future stream of income. There are elements of such reasoning in Marx, when he suggests that it is in the interest of the capitalist class to restrain its greed because otherwise the physical reproduction of the workers will be threatened,[23] and in the interest of the working class to restrain its wage demands in order not to jeopardize economic growth and future wage increases.[24] More recently, Kelvin Lancaster has proposed an analogous model in which the capitalists are restrained by the fear that the workers might retaliate against high levels of capitalist consumption with high wage demands and welfare payments.[25] Unlike Marx's hints at a temporally defined model, the Lancaster model is a genuinely strategic one, in which the decisions of both classes are interdependent in the sense of being "best replies" against each other.

In conclusion, I should say that the above discussion has not yet provided any grounds for normative statements about the injustice of exploitation. I have been concerned to bring out what exploitation *means*, in the technical Marxian sense of working more than the amount of labor embodied in the goods one can purchase for one's income, and to sketch some of the ways in which it can *come about*, by competition or collective bargaining based on differential ownership of the means of production. I have stated that for Marx this was no doubt also a case of exploitation in the wider sense of taking unfair advantage, but I have yet to state and discuss the criteria of fairness that are involved.

2. Freedom, Coercion, and Force Under Capitalism

Is the worker coerced or forced to sell his labor power? If so, how can this be made compatible with the fact that capitalism, unlike earlier modes of production, offers a good deal of freedom to the worker? I shall begin with the last question, and explore the sense in which and the limits within which the worker has a freedom of choice in capitalism. I then ask whether the worker can be said to be *coerced* to sell his labor power, assuming that this expression implies the existence of an agent coercing him. Finally, focusing on the cases in which this question is answered negatively, I shall consider whether the worker might not yet be *forced* to sell his labor power, assuming this phrase to be neutral with respect to the existence of an agent forcing him.

Following Marx, the worker has freedom of choice with respect to (at least) three different economic decisions. First, he is free to leave the working class altogether; second, he is free to choose his employer; and third, he is free to spend his wage as he pleases. I shall discuss these in turn, but first let me make a distinction between two senses of freedom. One we may refer to as "formal freedom": It simply consists in the absence of coercion, in the broad sense indicated below. The other I call "real ability," and is defined by the fact that the real ability to do x and the desire to do x implies doing x.[26] Formal freedom to do x and the desire to do x, on the other hand, do not imply doing x, unless the required material or personal resources are present. Real ability is unconditional; formal freedom is conditional in the sense that it requires resources to be effective.

Marx argues that in "bourgeois society every workman, if he is an exceedingly clever and shrewd fellow, and gifted with bourgeois instincts and favoured by an exceptional fortune, can possibly be converted himself into an *exploiteur deu travail d'autrui*."[27] As is evident from the conditional clause, this is a mere formal freedom, whose transformation into real ability depends inter alia on personal talents. The freedom to choose one's employer, on the other hand, is a real ability, under the competitive conditions usually assumed by Marx.[28] Hence we see that the worker is free in the more important sense (i.e., real ability) with respect to the less important freedom (the freedom to choose one's employer), while free in the weaker sense with respect to the more important freedom. Marx argued that the latter freedom tends to generate the illusion that the worker is free not only with respect to the individual capitalist, but with respect to capital as such.[29] This illusion is reinforced by the formal freedom with respect to capital as such, i.e., the conditional freedom to leave the working class altogether. Marx sometimes suggests that it is further reinforced by the (unconditional) freedom of the worker as a consumer,[30] but he equally suggests that this freedom tends to develop the self-control and autonomy of the worker, making him fit for his future revolutionary role.[31]

G. A. Cohen has argued that the workers are unconditionally free to leave the working class, yet in another sense are unfree to do so.[32] Starting from the empirical observation that in contemporary Britain a great many poor immigrants are able to enter the petty bourgeoisie, through their willingness to work long hours, he argues that this option is in fact open to any worker. There are, he argues, more exits available from the working class than there are actual exiters, although far fewer than there are workers, i.e., potential exiters. *Any* worker may leave the class, but not *all* of them can do so.[33] The reason why any worker *has* the unconditional freedom to leave the working class is that almost all workers choose not to *use* it. Cohen suggests, moreover, that a possible explanation for their not using it may be solidarity: No worker wants to use an option that is not collectively available. In his phrase, the workers are collectively forced to sell their labor power, although individually free not to do so. The tendency to confuse individual and collective freedom is an additional reinforcement of the illusion of independence mentioned above.

I now turn to the question whether the worker is coerced into selling his labor power. To discuss this, I must first explain what I mean by coercion. The paradigm case of coercion is making someone do something he would otherwise not have done by threatening him with physical punishment, but I shall use the term in a much wider sense. It then covers all cases of threats, whether in the form of inflicting punishment or withholding benefits. It covers, moreover, threats that invoke economic as well as physical sanctions or benefits. It covers, finally, a more general class of manipulations of the environment: intentionally depriving the coerced agent of some options that he would otherwise have had. This may or may not go together with adding an extra option—i.e., an offer—to the original feasible set.[34] The common feature of these cases is that an agent A performs an action x that has the intended and actual consequence of making another person B perform an action y that differs from the action z that B would have performed had A instead pursued his "normal" course of action w. We must also stipulate that B prefers the counterfactual situation in which A does w and he does z to the actual one in which A does x and he does y. We need not add, however, that A prefers the actual situation to the counterfactual one, although standardly this will indeed be the case. (A may be coercing B just to flex his muscles.) Clearly, much depends on how we determine the "normal" course of action for A. It may be defined in some cases as what A usually does, in other cases as what he would have done had B not been present. I shall not here try to resolve this question of the proper baseline for imputations of coercive behavior, except to note that it should not be defined as the course that A *ought* to have taken.[35] This would make it impossible, for instance, to say that the police justly coerce people to abstain from crimes.

If this account of coercion is accepted, at least in broad outline, one implication immediately follows: When an individual capitalist makes a wage offer to an individual worker in a competitive labor market, the latter is not coerced into accepting it. This was the case that Marx, mainly for methodological reasons, took as the paradigmatic one. He tended, in fact, to disregard the intermediate cases between physical compulsion and uncoerced labor contracts. Such intermediate cases arise in "thin markets," i.e., when there is some degree of monopoly or monopsony.[36] If a capitalist has a local monopsony as a purchaser of labor power, he can coerce the worker into accepting lower wages than he would have to offer to attract workers from elsewhere. Yet even in this case the worker is not necessarily coerced into selling his labor power, only into selling it at a particularly low price. An example of the worker being coerced into selling his labor power could be that the capitalist first takes steps to render the alternative of self-employment an unfeasible or unattractive one, and then makes his wage offer.

Consider now the case of collective bargaining. Against the contention that the workers are coerced into such bargaining, a standard objection is that nothing prevents the unions from setting up their own firm. They have the capital, and indeed the manpower to do so. If they choose not to do so, it must be because they expect that they would do less well for themselves than they will as wage laborers, for instance because they lack organizational skill or, more farfetchedly, because they do not trust themselves to retain some of the current revenue for investment.[37] Yet there is another possible explanation, paralleling the suggestion made above with respect to individual workers. The capitalist class might actively seek to undermine the profitability of worker-owned firms, e.g., by making external financing more difficult or by underselling them (over and above what takes place in competition between capitalist firms). In that case it would be true to say that workers are coerced into selling their labor power.[38]

A more complex case is the following. The workers in a given firm or industry are unorganized. If they were to organize themselves, they might set up their own firm; hence the employers take steps to prevent them from organizing themselves. I do not have in mind here such political measures as anticombination acts, which fall outside the present discussion. Rather, the employers might use their economic power to influence the variables that determine the probability of successful collective action by the workers. As an example, one may cite the use of "divide and conquer" tactics, e.g., by hiring workers from different ethnic or national backgrounds. If this is done purposively to prevent the workers from liberating themselves from the "invisible threads" of the wage contract, they are indeed coerced into selling their labor power. I believe, however, that this is mainly a theoretical possibility. Far more important, employers might use such tactics because organized workers could command a higher wage, not because they could break away from the wage relationship altogether. In that case, the workers are coerced into accepting a low wage, not into selling their labor power.

Is the worker forced to sell his labor power? This notion can be taken in one of three distinct senses. First, given the various constraints facing him, the worker has only two options: selling his labor power or starving to death. Second, while the worker can survive without selling his labor power, he can do so only under conditions that are so bad that the only acceptable option is to sell his labor power. Third, the worker must sell his labor power to optimize, but there may be acceptable ways of surviving that do not involve wage labor. The third sense may be set aside as distinctly spurious. Being forced to sell one's labor power in order to optimize does not count as being forced to sell one's labor power unless one is also forced to optimize,[39] in either of the first two senses.

As to the first sense, observe that this idea is not equivalent to that of wages being at subsistence. Wages might be above subsistence, and yet the only alternative to wage labor could be below subsistence, if the worker has no access to capital. Conversely, wages might be at subsistence because of the existence of a mass of peasants similarly living at subsistence, forcing wages down to their level but also providing an alternative occupation to wage labor. Hence evidence concerning trends in the wage level is not direct evidence on the issue whether workers are forced to sell their labor power or starve. One might invoke the process of primitive accumulation, but this largely implies that the workers were coerced into wage labor, rather than forced by "the dull compulsion of economic relations." In any case, the idea of starvation is irrelevant for modern capitalist economies.

The most reasonable way of understanding the contention that the worker is forced to sell his labor power is by taking it in the second of the senses indicated above. The existence of alternative occupations that might allow him to survive is irrelevant if they are so unattractive that no one could be expected to choose them. Of course, this depends on how we define what is acceptable and what is not.[40] I do not have any ideas about how to do this, except for some general remarks. The notion of what is acceptable will have to be defined both in relative and in absolute terms. If wages are high, a person may be said to be forced to sell his labor power if the alternative just allows him to survive, but if wages are at subsistence, the existence of such an alternative implies that he is not forced to sell his labor power. On the other hand, some alternatives are so good that even should the wage offer be raised to astronomical levels, the worker is not forced to take it. The worker is forced to sell his labor power if (1) the alternative is below some critical level and (2) the offered wage is well above the alternative. Presumably we do not want this critical level to be determined by moral considerations,[41] but I find myself unable to spell out the nonmoral criteria that underlie our intuitions in this respect.

What is the moral relevance of being forced to sell one's labor power? There is a well-known bourgeois answer to this question: You've made your bed, so you can lie in it. The answer can be rephrased in terms of a distinction between static and dynamic considerations. A worker may at any time of his life be forced to sell his labor power, but at any time he could take steps that at a later time would make him free not to do so. If moving out of the working class is only a matter of time preferences, i.e., a preference for saving over consumption, this answer has some force. It is further discussed in section 3 below. If, however, it is a matter of being exceptionally gifted, the answer is blatantly ideological, since it turns on the confusion between conditional and unconditional freedom. If, finally, the reason why the worker remains a worker is solidarity with his fellow workers, the answer turns on a confusion between individual and collective freedom.

3. Capitalist Injustice and Socialist Justice

In this section I shall try to set out Marx's theory of justice, partly with a view to explaining why it condemns exploitation as unjust, partly to examine its validity. I shall first discuss the widespread idea that Marx had no theory of justice, because he thought the notions of right and justice would be transcended in the fully developed communist society. I then go on to consider the idea that property is theft, with an application to two central cases of exploitation. I end by discussing the principles from *Critique of the*

Gotha Program: "to each according to his contribution" in the lower phase of communism, "to each according to his need" in the higher phase.

Marx's critique of justice should be distinguished from his general critique of *ideals*. Writing in *The Civil War in France* that the workers "have no ideals to realize,"[42] he appears to suggest that the class struggle is in no way moved by normative considerations. Yet any reader of *Economic and Philosophical Manuscripts* or *Grundrisse* knows that Marx himself held very strongly the ideal of autonomy or self-realization. The most plausible reading of the cited phrase is that Marx believed ideals to be politically inefficacious, not that he believed them to be nonexistent or strictly relative in nature. It has been suggested, however, that moral and nonmoral goods, e.g., justice and autonomy, differ in this respect.[43] The value of self-realization is unconditionally good, that of justice only "good because necessary" within a given society. There are certainly plenty of texts in which Marx appears to deny the existence of transhistorical ideals of justice, e.g., by asserting the justice of capitalist exploitation[44] or by suggesting that fully developed communism is a society in which rights are transcended rather than transformed.[45] Yet closer inspection of his views concerning both capitalism and communism shows that he was simply wrong about what he was doing. Marx may have thought that he had no theory of justice, but his actual analyses only make sense if we impute such a theory to him.

Why I think Marx's analyses of capitalism require an underlying criterion of justice will appear below. As to the analysis of communism, the passage in *Critique of the Gotha Program* in which Marx asserts the withering away of justice and rights in fully developed communism comes close to being self-contradictory. Here he first explains why the contribution principle is inadequate, because, for instance, it does not take account of differences between the workers: "One is married, another not; one has more children than another, and so on and so forth." He then goes on to conclude:

> But these defects are inevitable in the first phase of communist society as it is when it has just emerged after prolonged birth pangs from capitalist society. Right can never be higher than the economic structure of society and its cultural development conditioned thereby.
>
> In a higher phase of communist society, after the enslaving subordination of the individual to the division of labor, and therewith also the antithesis between mental and physical labour, has vanished; after labour has become not only a means of life, but life's prime want; after the productive forces have also increased with the all-round development of the individual, and all the springs of social wealth flow more abundantly—only then can the narrow horizon of bourgeois right be crossed in its entirety, and society inscribe on its banners: from each according to his ability, to each according to his needs.[46]

When Marx here refers to the "defects" of the contribution principle, he is implicitly invoking a higher principle of justice. Moreover, he then goes on to spell out the principle: to each according to his needs. No doubt Marx thought that in this passage he set out an argument against any abstract theory of justice, and did not notice that he could do so only by invoking himself a theory of the kind he wanted to dispense with.

Is property theft? Marx often refers to the transaction between capitalist and worker as "robbery," "embezzlement," "theft," etc. One passage is especially striking. It occurs in a discussion of expanded reproduction, where Marx supposes the existence of an "original capital" of £10,000, which then creates a surplus of £2,000. Even if the former were acquired honestly, the latter, according to Marx, is not:

> The original capital was formed by the advance of £10,000. How did the owner become possessed of it? "By his own labour and that of his forefathers," answer unanimously the spokesmen of Political Economy. And, in fact, their supposition appears the only one consonant with the laws of the production of commodities.
> But it is quite otherwise with regard to the additional capital of £2,000. How they originated we know perfectly well. There is not a single atom of its value that does not owe its existence to unpaid labour. The means of production, with which the additional labour-power is incorporated, as well as the necessaries with which the labourer is sustained, are nothing but component parts of the surplus-product, of the tribute exacted annually from the working-class by the capitalist class. Though the latter with a portion of that tribute purchases the additional labour-power even at its full price, so that equivalent is exchanged for equivalent, yet the transaction is for all that only the old dodge of every conqueror who buys commodities from the conquered with the money he has robbed them of.[47]

The argument is somewhat disingenuous or question-begging. To see this, consider G. A. Cohen's gloss on the last sentence: "Capitalists pay wages with money they get by selling what workers produce."[48] But of course workers produce with the help of capital goods, that by the assumption of the argument are the legitimate possession of the capitalist. I return to this issue shortly. First I want to consider the passage as evidence that Marx thought the capitalist appropriation of surplus value an unjust one. Cohen, in his further comment on the passage, argues that "[n]ow since . . . Marx did not think that by capitalist criteria the capitalist steals, and since he did think he steals, he must have meant that he steals in some appropriately nonrelativist sense. And since to steal is, in general, wrongly to take what rightly belongs to another, to steal is to commit an injustice, and a system which is 'based on theft' is based on injustice."[49]

I shall argue that this view, while not quite false, is misleading. Marx himself explains why it is inappropriate to say that the capitalist robs the worker:

> In my presentation, the earnings on capital are not in fact "only a deduction or 'robbery' of the worker." On the contrary, I present the capitalist as a necessary functionary of capitalist production, and show at length that he does not only "deduct" or "rob" but forces the production of surplus value, and thus helps create what is deducted; further I show in detail that even if in commodity exchange *only equivalents* are exchanged, the capitalist—as soon as he pays the worker the actual value of his labour-power—earns *surplus value* with full right, i.e. the right corresponding to this mode of production.[50]

The notion of theft as usually employed presupposes that the stolen object exists prior to the act of stealing it. It is because the object exists that someone might want to steal it. In capitalist exploitation it is the other way around: It is because the surplus can be appropriated or robbed that the capitalist has an incentive to create it. Had there been no capitalist, the workers would not be robbed, but nor would they have anything he could rob them of. Hence I submit that it is misleading to speak of theft in this case. This terminology plays on the moral connotations of standard cases of theft, in order to condemn nonstandard cases. The latter may or may not be relevantly different from a moral point of view, but the question should at least be confronted, not obscured, as it is by this language. In my view the issue should be formulated as one of distributive justice: Exploitation is wrong because it violates the principle "to each according to his contribution." The capitalist gets something for nothing, or much for little, at the expense of others. I shall first apply the contribution principle to two polar cases of exploitation, and then discuss two correlated objections.

First, consider the pure capitalist coupon-clipper, who hires a manager at a poor wage to exploit the workers for him. Disregarding for the time being the question of how the capitalist came to acquire his capital, this violates the contribution principle, since the capitalist makes no contribution (in terms of work), yet receives an income. (To say that he contributes capital would be relevant only if his capital was accumulated "by his own labor and that of his forefathers," which is the issue I prefer to postpone for a moment.) The capitalist is not entitled to profit on his capital. This does *not* mean that the working class is somehow collectively entitled to the whole product, because directly or indirectly its labor accounts for all that is produced. The "indirect" contribution of past labor to present capital is quite irrelevant if the past workers are no longer alive. There is no collective historical subject called "the working class" whose current incarnation is entitled to the current product by virtue of the contributions of past incarnations. The issue should be posed squarely as one of the distribution of the current product among those currently living. Of the latter, only the workers make a contribution; hence no one else is entitled to any part of the product.[51]

At the other pole, consider the pure capitalist entrepreneur, who has no capital, but exploits the worker by virtue of his organizational skill. By bringing together workers whose abilities complement one another, he is able to make them much more productive collectively than they could be in isolation. He "helps create what is to be deducted." Yet this does not entitle him to an income vastly greater than that of his workers. One is not morally entitled to everything one is causally responsible for creating. The thief has no claim to the proceeds from the sale of theft-alarm devices, nor the slavedriver to the produce of his slaves, nor finally the broker or mediator to the gains that he makes possible by bringing together people of complementary skills. Similarly, the capitalist entrepreneur should at most be rewarded for the actual effort of bringing the workers together, not for the work done by those whom he assembles. (I say "at most" because he would not be entitled to anything if he is also instrumental in preventing the workers from setting up their own firm.)

To these polar cases there correspond two powerful and widespread objections to the view that exploitation is unjust. With respect to the first, we must face the problem whether there could not be a "clean path" to capitalist accumulation,[52] morally unobjectionable unlike the "primitive accumulation" in early capitalism. If some workers, who for the sake of argument we may assume differ from others only in their time preferences, choose to save and invest rather than consume immediately, could anyone object if they offer others to work for them at a wage above what the latter could earn elsewhere? (To simplify matters, let us assume that our self-made capitalist arises within an initially egalitarian communist economy, not within a capitalist economy in which the alternative wage would be part determined by past and current injustice.) This is a variant of Nozick's "Wilt Chamberlain" argument:[53] Can anyone forbid capitalist acts between consenting adults? There are at least two grounds on which one could justify intervention to prevent this. First, the individual worker might be imperfectly informed, by no fault of his own, about the consequences of accepting the offer.[54] Second, even if it were in the fully informed interest of the worker to accept the offer, it might not be in the collective interest of the class of workers to accept it.[55] Hence, if the workers are unorganized by no fault of their own, and a fortiori if the capital owner was instrumental in bringing about their lack of organization, the Wilt Chamberlain argument breaks down. I must add, however, that if workers are both well informed and well organized, the argument appears irrefutable. One might try to temper it by arguing for curtailment of inheritance rights,[56] but it is not easy to do so in a way that avoids violation of the Pareto principle. My conclusion on this issue, therefore, must be twofold. First, in present-day capitalism the objection is largely irrelevant, since the situation is unjust through and through. Second, in an egalitarian economy there is a possibility, hardly quantifiable, that well-informed and well-organized workers would not start upon the slippery slope to income inequalities.

The second case points to the *incentive problem* that is at the heart of current discussions about the viability of socialism. How could it be unjust to reward someone for a task that he would not have undertaken in the absence of the promise of a reward? The problem of organizational skill is only one special case of this general issue. Again the objection can be stated in terms of Pareto efficiency: No one is made worse off by people reaping a reward for the use of skills that would otherwise have lain dormant. If one accepts this general type of argument, the best one can do is along the lines of Rawls's "difference principle," i.e., accepting inequalities up to the point where further inequality would make the worst-off group even worse off.[57]

Marx would probably have dismissed these problems as belonging only to the initial stage of communism, in which material incentives are still needed to elicit work or the deployment of skills. In the higher phase this will be forthcoming out of solidarity with the community[58] or because work has become "life's prime want." This, however, is an unproven and unprovable statement. At present, higher communism does not appear to be historically feasible, if we are to judge from the experience of the countries that call themselves socialist. On the basis of the principle that "ought implies can," one might then be tempted to reject the idea that there is anything unjust about exploitation. To say that exploitation is unjust is to say that it ought to be abolished, which only makes sense if it can be abolished, which is false. It is not obvious, however, that historical feasibility is the relevant sense of "can" in this context. The nonexploitative state is feasible in a different and more relevant sense, that is, physical feasibility. Since workers under capitalism work hard and entrepreneurs use their skills, we know that the proposed alternative is physically feasible.[59] It is not utopian in the sense in which it is utopian to assert, as did Marx, that under communism everybody could be a Raphael or a Leonardo.[60] Hence I suggest that "ought implies can" holds only if "can" is taken in the narrow sense of physical feasibility. If it is taken in the broader sense of historical feasibility, the principle works equally well the other way around: That something is perceived as morally obligatory may contribute to making it historically feasible, given the physical possibility. Historical feasibility is a relative and highly volatile notion. It should not be absolutized to serve as an argument for the perpetuation of inequalities that may be unavoidable today, but need not remain so indefinitely.

Let me consider finally the two principles of distribution asserted in *Critique of the Gotha Program*, the contribution principle and the needs principle. The former is a Janus-like notion. Looked at from one side, it serves as a criterion of justice that condemns capitalist exploitation as unjust. Looked at from the vantage point of fully developed communism, it is itself inadequate by the higher standard expressed in the needs principle. An able-bodied capitalist who receives an income without working represents an unjustified violation of the contribution principle—a violation, that is, not justified by the needs principle. By contrast, an invalid who receives welfare aid without contributing anything in return represents a violation of the contribution principle that is justified by the needs principle.[61] I believe that the best way of making sense *both* of Marx's critique of capitalism and of the remarks on communism in *Critique of the Gotha Program* is by imputing to him a hierarchical theory of justice, in which the contribution principle provides a second-best criterion when the needs principle is not yet historically ripe for application.[62]

I now turn to the needs principle itself. From what Marx says in *Critique of the Gotha Program*, it is most plausibly understood as a principle of equal welfare. He says, for instance, that it is a defect of the contribution principle that a worker with many children will receive the same income as a worker with few, presumably because each member of the former's family will have a lower level of welfare. The needs principle, if it is to correct this defect, must ensure equality of welfare. Alternatively, the needs principle could be read as saying that each person receives the maximal amount of welfare he is capable of enjoying, assuming such maxima, which might differ across individuals, to exist. This idea is perhaps more plausible exegetically, but too utopian to merit further discussion. I shall focus on the more realistic idea of equal welfare, and consider some objections to it that cumulatively make it rather unattractive as a principle of justice.

Observe first that the needs principle also embodies a contribution principle, although a different one from the principle regulating the initial phase of communism. If a person decides to work less in order to have more leisure, he must expect to receive correspondingly less income. This is so for two reasons. First, as a result of his decision less is produced, and hence even with an equal distribution of goods and services there will be less for everybody. Next, such a person should also receive fewer goods and services than a person whose income-leisure trade-off makes him work longer hours. They achieve the same welfare levels (including the maximal level of equal welfare for all) at different income-leisure combinations.

The issue is complicated by the notion of work becoming "life's prime want." I believe this is to some extent true of everybody and to some extent false of everybody. For every person there comes a point when he would rather stop working than continue, if only because he needs to sleep and eat. Similarly, although more controversially, every person would rather do some work than do no work at all. When forced to work very hard, one may think that a life of complete leisure is the best, but in the first place many people who have that option do not use it, and in the second place people who are forced to use it, i.e., the unemployed, typically do so because they are forced to, not because they welcome the opportunity to earn an income without working.[63] Hence the question of work becoming life's prime want is a question of *when* the marginal utility of work crosses the line from positive to negative, not *whether* it does so. A person, then, might prefer to work long hours because he enjoys the work, not because it allows him to earn more. Strict adherence to the principle of equal welfare should then allow him less income than someone who, for the sake of more income, works long hours in an occupation he finds irksome. This, clearly, creates difficulties for the application of the principle, since it might be hard for the person concerned, not to speak of others, to tell whether he works long hours because he likes the job or because he wants the income it provides him. The anticipation of the income might make him enjoy the work more, and he might falsely believe that his enjoyment is due to the nature of the work itself.[64]

A more fundamental difficulty is posed by the fact that some people have expensive needs. These fall in three classes. First, there are the needs stemming from mental and physical handicaps either present from birth or acquired involuntarily in later life. Next, there are the consumption needs that to a large extent are within the control of the individual. Fat people need more food, but they need not be fat. Some people have a craving for luxury goods, but they could undertake a planned change of preferences. People with large families need large incomes, but they could have chosen to have fewer children. The last example is a borderline case. It could also belong to the third class, the need to realize oneself through the sometimes expensive exercise of one's capacities. To write poems requires little by way of material resources, to make films a great deal more.

I am not saying that all of these cases present a problem for the needs principle. It was, after all, designed precisely to take care of such instances. At least this holds for the first class of expensive needs, and perhaps to some extent for the second. Yet not all sorts of extravagant consumption tastes merit support from society. If free rein was given to the development of tastes, with a guarantee that they would be fulfilled to an extent compatible with the same level of welfare for all, expensive tastes might emerge in an amount that would make it possible to satisfy them only very partially. Hence, to prevent this kind of anarchy of preferences, people could be told at the early stages of preference formation that society will not underwrite all sorts of expensive tastes. Since consumption tastes belong in general to the periphery of the individual rather than to the core, this would not seem too objectionable. Nevertheless, it would involve a very different understanding of the needs principle from the usual one. The principle would here be invoked to shape preferences so that it can be satisfied: "To each according to needs that allow equal satisfaction of needs." It is not obvious that this is in any way superior to giving everyone the same amount of resources, and then leaving them free to decide on how they want to use them.[65]

The anarchy problem could also arise with respect to the third set of expensive needs. In capitalism many people are frustrated in their self-realization because they lack the means to do what they would most like to do. If they knew that society would underwrite their preferred activity, so many might choose expensive ways of realizing themselves that few would be able to do so to a large extent. This, however, cannot be dealt with analogously to the previous problem. *Self*-actualization is so close to the core of the individual that one cannot expect that people will cease wanting to do the things that society tells them are too expensive; they will only cease trying to do them. Hence it is hard to see how one could avoid the source of frustration and inequality of welfare that stems from not everyone being able to do what they would most like to do. In addition, there is the problem that even were they able to do what they most want to do, they might be frustrated when they discover that they are not very good at doing it. It would be facile and Panglossian to suggest that the frustration due to lack of resources has the useful consequence of preventing people from experiencing the more profound frustration due to lack of talent, but it does seem true that these kinds of frustration vary inversely with one another, and that if the first kind of frustration were eliminated for all the second kind would create unavoidable welfare inequalities. Once again, equality of resources might be a better aim for society to set itself.

4. Epilogue

I have little to say by way of conclusion. The above discussion is clearly very tentative. It represents an attempt to rethink some basic Marxian notions in the light of the challenges of Rawls, Nozick, Dworkin, and others over the last decade or so. These authors have not succeeded fully in disturbing the dogmatic slumber of Marxism, but there are signs that it is becoming increasingly difficult to reassert the traditional views without more vigorous arguments than the traditional ones. In addition, of course, the increasingly repulsive character of many socialist regimes makes it obligatory for Marxists to reexamine the feasibility of their traditional ideals, and the desirability of the feasible arrangements. Broadly speaking, Marxist political theory is on the defensive for theoretical as well as practical reasons. It would be too much to say that I have mounted a counteroffensive, but perhaps I can claim to have tried to stabilize the lines of defense. If one were to accept the possibility of a clean path to capitalist accumulation, it would still be true that accumulation in actually existing capitalism has a long and unclean history that, by the principle of rectification invoked by the foremost champion of political libertarianism, would justify massive redistribution from capitalists to workers.[66] If one were to accept that a society not based on material incentives is historically unfeasible at present, one could still claim that the notion of justice need not be constrained by such feasibility.

Notes

Many, perhaps most, of the ideas in this paper are unoriginal. They derive from the work of G. A. Cohen and John Roemer, and from numerous discussions I have had with them over the last few years. I have full responsibility, of course, for the use made of their ideas. I would also like to thank Ottar Dahl, Philippe van Parijs, and Robert van der Veen for helpful criticism and comments.

1. Karl Marx, *Capital* (New York: International Publishers, 1967), 3:795.
2. Ibid., 791.
3. Ibid., 795.
4. Karl Marx, *Capital* (New York: International Publishers, 1967), 1:737.
5. Marx finds exploitation both in slavery (*Capital* 3:809) and in feudalism (*Capital* 1:715). These are, however, isolated instances.
6. *The German Ideology*, in Marx and Engels, *Collected Works* (London: Lawrence and Wishart, 1975 ff.), 5:409.
7. Ibid., 409, 410, 416.
8. See Stanley Moore, *Marx on the Choice between Socialism and Communism* (Cambridge: Harvard University Press, 1980), 14 ff. and passim.
9. Karl Marx, *Theories of Surplus-Value* (London: Lawrence and Wishart, 1972), 3:106; see also John Roemer, *A General Theory of Exploitation and Class* (Cambridge: Harvard University Press, 1982), 206.
10. Roemer, *A General Theory*. In parts 1 and 2 of this work Roemer develops a series of models of exploitation that differ in the *motivation* imputed to the agents (subsistence versus accumulation) and in the *markets* in which the transactions between agents take place (nonlabor commodity market, labor market, credit market).
11. Ibid., 113.
12. See ibid., 44–45, for a discussion of multiple price equilibria and their relation to exploitation.

13. Ibid., theorems 4.3, 4.6, and 4.7.
14. See ibid., 131–32, for an explanation of this indeterminacy.
15. According to the *general* theory of exploitation proposed in part 3 of Roemer's book, a group is capitalistically exploited if it would be better off, and its complement worse off, were it to withdraw from society with its per capita share of the means of production. This, for instance, would mean that the unemployed form an exploited group, contrary, I think, to intuition. Roemer's recent article "Property Relations vs. Surplus Value in Marxian Exploitation" (*Philosophy and Public Affairs* [1983]) adds the condition that the complementary group should also be worse off were it to withdraw with its *own* endowments (not its per capita share). According to this definition the unemployed are not exploited, but rather, as Roemer now says, "Marxian-unfairly treated." In my "Roemer vs. Roemer" (*Politics and Society* [1982]) I give an example of a group that satisfies all three conditions of Roemer's revised definition of exploitation, and yet could not be said to be exploited in any intuitive sense. In that article I also give my reasons for believing that no definition of exploitation in terms of counterfactual statements can capture the essentially *causal* nature of that concept.
16. *Capital* 3:829.
17. Max Weber, *Economy and Society* (New York: Bedminster Press, 1968), 305.
18. *Capital* 1:611.
19. See also C. C. von Weizsäcker, "Modern Capital Theory and the Concept of Exploitation," *Kyklos* (1975).
20. This must be modified in one important respect. The size of the surplus could be a good indicator of the injustice stemming from unequal access to investment decisions. Some writers (e.g., Leszek Kolakowski, *Main Currents of Marxism* [Oxford: Oxford University Press, 1978], 1:305) take this "exclusive power of decision" to *be* exploitation, but I think the more usual definition in terms of excess labor worked is to be preferred. One could well argue, however, that in contemporary capitalism inequalities of *power* matter more than inequalities of *consumption*, but I cannot here go into this issue.
21. On divide and conquer, see Lloyd Shapley and Martin Shubik, "Ownership and the Production Function," *Quarterly Journal of Economics* (1967), and John Roemer, "The Simple Analytics of Divide and Conquer," working paper no. 203 from the Department of Economics, University of California at Davis.
22. For a brief exposition with application to exploitation, see my "Marxism, Functionalism, and Game Theory," *Theory and Society* (1982).
23. *Capital* 1:239.
24. Karl Marx, "Wages," in *Collected Works* 6:420, 428, 435.
25. Kelvin Lancaster, "The Dynamic Inefficiency of Capitalism," *Journal of Political Economy* (1973).
26. More precisely, my being really able to do x, and preferring x over all other actions, implies my doing x. Given this definition of real ability, one can go on to say that my being really able to do x, and preferring x over all other things that I am really able to do, implies my doing x.
27. *Results of the Immediate Process of Production*, appendix to *Capital*, vol. 1 (New York: Vintage Books, 1977), 1079.
28. Ibid., 1032–33.
29. *Capital* 1:574, 614.
30. Karl Marx, "Reflections," in *Collected Works* 10:591.
31. Karl Marx, *Results of the Immediate Process of Production*, 1033.

32. See his articles "Capitalism, Freedom, and the Proletariat," in Alan Ryan, ed., *The Idea of Freedom: Essays in Honour of Isaiah Berlin* (Oxford: Oxford University Press, 1979); "Illusions about Private Property and Freedom," *Issues in Marxist Philosophy* 4 (Sussex: Harvester Press, 1981); "The Structure of Proletarian Unfreedom," *Philosophy and Public Affairs* (1983).

33. For the logical structure involved, see my *Logic and Society* (Chichester: Wiley, 1978), 97 ff.

34. See David Zimmerman, "Coercive Wage Offers," *Philosophy and Public Affairs* (1981): 133.

35. Ibid., 127 ff.

36. I owe this point (and the phrase "thin markets") to Pranab Bardhan.

37. See Finn Kydland and Edward Prescott, "Rules Rather than Discretion," *Journal of Political Economy* (1977): 486.

38. Against this Robert Nozick (*Anarchy, State, and Utopia* [Oxford: Blackwell, 1974], 252–53) writes: "And don't say that it is against the class interest of investors to support the growth of some enterprise that if successful would end the enterprise system. Investors are not so altruistic. They act in their personal and not their class interest." This may indeed be so, but the history of capitalism shows that investors nevertheless are able to organize themselves *politically* on behalf of their class interests.

39. Roemer, *A General Theory*, 81.

40. Cohen, "The Structure of Proletarian Unfreedom."

41. See Cohen, "Capitalism, Freedom, and the Proletariat."

42. *Marx-Engels Werke* (Berlin: Dietz, 1964 ff.), 17:343.

43. This is the argument of George Brenkert, "Freedom and Private Property in Marx," *Philosophy and Public Affairs* (1979): 135–36, and of Allen Wood, *Karl Marx* (London: Routledge, 1981), 126 ff.

44. E.g., *Capital* 1:194; *Capital* 3:339–40. Ziyad Husami, "Marx on Distributive Justice," *Philosophy and Public Affairs* (1978): 36, note 11, argues that these passages are not to be taken literally. I agree, however, with Allen Wood ("Marx on Right and Justice: A Reply to Husami," *Philosophy and Public Affairs* [1979]) that the relativistic reading is the only unstrained one. On the other hand I agree with Husami against Wood on the substantive issue: Marx had a theory of justice, even if he denied that he had one.

45. See the passage referenced in the following note.

46. *Marx-Engels Werke* 19:21.

47. *Capital* 1:582.

48. G. A. Cohen, review of Allen Wood, *Karl Marx*, in *Mind* (1982).

49. Ibid.

50. "Marginal Notes on Wagner," in *Marx-Engels Werke* 19:359.

51. I am indebted to Ottar Dahl for making me see the inadequacy of what one could call "normative collectivism."

52. For this idea, see Richard Arneson, "What's Wrong with Exploitation?" *Ethics* (1981): 204; G. A. Cohen, "Freedom, Justice, and Capitalism," *New Left Review* 126 (1981): 13; and John Roemer, "Are Socialist Ethics Consistent with Efficiency?" *Philosophical Forum* (1983).

53. Nozick, *Anarchy, State, and Utopia*, 161–62.

54. See my *Ulysses and the Sirens* (Cambridge: Cambridge University Press, 1979), 83.

55. G. A. Cohen, "Robert Nozick and Wilt Chamberlain: How Patterns Preserve

Liberty," in John Arthur and William Shaw, eds., *Justice and Economic Distribution* (Englewood Cliffs, NJ: Prentice-Hall, 1978).

56. See Roemer, "Are Socialist Ethics Consistent with Efficiency?"

57. Strictly speaking, application of the difference principle leads to Pareto improvement only if one has what Rawls calls a "chain connection" between the welfare of individuals; see Rawls, *A Theory of Justice* (Cambridge: Harvard University Press, 1971), 80 ff.

58. For an argument along these lines, see Amartya Sen, *On Economic Inequality* (Oxford: Oxford University Press, 1973), 96 ff.

59. See Roemer, *A General Theory*, 241 ff.

60. See the exposition and discussion of his views in chapter 1 of my *Making Sense of Marx*, forthcoming from Cambridge University Press, 1984.

61. What about the case (suggested by G. A. Cohen) of the invalid capitalist whose unearned income is exactly that to which he is entitled by the needs principle? By the definition of exploitation, he exploits his workers, but one might argue that the ensuing income distribution is nevertheless just. On closer inspection, however, this is seen to be false. Although *his* income corresponds to the canons of justice, the workers he employs receive less than they should, since his income is deducted from *their* wages, not from a social welfare fund to which all workers contribute. In any case the source of injustice mentioned in note 20 above would remain.

62. See Roemer, *A General Theory*, 265 ff., and Serge-Christophe Kolm, *Justice et Equité* (Paris: Editions du CNRS, 1972), 114 ff.

63. I realize that both of these arguments are incomplete, and that the (alleged) facts are open to other explanations.

64. This could be so, for instance, because of the tendency to reduce cognitive dissonance.

65. See Ronald Dworkin, "What Is Equity? Part 2: Equality of Resources," *Philosophy and Public Affairs* (1981).

66. Nozick, *Anarchy, State, and Utopia*, 152–53.

A Democratic Theory of Economic Exploitation Dialectically Developed

DAVID SCHWEICKART

IT IS STARTLING TO realize that the concept of economic exploitation, which has been the focus of intense philosophical debate for what seems like decades now, was barely touched on in John Rawls's 1971 masterwork, *A Theory of Justice*, the book that ushered in the present era of Anglo-American social and political philosophy. The subject was broached just once by Rawls, and only to be dismissed as being of such secondary importance as to be "out of place here."[1] The concept, however, had begun to attract the attention of a generation of students and young faculty who were rediscovering Marx, to the point that it could not much longer be ignored, not even in Harvard Yard. Robert Nozick, in his famous junior-colleague, neoconservative rebuttal to the liberal Rawls, devoted a full nine pages to attacking "Marxian exploitation," concluding that "Marxian exploitation is the exploitation of people's lack of understanding of economics."[2]

Many articles followed, most concerned with defending some version of Marx's theory against Nozick's rather crude critique. The debate changed decisively in 1982 with the publication of John Roemer's *General Theory of Exploitation and Class*.[3] Roemer, a mathematical economist of uncommon talent, provided a brilliant technical articulation of a labor-value theory of exploitation (dispensing with the often criticized labor theory of value),

From David Schweickart, "A Democratic Theory of Economic Exploitation Dialectically Developed," in Roger S. Gottlieb, ed., *Radical Philosophy* (Philadelphia: Temple University Press, 1993), 101–22, with the permission of Temple University Press.

then argued that an alternative "property-relations" theory is superior, being at once faithful to the basic moral intuitions of Marx, more general in scope, and less subject to counterexample.

Roemer's book and his many supporting articles spawned a minor industry, which I will not attempt to survey. Let me say simply that I think Roemer is right that there are serious problems with the labor-value theory of exploitation, at least as it is commonly understood. But Roemer does not take his analysis far enough—or rather, he takes it in the wrong direction. In what follows I argue that his property-relations theory of exploitation represents a dialectical advance over the labor-value theory, just as the labor theory represented a dialectical advance over the Smithian theory that preceded it, but that the property theory itself needs to be superseded by a "democratic theory" of exploitation. This democratic theory now has important practical relevance, immediate in the case of Eastern Europe, less immediate but quite real in the case of Western capitalism.

I set out my argument as a "dialectical" argument. Since the word "dialectic" is unfamiliar in many quarters and evokes active hostility in others, let me clarify what I mean. In a sense, dialectics is storytelling, that is, a form of discourse having a narrative structure. In what follows I tell a story about how, in response to certain conditions, a certain theory arose; how deficiencies became increasingly evident; how, in order to overcome these deficiencies, the theory was replaced by a new theory that did not suffer the same deficiencies; how this theory developed new deficiencies, calling for yet another theory, and so on. Although specific historical circumstances are relevant to the story I tell, a dialectic account is intended to be not a historical narrative per se, but a tracing of the "logic" of certain conceptual transformations.[4] (As is noted, the actual historical sequence does not always match the logical sequence.) To my way of thinking, a dialectical account allows for a richer analysis of the concept of exploitation than is provided by either a strictly historical account or an ahistorical analysis of alternative theories.

Before getting to the argument proper, let me offer a general definition of exploitation, then some preliminary remarks about theories of exploitation.

Let us take the following as a definition: X exploits Y if and only if X takes unfair advantage of Y. This definition highlights two aspects of phenomena we wish to investigate: that one agent has benefited at the expense of another agent, and that something morally wrong has occurred. To narrow the domain of our investigation, we concentrate on *economic* exploitation, that is, on those cases where the benefits in question are tied directly to the production and consumption of material goods and services—although, as we shall see, the logic of our exploration will push us beyond this restriction.

A definition of exploitation is one thing. A theory of exploitation is another. It is instructive to ask why one needs a *theory* of exploitation. It is my view that a theory of exploitation is required when the exploitation is not obvious, when the situation appears to be just, yet something seems wrong. One needs a theory to get beneath appearances to an underlying reality. (The sun *appears* to revolve around the earth; we need a theory to explain how it could be otherwise.)

A theory of exploitation should do three things. It should clarify the nature of the injustice, that is, make clear what normative principles are being violated and, if necessary, defend those principles. It should elucidate the mechanisms and institutions through which exploitation occurs, that is, explain how certain structures generate exploitative relationships and how certain structures mask the nature of those relationships. Finally, it should present an alternative vision, that is, a model of a nonexploitative society. As we shall see, each of the theories we consider can be understood to be attempting these tasks. How well a theory succeeds will condition our evaluation of that theory.

Lockean/Neo-Lockean Exploitation

Let us begin not with "Marxian exploitation," but with what might be called a theory of "feudal exploitation," a theory associated with the Enlightenment attack on feudal privilege. Let us think of feudalism as a social order in which serfs work their own land but may neither leave it nor sell it without their lord's permission. In addition, they are compelled either to pay a tithe to their lord or to work gratis on his land for a certain period of time each year. These payments are legitimized as payment for protection. So long as this protection really is necessary, a case might be made that there is no exploitation, but once the serfs no longer need the lord yet are compelled to submit to the feudal regulations anyway, then they are being (feudally) exploited.

The three facets of a theory of exploitation are evident here. The moral principle being violated is the right of an agent to dispose of her own labor and property without interference, so long as no one else's property rights are violated. The key mechanism of exploitation is the lord's control of the means of coercion, though this is supplemented by an ideology of nobility rights and natural place. The nonexploitative alternative envisaged is laissez-faire capitalism.

A major difficulty with the theory in this form is the problem of specifying what counts as "one's own" property. Presumably, the feudal lord would dispute the claim that the properties of his serfs are exclusively theirs. A full theory of feudal exploitation requires a theory of property rights.

Historically, this issue was settled by means of revolution. Philosophically, the key figure is Locke, who argues that property rights are natural, taking precedence over the acquired, consent-based rights of political authorities. Locke takes pains to give an account as to how "the world, given as it was to the children of men in common," should come legitimately to be the private property of individuals "without any express compact of all the commoners."[5] Locke cites the mixing of one's labor as the basis of just property acquisition, subject to the restrictions that one not accumulate so much that it spoils and that one leave "enough and as good" for others.

Rather than analyzing Locke's account, which from our vantage point seems laughably full of holes, let us look at its contemporary reincarnation: Robert Nozick's "entitlement theory," which jettisons Locke's quaint "labor mixing" idea and his spoilage restraint. Nozick correctly identifies the logical core of Locke's idea: "Individuals have rights," Nozick proclaims. "So strong far reaching are these rights that they raise the question of what, if anything, the state and its officials may do."[6]

Nozick proceeds to argue that if property is justly acquired and freely transferred, then no political authority may touch that property, not even via taxation, without the specific consent of the property owner. (Whether or not the political authority has been constituted democratically is irrelevant.)[7] Property is justly acquired if by voluntary exchange or by claiming that which belongs to nobody else, the latter acquisition subject to the "Lockean proviso" that there be "enough and as good remaining."[8]

Nozick's entitlement theory has been subject to withering rebuttal. Two main lines of argument stand out. The first and most obvious notes that the theory is irrelevant to real-world concerns, since the current distribution of wealth can in no way be thought to be the product of just acquisitions. Early capitalist accumulation derived from the theft of common land, the slave trade, the extermination of native peoples, and other assorted horrors. Just acquisition and voluntary exchange had little to do with it. (Nor have they to do with much of the subsequent capital accumulation, as countless financial scandals, our own savings and loan debacle among them, make evident.)

The second line of argument is more basic to our theoretical investigation. The dynamic of pure laissez-faire tends to bring about institutions and effects clearly at odds with the common good. In particular there is nothing in a (neo-)Lockean "entitlement theory" of exploitation to block the establishment of monopoly power. So long as fraud and physical coercion have been avoided, monopolies cannot be condemned, no matter how much wealth they amass, no matter how wasteful, no matter how far above costs they set their prices. If producers freely agree to fix prices or if a monopoly concern buys out its competitors or drives them out of business by selling below costs for a while, no objection may be raised.

Critics ask the obvious question: Why should property rights have such absolute weight? Surely it is legitimate to do what all societies in fact do: place some restrictions, in the name of the common good, on what people may do with "their" property. To this objection Lockeans have no adequate reply. The theory has hit a dialectical contradiction: A theory grounding itself in an appeal to universal human freedom justifies institutions that, if allowed to develop freely, negate the effective freedom of almost everyone.

SMITHIAN/NEOCLASSICAL EXPLOITATION

Smithian/neoclassical theory may be understood as a response to this contradiction. Adam Smith initiated the great search for a theory of *value*. To be sure, Smith was interested in the positive question—Why does the "invisible hand" of competition set the price of corn at x instead of at 2x?—but the positive issue is intertwined with a normative one. If, as Smith argues, there is a "natural price" for each commodity, then there is a case for intervention when certain institutions prevent the market price from settling at this natural price. Monopoly is identified as a culprit, as are certain governmental practices. Against these Smith directs his attack. The state should refrain from interfering with the workings of the free market *unless* intervention is necessary to keep markets free, that is, competitive, that is, nonmonopolistic.[9]

In the Smithian theory monopolies are exploitative, since they cause prices to deviate from their natural values. But what is this "natural value"? Smith offers the "adding-up" theory:

> When the price of any commodity is neither more or less than what is sufficient to pay the rent of the land, the wages of labour, and the profits of the stock employed in raising, preparing, and bringing it to market, according to their natural rates, the commodity is then sold for what may be called its natural price.[10]

But this theory is unsatisfactory without cogent theories of rent, wages, and profits. These, either positive or normative, Smith fails to provide. Why should society attempt to ensure that commodities sell at their "natural" prices, when certain components of that price might be problematic? To Smith it seems obvious (and his intuitions are not wrong on this point) that natural prices are (usually) better than monopoly prices; but in "solving" the value question as he does, he merely brings to the surface the deeper positive and normative questions.

Historically, the search for a more adequate theory of value passed from Smith to Ricardo and then to Marx. The resulting "labor theory of value," its roots stretching back through Ricardo and Smith to Locke, was then abruptly challenged toward the end of the nineteenth century by the "neo-classical revolution," which introduced the paradigm that still dominates mainstream economics today.

The historical dialectic in this instance does not match the conceptual dialectic, since, as we shall see, the labor theory is normatively more advanced than the neoclassical theory. It is best to understand neoclassical theory as an attempt to resolve, *within* a Smithian framework, the difficulties with Smith's theory suggested above. Neoclassical theory may be understood to be a sophisticated development of Smith's theory, just as neo-Lockean theory may be understood (as its advocates indeed understand it) to be a sophisticated revision of Locke. As in the case of the neo-Lockeans, the neoclassicals have different targets in mind than their forefather, but they too can be seen to grapple with the conceptual difficulties passed on to them.[11]

The great conceptual difficulty passed on to Smith's heirs was the problem of justifying the various components of his natural price. The problem is fundamentally normative, since the free market income of each class is determined by the respective components of a commodity's natural price. If the invisible hand, unimpeded by state interference or monopoly, sets prices at their "natural" values, and if there is no political redistribution of income, then the income of each class, indeed, of each individual, will be determined by the "natural" rates of rent, wages, and profit. But are these "natural" rates *fair* rates? Calling them "natural" won't suffice as a moral argument. It won't suffice now, nor would it suffice in the late nineteenth century when the issue was re-opened. If it was untenable after Jeremy Bentham and John Stuart Mill to identify moral with natural, it was even less tenable, in the face of a growing socialist movement, to regard the invisible hand as unproblematically just.

The intellectual problem confronting the heirs of Smith was daunting. It cannot be denied: The neoclassical solution was brilliant. The ethical ground was shifted from a dated, unconvincing appeal to nature to the more plausible canon of productive contribution: If you and I contribute jointly to the production of a commodity, we should divide the proceeds in proportion to our respective contributions.

But if the ethical appeal is to productive contribution, the theoretical difficulty seems insurmountable. Suppose we have a commodity, say a bushel of wheat, which we regard as the joint product of land, labor, and capital. How can we determine that x percent is due to the land, y percent to labor, and z percent to capital, where $x + y + z = 100$, apart from making the purely circular move of *defining* the contribution of land to be whatever the market rent happens to be, the contribution of labor to be whatever the market wage rate happens to be, and so on? How can one possibly define the "contribution" of a factor of production independently of the market mechanism in such a way as to be able to demonstrate (a) that the contributions add up to 100 percent and (b) that the free market will in fact return to each factor its respective contribution?

Amazingly enough, the neoclassical theorists met this challenge. Briefly put: The contribution of a factor is defined to be the *marginal product* of that factor. If, for example, it takes X acres of land worked by Y laborers using $Z worth of capital to produce a thousand bushels of wheat, then we define *the contribution of each acre* to be the increase in wheat that could be effected if the same workers employing the same capital worked X + 1 acres of land; we define *the contribution of each worker* to be the increase that could be effected if Y + 1 workers worked the same land with the same capital; and we define *the contribution of capital* to be the increase due to the same workers working the same land with one more unit of capital. If we make enough assumptions about substitutability of factors, diminishing returns, and so forth, then a mathematical theorem (Euler's Theorem) can be invoked to show that the sum of the contributions will be a thousand bushels. If we make enough additional assumptions to ensure perfect competition, it can be shown that the rent per acre set by the market will be precisely the contribution of that acre, the wage set by the market will be the contribution of the worker, and the interest set by the market will be the contribution of capital. Not only that, it can be demonstrated that monopoly power will enable a factor owner to receive more than he contributes—thus justifying Smith's original intuition.

We have here a theory of exploitation—historically, a rejoinder to the Marxian theory; conceptually, a dialectical development form the Lockean theory. The moral principle, that agents should receive in accordance with their productive contributions, is an advance over the problematic Lockean principle of unrestricted voluntary exchange. The exploitative mechanisms are identified: any interference with perfectly competitive pricing. A vision of nonexploitation is proposed: perfectly competitive capitalism. (This form of capitalism is something different from laissez-faire, since the government is now authorized to come between mutually consenting agents, e.g., producers engaged in price fixing, so as to promote competitive conditions.)

An amazing feat, the neoclassical solution, but unfortunately inadequate to the fundamental problem. The fundamental problem, recall, is normative. Hence, the definition of "productive contribution" must not only satisfy conditions (a) and (b) above. The definition must also be *morally relevant*.

The marginal product definition fails on this count. I have treated this issue at length elsewhere.[12] Suffice it to say that *even if* we want to say that land and capital "contribute" to the final product, we cannot say the same for the land*owner* or the capital*ist*.

The basic problem is this. In neoclassical theory, which sharply distinguishes the functions of capitalist and landowner from those of entrepreneur and manager, neither capitalist nor landowner engages in anything that might be called a productive activity. Their roles are purely passive. They allow land to be used by whoever will pay the highest rent; they allow capital to be used by whoever will pay the highest interest. The very conditions that must be assumed so as to prove that the free market will return to each factor its productive contribution rule out considering capitalists or landowners as being the bearers of risk or the exercisers of entrepreneurial skill—the very factors that would seem to be necessary if property income is to be *morally* justified. The Smithian/neoclassical theory also founders on a dialectical contradiction.

THE LABOR-VALUE THEORY OF EXPLOITATION

The neoclassical attempt to refurbish Adam Smith's theory of exploitation fails, but the project of building a theory of exploitation on the canon of contribution has not been exhausted. The activities of capitalists and landowners (at least within the neoclassical framework) may not qualify as productive contributions, but the activities of workers surely do. No matter what the theoretical framework, it must be granted that workers engage in productive activity.

Perhaps labor is the *only* productive activity. Such is the claim of the labor-value theory of exploitation. This is the theory usually associated with Marx. Marx argues that labor is the source of all value and yet workers receive only a portion of that value. He argues that wage labor masks the fact that workers, collectively, are paid not the value of what they produce, but rather the value of what it takes to produce (and reproduce) them as a laboring class.[13]

The standard response to this argument is dismissal, on the grounds that it appeals to a discredited theory of value. It is alleged that Marx's argument depends on the faulty assumption that prices in a market economy are proportional to labor inputs, which, in general, they are not. It should be well known by now (although it is not) that this response is wholly inadequate. For the "Fundamental Marxian Theorem"—that positive profits require a positive rate of exploitation—is independent of the assumption that prices are proportional to labor values. The mathematical Marxists (Morishima, Roemer, and others) have demonstrated this quite conclusively.[14]

There is, however, a significant lacuna in Marx's argument. If it is to be understood as (at least in part) a *moral* argument, then it must contain a moral premise. Marx leaves this premise unspecified.

For anyone who has read Marx's basic argument carefully, an obvious candidate comes to mind, a straightforward extension of the normative principle underlying Smithian exploitation: *If a person works x hours to produce goods or services consumed by others, then she should receive in return goods and services that it took others x hours to produce.*

This principle is a version of the canon of productive contribution. If several agents contribute their labor to a joint product, then they should receive a share of the product that is proportional to their contribution. This version, however, carries with it a presumption that the general canon does not. The ethical principle on which the labor-value theory of exploitation is based implies that labor *alone* is a productive activity.

There are reasons for thinking that Marx himself would balk at this ethical principle, reasons that I do not pursue here.[15] He would, however, assent to the claim that labor is the only productive activity. I think he is right to do so. Marx denies that the activities associated with the owners of the other factors of production are productive activities. He distinguishes, as do most subsequent economists, capitalist qua capitalist from managers and entrepreneurs. Once one makes this distinction, one must at least grant that the capitalist qua capitalist and landlord qua landlord contribute minimally to the production process, certainly much less than would be required for a justification of their incomes.

Marx not only denies the capitalist's appeal to the canon of contribution; he takes issue with most of the other standard justifications of property income. He shows that capital accumulation did not come about "cleanly" nor did the working class emerge voluntarily. Marx shows that even when an individual's initial capital is based on his own labor, the normal workings of the system will in time return to him income far in excess of his original contribution. He also shows that appeals to the capitalist's "sacrifice" or "abstinence" are spurious.[16]

I find Marx convincing on these matters. Moreover, I do not think capitalism can be saved by appealing to risk or to "time preference"—defenses not considered by Marx, but similar in structure and spirit to the ones he does address. I do not develop these issues here, since I have done so elsewhere.[17] I am persuaded that the labor-value theory of exploitation, suitably elaborated, can effectively debunk all justifications of capitalism save one: the quasi-utilitarian argument that capitalism is the best of all *feasible* worlds. As we shall see, justifications based on this claim are the target of a more dialectically advanced theory.

Although its negative arguments against appeals to the canon of contribution by any class but the (broadly defined) working class are impressive, it does not follow that the labor-value theory of exploitation is secure in its moral foundation. In formulating his powerful critique of wage labor, Marx makes the simplifying assumption that labor is homogeneous. For purposes of critique, this assumption serves well, but when one moves from critique to affirmation (to the negation of the negation), difficulties surface. If we accept the moral principle on which the labor-value theory of exploitation is based, a nonexploitative society would be one in which each worker receives the full value of her product. That is, if she contributes eight hours to society, then she should receive goods and services that took eight hours to produce.

But this implies that all labor must count the same, regardless of its *quality*. For the only plausible mechanism for guaranteeing that the labor-value principle is satisfied throughout society is to have every worker paid at the same rate, regardless of skill and regardless of the degree of unpleasantness.[18] Many readers (though perhaps not all) will object that such an arrangement would not be *fair*. But there exists an even more compelling objection: Such an economy is not viable. Not only would such radical egalitarianism require that moral incentives (or coercion) completely replace economic incentives, but it would also require a degree of central planning that cannot be made to function efficiently. (The theoretical arguments long advanced concerning the authoritarianism and inefficiency of central planning have been dramatically confirmed by the recent collapse of the Soviet model.)[19]

Although much more could be said about the labor-value theory of exploitation, I think I have said enough to establish the thesis of this section: The labor-value theory of exploitation, although an advance over the Smithian/neoclassical theory, is unsatisfactory. Its negative moment is sound: Neither capitalists qua capitalists nor landowners qua landowners engage in productive activity. But the ethical principle on which it is based is untenable, above all because the positive vision of a nonexploitative economy deriving from this principle is not only morally problematic; it is economically unfeasible. Since a meaningful theory of exploitation must be rooted in the real world, not only as a critical exposé of real justice, but as a positive exposition of a viable alternative, a better theory of exploitation is demanded.

THE PROPERTY-RELATIONS THEORY OF EXPLOITATION

John Roemer proposes such a theory. Its general structure is this. Class S is exploited by the complementary class S' whenever

1. There is a feasible alternative state in which coalition S would be better off than in its present situation;
2. Under this alternative coalition S' would be worse off than at present;

3. Coalition S' is in a relationship of dominance to coalition S. This dominance enables it to prevent coalition S from realizing the alternative.[20]

Some clarifications are in order. Roemer designates his general theory of exploitation a "property-relations" theory. Within this general theory he specifies successive forms of exploitation: feudal, capitalist, and socialist. All these forms satisfy the three conditions above. What distinguishes them are the different ways in which the *alternatives* are formulated—the different "withdrawal conditions." One of the merits Roemer claims for his theory is its generality. I do not concern myself with this claim here. Here I analyze as the "property-relations theory of exploitation" what Roemer calls "capitalist exploitation." The alternative that characterizes "capitalist exploitation" is for S to withdraw from the larger society with *its per capita share of the alienable assets*—natural resources and capital goods.

Roemer is explicit in his assertion of the superiority of the property-relations theory to the labor-value theory (called by him the "unequal exchange" theory).[21] If we look back to our critique of the labor theory, his verdict seems on the mark. The property-relations theory does not seem to entail an undesirable or unfeasible alternative. Built into its definition is a feasible alternative freely chosen. The difficulties we encountered with heterogeneous labor do not arise. If class S would be better off—whatever the qualitative composition of its labor contributions—by withdrawing with its per capita share of society's alienable assets, but is prevented from doing so by S' (who would be made worse off), then S is exploited.

Roemer's theory pushes beyond the labor-value theory not by revision but, in true dialectical fashion, by revolution—placing property, rather than labor, at the center of the exploitation question. Roemer agrees with the general Marxian condemnation of capitalism. He disagrees, however, that the key to the exploitative nature of capitalism is wage labor. The key, he argues, is unequal property ownership.

Roemer advances some strong, sophisticated arguments in support of his highly controversial thesis. He demonstrates that it is possible to have labor exploitation (i.e., agents consuming commodities that embody less labor than they contribute) without wage labor. He shows, for example, that if we have a society where initial property endowments are unequal, it makes no difference whether those with more capital hire laborers or simply loan out their capital. Exactly the same agents will exploit and be exploited.[22]

He pushes the argument further. Suppose we have two islands equally endowed with labor, each with full knowledge of available technologies, but differentially endowed with initial capital. Suppose there is neither labor migration between these islands nor any capital flow, only free trade of commodities. Roemer demonstrates that if each island apportions its labor to maximize its consumption, then unequal exchange, that is, labor exploitation, will occur.[23]

How do these arguments bear on the issue with which we are concerned, namely, the adequacy of the property-relations theory of exploitation? Central to our investigation is Roemer's claim that his property-relations theory is more adequate normatively than the labor-value theory. Unlike the labor-value theory, his theory does not require that all agents be paid at the same rate. For Roemer, the morality of the unequal reward thus comes down to the legitimacy of one's initial wealth. That is to say, if the inequality of initial assets is just, then the unequal consumption is just. If the initial distribution is not just, then neither are the resulting entitlements.

Roemer's idea here is not unattractive. It would seem to be in better accord than the labor theory with certain of our considered moral judgments. For example, if two islands develop their resources autonomously, one more effectively than the other, we do not want to say that voluntary trade between them is exploitative simply because the commodities of the more developed island embody less labor than those for which they are exchanged. If such trade is deemed exploitative, then the advanced island could avoid exploiting the other only by refusing to trade—even when both parties would benefit by the trade—or by disadvantaging itself. Surely the former course makes no sense. Surely justice (as opposed to benevolence) cannot require the latter.

I think Roemer is right that the implications of the labor-value theory of exploitation sometimes conflict with our sensible intuitions. His theory avoids many of the difficulties of the earlier theory. But this theory lands him in a trap—if you will, in a dialectical contradiction. To avoid the implausibly egalitarian implications of the labor-value theory (that all labor should be rewarded equally), he posits a theory whose implications turn out to be—even more egalitarian.

For consider the normative principle on which the property-rights theory is based. Recall that a class is exploited if three conditions obtain: It would be better off withdrawing from the larger society with its per capita share of society's alienable assets; the complementary class would be worse off; the complementary class blocks the withdrawal.

What is the ethical principle operative here? The conditions that S be better off and S' worse off function not normatively but to indicate that S' is benefiting at the expense of S. The blocking condition inserts causality, so that an agent may be deemed responsible. That leaves us with the normative principle itself, which must be: *the right of any individual or group to a per capita share of the alienable assets of society.*

This is a strongly egalitarian principle. It is stronger than the famous Rawlsian difference principle, which it closely resembles. According to Rawls, "all social primary goods . . . are to be distributed equally unless an unequal distribution of any or all of these goods is to the advantage of the least favored."[24] The property-theory principle implies that inequalities are justified only if *no* subgroup (not merely the least favored) would be better off with an equal distribution.

We notice that something rather odd has transpired. In avoiding the excessive egalitarianism of the labor-value principle, we find ourselves with a principle that seems even more egalitarian. If we balked at assigning equal value to all labor, regardless of quality or circumstance, why should we not balk at an alleged equal entitlement to all alienable assets? If I work harder than you or longer than you or more skillfully than you in creating material assets, why are you entitled to a per capita share?

In fact, the property-relations theory of exploitation contains within itself a contradiction. On the one hand, it does not want to commit itself to equality of outcome. If we begin with equal endowments but employ them differently (more or less skillfully, more or less intensely, more or less wisely), then unequal outcomes should not be deemed exploitative. On the other hand, these unequal outcomes form the basis for the "initial endowments" of the next period—which are supposed to be equal.

Roemer, in his latest work, senses the strong egalitarian position toward which the logic of his theory leads. He bites the bullet in the penultimate chapter of *Free to Lose*, wherein he constructs a highly original proof of a rather strange theorem:

> On the class of economic environments X, there is only one economic constitution F that satisfies the five axioms Pareto Optimality, Land Monotonicity, Technological Monotonicity, Limited Self-Ownership, and Protection of the Infirm. That unique constitution assigns in any environment the Pareto optimal allocation of corn and labor that equalizes the utility levels of the agents.[25]

This is not the occasion to analyze this theorem. Suffice it to note its import. The only "economic constitution" (i.e., principle of allocation of resources) that satisfies a set of constraints that Roemer thinks anyone of an anticapitalist bent should find nonproblematic is an allocation that "equalizes the utility levels of the agents" (i.e., makes everyone equally happy). This is egalitarianism with a vengeance. A more egalitarian prescription is scarcely imaginable.

This is too strong an egalitarian commitment. Such a commitment conflicts with many of our considered intuitions. More important, it conflicts with the nonutopian impulse of the Marxian socialist tradition, an impulse that is particularly important today when the issue of feasible socialism is being hotly debated. We have here another curious dialectical reversal. A strength of the property-relations theory over and against the labor theory is its insistence that a feasible alternative exist before exploitation can be charged. This alternative, however, turns out to be wholly abstract. If we try to think concretely about alternatives, we find ourselves running up against an excessive restriction. To avoid the charge of capitalist exploitation, the feasible alternative must be such that no group can make itself better off by withdrawing with its per capita share of the alienable assets— regardless of how much or how little it contributed to the formation of those assets. This restriction rules out not only capitalism, but any form of feasible socialism as well—in particular, market socialism. To be sure, the issue of market socialism is controversial, but a theory of exploitation that decides the issue a priori is surely defective.[26]

What is called for is a theory of exploitation that is more adequate to real-world socialism and more firmly grounded normatively. What is needed is a theory that combines elements of the labor-value theory with elements of the property-relations theory in a synthesis that exceeds the sum of its parts. Precisely such a theory, I submit, is the following.

A DEMOCRATIC THEORY OF ECONOMIC EXPLOITATION

The democratic theory of exploitation rests on a principle that is not a principle: Individuals should, in some sense, legislate the rules that bind them. This principle is too vague to be a real principle. The principles that underlay all the previous theories of exploitation were sharp and clear: property rights, quantitative contribution, equality of wages, a per capita share of alienable assets. This principle is more a heuristic than a well-defined norm. It guides our thinking but does not command.

It is also self-reflexive, in a way that the other principles are not. How do we determine in *what* sense individuals should legislate their rules? We do it democratically. Individuals must, in some sense, democratically decide on the economic rules and goals and institutions that will constrain their subsequent behavior; they must decide the appropriate spheres for various sorts of democratic mechanisms.

So long as we focus on the normative principle itself, the democratic theory seems hopelessly vague. But the crucial dialectical innovation of this theory is to shift the starting point from the normative principle to the alternative vision. We begin not with an abstract principle, but with a far more concrete project: the specification of a model of an economically feasible, morally desirable alternative to capitalism.[27] In all the previous theories, the model of a nonexploitative economy could be derived more or less rigorously from the normative foundation. Not so with democratic exploitation. The model itself must be constructed not via logical deduction from first principles, but by drawing on theoretical, historical, and empirical research, all the while guided by the democratic heuristic.

This project, although not widely known, is in fact well advanced. Increasingly, since about 1970, various radical thinkers and activists have been investigating the theory and practice of *economic democracy*.[28] The central concept here is *workplace democracy*. Why, it began to be asked, do workers not elect their bosses? If ordinary citizens in Western democracies are competent enough to elect their mayors, governors, presidents, and a host of other political officials, are they not competent enough to elect their workplace managers?

As it turns out, the answer to this empirical question is unambiguous: They are. As it turns out, there are large (and growing) numbers of experiments—participation schemes, cooperative enterprises, networks of cooperative enterprises—that prove beyond a reasonable doubt that workplace democracy is *efficient*, at least as efficient as and often more so than ordinary capitalist management.[29] Democracy, it turns out, has positive economic as well as political and moral significance.

Starting from the basic, well-grounded premise that workplace democracy works, the task then becomes to determine what sorts of structures are necessary to link a system of democratic enterprises into an optimally viable, desirable democratic economy. This question, of course, is less amenable to direct empirical investigation and hence is more speculative. Still, I think we are now in position to state with considerable confidence what the basic institutions of economic democracy should be.[30]

Obviously, this is not the place for more than the briefest sketch, but let me at least provide that.[31] A feasible, desirable, fully democratic economy must be an appropriate synthesis of three elements: *workplace democracy, a free market for economic goods and services*, and *social control of investment*. Workers should control their enterprises, one-person, one-vote. In larger enterprises this entails electing a workers' council that appoints the management. Enterprises should sell to one another and to consumers freely, with supply and demand (for the most part) determining prices. (Economic democracy is a market economy—though *not* a capitalist economy.) What the invisible hand of supply and demand should not determine is the nature and rate of new investment. For a large variety of compelling reasons—ethical, ecological, economical—a better mechanism is needed. Although there is no consensus on specific details, it is clear that national, state, and local legislatures must play an active role in generating the investment fund (via enterprise taxation) and in setting general priorities for its dispensation.

One may conceptualize these briefly described institutions as a synthesis of three different forms of democracy. In a real if limited sense the market mechanism is a democratic institution. Individuals vote their preferences with their purchases. The productive apparatus responds to consumer demand. Workplace democracy is democracy of a different sort, democracy on the model of the ancient Greek polis or the early town meetings in this country, that is, direct democracy. The arena is small enough for all individuals so inclined to voice their views and try to persuade others; the issues are near at hand and the results often swiftly perceived. By contrast, social control of investment is necessarily a mediated, representative democracy. The need for coherence and consistency in investment planning and for balancing costs, benefits, entrepreneurial incentives, regional versus national interests, and the like precludes the direct, popular formulation of investment priorities, though not, of course, popular input. Economic democracy is thus a synthesis of individualist, direct, and representative democracy, giving individuals the opportunity for democratic participation as consumers, as workers, and as citizens.

It is clear on reflection that the democratic theory of exploitation is a synthesis and sublation of the previous two theories (see table 1 for a summary of the dialectical argument). The labor-value theory of exploitation is right that neither capitalists nor landowners are necessary for a healthy economy. (Quite the contrary!) It is right too in its condemnation of wage labor. The property-relations theory is right to focus attention on property rights, for these rights, as currently constituted, block the emergence of a democratic economy. They serve as the fundamental bulwark of capitalism. (Why can't workers elect their bosses? Why must democracy stop at the factory gate? Because the factory does not belong to them. Why can we not set priorities democratically as to the development of our economy? Because investment decisions are made by the "private" sector, i.e., by the owners of the means of production. Why can't we change things? Because money dominates politics, and that money—most of it—derives from property.)

Both the labor-value theory and the property-relations theory, however, are too narrowly normative. That is to say, each centers on a normative principle, sharply defined, and this renders each theory inadequate in the face of what is perhaps now *the* fundamental question for radical theorists: Is there a viable alternative to capitalism? Democratic theory preserves the valid insights of the earlier theories but confronts this question head on— and in my view, successfully.

Table 1. Summary of the Dialectical Argument

Theory of Exploitation	Normative Principle	Exploiting Institution	Alternative Vision	Basic Contradiction
Lockean/ Neo-Lockean	Just acquisition/ Free exchange	The state	Laissez-faire	Monopolies
Smithian/ Neoclassical	Productive contribution	Monopolies	Perfect competition	Capitalists don't contribute
Labor value	Equal exchange of labor	Wage labor	Equal wages	Heterogeneous labor/Incentives
Property relations	Eqaul access to alienable assets	Unequal property	Equal assets	Excessive egalitarianism
Democratic	Legislative self-binding rules	Capitalism	Economic democracy	

A CONCLUDING REMARK

I do not mean to suggest that the democratic theory of exploitation is the final form of exploitation theory. History has not come to an end. The democratic theory is itself unfinished. The reader cannot fail to notice a great many gaps in my argument, and large areas only roughly sketched.

But even when the gaps are closed and details provided (as I am confident they can be), the theory here presented remains radically incomplete. For there is a huge area of exploitation, also the focus of much attention by radical theorists and activists, that this account has left invisible: namely, sex/gender exploitation. This is not the place to venture even a sketch of what the next stage of exploitation theory will look like, but I am persuaded that it will be a dialectical advance that infuses the democratic theory just presented with feminist theory so as to clarify, critique, and mark an alternative not only to sex/gender exploitation itself, but to a range of other problems that feminist theory has shown to be linked to that exploitation: social violence, militarism, carelessness (in all its meanings), the despoilation of our planet, and so on.

Theoretically and practically, there is much to be done.

Notes

1. John Rawls, A Theory of Justice (Cambridge: Harvard University Press, 1971), 310.
2. Robert Nozick, Anarchy, State, and Utopia (New York: Basic Books, 1974), 262.
3. John Roemer, A General Theory of Exploitation and Class (Cambridge: Harvard University Press, 1982).

4. A model for what I am doing is Marx's account early in *Capital* of the development of the form of value from the elementary form to the extended form to the general form to the money form (*Capital*, [New York: International Publishers, 1967], 1:48–70).

5. See John Locke, *Second Treatise of Government*, Samuel Moore and Edward Aveling (Indianapolis: Hackett, 1980), 18–30.

6. Nozick, *Anarchy, State, and Utopia*, ix.

7. It may be noted that although logically Nozick is arguing against "feudal exploitation," the real concern has shifted enormously since Locke. Locke articulates a defense of bourgeois property against its usurpation by aristocratic authorities. Neo-Lockeans such as Nozick are concerned to defend bourgeois property against the threat of democratic redistribution. It is not the king that Nozickeans fear but popular majorities.

8. Nozick, *Anarchy, State, and Utopia*, 150–82. Nozick pays much attention to the Lockean proviso, hoping to give it current applicability. Since my critique of Nozick centers elsewhere, we need not analyze this (vain, in my view) attempt.

9. Actually, Smith has little faith that law can fend off directly the deep tendency toward monopoly. "People of the same trade seldom meet together, even for merriment and diversion, but the conversation ends in a conspiracy against the public, or in some contrivance to raise prices. It is impossible to prevent such meetings, by any law which either could be executed, or would be consistent with liberty and justice." He does believe, however, that certain public works, above all roads and canals, can enhance competition (Adam Smith, *The Wealth of Nations* [Middlesex: Penguin, 1970], 232–33, 251).

10. Ibid., 157

11. I observed that the neo-Lockeans are more concerned to check democratic "excesses" than monarchical ones. I would venture that the "monopoly" of most concern to neoclassicals is not that of enterprises but (at least until very recently) that of labor. See Milton Friedman's treatment of business monopolies and labor unions in *Capitalism and Freedom* (Chicago: University of Chicago Press, 1962), ch. 8.

12. See David Schweickart, *Capitalism or Worker Control? An Ethical and Economic Appraisal* (New York: Praeger, 1980), 5–19.

13. Marx, *Capital*, esp. 146–98.

14. Michio Morishima, *Marx's Economics: A Dual Theory of Value and Growth* (Cambridge: Cambridge University Press, 1973); John Roemer, *Analytic Foundations of Marxian Economic Theory* (Cambridge: Cambridge University Press, 1981).

15. Marx is far too subtle and dialectical a thinker to base his case against capitalism on a single normative principle. But to set out the structure of Marx's argument in its full complexity is beyond the scope of this chapter.

16. See Marx, *Capital*, 713–61, 579–88, and 591–99, for the various arguments.

17. See my *Against Capitalism* (Cambridge: Cambridge University Press, 1993), ch. 1.

18. Students of Marx might protest that in *Capital* Marx allows that skilled labor count as a multiple of unskilled labor (44). But with Marx there is intent on constructing a (quasi-)positive theory, not a normative one. In a market economy, prices will not reflect labor values unless skilled labor counts for more than simple labor. Whether it *should* count for more (in a nonexploitative society) is a separate matter, one to which the labor-value theory of exploitation (as I have formulated it) gives a definite, if problematic, answer.

19. It should not be thought that only procapitalists have made such arguments, nor should one identify the Soviet model with socialism. Many radical thinkers have argued, and for a long time, that a desirable, feasible socialism should be structured very differently from the Soviet model. This issue is taken up more fully below.

20. Roemer, *General Theory*, 194–95.

21. For a concise presentation of his case, see John Roemer, "What Is Exploitation?" *Philosophy and Public Affairs* (Winter 1989): 90–97. He has, however, had some "Second Thoughts on Property Relations and Exploitation," *Canadian Journal of Philosophy*, supp. vol. 15:257–66.

22. Cf. Roemer, *General Theory*, 87–95; see also Roemer, *Free to Lose: An Introduction to Marxist Economic Philosophy* (Cambridge: Harvard University Press, 1988), 90–98.

23. See John Roemer, "Unequal Exchange, Labor Migration, and International Capital Flows: A Theoretical Synthesis," in P. Desai, ed., *Marxism, Central Planning, and the Soviet Economy: Economic Essays in Honor of Alexander Erlich* (Cambridge: MIT Press, 1983), 34–62. See also Roemer, *Free to Lose*, 99–103.

24. Rawls, *A Theory of Justice*, 303.

25. Roemer, *Free to Lose*, 167.

26. It is worth noting that Roemer has recently shifted his attention from exploitation to precisely the question of market socialism. See his "The Morality and Efficiency of Market Socialism," *Ethics* 102 (April 1992): 448–64. See also Pranab Bardhan and John Roemer, "Market Socialism: A Case for Rejuvenation," *Journal of Economic Perspectives* 6 (Summer 1992): 101–16. In Roemer's view no market socialism is "just," but designing a feasible alternative to capitalism is an appropriate and important task for a socialist theorist today.

27. Normative considerations—the democratic principle noted above and others as well—guide the construction of the model and enter explicitly into its defense. But we do not *begin* with abstract principles.

28. The literature is now too vast to cite here. The most important early theorist was Cornell economist Yaroslav Vanek, whose technical treatise, *The General Theory of Labor-Managed Market Economics* (Ithaca: Cornell University Press, 1970), and popular companion piece, *The Participatory Economy* (Ithaca: Cornell University Press, 1971), set the terms for almost all subsequent analysis. An important recent contribution from a more philosophical perspective is Carol Gould, *Rethinking Democracy: Freedom and Social Cooperation in Politics, Economy, and Society* (Cambridge: Cambridge University Press, 1988). My own *Against Capitalism* contains an extended bibliography.

29. For a recent analysis of some forty-three separate studies, see David Levine and Laura D'Andrea Tyson, "Participation, Productivity, and the Firm's Environment," in Alan Blinder, ed., *Paying for Productivity: A Look at the Evidence* (Washington, D.C.: Brookings Institute, 1990), 183–244.

30. Setting out such a model should not be thought to contradict the reflexivity of the democratic principle. The institutions to be set out all give scope to democratic decision making, and they are all open with respect to many details. Moreover, they are merely being advocated here, not legislated—but with the confidence that they would be readily embraced by the vast majority, if thoroughly and fairly debated. (Joyce Rothschild and Allen Whitt cite a 1984 study that finds "the social basis of support for workplace democracy to include nearly all segments of society, especially blue-collar workers and professional/technical

workers. The only class that does not support the redistribution of power in the workplace are managers and owners." *The Cooperative Workplace: Potentials and Dilemmas of Organizational Democracy and Participation* [Cambridge: Cambridge University Press, 1986], 186).

31. For many more details and an exhaustive defense, see my *Against Capitalism*.

PART II

Marxian Exploitation

Exploitation

ANWAR SHAIKH

IN THE MOST GENERAL sense, to exploit something means to make use of it for some particular end, as in the exploitation of natural resources for social benefit or for private profit. Insofar as this use takes advantage of other people, exploitation also implies something unscrupulous. If the other people are endemically powerless, as in the case of the poor in relation to their landlords, creditors, and the like, then the term "exploitation" takes on the connotation of oppression.

Marx uses the word "exploitation" in all the above senses. But he also defines a new concept, the *exploitation of labor*, which refers specifically to the extraction of the surplus labor upon which class society is founded. In this latter sense, exploitation becomes one of the basic concepts of the Marxist theory of social formations.

EXPLOITATION AND CLASS

Society consists of people living within-and-through complex networks of social relations which shape their very existence. Marx argues that the relations which structure the social division of labor lie at the base of social reproduction, because the division of labor simultaneously accomplishes two distinct social goals: first, the production of the many different objects which people use in their myriad activities of daily life; and second, the reproduction of the basic social framework under which this production takes place, and hence of the social structures which rest on this foundation. Social

From Anwar Shaikh, "Exploitation," in John Eatwell, Murray Milgate, and Peter Newman, eds., *The New Palgrave*, vol. 2 (London: Macmillan, 1987), 249–51, with the permission of Macmillan Press Ltd.

reproduction is always the reproduction of individuals as *social individuals*.

Class societies are those in which the rule of one set of people over another is founded upon a particular kind of social division of labor. This particularity arises from the fact that the dominant class maintains itself by controlling a process through which the subordinate classes are required to devote a portion of their working time to the production of things needed by the ruling class. The social division of labor within a class society must therefore be structured around the extraction of *surplus labor*, i.e., of labor time over and above the required to produce for the needs of the laboring classes themselves. In effect, it is the subordinate classes which do the work for the reproduction of the ruling class, and which therefore end up *working to reproduce the very conditions of their own subordination*. This is why Marx refers to the extraction of surplus labor in class societies as the exploitation of labor (Marx 1867, part 3 and appendix). It should be clear from this, incidentally, that the mere performance of labor beyond that needed to satisfy immediate needs does not in itself constitute exploitation. Robinson Crusoe, laboring away in his solitude in order to plant crops for future consumption or to create fortification against possible attacks, is merely performing some of the labor necessary for his own needs. He is neither exploiter nor exploited. But all this changes once he manages to subordinate the man Friday, to "educate" him through the promise of religion and the threat of force to his new place in life, and to set him to work building a proper microcosm of English society. Now it is Robinson who is the exploiter, and Friday the exploited whose surplus labor only serves to bind him ever more tightly to his new conditions of exploitation (Hymer 1971).

Although the exploitation of labor is inherent in all class societies, the form it takes varies considerably from one mode of production to another. Under slavery, for instance, the slave belongs to the owner, so that the whole of his or her labor and corresponding net product (i.e., product after replacement of the means of production used up) is ostensibly appropriated by the slaveowner. But in fact the slave too must be maintained out of this very same net product. Thus it is the surplus product (the portion of the net product over that needed to maintain the slaves), and hence the surplus labor of the slaves, which in the end sustains the slaveowning class. In a similar vein, under feudalism the surplus labor of the serf and tenant supports the ruling apparatus. But here, the forms of its exaction are many and varied: sometimes direct, as in the case of the quantities of annual labor and/or product which the serf or tenant is required to hand over to Lord, Church, and State; and sometimes indirect, as in the payment of money rents, tithes, and taxes which in effect require the serf or tenant to produce a surplus product and sell it for cash in order to meet these imposed obligations.

The material wealth of the dominant class is directly linked to the size of the surplus product. And this surplus product is in turn greater the smaller the standard of living of the subordinate classes, and the longer, more intense, or more productive their working day. Both of these propositions translate directly into a higher ratio of surplus labor time to the labor time necessary to reproduce the laborers themselves, that is, into a higher *rate of exploitation* of labor: Given the productivity of labor and length and intensity of the working day, the smaller the portion of the product consumed by the producing class, the greater the portion of their working day which is in effect devoted to surplus labor; similarly, given the consumption level of the average peasant or worker, the longer, more intense, and/or more productive their labor, the smaller the portion of their working day which has to be devoted to their own consumption needs, and hence the greater the portion which corresponds to surplus labor.

Because the magnitude of the surplus product can be raised in the above ways, it is always in the direct interest of the ruling class to try and push the rate of exploitation toward its social and historical limits. By the same token, it is in the interest of the subordinate classes not only to resist such efforts but also to fight against the social conditions which make this struggle necessary in the first place. The exploitative base of class society makes it a fundamentally antagonistic mode of human existence, marked by a simmering hostility between rulers and ruled, and punctuated by periods of riots, rebellions, and revolutions. This is why class societies must always rely heavily on ideology to motivate and rationalize the fundamental social cleavage upon which they rest, and on force to provide the necessary discipline when all else fails.

CAPITALISM AND EXPLOITATION

Capitalism shares the above general attributes. It is a class society, in which the domination of the capitalist class is founded upon its ownership and control of the vast bulk of the society's means of production. The working class, on the other hand, is made up of those who have been "freed" of this selfsame burden of property in means of production, and who must therefore earn their livelihood by working for the capitalist class. As Marx so elegantly demonstrates, the *general social condition* for the reproduction of these relations is that the working class as a whole be induced to perform surplus labor, because it is this surplus labor which forms the basis of capitalist profit, and it is this profit which in turn keeps the capitalist class willing and able to reemploy workers. And as the history of capitalism makes perfectly clear, the whole process is permeated by the struggle between the classes about the conditions, terms, and occasionally even about the future of these relations.

The historical specificity of capitalism arises from the fact that its relations of exploitation are almost completely hidden behind the surface of its relations of exchange. At first glance, the transaction between the worker and capitalist is a perfectly fair one. The former offers labor power for sale, the latter offers a wage rate, and the bargain is struck when both sides come to terms. But once this phase is completed, we leave the sphere of freedom and apparent equality and enter into "the hidden abode of production" within which lurks the familiar domain of surplus labor (Marx 1867, ch. 6). We find here a world of hierarchy and inequality, of orders and obedience, of bosses and subordinates, in which the working class is set to work to produce a certain amount of product for its employers. Of this total product, a portion which corresponds to the materials and depreciation costs of the total product is purchased by the capitalists themselves, in order to replace the means of production previously used up. A second portion is purchased by the workers with the wages previously paid to them by their employers. But if these two portions happen to exhaust the total product, then the capitalists will have succeeded in producing only enough to cover their own (materials, depreciation, and wage) costs of production. *There would be no aggregate profit.* It follows, therefore, that for capitalist production to be successful, i.e., for it to create its own profit, workers must be induced to work longer than the time required to produce their own means of consumption. They must, in other words, perform surplus labor time in order to produce the surplus product upon which profit is founded.

The above propositions can be derived analytically (Morishima 1973, ch. 7). More important, they are demonstrated *in practice* whenever working time is lost through labor strikes or slowdowns. Then, as surplus labor time is eroded, the normally hidden connection between surplus labor and profit manifests itself as corresponding fall in profitability. Every practicing capitalist must learn this lesson sooner or later.

Orthodox economics, encapsulated within its magic kingdom of production functions, perfect competition, and general equilibrium, usually manages to avoid such issues. Indeed, it concerns itself principally with the construction and refinement of an idealized image of capitalism, whose properties it then investigates with a concentration so ferocious that it is often able to entirely ignore the reality which surrounds it. Within this construct, production is a disembodied process undertaken by an intangible entity called the firm. This firm hires "factors of production" called capital and labor in order to produce an output, paying for each factor according to its estimated incremental contribution to the total output (i.e., according to the value of its marginal product). If all goes well, the sum of these payments turns out to exhaust exactly the net revenues actually received by the firm, and the ground is set for yet another round.

Notice that this conception puts a thing (capital) and a human capacity (labor power) on equal footing, both as so-called factors of production. This enables the theory to deny any class difference between capitalists and workers by treating all individuals as essentially equal because they are all owners of at least one factor of production. The fact that "factor endowments" may vary considerably across individuals is then merely a second-order detail whose explanation is said to lie outside of economic theory. Next, by treating production as some disembodied process, the human labor process is reduced to a mere technical relation, to a production function which "maps" things called inputs (which include labor power) into a thing called output. All struggle over the labor process thus disappears from view. Finally, since capital and labor are mere things, they cannot be said to be exploited. However, to the extent that the payment for some factors falls short of equality with its particular marginal product, the *owner* of this factor may be said to be exploited. In this sense, exploitation is defined as a discrepancy between an actual and an ideal "factor payment" (it can be established that a very similar construction underlies notions of unequal exchange such as those in Emmanuel 1969). More important, exploitation as defined above can in principle apply just as well to profits as to wages. Capitalism thus emerges as a system in which capitalists are just as liable to be exploited by workers as vice versa (Hodgson 1980, sec. 2). With this last step, the very notion of exploitation is reduced to utter triviality.

EXPLOITATION, GENDER, AND RACE

We have focused on the notion of exploitation as the extraction of surplus labor because this relation is the foundation upon which class society is built, in the sense that the other legal, political, and personal relations within the society are structured and limited by this central one. This does not mean that these other relations lack a history and logic of their own. It only means that within any given mode of production, they are bound to the system by the force field of this central relation, and characteristically shaped by its ever-present gravitational pull.

In the same vein, the notion that class society is marked by oppression along class lines obviously does not exclude other equally egregious forms of subjugation. It is evident, for instance, that the oppression of women by men is common to all known societies, and to all classes within them. Thus any proper understanding of the oppression of workers by capitalists must also encompass the oppression of working-class women by men of all classes, as well as the oppression of ruling-class women by men of their own class.

But even this is not enough. It is not sufficient to say that class and patriarchy are coexistent forms of oppression. We need to know also how they relate to one another. And it is here that Marxists generally give preeminence to class, not because class oppression is more grievous, but because of the sense that it is the nature of the class relation which modulates and shapes the corresponding form of patriarchy. That is to say, Marxists argue that capitalist patriarchy is distinct from feudal patriarchy precisely because capitalist relations of production are characteristically different from feudal ones.

Needless to say, there is still considerable controversy about the exact relationship between patriarchy and class (Barret 1980), as there is about the relation of race to either of them (Davis 1981). These are issues of great theoretical significance. Most important, a united struggle against these various forms of oppression has truly revolutionary potential.

References

Barret, M. 1980. *Women's Oppression Today: Problems in Marxist Feminist Analysis.* London: Verso.

Davis, A. Y. 1981, *Women, Race, and Class.* New York: Vintage, 1983.

Emmanuel, A. 1969. *Unequal Exchange: A Study of the Imperialism of Trade.* New York: Monthly Review Press.

Hodgson, G. 1980. "A Theory of Exploitation without the Labor Theory of Value." *Science and Society* 44, no. 3 (Fall): 257–73.

Hymer, S. 1971. "Robinson Crusoe and the Secret of Primitive Accumulation." *Monthly Review* 23, no. 4 (Sept.): 11–36.

Marx, K. 1867. *Capital,* vol. 1. London: Penguin Books, 1976.

Morishima, M. 1973. *Marx's Economics.* Cambridge: Cambridge University Press.

Exploitation

NANCY HOLMSTROM

ACCORDING TO MARX ONE of the primary evils of capitalism (and any other class society) is that it is exploitative—and necessarily so. Socialist and communist societies will (necessarily) not be exploitative and this is one of the reasons why they will in some sense be better. To understand such claims we have to determine exactly what Marx means by "exploitation" and what it is about exploitation that Marx finds to be bad. Neither of these questions is as simple as it might seem.

A common misunderstanding of Marx is this: Exploitation consists simply in an unequal distribution of social wealth. Workers are exploited because they get so much less of the pie than do capitalists. Another interpretation of Marx's concept is that exploitation consists in the fact that workers do not get the whole pie. They produce all value and, therefore, deserve to get it all back. I will show that both of these interpretations are inadequate or simply mistaken. An error common to both is an overemphasis on distribution.

Let someone ask: Why is exploitation under capitalism (or any other economic formation) bad? The answer we are strongly inclined to give is: Because it is unfair or unjust. But some have argued—among them, Allen Wood[1]—that this obvious answer is not Marx's answer, and indeed it is wrong given Marx's specific theory of capitalist exploitation. But then why is exploitation an evil?

I will first explain Marx's theory of exploitation in capitalism and his general concept. We will then be able to see in what ways exploitation is an evil for Marx, whether or not it is unfair or unjust. I will, however,

From Nancy Holmstrom, "Exploitation," Canadian Journal of Philosophy 7, no. 2 (1977): 353–69, with the permission of the journal and the consent of the author.

contend that the arguments purporting to show that exploitation, as conceived by Marx, is not unjust are not conclusive. However, I will also contend that, for Marx, what primarily makes exploitation an evil is not its injustice.

1

In order to elucidate Marx's concept of exploitation, it will help first to explain what Marx means by *necessary*, *surplus*, and *free* labor. The force of my explanation will be limited at this point and should become clearer as we go on. Necessary labor is that labor—and no more—which will satisfy the subsistence needs[2] of the workers and of their dependents. In Marx's view there will always be some necessary labor even under socialism and communism. "Just as the savage must wrestle with Nature to satisfy his wants, to maintain and reproduce life, so must civilized man, and he must do so under all social formations and under all possible modes of production."[3] Now in class societies (societies not controlled by the working class), workers are required to do more than necessary labor. "Surplus labor," as Marx uses the term, means all labor over and above subsistence labor. In socialist and communist societies, there will be no surplus labor required. Marx believed that there would be surplus labor in socialism and communism, but only because people would desire to do it. In fact, he believed that the primary distinguishing property of human beings was the capacity and need to do creative work.[4] However, given that the goal of production in socialism and communism is simply the satisfaction of needs, no one will be required to do any labor that is not necessary. The only labor required will be some necessary labor, the amount of which will be greatly reduced because of increased productivity.

The idea that there are degrees of freedom and lack of freedom is implicit in Marx's discussions of these points. Labor that is necessary (required by nature) is not free in the fullest sense possible. However, this does not doom it to being unfree or forced labor. Speaking about the realm of necessity, Marx says: "Freedom in this field can only consist in socialized man, the associated producers, rationally regulating their interchange with Nature, bringing it under their common control, instead of being ruled by it as by the blind forces of Nature; and achieving this with the least possible expenditure of energy and under conditions most favorable to, and worthy of their human nature."[5] Necessary labor, then, can be free or unfree. There is a freedom that is compatible with necessity, which requires control over the activity by the agents and the absence of control by others. Necessary labor in socialist and communist societies will meet this condition. Necessary labor that is not under the control of those doing it, but under alien control, is unfree.

Marx makes it clear that freedom which is compatible with necessity is not the fullest kind of freedom possible. It remains necessary. "Beyond it begins that development of human energy which is an end in itself, the true realm of freedom, which, however, can blossom forth only with the realm of necessity as its basis. The shortening of the work day is its basic prerequisite."[6] Let us call the labor that is free, though necessary, "relatively free" labor, as opposed to "really free" labor, which is not necessary.[7] This kind of surplus labor which is really free labor will only be possible for the majority of people in socialist and communist society. More on this later.

2

The first time that the word "exploitation" appears in *Capital I* is in chapter 9, "The Rate of Surplus Value," in the title of section 1, "The Degree of Exploitation of Labor Power." It first occurs in the text when he says: "The rate of surplus value is therefore an exact expression for the degree of exploitation of labor power by capital, or of the laborer by the capitalist."[8] We have to determine, then, why Marx first introduces the term "exploitation" in this context and exactly what the rate of surplus value is.

Marx's theory of surplus value is his explanation of the origins of profits in capitalism. Capitalism is a system of commodity production. It is a system in which things are bought and sold on a market, in which labor power is a commodity. The production of profit is the purpose of production for the capitalist. What the capitalist produces always has some use; it satisfies some want or other. In Marx's terminology, this is to say that all commodities have some use value. But this is not the reason why the capitalist produces what he does. What the capitalist produces must also have some value for exchange, which Marx calls *exchange value*. A capitalist will not produce something that has use value but no exchange value, such as unsubsidized housing of good quality for poor people. The exchange value (usually abbreviated as "value"), at which the capitalist aims, must, moreover, be greater than the value of the means of production and the labor power that went into its production, or else there would be no point to the process for the capitalist. The capitalist pays out money for the means of production, which Marx calls *constant capital* or c, and for labor power, which Marx calls *variable capital* or v. The value of the product, then, must be greater than c plus v. The additional value has its source in the peculiar nature of the commodity labor power. Like any other commodity, labor power is assumed to be sold at its value most of the time. The (exchange) value of a commodity, according to the Marxist theory, is the simple, abstract, socially necessary labor time required to produce it.[9] This is the labor theory of (exchange) value. In the case of labor power, its value includes the necessities of life not only for the worker, but also for the worker's family, so as to ensure the future supply of labor power. The workers produce this value in only a portion of the time that they work: The labor done during this time is necessary labor. The value that they produce during the rest of the time, during surplus labor time, is surplus value, which we will call *s*. This is the source of profit. It creates value greater than its own value, which is the reason why labor power is called variable capital.

The ratio of surplus value to the value of labor power, s/v, is the rate of surplus value. When we understand how the value of labor power is determined, we can see that this ratio is equivalent to the ratio of surplus labor to necessary labor. Since the wage that the worker receives is for the necessary labor time and only for necessary labor time (assuming labor power is sold at its value), this same ratio is also equivalent to the ratio of unpaid to paid labor. This division of the work day under capitalism into necessary and surplus labor time, with the latter unpaid, is concealed by the wage relationship. The worker receives a wage and works a full day, which suggests that the wage is payment for a day's labor. However, what workers really sell to the capitalists, according to Marx, is not labor, but the capacity to labor or labor power, which capitalists then use as they wish for the day. It was this discovery of Marx's that enables one to discern the division of the work day under capitalism into necessary and surplus labor time.

Let us turn now to the question of the freedom of labor under capitalism. Labor under capitalism would appear to be free. This appearance, however, according to Marx, is an illusion, which results from several facts. The individual laborer is not tied to any particular capitalist, as is a slave or a serf, but can work for various different capitalists and usually does so. There are no chains and no laws that force workers to work for a particular boss or even to work at all. It appears that what makes them work is their desire to satisfy certain needs, so that they choose the capitalist who offers them the best deal. Sometimes they get a better deal than at other times. Thus the relationship appears to be a free exchange between equals, one buying and the other selling. In fact, Marx believes, the exchange is an unfree one, because it is based on force. Although they are not tied to any particular capitalist, workers under capitalism are tied to the class of capitalists. The laborer under capitalism who is free of feudal bonds is also "free" from ownership of the means of production.[10] Persons who have no access to the means of production other than their own capacity to labor do not need to be forced to work by chains or by laws. The "freedom" they have compels them to sell their labor power to those who own the means of production and to put themselves under their dominion.[11] Workers who have once sold their labor power to the owners of the means of production are then forced by them to do nonnecessary surplus labor during part of the work day. This surplus labor is, by definition, unnecessary to them and they are uncompensated for it. Hence Marx says that surplus labor "in essence . . . always remains forced labor no matter how much it may seem to result from free contractual agreement."[12] The source of the capitalists' dominion over unpaid labor is the separation of most of the population from the means of production and the accumulation of those means by a few. This was originally accomplished for the most part by "conquest, enslavement, robbery, murder, briefly, force."[13]

The labor that workers do during the rest of the day is necessary and is compensated in the form of the necessities of life. In a sense they are working for themselves during this time. Hence, necessary labor has less of a forced nature than surplus labor. Nevertheless, it is unfree. As explained earlier, necessary labor can be (relatively) free for Marx only if it is under the control of those who are doing it. In capitalism, however, workers are under the dominion of capitalists who, Marx says, are merely the personifications of capital (the capitalist mode of production). Production is not brought under the conscious collective control of all members of society. Instead "anarchy reigns in the field of production." The market is seen as functioning according to natural necessity, beyond human control. Inside the factory, workers work under the despotism of capital during necessary labor as well as surplus labor time. So both necessary and surplus labor are unfree under capitalism, but the latter has an additional element of compulsion. The same ratio of surplus value to the value of labor power can, therefore, also be expressed as the ratio of forced labor to labor that is relatively unforced but still unfree.

The product of the workers' surplus, unpaid and forced labor, is then appropriated by the owner of labor power and the means of production, the capitalist. This surplus value is the source of their profit.[14] The actual producers have no control over the surplus. The profits of capitalists, then, according to Marx's theory, are generated by surplus, unpaid and forced labor, the product of which the producers do not control. This is exploitation as Marx uses the term.

We can see then why Marx introduced the term "exploitation" in the context of discussing the origin of capitalist profits. Profits come from surplus value and the extraction of surplus value involves the appropriation of the product of forced, unpaid, surplus labor. It is not the fact that capitalists have some, or even a very large, income that is exploitative. It is the fact that the income is derived through forced, unpaid, surplus labor, the product of which the producers do not control, which makes it exploitative.

Although the concept is first explained with reference to capitalism, Marx did not think that exploitation was unique to capitalism. In fact, he says that "the essential difference, between, for instance, a society based on slave labor, and one based on wage labor, lies only in the mode in which this surplus is in each case extracted from the actual producers, the laborer."[15] While the existence of exploitation in capitalism had to be discovered by science,[16] and specifically through the discovery of surplus value, the discovery of exploitation in feudal society requires no deep analysis. The division of a serf's labor into necessary and surplus labor is quite apparent. Serfs worked part of the time on their own land and kept the product of that labor. This was necessary labor, which is essentially labor for themselves. During that time, however, they were subject to all sorts of constraints set by the lord, which made their necessary labor unfree. To be allowed to do this necessary labor, they had, moreover, to work on the lord's land as well, and the product of this labor went to the lord. That serfs were forced to do this nonnecessary labor for the lord was made brutally apparent to any serf who failed to do it. In the feudal mode of production, then, it is quite clear that workers were forced to do unpaid surplus labor the product of which they did not control, hence that they were exploited. In a system of production based on slavery, the despotism exerted over the slaves in all their labor is very apparent. That the product of slave labor is appropriated by the persons forcing them to work is also clear. What is concealed by the relationship between the slaves and their masters is that part of the slaves' labor is for themselves in that part of the product is returned to them in the form of all or some of the necessities of life. This labor is certainly unfree, although there is a sense in which it is less compelled than the nonnecessary, uncompensated labor they do the rest of the time. Slavery thus also involves exploitation: Part of the labor that is done is forced unpaid surplus labor the product of which is under the control of nonproducers.[17]

The features common to exploitation, as I have explained it, that it involves forced, surplus, and unpaid labor, the product of which is not under the producers' control, are not four unconnected features. While not logically connected, perhaps, they can be seen to imply one another given Marx's empirical assumptions. If the producers receive merely the necessities of life, then what they produce beyond that is surplus and is uncompensated or unpaid. To be paid or compensated does not simply mean getting a certain amount of money or material goods. A large stockholder in a corporation does not necessarily directly get any more money or material goods if the value of his stock goes up. Nevertheless, he profits, he is compensated, because he has (partial) control over something that has increased in value. If the producers are not compensated for their surplus labor, then it follows both that they do not receive the surplus they have produced and that they have no control over the surplus product. People will seldom knowingly produce more than they need if they have no control over it and are not otherwise compensated. Therefore, labor which has these three features will also, most probably, be forced labor. Thus in speaking about exploitation in general, Marx said that the essential difference between different exploitative systems lay only in the mode in which the surplus was extracted from the producers. This description implies all four features of exploitation: that it is the production of a surplus, appropriated from the producers, uncompensated for, and forced.

Exploitation will occur in all societies in which a minority controls the means of production, in other words, all class societies. This is the basic cause of exploitation. According to Marx, a ruling class developed as soon as it became possible to produce more than was needed for subsistence, to produce a surplus. The ruling class is the class that controls the means of production. This control enables them to force the producers to produce more than they receive. Controlling the means of production, including the producers, the ruling class also controls and lives off the product of the surplus, unpaid and forced labor of the producers. The mode in which this surplus is extracted differs from one class society to another.

3

Marx's theory of exploitation in capitalism and his general concept of exploitation have been explained. I would like now to go into further clarifications of the concept and show why certain alternative interpretations are mistaken.

In our interpretation of Marx's concept of exploitation, little importance has been given to the distribution of income. To do otherwise would be inconsistent with Marx's emphasis on the sphere of production as opposed to the sphere of circulation. It would also be inconsistent with his explicit statement that principles of distribution will always be consequences of a given mode of production.[18] It is true that in an exploitative society nonproducers appropriate the product of producers and also that workers who are exploited do unpaid labor. It is also true that the relationship between profits and wages is connected with the degree of exploitation. However, these facts do not support an analysis of exploitation that makes distribution of income central to the concept.

High wages do not mean that workers are not exploited or even that they are exploited to a lesser degree. However, the ratio of capitalist profits to workers' wages (relative wages) may be seen to be connected with the rate of exploitation, if we accept a key assumption. If labor power is sold at its value (which is the key assumption), the ratio of surplus to necessary labor is equivalent to the ratio of unpaid to paid labor. Since profits come out of surplus value, and since wages are the value of labor power, the ratio of profits to wages will be equivalent to the rate of surplus value or the rate of exploitation. Marx assumed that the ratios of surplus to necessary labor, surplus value to the value of labor power, unpaid to paid labor, and forced to less forced labor were all equivalent because he assumed that labor power, like other commodities, would generally be sold at its value, an assumption shared by almost all economists. However, although there will always be a portion of labor that is unpaid, these ratios will not all be equivalent if labor power is not sold at its value. Neither the fact of exploitation nor its rate would be affected. If wages were to do the unlikely thing and go above the value of labor power, this would not make the worker less exploited, and if, more likely, it went below its value, this would not make the worker more exploited. Although the ratio of profits to wages is connected with the rate of exploitation, this is due to its connection with the ratio of surplus labor to necessary labor and of forced unpaid labor to paid labor. The high relative income of capitalists to that of workers is not definitive of exploitation.

The degree of exploitation is determined by the ratio of surplus to necessary labor. The greater the proportion of time that the worker is forced to work to produce a surplus for the capitalist, the greater the rate of exploitation. Workers who work a six-hour day and produce their own value in one hour are more exploited than workers who work a twelve-hour day and produce their own value in eight hours. Both the rate of exploitation and the absolute amount of exploitation are greater in the former case. The decrease of the amount of surplus labor down to zero, or down close to zero, is ruled out by the needs of the system. There would be no production if there were no profit derived from production. Thus exploitation can never be eliminated in capitalism. Furthermore, it will always be in the interests of capitalists to try to increase the ratio of surplus to necessary labor, the ratio of profit to investment, and in the interests of workers to decrease it. Hence, the inevitability of class antagonism. This consequence of my interpretation of what it is for one person to *exploit* others makes it clear why Marx believed in the necessity of a revolution. On many other interpretations, it is less clear why Marx was a revolutionary.

Exploitation is inevitable not only in capitalism but in any class society, including a society ruled by a bureaucracy. The question of whether the bureaucrats' material conditions are better or worse is irrelevant to questions of whether the workers are exploited. It is also irrelevant to study the nature of those in control. So long as workers do not control the means of production they will be exploited; they will be forced to work part of the time for no return, and they will not have control over the surplus they produce.[19]

The reality of exploitation is also not affected by how the surplus is used by those who appropriate it. Under feudalism most of the surplus was directly consumed by the individual feudal lords who appropriated it. Under capitalism most of the surplus goes to maintaining and developing the means of production and buying labor power. Only a small portion is directly consumed by the capitalist class. *Even if some fledgling capitalist reinvested so much of the surplus that his standard of living was no higher than that of his employees, this would not change the fact that he was exploiting them.* They would still be forced to work and produce a surplus that he then appropriates.

Another interpretation of exploitation that makes distribution central is the interpretation which takes exploitation to consist in the fact that workers do not receive back all the wealth[20] that is produced.[21] Behind this interpretation is the idea that, according to Marx, labor is the source of all wealth, and hence workers should get back all the wealth that is produced. Marx, however, directly contradicts both these views in *The Critique of the Gotha Program.*[22] He says that nature, as much as labor, is the source of wealth, and he makes clear that the elimination of exploitation would not mean returning to workers all the wealth they produce. In a socialist society, Marx explains, before workers receive back the proceeds of their labor, deductions have to be made for a number of social needs and for the maintenance and development of the means of production. Since these social needs include the care of those unable to work, the producers do not receive it all back indirectly either. Nor does the producing class receive it all back, since Marx does not limit support of those unable to work to members of the producing class. The principle of distribution that will be operative in socialism is "to each according to his labor." The principle that will be operative in a communist society is "to each according to his needs." Neither of these principles implies that workers receive back all the wealth that they produce.

This raises the question of whether some labor in socialism and communism will be unpaid. To the extent that workers do not receive as disposable income all the wealth that they produce, then some of their labor will be unpaid. One of the conditions of exploitation, unpaid labor, would then be a feature of socialism and communism as well as of class societies. Yet Marx did not think that socialism and communism were exploitative societies. This is because being unpaid is not a sufficient condition of exploitation. The other conditions of exploitation are necessary and they are not fulfilled in socialist and communist societies. There is no forced labor. The surplus is under the control of those who produce it. There is no class of nonproducers who appropriate what workers have produced. Workers do not consume it all, directly or indirectly, but they control it as a class. This point suggests another interpretation of what it is to be paid. Earlier in the paper I pointed out that the wealth of stockholders in a corporation is not simply equal to their immediate disposable income. They have wealth in the corporation. This does not imply, however, that they would be permitted to walk off with some of the machinery that belonged to the corporation, the value of which was somehow calculated to be equal to their share in the corporation. They are considered to have wealth in the corporation where wealth means command over resources. In this sense, because workers in socialist and communist societies have control over all the wealth that is produced, they can be said to be fully paid.[23] To conclude this point, we can say that whether or not workers in socialist and communist societies do any unpaid labor depends on what it means to be *paid*. In one sense, they are fully paid, in another, they are not. Since being unpaid in the narrow sense is not sufficient for exploitation, it does not matter which interpretation of being paid is correct. On either one, it follows that socialist and communist societies are nonexploitative. Since this is clearly what Marx thought, any other implication should raise doubts about itself.

4

We turn now to the question of why Marx thought exploitation an evil. This question is easy to answer now that the concept of exploitation has been clarified.

When X exploits, Y, Y is forced to do unnecessary, unpaid labor and does not control the product of that labor. Force, domination, unequal power, and control are involved in exploitation both as preconditions and as consequences. This is why Marx thinks exploitation an evil. And, as Wood says, this servitude[24] is "the more insidious because it is experienced as such without being understood as such."[25]

Those who control the means of production appropriate the product of forced labor. Crocker[26] calls this undemocratic control of production and says that this is why Marx condemned exploitation. This explanation is inadequate because it obscures the connection that exploitation has to the labor theory of value and to alienation. Although it is true that the majority does not have control of production in class societies, more to the point is the fact that producers do not have control. The labor theory of value says the value of a product is a function of the labor that went into it. Being congealed labor, the product is in some sense part of the producers. When it is taken away from them, they are thereby diminished, impoverished, denuded. The connections with Marx's theory of alienation are obvious, but are not obvious if we describe exploitation simply as undemocratic control of production. This characterization of exploitation is also one-sided in that it fails to bring out the fact that workers who are exploited are themselves under the control of non-producers. Because they must sell their labor power to the capitalist, their productive activity, their very capacity for life activity comes under the control of the capitalist. Again we see the systematic connection between exploitation and alienation.[27]

Now in addition to involving force and domination, isn't exploitation also unjust? Wood has argued quite persuasively that Marx did not think so. According to Wood, Marx held justice to be a juridical concept which only makes sense in terms of its function within a given mode of production. In what is probably the most important passage from Marx that Wood uses to support his interpretation, Marx says, "The justice of transactions arise as natural consequences from the relations of production. . . . This content is just whenever it corresponds to the mode of production, is adequate to it. It is unjust whenever it contradicts that mode."[28] The transaction that goes on between capitalist and worker is the buying of the worker's labor power by the capitalist, usually at its full value. "This is," says Wood, "according to the Ricardian formula and the strictest rules of commodity exchange, a just transaction, an exchange of equivalent for equivalent. Surplus value, to be sure, is appropriated by the capitalist without an equivalent. But there is nothing in the exchange requiring him to pay any equivalent for it."[29] If the capitalist receives more value from this commodity than he started with, Marx calls this "peculiar good fortune for the buyer (of labor power) but no injustice at all to the seller."[30] Such statements are usually ignored by interpreters who claim that Marx thought exploitation to be unjust. Wood suggests that what they often have in mind is that it is unjust if workers do not receive back all the value that they produce, and, as we have seen, this is a mistake. Wood also argues correctly that "for Marx justice is not and cannot be a genuinely revolutionary notion."[31] An interpretation which construes Marx to base his critique of capitalism on its injustice would most likely lead to reformist conclusions, since the emphasis would tend to be on enlightening people to its injustice. It does not follow, however, as Wood seems to think, that merely to hold exploitation to be unjust has reformist consequences.

An initial problem with Wood's interpretation is that it is not clear that the transaction between worker and capitalist should be looked at in the way Wood does. Allen[32] and Fried[33] both point out that the worker is not paid what he is supposed to be paid according to bourgeois ideology. The transaction that is supposed to be going on is not just by capitalist standards. So there is an inevitable gap between principle and practice in bourgeois society.

The main problem with the interpretation, however, in my opinion, is that Wood views the exchange between capitalist and worker too narrowly, abstracted totally from its background. Some of the key passages that Wood cites in support of his interpretation of the exchange between capitalist and worker as just, do not, upon careful inspection, support his interpretation. One of the most important of these is to be found at *Capital I*, p. 176, where Marx talks of the exchange between capitalist and worker as an exchange of equivalent for equivalent which is just, according to the standards of commodity production. Now Marx also says in the same paragraph that workers freely sell their labor power to the capitalist. I think that a useful analogy can be drawn between Marx's views about the freedom of the transaction and the equivalence of the exchange. As for the freedom of the transaction, Marx says, "the 'free' laborer . . . *agrees, i.e., is compelled* by social conditions, to sell the whole of his active life, his very capacity to work, for the price of the necessities of life, his birthright for a mess of pottage"[34] and also that "surplus labor always remains forced labor—no matter how much it may *appear* to result from free contractual agreement."[35] According to Marx, the exchange between capitalist and worker appears free only if we take a narrow look just at the exchange itself as occurring between an individual worker and capitalist. Looking at the social background of the exchange, and looking at the relationship, not between an individual worker and an individual capitalist, but between the working class and the capitalist class, we get a very different picture. What looks free and independent is in reality totally dependent and unfree.

Applying this point to the question of whether capitalists and workers exchange equivalents, we also get a different answer if we look at the background of the exchange and at the relationship between classes rather than between individuals. This is suggested by Marx when he says "only buyer and seller, mutually dependent, face each other in commodity production." However, he says, "the matter looks quite different if we consider capitalist production in the uninterrupted flow of its renewal and if, in place of the individual capitalist and the individual worker, we view them in their totality, the capitalist class and the working class confronting each other. But in doing so, we should be applying standards quite foreign to commodity production."[36] If matters are looked at in that way we would understand why Marx refers to the surplus product as "the tribute annually exacted from the working class by the capitalist class," and goes on to say that, "though the latter with a portion of that tribute purchases the additional labor power even at its full price, so that equivalent is exchanged for equivalent, the transaction is for all that only the old dodge of every conquerer who buys commodities with the money he has robbed them of."[37] We would hardly call such a transaction just even if equivalent is exchanged for equivalent. But is equivalent exchanged for equivalent? Marx says elsewhere that "capital retains this surplus labor without an equivalent."[38] Looking at the exchange between individual members of the conquered and conquering groups, one might say yes. However, looking at the "exchange" between the conquered and conquering groups as a whole, it is clear that equivalent is not exchanged for equivalent. In fact, it is not really an exchange at all!

Going back to the passage Wood cites, where Marx says that equivalent is exchanged for equivalent, these points suggest that Marx is there describing how matters superficially appear, but not how they really are. This suggestion is confirmed later, on the same page, when Marx describes the sphere where transactions take place as the sphere "which furnishes the 'Free Trader Vulgaris' with . . . the standard by which he judges a society based on capital and wages. . . . This sphere is a very Eden of the innate rights of man. The alone rule Freedom, Equality, Property and Bentham." So the context of the passage that Wood cites in isolation is one of ridiculing such ideas as illusions of bourgeois ideology. Having surveyed the background of this so-called exchange as Marx sees it, we now see that calling it a just exchange could only be done tongue-in-cheek, or to mean: "This is *taken* to be just."

Another questionable interpretation has been placed on Marx's criticism of the demand for and even the notion of a fair day's wage in *The Critique of the Gotha Program*. Wood holds that Marx's criticism was due to the fact that workers were already receiving a fair day's wage, and yet were still exploited. Another, at least equally plausible interpretation, is that the notion of a fair day's wage is a contradiction in terms, since all wages involve unpaid labor, based on force, and hence, are all unfair.

Wood interprets such statements as "right can never be higher than the economic structure of society and the cultural development conditioned by it,"[39] as well as the statement from *Capital III* quoted earlier, to mean that it is inappropriate to use the standards of one mode of production to criticize another mode of production. However, it can also be interpreted as Fried does, to mean that what standards of right can actually be exemplified depends on the mode of production. It is all right, she says, to use the standards of one to criticize another, but only in combination with the struggle to change the mode of production to one where the other standard could be put into practice.

A provocative consequence of Wood's interpretation is that, according to Marx, reforms that would take away surplus value would be "injustices of the most straightforward and unambiguous kind."[40] But surely Marx would never have said this. In fact, he would have considered it just the sort of ideological mystification that he was concerned to expose and to ridicule.

I conclude that whether Marx thought exploitation to be an evil because it was unjust, as well as for different reasons, is not clear.[41] However, there were other independent reasons why Marx considered exploitation an evil. It is evil, Marx held, because it involves force and domination in manifold ways and because it deprives workers of control that should be theirs.

Socialist and communist societies as conceived by Marx will necessarily exclude exploitation. This is one of the reasons why they will be better than any class society.

Notes

Bernard Gendron was extremely helpful to me in writing this paper. I also profited from discussions with Gary Young who argues for a stronger position against Wood than I do in this paper "Marx and the Injustice of Capitalist Production" (unpublished). The account of exploitation I develop here is similar to accounts given by Lawrence Crocker in "Marx's Concept of Exploitation," in *Social Theory and Practice* (Fall 1972), and Allen Wood in "The Marxian Critique of Justice," in *Philosophy and Public Affairs* 1 (1972), but there are important differences as well, some of which will emerge in the paper. A preliminary version of this paper was given at a meeting of the Marxist Activist Philosophers in October 1975.

1. Allen Wood, "The Marxian Critique of Justice," *Philosophy and Public Affairs* 1 (1972).
2. These will vary according to physical conditions, such as climate, and also according to social and historical conditions. There is also, Marx says, a conventional element.
3. *Capital*, vol. 3 (New York: International Publishers, 1967), 820.
4. Cf., e.g., *Grundrisse* (Penguin), 611.
5. Ibid., 820.
6. Ibid., 820. Cf. *Grundrisse*, 611.
7. I am deliberately avoiding the question of Marx's position on the metaphysical question of freedom. The position I have ascribed to him is compatible with various positions on the question.
8. *Capital*, vol. 1 (New York: International Publishers, 1967), 218.
9. "Socially necessary" labor means the labor that is required to produce a product, given the specific conditions in which the labor takes place, i.e., given "the normal conditions of production, and . . . the average degree of skill and intensity prevalent at the time." *Capital* 1:39.
10. Ibid., 169.
11. "It takes centuries ere the 'free' laborer, thanks to the development of capitalistic production, agrees, i.e., is compelled by social conditions, to sell the whole of his active life, his very capacity to work, for the price of the necessities of life, his birthright for a mess of pottage." Ibid., 271.
12. *Capital* 3:819. Also, "It will not be forgotten, that, with respect to the labor of children, even the formality of a voluntary sale disappears." *Capital* 1:578, fn.1.
13. *Capital* 1:714.
14. The rest of the surplus value goes to other capitalists in the form of rent and interest.
15. *Capital* 1:217.
16. Ibid., 542.
17. Ibid., 539–40.
18. "It was in general incorrect to make a fuss about so-called *distribution* and put the principal stress on it. Any distribution whatever of the means of consump-

tion is only a consequence of the distribution of the conditions of production themselves. The latter distribution, however, is a feature of the mode of production itself." *Critique of the Gotha Program*, in *Selected Works* (New York: International Publishers, 1974), 325.

19. See, for example, Tony Cliff, *State Capitalism in Russia* (London. Pluto Press, 1974).

20. I use the word "wealth" rather than "value" because the latter, which is equivalent to "exchange value," is inappropriate to socialist and communist societies, being the specific form that wealth takes in capitalist societies. The necessity for this terminological precision was impressed upon me by David Smith.

21. Robert Nozick's interpretation of Marx's concept of exploitation is similar to this. Although he never states what he takes Marx's definition to be or cites any texts, he nevertheless states that "the charm of simplicity of this theory's *definition* of exploitation is lost when it is realized that according to the definition there will be exploitation in *any* society in which investment takes place for a greater future produce . . . and in any society in which those unable to work, or to work productively, are *subsidized* by the labor of others." *Anarchy, State, and Utopia* (New York: Basic Books, 1974), 253.

22. 319, 322–25 in particular.

23. This point was suggested to me by Bernard Gendron.

24. Marx says, "Surplus labor . . . in essence always remains forced labor" (*Capital* 3:819), and in numerous passages he refers to labor under capitalism as wage slavery and to workers under capitalism as wage slaves.

25. Wood, "Marxian Critique of Justice," 278.

26. Lawrence Crocker, "Marx's Concept of Exploitation," *Social Theory and Practice* (Fall 1972).

27. Marx thought that the elimination of capitalism and its replacement by socialism was possible at the time he was writing. However, even if he had thought it impossible at that time he would not have taken this to destroy the basis of his condemnation. He would still have thought it an evil, the elimination of which would result in a higher form of society. He describes the social form that will follow capitalism as a "higher" form, e.g., in *Capital* 1:592. Consider what he says about slavery: "The *recognition* of the products as its own, and the judgment that its separation from the conditions of its realization is improper— forcibly imposed—is an enormous (*advance in*) awareness, itself the product of the mode of production resting on capital, and as much the knell to its doom as, with the slave's *awareness* that he *cannot be the property of another*, with his consciousness of himself as a person, the existence of slavery becomes a merely artificial vegetative existence, and ceases to be able to prevail as the basis of production." (My emphasis)

28. *Capital* 3:339.

29. Wood, "Marxian Critique of Justice," 262.

30. *Capital* 1:194.

31. Wood, "Marxian Critique of Justice," 271.

32. Derek Allen, "Is Marxism a Philosophy?" *Journal of Philosophy* 71 (1974).

33. Marlene Fried in "Marxism and Justice," comment on Allen, at American Philosophical Association Eastern Division Meetings, Dec. 1974.

34. *Capital* 1:271.

35. *Capital* 3:819.

36. *Capital* 1:586.

37. *Capital* 1:582.
38. *Capital* 3:819.
39. *Critique of the Gotha Program,* 324.
40. Wood, "Marxian Critique of Justice," 268.
41. Much the same conclusion is argued for in William McBride's very useful paper in *Ethics* 85 (1975), which I read after writing this paper.

PART III

Marxian Exploitation under Debate

The Labor Theory of Value and the Concept of Exploitation

G. A. COHEN

It is we who ploughed the prairies, built the cities where they trade,
Dug the mines and built the workshops, endless miles of railroad laid,
Now we stand outcast and starving, 'mid the wonders we have made . . .
—"Solidarity," by Ralph Chaplin (to the tune of
                                    "Battle Hymn of the Republic")

THIS CHAPTER SHOWS THAT the relationship between the labor theory of value and the concept of exploitation is one of mutual irrelevance. The labor theory of value is not a suitable basis for the charge of exploitation directed by Marxists against capitalism, and the real foundation of that charge is something much simpler which, for reasons to be stated, is widely confused with the labor theory of value.

1

I begin with a summary presentation of the labor theory of value, as we find it in the first volume of *Capital*.[1] I define the term "value," and then I

From G. A. Cohen, "The Labor Theory of Value and the Concept of Exploitation," *Philosophy and Public Affairs* 8, no. 4:338–60, copyright 1979 by Princeton University Press (expanded and revised as "The Labour Theory of Value and the Concept of Exploitation" in G. A. Cohen, *History, Labour, and Freedom* [Oxford: Clarendon Press, 1988]), 209–38. Reprinted from *History, Labour, and Freedom* by permission of Princeton University Press and the consent of the author.

indicate what the labor theory says about what it denotes. What follows is one way of organizing the ideas laid out in the first few pages of Marx's magnum opus. Having completed my own presentation of those ideas, I shall describe a different way of presenting them, which I do not think is right.

It is convenient to define value by reference to exchange value, with which I therefore begin.

Exchange value is a property of things which are desired; in Marxian language, then, it is a property of use values.[2] It is, however, a property, not of all use values, but of those use values which are bought and sold, which undergo market transactions. Such use-values Marxism calls "commodities." Exchange value, then, is a property of commodities.

What property is it? The exchange value of a commodity is its power of exchanging against quantities of other commodities. It is measured by the number of commodities of any other kind for which it will exchange under equilibrium conditions. Thus the exchange value of a coat might be eight shirts, and also three hats, and also eighty pounds sterling.

Exchange value is a relative magnitude. Underlying the exchange-value of a commodity is its value, an absolute magnitude. A commodity a has n units of commodity b as its exchange value just in case the ratio between the values of a and b is $n{:}1$. The exchange values relative to one another of two commodities will remain the same when each changes in value if the changes are identical in direction and proportion.

The central claim of the labor theory of value is that magnitude of value is determined by socially necessary labor time. To be more precise: The exchange value of a commodity varies directly and uniformly with the quantity of labor time required to produce it under standard conditions of productivity, and inversely and uniformly with the quantity of labor time standardly required to produce other commodities, and with no further circumstance. The condition alone states the mode of determination of value *tout court*.

The labor theory of value is not true by the very definition of value, as value was defined above. In alternative presentations of the opening pages of volume 1, value is *defined* as socially necessary labor time. But a stipulative definition of a technical term is not a theory, and when value is defined as socially necessary labor time, it cannot also be a central theoretical claim of the labor theory that socially necessary labor time determines value. Still, those who favor the alternative definition sometimes do proceed to a substantive theoretical thesis, to wit, that value determines equilibrium price: In equilibrium price equals value, the latter being defined in terms of socially necessary labor time.

The size of this dispute can be exaggerated. We have two propositions:

1. Socially necessary labor time determines value.
2. Value determines equilibrium price.

I say that (2) is true by definition. Others say that (1) is.[3] But whoever is right, the conjunction of (1) and (2) entails that

3. Socially necessary labor time determines equilibrium price,

and (3) is not true by definition, on any reckoning. As long as it is agreed that the labor theory of value, in its volume 1 version, says (3), and that (3) is not true by definition, I do not wish to insist on my view that the definitional truth is (2) rather than (1). Almost all of what follows could be restated so as to accommodate the other definition. (One bad reason why the other definition finds favor will be presented in section 7, which also offers a textual defense of my treatment of (2) as true by definition.)

We now turn to a supposed[4] corollary of the labor theory of value, the labor theory of surplus value.

The labor theory of surplus value is intended to explain the origin of nonwage income under capitalism. Call the energies and faculties the worker uses when laboring his *labor power*. Now note that under capitalism labor power is a commodity. It is sold in daily or weekly packets by the worker to the capitalist. Being a commodity, it has a value, and, like any commodity, its value is, according to (1), determined by the amount of time required to produce it. But the amount of time required to produce it is identical with the amount of time required to produce the means of subsistence of the worker, since a person's labor power is produced if and only if he is produced. Thus "the value of labor power is the value of the means of subsistence necessary for the maintenance of its owner."[5] The origin of nonwage income is, then, the difference between the value of labor power and the value produced by him in whom it inheres. When capitalists profit, they do so because the amount of time it takes to produce what is needed to keep producers in being for a certain period is less than the amount of time the latter spend producing during that period.

The capital paid out as wages is normally equal to the value of the producer's labor power. It is known as *variable capital*. The value produced by the worker over and above that represented by variable capital is called *surplus value*. The ratio of surplus value to variable capital is called the *rate of exploitation*:

The rate of
$$\text{exploitation} = \frac{\text{surplus value}}{\text{variable capital}}$$

$$= \frac{\text{surplus value}}{\text{value of labor power}}$$

$$= \frac{\text{time worked } - \text{ time required to produce the worker}}{\text{time required to produce the worker}}$$

2

Why is the term "exploitation" used for what the rate of exploitation is a rate of? Is it because the term, as used in that phrase, denotes a kind of injustice? It is hard to think of any other good reason for using such a term.

Yet many Marxists say that the Marxian concept of exploitation is a *purely* scientific one, with no moral content. They say that to assert, in the language of Marxism, that A exploits B is to offer no condemnation or criticism of A, or of the arrangements under which A operates. For them, (4) is false:

4. One reason for overthrowing capitalism is that it is a regime of exploitation (and exploitation is unjust).

Two kinds of Marxist deny (4). The first kind does so because he denies that there is *any* reason to do with values for overthrowing capitalism. People seek to overthrow it because of their class situation, or because of their morally ungrounded identification with the class situation of other people.

The second kind of Marxist (4)-denier believes that there are indeed values which should lead people to struggle against capitalism, but that justice is not one of them, since justice, he says, is not a Marxian value. What is wrong with capitalism is not that it is unjust, but that it crushes human potential, destroys fraternity, encourages the inhumane treatment of man by man, and has other grave defects generically different from injustice.

Now I am certain that many Marxists have held (4), and that Karl Marx was one of them. But I shall not here defend that claim. Marxists who reject it will find this chapter less challenging, but I hope that they will read it anyway. For while my main topic is the relationship between (4) and the labor theory of value, in pursuing it I uncover deep and neglected (or, at least, underplayed) ambiguities in the labor theory of value itself, and no Marxist will deny that many Marxists do affirm the theory of value.

3

I begin with an argument which is based on the labor theory of value, and whose conclusion is that the worker is exploited, where that is taken to entail an injustice. We can call it the Traditional Marxian Argument. It may be attributed to those believers in (4) who hold that the labor theory of value supports (4):

    5. Labor and labor alone creates value.

    6. The laborer receives the value of his labor power.

    7. The value of the product is greater than the value of his labor power.

∴ 8. The laborer receives less value than he creates.

∴ 9. The capitalist appropriates the remaining value.

  10. The laborer is exploited by the capitalist.

Premise (5) comes from the labor theory of value, and the labor theory of surplus value supplies premises (6), (7), and (9).

In the foregoing statement of the Traditional Argument, and elsewhere in this chapter, I speak of "*the* labourer" and "*the* capitalist": I thereby depict a relationship between social classes as a relationship between individuals who represent them. Anyone who finds that device objectionable can mentally pluralize "laborer" and "capitalist" throughout, but even an orthodox zealot *should* not object to the device, since, in individualizing the class relationship, I am imitating Marx's *Capital* practice.[6]

The Traditional Marxian Argument, as formulated above, derives a conclusion imputing injustice from a set of factual-cum-theoretical premises. The Argument needs to have some premises about injustice added to it in order not to be, as it is in its formulation above, elliptical or incomplete (and the same holds for the Simpler Marxian Argument and the Plain Argument, which are introduced below). Some reflections on what the needed further premises should say are offered in section 11 below.

4

The Traditional Argument employs the labor theory of surplus value, which yields premises (6), (7), and (9). But they can be replaced by a truism, which will contribute as much as they do to securing the conclusion that the laborer is exploited. The result is this simpler Marxian argument (statement [11] is the truism):

    5. Labor and labor alone creates value.

  11. The capitalist appropriates some of the value of the product.

∴ 8. The laborer receives less value than he creates, and

  12. The capitalist appropriates some of the value the laborer creates.

∴ 10. The laborer is exploited by the capitalist.

The labor theory of *surplus* value is, then, unnecessary to the moral claim Marxists make when they say that capitalism is exploitative. It does not matter what *explains* the difference between the value the worker produces and the value he receives.[7] What matters is just that there *is* that difference. (Note that, although the Simpler Marxian Argument drops the labor theory of surplus value, there is still a recognizable concept of surplus value in it, namely, the difference between the value the worker produces and the value he receives; and the value he receives can still be called variable capital.)[8]

5

We began with the labor theory of value, the thesis that the value of a commodity is determined by the socially necessary labor time required to produce it. We have arrived at an argument whose conclusion is that the laborer is exploited by the capitalist, and which supposedly draws one of its controversial premises from the labor theory of value. That is premise (5), that labor and labor alone creates value. But we shall now show that the labor theory does not entail (5). It entails, moreover, that (5) is false.[9]

Suppose that a commodity has a certain value at a time *t*. Then that value, says the labor theory, is determined by the socially necessary labor time required to produce a commodity of that kind. Let us now ask: Required to produce it *when*? The answer is: At *t*, the time when it has the value to be explained. The amount of time required to produce it in the past, and, a fortiori, the amount of time actually spent producing it are magnitudes strictly irrelevant to its value, if the labor theory is true.

Extreme cases make the point clear. (a) Suppose that there is a use value *a*, which was produced in the past, when things such as *a* could come into being only through labor, but that labor is no longer required for things such as *a* to appear (perhaps *a* is a quantity of manna, produced by people at a time before God started what we can imagine is His now usual practice of dropping it). Then, according to the labor theory of value, *a* is valueless, despite the labor "embodied" in it. (b) Contrariwise, suppose that there is a commodity *b* now on the market, and that *b* was not produced by labor, but that a great deal of labor is now required for *b*-like things to appear (*b* might be a quantity of clean air bottled before it became necessary to manufacture clean air). Then *b* has a value, even though no labor is "embodied" in it.[10]

These statements follow from the labor theory of value. The theory entails that past labor is irrelevant to how much value a commodity now has.[11] But past labor would not be irrelevant if it created the value of the commodity. It follows that *labor does not create value, if the labor theory of value is true.*

Let us call the thesis that value is determined by socially necessary labor time—that is, the labor theory of value—*the strict doctrine*, and let us say that such sentences as (5), or ones which speak of value as embodied or congealed labor, belong to the *popular doctrine*. Strict and popular doctrine are commonly confused with one another, for several reasons. The least interesting reason—more interesting ones will be mentioned later—is that Marx often set formulations from the two doctrines side by side. Examples:

> The value of a commodity is to the value of any other commodity as the labour-time necessary for the production of the one is related to the labour-time necessary for the production of the other. "As exchange-values, all commodities are merely definite quantities of congealed labour time."

> So far as the *quantity of value* of a commodity is determined, according to my account, through the *quantity of labour-time contained in it* etc., then [it is determined] through the normal amount of labour which the production of an object costs etc.[12]

I am not saying that Marx was unaware of the difference between the strict and the popular doctrine. This sentence proves otherwise:

> What determines value is not the amount of labour time incorporated in products, but rather the amount of labour time currently necessary.[13]

"Currently necessary": at the time, that is, when the commodity has the given value. The relevant socially necessary labor time is that required now, not that required when it was produced:

> The value of any commodity ... is determined not by the necessary labour-time that it itself contains, but by the *socially* necessary labour-time required for its reproduction.[14]

So I do not say that Marx was ignorant of the difference between the two doctrines. But I do say that the difference is damaging to key Marxian theses. It has grave implications, which are widely unnoticed and which were not noticed by Marx. Our chief concern is with implications for the idea of exploitation. There are also implications for pure economic theory, some of which will occupy me in a subsequent digression (see section 7). But first let us look more carefully at the differences between the two formulations.

There are two reasons why the amount of labor which was actually spent on a particular product might differ from the amount now standardly required to produce that kind of product. The first is a nonstandard level of efficiency in the actual labor process, which can be more or less efficient than the social norm. The second is technological change, which alters that norm.

Consider the case of inefficient labor. Marxists have always regarded it as a particularly inept criticism of the labor theory of value to object that it entails that an inefficiently produced product has more value than one produced efficiently and therefore in less time. And the asserted consequence does indeed fail to follow from the strict doctrine. But why should it not follow from the popular doctrine? If labor creates value by, as it were, congealing in the product, then if more labor is spent, must not more labor congeal, and will there not then be more value in the product?

The case of inefficient labor shows the incompatibility between the strict and popular doctrines. Marxists know about that case, but they are nevertheless reluctant to reject the popular doctrine. After all, the reason why both doctrines exist in Marxist culture, why neither one is enough, is that each has intellectual or political functions (or both) of its own to fulfill.[15] Accordingly, faced with problems such as that of inefficient labor, many Marxists propose a mixed formulation, the purpose of which is so to modify the popular doctrine that it is brought into line with the strict doctrine. And so it is said, in response to the case of inefficient labor, that

13. The worker creates value *if, and only in so far as*, his labor is socially necessary.

To the extent that actual labor time exceeds what is standardly required, labor is not value-creating. The formulation is obviously intended to preserve the popular idea of creation, without contradicting the strict doctrine. But I shall show that this cannot be done. The strict doctrine allows no such mixed formulations.[16]

The strict doctrine certainly rules out (13), since (13) cites the wrong amount of socially necessary labor time, namely that which is required when the commodity is being created,[17] rather than that which is required when the commodity is on the market. To have any prospect of being faithful to the strict doctrine, a mixed formulation must say not (13) but some such thing as this:

14. The worker creates value *if, and only in so far as*, the amount of labor he performs *will be* socially necessary when the product is marketed.

Marxists think that (14) follows from the strict doctrine because they mistakenly suppose that (14) follows from something the strict doctrine does indeed entail, but which is of no relevant interest, namely,

15. Value is determined by (that is, *is inferable from*) expended labor time when the amount expended is what will be socially necessary when the product is marketed.

Statement (15) does follow from the strict doctrine, just as (16) follows from the true doctrine about barometers:

16. The height of a mercury column on day 2 is determined by (that is, *is inferable from*) the atmospheric pressure on day 1 when day 1's atmospheric pressure is what day 2's atmospheric pressure will be.

Statement (16) is entailed by the truth that day 2's atmospheric pressure makes the height of the mercury column on day 2 what it is. But (16) does not entail that day 1's atmospheric pressure makes the height of the mercury column on day 2 what it is. And (15), similarly, gives no support to (14).

The general point is that if a magnitude *m* causally depends upon a magnitude *m'*, and it is given that a magnitude *m"* is equal to *m'*, then whatever *m"* is a magnitude of, magnitude *m* will be inferable from magnitude *m"*. There could then be an illusion that magnitude *m"* *explains* magnitude *m*. Just that illusion, I claim, seizes anyone who supposes that (14) is consistent with the strict doctrine.

An additional problem for the mixed formulation is a case of abnormally efficient labor, or of labor which used means of production superior to those now available, where in each instance *less* labor than is now socially necessary was expended. One cannot begin to claim in such a case that value is created by labor subject to the constraint that the amount expended will be socially necessary, since here not enough labor is expended. When there is *inefficiency*, there is a chance of pretending that some of the labor which occurred did not create value. Where there is special *efficiency*, there can be no similar pretence that labor which did not occur did create value.

We conclude that attempts to salvage the popular idea of creation by recourse to mixed formulations will not succeed.

6

The strict and popular doctrines differ because of the difference between a present counterfactual magnitude (the amount of labor that would now be required to produce something) and a past actual magnitude (the amount of labor that was actually spent producing something). In the last section I cited cases where the two magnitudes differ in size (because of deviations from standard efficiency, and technical change) to prove that they are magnitudes of different things. But even if people never worked (or even could not work) other than at standard efficiency, and even if technical change never occurred (or even could not occur), so that labor actually spent was always equal to socially necessary labor time, labor actually spent would not (because it could not) be socially necessary labor time, and the strict and popular doctrines would remain incompatible. The concept of the amount of time required to produce a commodity is not the same as the concept of the amount of time actually spent producing it, and the two remain different even under the assumption that the relevant amounts are identical. Some Marxist economists were bored by this chapter when it appeared as an article, because of their practice of assuming that the labor time that is actually spent neither exceeds nor falls short of that which is socially necessary. But, while that assumption might have a methodological justification in certain contexts, it cannot imply that the things whose amounts are here assumed to be the same are *themselves* the very same thing; no assumption whatsoever can set aside the conceptual difference between actual and counterfactual labor.

What was required in the past, and still more what happened in the past—these facts are constitutively irrelevant to how much value a commodity has, if the labor theory of value is true. But they are not epistemically irrelevant. For, since technical conditions change relatively slowly, socially necessary labor time in the recent past is usually a good guide to socially necessary labor time now. Typical past actual labor time is, moreover, the best guide to how much labor time was necessary in the past. Thereby what did occur, the labor actually spent, becomes a good index of the labor that is now required, and, therefore, a good index of the value of the commodity, if the labor theory of value is true. But it does not follow that labor (actually spent) creates the value of commodities.

On the contrary: I have shown that, if the labor theory of value is true, then it follows that labor does *not* create value. And we can now also draw a stronger conclusion. For it would be quixotic to seek a basis *other than* the labor theory of value for the proposition that labor creates value.[18] We may therefore conclude that labor does not create value, whether or not the labor theory of value is true.

Some will be disposed to ask: If labor does not create value, what does? But it is a prejudice to suppose that value must be *created*. Something must, of course, explain value and its magnitudes, but not all explainers are creators. One putative explanation of value magnitudes is the labor theory of value, the strict doctrine. But it identifies no creator of value, unless we suppose that explaining is creating. *What would now be needed to produce a commodity of a certain kind*—that is not a creator in any literal sense.

Why is the popular doctrine popular? One reason is that it appears more appropriate than the strict doctrine as a basis for a charge of exploitation. We shall see (sections 8 and 9) that neither doctrine in fact supports such a charge, but it is clear that the popular doctrine *seems* better suited to do so, just because it alone says that labor *creates* value. But a partly distinct reason for the popularity of the popular doctrine is that certain arguments against the strict doctrine tend to be met by an illicit shift to popular formulations. This will be explained in the next section, where the theme of exploitation is in abeyance, and where I argue that the strict doctrine is false. The discussion of exploitation is completed in sections 8–11, which do not presuppose the next one.

7

I want here to expose, in some detail, how Marx arrived at the popular and strict doctrines in the opening pages of *Capital*.

Capital begins with what Marx rightly regards as the elementary phenomenon of capitalism, which is the commodity. A commodity is an object which "satisfies human wants"[19] (and is therefore, in Marxian language, a *use value*), and which undergoes market exchange with other such objects, the ratios in which it exchanges with them constituting its *exchange value*. So a commodity is a use value which is a "bearer of exchange-value."[20]

Focus on the commodity leads to the first *explanandum* of *Capital*, which is the fact that commodities exchange against one another not haphazardly but, within given limits of time and place, in definite proportions.[21] It is required to explain why they exchange in the ratios they do, or, in more modern terms, their equilibrium prices. Why, for example, is one quarter of corn worth x hundredweight of iron?

Marx replies that if, as he puts it, "1 quarter corn = x cwt. iron," then in each "there exists in equal quantities something common to both. . . . Each of them, so far as it is exchange-value, must therefore be reducible to this third," which is its value, and of which exchange-value is but "the mode of expression."[22] Value, then, is the absolute magnitude which the relative magnitude exchange value reflects: The value of a given commodity is that property of it, whatever it may be, which, together with the value of other commodities, determines the given commodity's exchange value. *Note that the way in which Marx introduces the concept of value ensures that it is true by definition that value determines equilibrium price.*

Marx's question is: What determines value, so defined? His first step toward an answer is to deny, on obscure and indefensible grounds, that use value plays a role in determining magnitude of value.[23] Having thus set aside use value, he then claims that commodities "have only one common property left, that of being products of labour," and that labor must therefore be "the value-creating substance"; and from that he infers that the magnitude of a commodity's value depends on how much labor "is objectified or materialized in it."[24]

It is in this fashion that Marx arrives at the popular doctrine, the thesis that labor creates value. He reaches the popular thesis on the basis of premises none of which formulate propositions about how markets operate. But, having arrived at the stated popular conclusion, Marx now enters an observation, for which he gives no reason, but which is in fact justified by the way markets work. The observation is that the product of "unskilful and lazy" labor is not worth more.[25] That is so because no buyer in a competitive market will pay over the odds just because an undue amount of labor has been spent producing what he buys. But Marx does not give that or any other argument for his remark, which is quite unmotivated on the premises he has employed heretofore.[26]

The point about inefficient labor leads Marx to the conclusion that value is determined not, as the popular doctrine says, by the amount of time spent producing the commodity, or the labor embodied in it, but by the amount of time required to produce it under average conditions of productivity, which Marx calls "socially necessary labour time."[27] This is the strict doctrine, or the labor theory of value properly so called, and, as I have tirelessly insisted, it entails that the amount of time which was actually spent producing a commodity has absolutely no effect on its value.

The strict doctrine is the bastard issue of a union between premises which have nothing to do with markets and from which Marx derives the popular doctrine, and one truth (the one about inefficient labor) which reflects how markets operate. Now, *had Marx addressed his original* explanandum (see page 104) *from the point of view of market facts in the first place*, he might have noticed that circumstances other than socially necessary labor time contribute to explaining it, since socially necessary labor time is demonstrably not the only determinant of equilibrium price. One such further determinant is the pattern of ownership of means of production, which can affect values, through the distribution of bargaining power to which it gives rise. Products of means of production on which there is some degree of monopoly are likely for that reason to command a higher price in equilibrium than they otherwise would, and therefore to have a higher value, under the definition of value with which Marx began.

But if value is something the explanation of which must literally create it, then, since ownership of means of production literally creates nothing, it would follow that, despite appearances, the pattern of that ownership cannot affect value formation. And that is what a Marxist says. He says that labor alone creates *value*: The pattern of ownership can affect price, and hence how much value various owners *get*. But no part of what they get is created by ownership.

But this line of defense depends essentially on the idea that labor *creates* value. If we stay with the strict doctrine, which rightly does not require that anything *creates* value, it has no motivation whatsoever.

To make this more clear, I return to the three propositions in my initial presentation of the labor theory of value (see section 1):

1. Socially necessary labor time determines value.

2. Value determines equilibrium price.
3. Socially necessary labor time determines equilibrium price.

Recall my view that the definitional statement is (2), and that (1) is the substantive theory. (1) and (2) entail (3). I said that I would say why some prefer to see (1) as true by definition. Here is one reason why.

Counterexamples to (3) abound, such as the one I noted about the pattern of ownership of means of production, or the cases of divergences in period of production and organic composition of capital.[28] Statement (3) is false, and much of the second and third volumes of *Capital* is an attempt to cope with that fact.

Now, if (3) is false, one *at least* of (1) and (2) must be false. But, if (2) is true by definition, then (1) is false, and the labor theory of value is sunk. What Marxists therefore do is to treat (1) as true by definition—so that counterexamples to (3) cannot touch it—and then simply drop (2). They redefine value, which was supposed to be whatever underlies equilibrium price, *as* socially necessary labor time, and they mask from themselves the consequent triviality of the claim that socially necessary labor time determines value by resorting to popular discourse. Their maneuver with (1) and (2) in fact deprives the labor theory of all substance, but they conceal that consequence by construing (1) in a popular fashion, by (mis)reading it as though it says that labor *creates* value, which does not sound trivial, and they plead that the circumstances thought to be counterexamples to the labor theory do affect price but clearly have no power to bring value into being. They say that, whatever determines market ratios, and thereby who gets what amounts of value, labor alone creates what value there is to get. For how, they ask, could anything but labor, actual production, produce anything, and *how*, therefore, *could anything but labor produce value*? I reply that, once the trivializing shift has been made, one can no longer identify anything called "value" which labor could be said to produce.[29]

The popular doctrine supplies an appearance of substance when, under pressure of counterexamples, (1) is treated as true by definition, (2) is dropped, and the labor theory is, in reality, drained of all substance. Because of its simplifying assumptions, volume 1 of *Capital* can proceed under definition (2) of value. When the assumptions are relaxed, (1) and (2) cannot both be true. Hence, in volumes 2 and 3, statement (2) is abandoned.

At this point, it is instructive to look at a central part of Marx's critique of Ricardo. If I am right, it depends on popular formulations.

Ricardo defined value as Marx does at the beginning of *Capital*, as the absolute magnitude, whatever it may be, which underlies the relativities of equilibrium price. He then provisionally hypothesized that socially necessary labor time was that magnitude, and that it therefore determined equilibrium price. He went on to acknowledge, however, that variations in periods of production falsify his provisional hypothesis, and he consequently allowed that equilibrium price and, therefore, value deviate from socially necessary labor time.[30]

According to Marx, Ricardo was here misled by appearances; the real deviation is not of value from socially necessary labor time, but of equilibrium price from value (which *is* socially necessary labor time).[31]

Now, both Ricardo and Marx say that equilibrium price deviates from socially necessary labor time. What then is the theoretical difference between them? I believe that there is none, or, what comes to the same thing, that the difference can be stated only in popular discourse, to which Marx therefore here resorts. He says that variations in period of production and organic composition do not affect how much value is *created*, but only how much is *appropriated* at the various sites of its creation. But if one asks, "Exactly what is it that labor is here said to create?" then, I contend, there can be no answer, once value is no longer, as now it cannot be, defined as the absolute underlying equilibrium price.[32] Marx's quarrel with Ricardo is merely verbal, with a cover of metaphor concealing its emptiness.

The labor theory of value comes in two versions, strict and popular. The two contradict one another. But the labor theorist cannot, by way of remedy, simply drop the popular version. For despite their mutual inconsistency, each version can appear true only when it is thought to receive support from the other: "Labor creates value" seems (but is not) a simple consequence of the thesis that value is determined by socially necessary labor time, and that thesis appears to survive refutation only when it is treated as interchangeable with the idea that labor creates value.

8

In this section I shall identify the real basis of the Marxian imputation of exploitation to the capitalist production process, the proposition which really animates Marxists, whatever they may think and say. The real basis is not the commonly stated one, sentence (5), but a fairly obvious truth which owes nothing to the labor theory of value, and which is widely confused with (5). And since (5) is itself confused with the labor theory of value, the latter is confused with the fairly obvious truth to be stated.[33]

A by-product of my discussion, then, will be an explanation why the labor theory of value, which ought to be controversial, is considered even by very intelligent Marxists to be a fairly obvious truth. When Marxists think obviously true what others think not obvious at all, one side at least is very wrong, and an explanation of the error in terms of class position or ideological standpoint is not enough, because it does not show how the error is possible, by what intellectual mechanism it can occur. What follows will help to explain how it is possible for very intelligent Marxists to be utterly wrong.

Recall what has been shown. We have seen that if the labor theory of value is true, then labor does not create value. For if labor creates value, past labor creates value; and if past labor creates value, then past labor determines the value of the product. But the labor theory of value says that value magnitudes are determined by currently necessary labor time. It follows that past labor does not create value, if the labor theory of value is true. There is, moreover, no plausible alternative basis on which to assert that labor creates value. Hence it is false that labor creates value. And I shall show in section 9 that, even if it were true, it would not be a sound basis for a charge of exploitation.

Nor does the labor theory of value itself, strictly formulated, form such a basis. Any such impression disappears once we see that it does not entail that the workers create value. In fact, the labor theory of value does not entail that the workers create anything.

Yet the workers manifestly do create something. They create the product. They do not create *value*, but they create *what has value*. The small difference of phrasing covers an enormous difference of conception. What raises a charge of exploitation is not that the capitalist appropriates some of the value the worker produces, but that he appropriates some of the value of *what* the worker produces. Whether or not workers produce value, they produce the product, that which has value.

And no one else does. Or, to speak with greater care, producers are the only persons who produce what has value: It is true by definition that no human activity other than production produces what has value. This does not answer the difficult question, Who is a producer? But whatever the answer to it may be, only those whom it identifies can be said to produce what has value. And we know before we have the full answer that owners of capital, considered as such, cannot be said to do so.

Note that I am not saying that whatever has value was produced by labor, for I have not said that whatever has value was produced. I also do not deny that tools and raw materials are usually needed to produce what has value. The assertion is that laborers, in the broadest possible sense, are the only persons who produce anything which has value, and that capitalists are not laborers in that sense. If they were, capital and labor would not be distinct "factors of production":[34] The capitalist supplies capital, which is not a kind of labor.

Some will question the claim that owners of capital, considered as such, do not produce anything. An owner of capital can, of course, *also* do some producing, for example, by carrying out a task which would otherwise fall to someone in his hire. Then he is a producer, but not *as* an owner of capital. More pertinent is the objection that owners of capital, in their very capacity as such, fulfill significant productive functions, in risking capital, making investment decisions, and so forth. But whether or not that is true, it does not entail that they produce anything in the importantly distinct sense in issue here. It does not entail, to put it one way, that they engage in the activity of producing.

To act productively it is enough that one does something which helps to bring it about that a thing is produced, and that does not entail participating in producing it. You cannot cut without a knife, but it does not follow that, if you lack one and I lend you one, thereby enabling you to cut, then I am a cutter, or any other sort of producer. The distinction is between productive activities and producing activities. Capitalists arguably engage in the former, but once the distinction is clear, it is evident that they do not (unless they are not only capitalists) engage in the latter.

To be sure, *if*—what I here neither assert nor deny—the capitalist is a *productive* nonproducer, that will have a bearing on the thesis that he is an exploiter. It will be a challenge to a charge of exploitation whose premise is that he produces nothing. But it would be wrong to direct the challenge against the *premise* of that charge, that he produces nothing. As that is generally intended, it cannot be denied.

And it is this fairly obvious truth which, I contend, lies at the heart of the Marxist charge of exploitation. The real basis of that charge is not that only workers produce value, but that only they produce what has it. The real Marxian argument for (10) is not the Simpler Marxian Argument (see section 4), but this different one (the Plain Argument):

17. The laborer is the person who creates the product, that which has value.
11. The capitalist appropriates some of the value of the product.
18. The laborer receives less value than the value of what he creates,

and

19. The capitalist appropriates some of the value of what the laborer creates.
10. The laborer is exploited by the capitalist.

The Plain Argument is constructed in analogy with the Simpler Marxian Argument, under the constraint that premise (17) replaces premise (5). The arguments are totally different, but very easy to confuse with one another.

The Plain Argument is not a (distinctively) Marxian argument: It owes nothing to any version of the labor theory of value. Hence, in calling it the *real* Marxian argument for (10), I do not mean that it is a really *Marxian* argument, for it is not. I mean, rather, that it is the argument which really moves Marxists politically, and with which, as I shall show in the following section, they confuse the arguments that they officially propound.

9

I here defend my claim that it is labor's creation of what has value, not its (supposed) creation of value, which lies at the root of the Marxist charge that capitalism is a system of exploitation.

We have seen that labor does not create value. I now argue that, even if it did, that would have no bearing on the question of exploitation.

The proposition that labor creates value is, to begin with, unnecessary to the thesis that labor is exploited. For, if we suppose that something else creates value, the impression that labor is exploited, if it was there before, will sturdily persist. Thus, imagine that the magnitude of a commodity's value is wholly determined by the extent and intensity of desire for it, and that we can therefore say that desire, not labor, creates value.[35] But imagine, too, that labor creates the product itself, out of in all senses worthless raw materials, or—the product being a pure service—out of none. Do we now lose our inclination (supposing, of course, that a belief in the labor theory of value induced one in us) to sympathize with the laborer's claim to the product, and, hence, to its value, even though we are no longer supposing that labor creates that value? I do not think that we do. The worker continues to look exploited if he creates the valuable thing and does not get all the value of the thing he creates. What matters, normatively, is what creates that thing, or so transforms it that it has (more) value,[36] not what makes things of its sort have the amount of value they do, which is what the labor theory of value is really supposed to explain.

But the claim that labor creates value is not only unnecessary to the charge of exploitation. It is no reason whatever for laying such a charge. Once again, I make the point by imagining that desire creates value. If labor's creation of value would give the laborer a claim to value *because* he had created it, then so would the desirer's creation of value give him a claim on that basis. Yet would we say that desirers are exploited because they create the value of the product, and the capitalist receives part of that value? The suggestion is absurd.[37] It must then be equally absurd to think that laborers are exploited *because* they create value which others receive.

It is absurd, but it does not seem absurd, and the explanation of the discrepancy is that it is impossible to forget that labor creates what has value. Creating value, when we suppose that workers do that, seems to matter, because we naturally think that they could create value only by creating what has it, and the relevance of the latter is mistakenly transmitted to the former. Part of the case for saying that (17) is the real basis of the charge of exploitation is that (5) cannot be yet seems to be, and the relationship between (17) and (5) explains the illusion.

But there is also a more direct reason for thinking that the essential thing is labor's creation of what has value. Look at the excerpt from "Solidarity," which forms the epigraph of this chapter. It says nothing about value, and the labor theory is not required to appreciate its point, which is that "we" are exploited. It does say that "we" have made all these valuable things.

It is, then, neither the labor theory of value (that socially necessary labor time determines value), nor its popular surrogate (that labor creates value), but the fairly obvious truth (that labor creates what has value) rehearsed in the song, which is the real basis of the Marxist imputation of exploitation.

I have been discussing the exploitation of the propertyless wage worker under capitalism. But if anything is the *paradigm* of exploitation for Marx, it is the exploitation of the feudal serf, who does not, according to Marx, produce value, since his product is not marketed and is therefore not a commodity. The serf's exploitation is, according to Marx, entirely manifest. The proletarian's is more covert, and it is by arguing that his position may in fact be assimilated to the serf's that Marx seeks to show that he too is exploited.

The exploitation of the serf is manifest, because nothing is more clear than that part of what he produces redounds not to him but to his feudal superior. This is not so in the same plain sense under capitalism, where the product itself is not divided between capitalist and worker, but marketed.[38]

Now Marxists contend that the labor theory of value is required to uncover the exploitation of the wage worker, but I disagree. What is needed is not the false and irrelevant labor theory, but the mere concept of value, as defined, independently of the labor theory, in our sentence (2). It enables us to say that, whatever may be responsible for magnitudes of value, the worker does not receive all of the value of his product.

Marxists say that

20. The serf produces the whole product, but the feudal lord appropriates part of the product;

and

21. The proletarian produces all of the value of the product, but the capitalist appropriates part of the value of the product.

I accept (20), but I modify the first part of (21) so that it resembles the first part of (20), with this result:

22. The proletarian produces the whole product, but the capitalist appropriates part of the value of the product.

The exploitation of the proletarian is, on my account, more similar to the
exploitation of the serf than traditional Marxism says. There remains
the difference that in (22), by contrast with (20), there is an exercise of
the concept of value (though not, of course, of the labor theory of value).
That exercise is essential, since it is false that

23. The proletarian produces the whole product, but the capitalist appropriates part of the product.

(23) is false, since in one sense the capitalist appropriates all of what the
proletarian produces and in another sense he almost always appropriates
none of it. He appropriates all of it in that the whole of the product belongs to him before he sells it. But we can also say that he almost always
appropriates none of it, in that he almost always sells all of it. Hence, at
the level of the individual capitalist, a reference to value in characterizing
his exploitative appropriation is ineliminable.

If we now shift to the relationship between the capitalist and working
classes, we can describe capitalist exploitation without exercising the concept of value at all, and we can thereby assimilate the exploitations of serfs
and wage workers even more thoroughly. The following analogy holds:

24. Serfs produce all the products in feudal society, but feudal lords appropriate some of them;

and

25. Proletarians produce all of the products in capitalist society, but capitalists appropriate some of them.

The means of subsistence consumed by capitalists and the means of production which they use productively are all produced by workers. And there
we have the essential fact of capitalist exploitation, in a formulation which
involves no use of the concept of value.[39]

10

In the last two sections I have insisted that labor creates that which has
value, and I have continued to deny that labor creates value itself. Yet it
might be objected that the insistence contradicts the denial, that, in short,
(26) is true:

26. Since labor creates what has value, labor creates value.

But the objection is misguided. For *if* there is a sense of "labor creates value" in which (26) is true, it is not the relevant traditional sense, that intended by Marxists when they assert (5). "Labor creates what has value" could not entail "labor creates value" where the latter is a contribution to explaining the magnitude of the value of commodities, as (5) is supposed to be. How could it follow from the fact that labor creates what has value that the *amount* of value in what it creates varies directly and uniformly with the amount of labor expended?[40]

Is there a sense, distinct from that of (5), in which "labor creates value" does follow from "labor creates what has value"? Probably there is. If an artist creates a beautiful object out of something which was less beautiful, then we find it natural to say that he creates beauty. And it would be similarly natural to say of a worker who creates a valuable object out of something less valuable that he creates value. But that would not support the popular version of the labor theory of value, though it would, of course, help to explain why so many Marxists mistakenly adhere to it.

11

I have argued that the essential nonnormative claim in the argument that capitalism is a regime of exploitation is that the capitalist appropriates part of the value of the worker's product. That appropriation undeniably occurs, but, for it to constitute exploitation, it needs to be shown (see section 3 above) that it is an injustice, that the relevant transfer of value is unfair. In what follows I do not attempt to prove the unfairness charge, but only to lay out what needs to be shown for the charge to stick.

I believe that the crucial lacuna in the Plain Argument is a statement about the distributive background against which the labor contract is concluded.[41] Capitalists obtain some of the value of what workers produce because capitalists do and workers do not own means of production: That is why workers accept wage offers which generate profit for capitalists. The crucial question for exploitation is, therefore, whether or not it is fair that capitalists have the bargaining power they do. If it is morally all right that capitalists do and workers do not own means of production, then capitalist profit need not be the fruit of exploitation; and, if the precontractual distributive position is morally wrong, then the case for exploitation is made. The question of exploitation therefore resolves itself into the question of the moral status of capitalist private property. When apologists for capitalism deny that capitalists are exploiters on the ground that they contribute to the creation of the product by providing its means of production, the appropriate Marxist reply is not merely that workers alone produce, which the apologist can (and must) concede, nor that workers produce the value, which is false and irrelevant, but that the capitalist's "contribution" does not establish absence of exploitation, since capitalist property in means of production is theft, and the capitalist is therefore "providing" what morally ought not to be his to provide. Exploiting is a kind of taking without giving. The capitalist does not really give, because what he appears to give was unjustly taken in the first place. Again, capitalists may well qualify as productive in certain ways (see section 8 above), but so, too, may slaveowners. But, unless their ownership of slaves is morally defensible, slaveowners nevertheless exploit, and so, too, do capitalists, unless their ownership of capital is morally defensible.

A flow of value, in either the popular or the plain sense, from the worker to the capitalist constitutes exploitation only if the contract it fulfills arises out of an unfair bargaining situation, and regardless, moreover, of whether or not that situation precisely *forces* the worker to sell his labor to the capitalist.[42] Once the truisms of the Plain Argument are to hand, the crucial question for exploitation concerns the justice of the distribution of the means of production.[43] And that would be the crucial question even if (contrary to what I have argued) the thesis that workers create value were both true and relevant to the charge of exploitation. For, even so, workers could not create value without means of production, and if capitalists were morally entitled to those means, then they would surely be entitled to set terms for their use under which they receive some return for allowing them to be used.[44] So the thesis that labor creates value requires the same supplementation as the Plain Argument when it is used as a basis for arguing that workers are exploited.

In my view, the worker is indeed exploited by the capitalist, since the latter secures profit through private ownership of means of production, and private ownership of means of production is morally illegitimate. I shall not here try to establish its moral illegitimacy, but note that the foregoing statement is consistent with the claim, which some Marxists might wish to make, that private ownership of capital is unjust precisely *because* it enables capitalists to extract value from what workers produce. That would be one way of impugning the moral status of private ownership of capital, but there are also other ways, which I prefer, and which I have explored elsewhere.[45]

12

Table 1 sets out my theses about three propositions which have figured centrally in this chapter. The phrase "is a suitable basis for a charge of exploitation," which heads the table's fourth column does not here mean "establishes that capitalists exploit workers," but "is the essential nonnormative ingredient in a sound argument for the conclusion that capitalists exploit workers."

Table 1

	is true	follows from (1)	contradicts (1)	is a suitable basis for a charge of exploitation
(1) = the labor theory of value = value is determined by socially necessary labor time = the strict doctrine	T1: No	T2: Yes	T3: No	T4: No
(5) = labor creates value = the popular doctrine	T5: No	T6: No	T7: Yes	T8: No
(17) = labor creates the product, that which has value	T9: Yes	T10: No	T11: No	T12: Yes

I now summarize my arguments for the table's twelve theses:

T1: *The labor theory of value is false.* Standard counterexamples prove that socially necessary labor time is not the only determinant of equilibrium price. The strict doctrine is, therefore, false. Marxists nevertheless maintain that the labor theory of value is true by insisting, in face of the counterexamples, that, whatever determines equilibrium price, only labor creates value. But that defense of the labor theory is cast in terms of the illicit popular doctrine. It also unjustifiably divorces values from price, by reference to which value was initially defined. (See section 7 above.)

T2 and T3 are entered here merely to complete the table. They record the self-evident truths that the labor theory of value follows from and does not contradict itself.

T4: *The labor theory of value is not a suitable basis for a charge of exploitation.* Workers are exploited only if they produce something. But the strict doctrine does not entail that they produce anything: it merely specifies how to determine the value of commodities, without saying anything about how commodities come into being. Commodities are, of course, produced by labor, and that, as T12 says, *is* a suitable basis on which to found a charge of exploitation. But the plain fact that labor produces commodities is, though obvious, not entailed by the labor theory of value. (See section 8 above.)

T5: *Labor does not create value.* As T7 says, the labor theory of value (i.e., the strict doctrine) entails that labor does not create value. But no one asserts that labor creates value on any basis other than the labor theory of value. One may safely conclude that labor does not create value. (See pages 103, 108 above.)

T6: *The labor theory of value does not entail that labor creates value.* This follows from T7 (together with the fact that the labor theory of value is not self-contradictory).

T7: *The labor theory of value entails that labor does not create value.* If labor created value, it would determine its magnitude (when, that is, "labor creates value" is endowed with the sense that Marxists give it: for a different and irrelevant sense of "labour creates value" see section 10 above). But the labor theory of value says that socially necessary labor time determines value magnitudes, and socially necessary labor time, the amount of time required to produce a given commodity, is not the same thing as the amount of time actually spent producing it. If, accordingly, the first determines the commodity's value, the second does not. (See sections 5 and 6 above.)

T8: *The claim that labor creates value is not a suitable basis for a charge of exploitation.* Suppose that labor's (alleged) creation of value were a suitable basis for saying that workers are exploited. It would follow, by parity of reasoning, that, if desire created value, then desirers would be exploited if they did not receive, gratis, the product whose value is due to their desire. Yet if one supposes that value is entirely due to demand, which reflects desire, one need not then believe that those who produce what is demanded lose their claim to it, even if they do not desire it. (The producers might want it even though they do not, in the relevant sense, desire it, in order to exchange it for something they do desire.) Whatever creates value is irrelevant to claims about exploitation, and it can seem relevant only when the idea of creating value is confused with the distinct idea of creating use value, or the product itself. (See section 9 above.)

T9: *Labor creates what has value.* This fairly obvious truth needs defense only against the ideological claim that capitalists too create what has value. But, if that claim were true, then capital and labor would not be distinct factors of production: Qua capitalists, capitalists supply capital, which is not a kind of labor. Capitalists may, of course, also labor, and thereby participate in the creation of what has value, as they do when, for example, they happen to manage their own enterprises. But that is an illustration of, not a counterexample to, T9. The putatively exploitative element in capitalists' income is what they get as a result of owning capital, not the additional amount some get as a result of engaging in labor themselves. (See section 8 above.)

T10 and T11 record the self-evident truths that *the labor theory of value neither entails nor contradicts the plain truth that labor creates what has value.*

T12: *The labor creates what has value is a suitable basis for a charge of exploitation.* Before arguing for T12, let me argue for an associated thesis, T12': *That labor creates what has value is the real basis of the Marxist charge of exploitation,* whatever Marxists may avow. For, as we saw, the labor theory of value (see T4) provides no basis for that charge, and that is why Marxists usually formulate the charge in popular terms, since the claim that labor *creates* value *seems* to support it. Reflection shows, however, that the popular doctrine *only seems* to provide a basis for the charge of exploitation. (See T8). T12' then explains why it seems to provide such a basis: Marxists confuse "labor creates what has value" with "labor creates value," even though the small difference of phrasing covers an enormous difference of conception. (The same confusion helps to explain why Marxists persist in thinking that so controversial a doctrine as the labor theory of value is *obviously* true: They confuse (1) with (5) and (5) with (17), and, thereby, (1) with (17). See page 108 above.)

Another argument for T12', and this one is also an argument for T12, is that the lines from "Solidarity" which head up this chapter evidently raise a charge of exploitation, even though they say nothing above the creation of value. They speak only about the creation of what has value, and they imply that workers are exploited because they are deprived of so much of the value of the wonders they have made by those who did not labor to make them (see section 8 above).

I have prosecuted my critique of the labor theory of value with consummate intransigence because I believe that it is a terrible incubus on progressive reflection about exploitation. Instead of desperately shifting about for some or other way of defending the labor theory,[46] Marxists and quasi-Marxists should address themselves to the crucial question, which is whether or not private ownership of capital is morally legitimate.

Notes

1. A less summary and more sequential—and more critical—presentation of the same material will found in sec. 7 below, where I also have occasion to remark on some famous differences between vol. 1 and other parts of *Capital.*
2. Fuller definitions of the technical terms introduced here will be found in appendix 2 of *Karl Marx's Theory of History: A Defence* (Oxford: Clarendon Press, 1978).
3. For example, Ronald Meek, in *Smith, Ricardo, and Marx,* 95. Meek treats (1) as true by definition and (2) as the substantive thesis. He acknowledges on 127 that the issue is contestable.
4. The labor theory of surplus value is not, in my view, validly derived from the labor theory of value, but there is no need to explain and defend that claim here.
5. Marx, *Capital* 1:284. Strictly speaking, the value of labor power is, according to Marx, the value of the means of subsistence needed to reproduce the labor supply, and it therefore includes the value of the means of raising children. This complication, which does not benefit the theory, will be ignored here.

6. See, for example, the superb and moving final paragraph of part 2 of vol. 1 of *Capital* (280).
7. It does not, that is, matter to the moral claim about exploitation, even if it is interesting from other points of view.
8. It is the concept of variable capital, and not that of the value of labor power, which is crucial in the key theoretical applications of the labor theory of value—for example, in the reproduction schemas, in the transformation of values into prices, and in the doctrine of the tendency of the rate of profit to fall. *Capital* allows at least short-term divergences between the value of labor power and variable capital per laborer; and, wherever there is such a divergence, it is the second, not the first, which must be inscribed in the relevant equations.
9. In the traditional sense of (5), according to which part of what is claimed in saying that labor creates value is that quantity of value is a function of quantity of labor. Other possible senses, such as that dealt with in sec. 10 below, are irrelevant here.
10. It might be objected that *b* cannot have a value for Marx, since he defines value for products of labor only. The textual point is probably correct (see *Capital* 1:129 for support), but no wise defender of Marx will want to urge in his defense the unfortunate lack of generality of the labor theory. Still, if anyone is impressed by the objection, let him imagine that *very little* labor went into *b*. The crucial point, which the extreme examples are only meant to dramatize, is that there is, according to the labor theory, "continuous change in value-relations," since the amount of labor required to produce something of a certain kind is subject to variation. See *Capital* 2:153.
11. Despite the misleading terminology in which it is cast, this is true even of Piero Sraffa's "dated quantities of labor" analysis. See *Production of Commodities by Means of Commodities*, ch. 6; Ian Steedman, *Marx after Sraffa*, 70, n. 3.
12. The first passage comes from *Capital* 1:130 (Marx is quoting from his earlier *Critique of Political Economy*). The second comes from the "Notes of Adolph Wagner," 184.
13. *Grundrisse*, 135. I have replaced the translator's "at a given moment" by "currently", which gives a more literal rendering.
14. *Capital* 3:238. (To reproduce a commodity is to produce another just like it.) Compare *The Poverty of Philosophy*: "It is important to emphasize the point that what determines value is not the time taken to produce a thing, but the *minimum* time it could possibly be produced in" (136).

     Now despite his express and theoretically mandated preference for the strict doctrine, Marx's presentation is replete with popular formulations (and so, too, is the Marxist tradition). See, for example, these pages of vol. 1 of *Capital*, which are the harvest of a pretty random search: 128–30, 135–36, 141–42, 155, 190, 202, 260, 294–96, 303, 307, 323, 325–26, 430, 433, 675–76, 680. In many cases, the popular formulations in question cannot be translated into strict ones without significant loss.
15. Despite their mutual incompatibility, one function of each doctrine is that it may be used, or, rather, misused, to support the other: See the last paragraph of sec. 7 below.
16. Marx frequently had recourse to mixed formulations: see, e.g., *Capital* 1:295, 303.
17. There may, of course, be no such unique quantity: So much the worse for (13).
18. In, that is, the traditional sense of "labor creates value," which is the relevant sense here: See n. 9 above.

19. *Capital* 1:125.
20. Ibid., 126.
21. Ibid., 127.
22. Ibid.
23. "This common element cannot be a geometrical, physical, chemical or other natural property of commodities. Such properties come into consideration only to the extent that they make the commodities useful, i.e. turn them into use-values. But clearly, the exchange relation of commodities is characterized precisely by its abstraction from their use-values. Within the exchange relation, one use-value is worth just as much as another, provided only that it is present in the appropriate quantity.... As use-values, commodities differ above all in quality, while as exchange-values they can only differ in quantity, and therefore do not contain an atom of use-value" (Ibid. 127–28).
24. Ibid., 129.
25. Ibid.
26. See the questions about inefficient labor and the popular doctrine which are posed at page 101 above.
27. *Capital* 1:129.
28. There is no originality in my invocation of these counterexamples, which have dogged the labor theory of value from its inception. I claim originality only for my diagnosis of how Marx and Marxists enable themselves to cleave to the labor theory in the face of the well-known counterexamples to it.
29. The italicized question reflects conflation of the confused idea that labor creates value with the correct idea that it creates what has it, to wit, the use-valuable product: See sec. 8 below.
30. See Ricardo's *Principles of Political Economy*, ch. 1; and see Mark Blaug, *Economic Theory in Retrospect*, 96 ff., for a brief accessible exposition.
31. See *Theories of Surplus Value* 2:106, 174–80; *Grundrisse*, 562–63; *Selected Correspondence*, 122.
32. Hence, if I am right, the transformation problem is a strictly incoherent problem, whether or not it has a mathematical "solution."
33. "Is confused with" is not a transitive relation, but the above statement is none the less true.
34. I use scare-quotes because there are good Marxian objections to the classification of capital and labor as distinct but comparable factors of production: Note that in a sense all that is required for production is capital, since capital buys not only means of production but also labor. That only hints at the objections, which are given in vol. 3 of *Capital*, ch. 48, and which do not affect the point made in the text above.
35. That may sound like an insane supposition, but it is not when, as here, it is the supposition that facts about desire, and not facts about labor time, determine exchange-value ratios. The reader who finds absurd the idea that desire creates value is probably himself confusing value creation with product creation, and therefore confusing the idea that desire creates value with the magical idea that it creates the desired product. Recall that value is not the same thing as use value. Desire could not, except through magic, create use value: it could not bring it about that something has the power of satisfy it. But bourgeois economists who think that desire contributes to the creation of value, by generating a willingness to pay for what is desired, are not believers in magic.

36. Whatever creates (or enhances the value of) a valuable thing in *that* sense creates (some of) its value, but that is not the sense of "creates value" in which labor is supposed to create value in the labor theory of value: See sec. 10 below.

37. Note that I am not saying that a person's desire for something is no reason why he should receive it. Of course it is a reason, albeit one singularly capable of being overriden. But a person's desire for something cannot be a reason for his receiving it *on the ground* that his desire for it enhances its value, even if his desire for it does enhance its value. That ground is surely unintelligible.

    One more caveat. I do not suppose in the above paragraphs or anywhere else that the correct principle of reward is according to productive contribution. One can hold that the capitalist exploits the worker by appropriating part of the value of what the worker produces without holding that all of that value should go to the worker. One can affirm a principle of distribution according to need, and add that the capitalist exploits the worker because need is not the basis on which he receives part of the value of what the worker produces. Compare Jon Elster: "A person is exploited if (i) he does not enjoy the fruits of his own labour and (ii) the difference between what he makes and what he gets cannot be justified by redistribution according to need" ("Exploring Exploitation," 3).

38. For further discussion and textual references, see *Karl Marx's Theory of History*, 333 f.

39. For more in the same vein, see my "More on Exploitation and the Labour Theory of Value," 318–19.

40. And if it did follow, then the labor theory of value, the strict doctrine, would be false.

41. It is the crucial lacuna in that it is the only *controversial* claim that needs to be added.

42. *Is* the worker forced to work for the capitalist? The answer to that question is rather complicated: see chs. 12 and 13 of my *History, Labour, and Freedom: Themes from Marx* (Oxford: Clarendon Press, 1988).

43. I believe that Marx, too, thought that this was the crucial question, and that a widespread failure to realize that he did is a result of a mistaken reading of an important passage in his *Critique of the Gotha Programme*: see 299–300 of ch. 14 of my *History, Labour, and Freedom*.

44. It does not follow that they are entitled to set any terms whatever for their use: One can believe that capitalists are legitimate owners of means of production but that offering wages below a certain level is nevertheless an attempt to exploit. But if, as Marxists believe, *all* profit, of whatever dimensions, is exploitation, then there can be no legitimate entitlement to private ownership of capital.

45. In my two articles on "Self-Ownership, World-Ownership, and Equality."

46. For a representative example of such desperation, see Holmstrom's "Marx and Cohen on Exploitation and the Labour Theory of Value," 299–302, to which I reply at "More on Exploitation and the Labour Theory of Value," 326–28, an article some parts of which (but not that one) have been incorporated into the present chapter.

References

Blaug, M. 1968. *Economic Theory in Retrospect*. London.

Cohen, G. A. 1983. "More on Exploitation and the Labour Theory of Value." *Inquiry* 26, no. 3.

———. 1986a. "Self-Ownership, World-Ownership, and Equality." In Lucash 1986.

———. 1986b. "Self-Ownership, World-Ownership, and Equality: Part 2." In Paul et al. 1986.

Elster, J. 1978. "Exploring Exploitation." *Journal of Peace Research* 15. no. 1.

Holmstrom, N. 1983. "Marx and Cohen on Exploitation and the Labour Theory of Value." *Inquiry* 26, no. 3.

Lucash, F., ed. 1986. *Justice and Equality Here and Now*. Ithaca, NY.

Marx, Karl. 1847. *The Poverty of Philosophy*. In *The Collected Works of Karl Marx and Frederick Engels*, vol. 6. London: Lawrence and Wishart, 1976.

———. 1857–58. Grundrisse, Harmondsworth, 1973.

———. 1861–63. *Theories of Surplus Value*. vol. 1 (London, 1969), 2 (London, 1969), 3 (London, 1972).

———. 1867 ff. *Capital*, vol. 1 (Harmondsworth, 1976), 2 (Harmondsworth, 1978), 3 (Harmondsworth, 1981).

———. 1879–80. "Notes on Adolph Wagner," In *Karl Marx: Texts on Method*, ed. T. Carver. Oxford, 1975.

Marx, Karl, and Frederick Engels. 1975. *Selected Correspondence*. Moscow.

Meek, R. 1977. *Smith, Ricardo, and Marx*. London

Paul, E., et al., eds. 1986. *Marxism and Liberalism*. Oxford.

Ricardo, D. 1971. *Principles of Political Economy and Taxation*. Harmondsworth.

Sraffa, P. 1960. *Production of Commodities by Means of Commodities*. Cambridge.

Steedman, I. 1977, *Marx after Sraffa*. London.

Should Marxists Be Interested in Exploitation?

JOHN E. ROEMER

> To work at the bidding and for the profit of another ... is not ... a
> satisfactory state to human beings of educated intelligence, who have
> ceased to think themselves naturally inferior to those whom they
> serve.
>
> J. S. Mill, *Principles of Political Economy*

> The capitalist mode of production ... rests on the fact that the
> material conditions of production are in the hands of non-workers in
> the form of property in capital and land, while the masses are only
> owners of the personal conditions of production, of labour power. If
> the elements of production are so distributed, then the present-day
> distribution of the means of consumption results automatically.
>
> Karl Marx, *Selected Works*

1. MOTIVATIONS FOR EXPLOITATION THEORY

MARXIAN EXPLOITATION IS DEFINED as the unequal exchange of labor
for goods: the exchange is unequal when the amount of labor embodied in
the goods which the worker can purchase with his income (which usually
consists only of wage income) is less than the amount of labor he expended
to earn that income. Exploiters are agents who can command with their
income more labor embodied in goods than the labor they performed; for
exploited agents, the reverse is true. If the concept of embodied labor is

From John E. Roemer, "Should Marxists Be Interested in Exploitation?" *Philosophy and Public
Affairs* 14, no. 1: 30–65, copyright 1985 by Princeton University Press. Reprinted by permission of Princeton University Press.

defined so that the total labor performed by a population in a certain time period is equal to the labor embodied in the goods comprising the net national product (NNP), and if the NNP is parceled out to the members of the population in some way, then there will be (essentially) two groups: the exploiters and the exploited, as defined above. (I say "essentially" because there may be some ambiguity; an agent may be able to purchase different bundles of goods, some bundles of which embody more labor than he worked, and other bundles of which embody less labor than he worked. This gives rise to a "gray area" of agents whom we might wish to consider neither exploited nor exploiting.)[1] Thus, exploitation theory views goods as vessels of labor, and calculates labor accounts for people by comparing the "live" labor they expend in production with the "dead" labor they get back in the vessels. Exploitation is an aspect of the pattern of redistribution of labor which occurs through the process of agents "exchanging" their current productive labor for social labor congealed in goods received. It may not always be easy or even possible to *define* the content of dead labor in the vessels, as when labor is heterogeneous or joint production of many goods from the same production process exists. There is a large literature on these questions, which shall not concern me here. For this article, I assume labor is homogeneous.

It is important to note that exploitation is not defined relationally. The statement "A exploits B" is not defined, but rather "A is an exploiter" and "B is exploited." Exploitation, as I conceive it, refers to the relationship between a person and society as a whole as measured by the transfer of the person's labor to the society, and the reverse transfer of society's labor to the person, as embodied in goods the person claims.

What are the uses of exploitation theory? Why is it considered the cornerstone of Marxian social science by many writers? More directly, what positive or normative conclusions might we draw about capitalism from observing that workers are exploited under capitalism? I can identify four main uses or justifications of exploitation theory:

1. The accumulation theory: Exploitation of workers explains profits and accumulation under capitalism; it is the secret of capitalist expansion.
2. The domination theory: Exploitation is intimately linked to the domination of workers by capitalists, especially at the point of production, and domination is an evil.
3. The alienation theory: Exploitation is a measure of the degree to which people are alienated under capitalism. The root of alienation is the separation of one's labor from oneself. If one's labor is put into goods which are produced for exchange (not for use by oneself or one's community), that constitutes alienation. Exploitation occurs because some people alienate more labor than others. It is differential alienation.

4. The inequality theory: Exploitation is a measure and consequence of the underlying inequality in the ownership of the means of production, an inequality which is unjustified.

There is another theory which is, I think, a special case of (4), and so will be numbered:

4'. The expropriation theory: Exploitation is a measure of expropriation, of one agent owning part of the product which should rightfully belong to another agent.

These four (or five) proposed explanations for our interest in exploitation theory are usually confounded. They should not be, however, because they constitute different claims. Adherents to exploitation theory tend to emphasize some of (1) through (4) when others of the list become subjected to embarrassments or counterexamples. I will argue that in the general case none of (1) through (4) can be sustained; there is, in general, no reason to be interested in exploitation theory, that is, in tallying the surplus value accounts of labor performed versus labor commanded in goods purchased. My arguments against (1) through (4) are, briefly, these: (1) All commodities are exploited under capitalism, not only labor power, and so the exploitation of labor does not explain profits; concerning (2), domination is an important issue under capitalism, but exploitation is irrelevant for its study; concerning (3), differential alienation can be measured using surplus value accounts, but I do not think such alienation is interesting unless it is a consequence of unequal ownership of the means of production. We are thus led to (4) which, I think, is the closest explanation for Marxists' interest in exploitation; but in the general case, I will show inequality in ownership of the means of production, even when ethically indefensible, is not properly measured by exploitation. In particular, it can happen in theory that those who own very little of the means of production are exploiters and those who own a lot are exploited. Hence exploitation (the transfer of surplus value) is not a proper reflection of underlying property relations.

There is an apparent similarity between this iconoclastic posture toward exploitation theory, and the attacks on the labor theory of value which have accelerated in the past decade.[2] In the final section, I evaluate this similarity, and claim it is quite shallow. While the labor theory of value almost always gives incorrect insights, exploitation theory in many cases coincides with a deeper ethical position—although on its own terms it does not provide a justification for that position. My verdict will be that exploitation theory is a domicile that we need no longer maintain: It has provided a home for raising a vigorous family who now must move on.

The reader should bear in mind that throughout the article "exploit" has a technical meaning, the unequal exchange of labor. When I claim that exploitation theory is without foundation. I do not mean capitalism is just. I believe capitalism is unjust (or ethically *exploitative*) because of sharply unequal ownership of the means of production. What I show in section 5 is that this inequality is not necessarily coextensive with the transfer of surplus value from workers to capitalists, and therefore it is inappropriate to ground an equality-based morality on the technical measure of exploitation. If I occasionally use "exploitation" in its ethical as opposed to technical sense, the word will be italicized as above.

2. DEFINITION OF TERMS: A SIMPLE MODEL

I have outlined above an identification problem with respect to the motivation for our interest in exploitation. In this section, this identification problem will be posed as starkly and schematically as possible, by exhibiting a simple model in which exploitation emerges simultaneously with accumulation, domination, differential alienation, and inequality in ownership of the means of production. This section, therefore, serves to define terms and to pose the problem more precisely.

Imagine an economy with 1,000 persons and two goods: corn and leisure. There are two technologies for producing corn, called the Farm and the Factory. The Farm is a labor-intensive technology in which no seed capital is required, but corn is produced from pure labor (perhaps by cultivating wild corn). The Factory technology produces corn with labor plus capital— the capital is seed corn. The technologies are given by:

Farm: 3 days labor → 1 corn output
Factory: 1 day labor + 1 seed corn → 2 corn output

Corn takes a week to grow (so the seed is tied up in the ground for that long). The total stock of seed corn in this society is 500 corn, and each agent owns ½ corn. The agents have identical preferences which are these: Each wants to consume 1 corn *net* output per week. After consuming his 1 corn, the agent will consume leisure. If he can get more than 1 corn for no more labor, he will be even happier: but preferences are lexicographic in that each wishes to minimize labor expended subject to earning enough to be able to consume 1 corn per week, and not to run down his stock of capital.

There is an obvious equilibrium in this economy. The typical agent works up his ½ corn in the Factory in ½ day, which will bring him 1 corn at the end of the week. Having fully employed his seed capital, he must produce another ½ corn somewhere, to replace his capital stock: This he does by working in the Farm technology for 1½ days. Thus he works 2 days and produces 1 corn net output. Every agent does this. Indeed, 2 days is the labor time socially necessary to produce a unit of corn, given that this society must produce 1,000 corn net each week. It is the labor embodied in a unit of corn. At this equilibrium there is no exploitation, since labor expended by each agent equals labor embodied in his share of the net output. Nor is there accumulation, for society has the same endowments at the beginning of next week; nor is there domination at the point of production, since no one works for anyone else; nor is there differential alienation of labor, since there is not even trade; and, of course, there is equality in initial assets.

Now change the initial distribution of assets, so that each of 5 agents owns 100 seed corn, and the other 995 own nothing but their labor power (or, to be consistent with our former terminology, nothing but their leisure). Preferences remain as before. What is the competitive equilibrium? One possibility is that each of the 995 assetless agents works 3 days on the Farm, and each of the 5 wealthy ones works 1 day in the Factory. But this is not an equilibrium, since there is a lot of excess capital sitting around which can be put to productive use. In particular, the wealthy ones can offer to hire the assetless to work in the Factory on their capital stock. Suppose the "capitalists" offer a corn wage of 1 corn for 2 days labor. Then each capitalist can employ 50 workers, each for 2 days, on his 100 seed corn capital. Each worker produces 4 corn in the Factory with 2 days labor. Thus each capitalist has corn revenues of 200 corn: Of that, 100 corn replace the seed used up, 50 are paid in wages, and 50 remain as profits. Capital is now fully employed. But this may or may not be an equilibrium wage: only $5 \times 50 = 250$ workers have been employed, and perhaps the other 745 peasants would prefer to work in the Factory for a real wage of ½ corn per day instead of slaving on the Farm at a real wage of ⅓ corn per day. If so, the real wage in the Factory will be bid down until the assetless agents are indifferent between doing unalienated, undominated labor on the Farm, and alienated, dominated labor in the Factory. Let us say, for the sake of simplicity, this equilibrating real wage is one corn for 2½ days Factory labor. (In the absence of a preference for Farm life over Factory life, the real wage will equilibrate at 1 corn for 3 days labor, that is, at the peasant's labor opportunity cost of corn, since in this economy there is a scarcity of capital relative to the labor which it could efficiently employ.) Now we have *accumulation* (or at least much more production than before, which I assume is not all eaten by the capitalists), since each capitalist gets a profit of $200 - 100 - 40 = 60$ corn net, and each worker or peasant gets, as in the first economy, 1 corn net. Hence total net product is 995 + $(5 \times 60) = 1,295$ corn, instead of 1,000 corn as before. We also have *domination* since some agents are employed by others, and by hypothesis, this gives rise to domination at the point of production. *Differential alienation* has emerged, since some agents (the workers) alienate a large part of their labor to the capitalists, while the capitalists and the peasants alienate no labor (although they work different amounts of time). *Exploitation* has emerged since the workers and peasants all expend more labor than is "embodied" in the corn they get, while the 5 capitalists work 0 days and each gets 60 corn.

Hence, the four phenomena in question emerge simultaneously with the exploitation, in the passage from the "egalitarian" economy to the "capitalist" economy. With respect to expropriation, we might also say that it has emerged in the second economy.

3. The Accumulation Theory

The unique positive (as opposed to normative) claim among (1) through (4) is the claim that our interest in exploitation is because surplus labor is the source of accumulation and profits. Explanation (1) uses "exploit" in the sense of "to turn a natural resource to economic account; to utilize," while theories (2), (3), and (4) use "exploit" in the sense of "to make use of meanly or unjustly for one's own advantage or profit."[3] A current in Marxism maintains that exploitation is not intended as a normative concept, but as an explanation of the modus operandi of capitalism; the production of profits in a system of voluntary exchange and labor transfers is the riddle which must be explained, and which Marx posed in *Capital I*. The discovery that exploitation of labor is the source of profits answers the riddle. (Even though all commodities exchange "at their values," a surplus systematically emerges at one point in the labor process. For the value which labor produces is greater than what labor power is worth, and hence what it is paid.) Indeed, the claim that exploitation theory should not be construed as normative theory has its source in Marx, as Allen Wood points out.[4]

The formal theorem supporting position (1) was first presented by Okishio and Morishima,[5] and the latter coined it the Fundamental Marxian Theorem (FMT). It demonstrates that in quite general economic models, exploitation of labor exists if and only if profits are positive. The FMT is robust; the error lies in the inference that its veracity implies that profits are *explained* by the exploitation of labor. For, as many writers have now observed, *every* commodity (not just labor power) is exploited under capitalism. Oil, for example, can be chosen to be the value numeraire, and embodied oil values of all commodities can be calculated. One can prove that profits are positive if and only if oil is exploited, in the sense that the amount of oil embodied in producing one unit of oil is less than one unit of oil—so oil gives up into production more than it requires back.[6] Thus the exploitation of labor is not the explanation for profits and accumulation any more than is the exploitation of oil or corn or iron. The motivation for the privileged choice of labor as the exploitation numeraire must lie elsewhere, as I have argued in other articles.[7] In trying to locate the specialness of labor which would justify its choice as the exploitation numeraire, one is inexorably led into arguments that labor is the unique commodity which can be "dominated" or "alienated"—the terrain of argument shifts to a defense of theories like (2) and (3). The dialogue goes something like this, where "Marxist" is defending theory (1):

Marxist: The exploitation of labor accounts for the existence of profits under capitalism. That's why we are interested in exploitation theory, not as normative theory.

Antagonist: But oil is exploited too under capitalism, and its exploitation is, as well, necessary and sufficient for profits. So labor's exploitation does not *explain* profits.

Marxist: No, you are not entitled to say oil is exploited, because oil is not dominated, oil is not alienated from its possessor in any interesting sense during production, one's oil is not a joint product with one's self, there are no problems in extracting the oil from the "oil power." Only labor has these properties and hence only labor is exploited.

Antagonist: Initially you claimed your interest in exploitation theory was as a positive theory only. But you rule out describing oil as exploited for reasons that can only imply exploitation has normative content. For surely the domination and alienation of labor and the attachment of labor to the self are germane not for evaluating whether labor is or is not used in the sense of "turning a natural resource to economic account," but only for deciding whether labor is "made use of meanly or unjustly for [one's own] advantage or profit." You claim to be interested in labor's exploitation only because labor is exploited in the first sense, but rule out calling other commodities exploited because they are not *exploited* in the second sense. I take it, then, your *true* justification for describing labor as exploited must lie in one of the normative theories of exploitation.

I conclude position (1) cannot be supported as the reason for our interest in exploitation theory.[8] Despite his avowed lack of interest in a normative justification of exploitation theory, the Marxist in the dialogue can only rescue exploitation theory from the jaws of the Generalized Commodity Exploitation Theorem by appealing to a special claim labor has on wearing the exploitation mantle, a claim that seems only to be defensible on grounds of the unfairness or unjustness or nastiness of the conditions of labor's utilization. As G. A. Cohen writes, "Marxists do not often talk about justice, and when they do they tend to deny its relevance, or they say that the idea of justice is an illusion. But I think justice occupies a central place in revolutionary Marxist belief. Its presence is betrayed by particular judgments Marxists make, and by the strength of feeling with which they make them."[9] And I would add, it is only by appealing to conceptions of justice that exploitation theory can be defended as interesting.

4. THE DOMINATION THEORY

For the remainder of this article, my concern will be to investigate the possibility of defending an interest in exploitation theory for the light it sheds on the three issues of domination, differential alienation, and inequality in ownership of the means of production. My interest in these three issues is normative. If, for example, exploitation can be shown to imply domination of workers by capitalists, and if we argue independently that domination is unjust, then exploitation theory provides at least a partial theory of the injustice of capitalism. (Only a partial theory, since other practices besides domination might be unjust, which exploitation theory would not diagnose.) Identifying the main evil of capitalism as domination, and even extraeconomic domination, is a theme of some contemporary Marxist work.[10] It is not my purpose to evaluate this claim (with which I disagree), but rather to postulate an ethical interest in domination, and ask whether that justifies an interest in exploitation theory.

It is necessary to distinguish two types of domination by capitalists over workers, domination in the maintenance and enforcement of private property in the means of production, and domination at the point of production (the hierarchical and autocratic structure of work). The line between the two cannot be sharply drawn, but let us superscript the two types domination^1 and domination^2, respectively. I will argue that each of domination^1 and domination^2 implies exploitation, but not conversely. Hence if our interest is in domination, there is no reason to invoke exploitation theory, for the direction of entailment runs the wrong way. Domination may be a bad thing, but there is no reason to run the circuitous route of exploitation theory to make the point. In certain situations, exploitation requires domination^1, but since we cannot know these cases by analyzing the exploitation accounts alone, there is no reason to invoke exploitation if, indeed, our interest in exploitation is only as a barometer of domination^1. Furthermore, our interest in domination^1 is essentially an interest in the inequality of ownership of the means of production, for the purpose of domination^1 is to enforce that ownership pattern. I maintain if it is domination^1 one claims an interest in, it is really inequality (however defined) in the ownership of the means of production which is the issue. Thus, an ethical interest in domination[1] shifts the discussion to the validity of position (4), while an interest in domination[2] has as its source the moral sentiments reflected in the epigraph from J. S. Mill, in the analogy implied by the term "wage slavery."

Domination[1] enforces property relations in two ways. The obvious way is through police power protecting assets, preventing their expropriation by those not owning them. Clearly, since differential ownership of the means of production gives rise to exploitation, this form of domination implies exploitation. The second way domination[1] enters into property relations is to give property its value in the absence of perfect competition. A property right is not a physical asset, it is the right to appropriate the income stream flowing from a certain physical asset. (As C. B. Macpherson points out, it is peculiarly under capitalism that physical assets are confused with the property rights that are related to them.)[11] In the absence of perfect competition, the value of property is not defined by the market. Under perfect competition, all agents are price (and wage) takers, no one has power to bargain or to set the terms of trade. Prices in equilibrium clear markets. Assuming the equilibrium is unique (a heroic assumption), property values are then well defined. But in the absence of perfect competition, there is room for bargaining, and the value of one's property rights may well be determined by extraeconomic domination.[12] (It is more accurate to say values are not defined by the traditional economic data, and at present there is no accepted theory of bargaining under imperfect competition which can determine them.) This is typically the case where markets for particular assets or commodities are thin. The state or landlord which (or who) controls the irrigation canal (an indivisible commodity, with a very thin market) can exact a monopolistic price for its use, giving rise to high peasant exploitation. Due to thin credit markets in rural areas of the underdeveloped countries, local landlords are able to charge usurious interest rates to peasants for consumption loans, increasing the rate of exploitation. To the extent that one thinks incomes from different types of labor under capitalism are politically determined, in order to assert control over the work force,[13] rather than as a reflection of relative scarcities, then domination[1] plays a role in determining exploitation. Domination[1] may determine what certificates people receive, through channeling them into different educational careers, and those certificates determine the value of the person's labor services.[14] In these cases, the peculiarity of domination[1], what contrasts it with feudal domination, is its effect on setting the value of services or assets in the *market* (and thereby influencing the degree of exploitation). Although the power relation inherent in domination[1] is finally realized through markets, contrasted with feudalism, it is similar to feudal exploitation, since one agent has *power* over another which he would not have in a fully developed, perfectly competitive market economy. Thus this exercise of domination[1] is not the essence of capitalism, if capitalism is essentially a competitive system. Certainly Marx's proclaimed task was to explain capitalism in its purest form: where the values of all commodities are explained by "fair trades," that is, values commanded on perfectly competitive markets.

In certain situations, conversely, exploitation implies domination[1]; I mean the trivial observation that exploitation is the consequence of differential ownership of the means of production which, in many cases, the exploited would alter were it not for police power preventing them from doing so. (Hence, if we observe exploitation, there must be domination[1].) It has been maintained, however, that exploitation need not imply domination[1]; Adam Przeworski argues that in some Western European countries workers have the power to expropriate capitalists, and hence they are not dominated[1], but they do not, because it is not in their perceived interests to do so.[15] Moreover, in sections 4 and 5 below I show that exploitation can exist without differential ownership of the means of production; therefore, presumably exploitation can exist even though all agents accept as just the property rights, and so domination[1] (police power to protect property) need not attain. In summary, my claims concerning domination[1] are these: (a) With respect to the exercise of power under conditions of imperfect competition, domination[1] exists and is perhaps important in capitalism, and more so in less developed capitalism, but it is characteristically noncapitalist, that is, being due to imperfect competition and thin markets; (b) it implies exploitation, but that provides no reason to be interested in exploitation theory, if our concern is really with domination[1]; (c) in some cases, perhaps the archetypical case, exploitation implies domination[1] in the sense of police power protecting property, but in that case it is not the domination that concerns us but the unjust inequality in the distribution of the means of production. If (c) is our reason for justifying an interest in exploitation theory, we are invoking position (4) and not position (2), since domination[1] in this case is only the means to maintain the unequal distribution of assets which is the basis for our condemnation of capitalism.

The more usual conception of domination is the second one; domination[2] does not involve the protection or creation of value in capitalist property, but rather the hierarchical, nondemocratic relations in capitalist workplaces. Of course, this hierarchy presumably creates (additional) profits, and therefore leads to an increased valuation of capitalist property, and hence is similar to the role of domination[1]; but in discussing domination[2] I am specifically concerned with the domination of the worker's self, the relation of subordination he enters into with the capitalist when he enters the workplace.

While our moral opposition to domination[1] shares its foundation with our moral opposition to feudalism, our opposition to domination[2] shares its foundation with our opposition to slavery. (The analogy is inexact, since many feudal practices involved domination[2] over the selves of serfs; for the sake of the analogy, I envisage "pure feudalism" as a system where feudal dues are paid because of extraeconomic coercion, but the serf never sees or interacts personally with the lord.)

Although domination[2] can create the conditions for profitability and therefore exploitation of labor, the converse is in general not the case. Exploitation does not imply the existence of domination[2]. I showed in my book that the class and exploitation relations of a capitalist economy using labor markets can be precisely replicated with a capitalist economy using credit markets,[16] where domination[2] does not exist. In Labor Market Capitalism, agents optimize, given their endowments of property, and end up choosing either to sell labor power, to hire labor power, or to produce for the market using their own labor power on their own account. Agents segregate themselves into five classes, based on the particular ways they relate to the labor market. The Class Exploitation Correspondence Principle demonstrates that everyone who optimizes by selling labor power is exploited, and everyone who optimizes by hiring labor is an exploiter. It was assumed in that analysis that agents make the decision to sell labor entirely on economic grounds; they do not calculate as part of their objective the disutility associated with being dominated[2], with working under a boss. In Credit Market Capitalism, there is no labor market, but a market for lending capital at an interest rate. At the equilibrium, some agents will lend capital, some will borrow capital, some will use their own capital for production. Again, agents segregate themselves into five classes defined by the particular ways they relate to the credit market. Again, the Class Exploitation Correspondence Principle holds: Any agent who optimizes by borrowing capital will turn out to be exploited. Moreover, the Isomorphism Theorem states that these two hypothetical capitalisms are identical insofar as class and exploitation properties are concerned. An agent who, under Labor Market Capitalism, was a member of a labor-selling class, and was therefore exploited, will be a member of a capital-borrowing class in Credit Market Capitalism, and will be exploited. This result replays the Wicksell-Samuelson theme that it is irrelevant, for the distribution of income, whether capital hires labor or labor hires capital; the mild sin of omission of these writers was not to point out that propertyless agents are exploited in either case, whether they be the hirers or sellers of the factor. In Labor Market Capitalism there is domination[2], but in Credit Market Capitalism, there is not.[17]

Moreover, an even sharper example may be constructed of an economy possessing no labor or credit market, but only markets for produced commodities which are traded among individual producers. In such an economy exploitation will result at equilibrium, in general, if there is initial inequality in the ownership of means of production. But in this exchange and production economy, there are no relations of domination[2] of any kind; the exploitation can be accomplished through "invisible trade." It is possible to argue that there is exploitation without class in this economy, since all producers enjoy the same relation to the means of production: They work only on their own.[18] Indeed, this example may be taken as the archetype of exploitation, or unequal exchange, between countries where neither labor nor capital flows across borders. Differential initial endowments of countries will give rise to exploitation in trade, even when no relations of domination[2] through international labor migration or capital lending take place.[19]

The previous paragraphs claim to demonstrate that the existence of exploitation does not imply the existence of domination[2], and hence our putative interest in exploitation theory cannot be justified on grounds of a more basic interest in domination[2]. Here I follow Marx, in modeling capitalism as a system where there are no market frictions, but where goods exchange competitively at their market-determined prices. In particular, it seems appropriate, for this thought experiment, to assume all contracts are costlessly enforceable and can be perfectly delineated. For Marx wished to show the economic viability of capitalism in the absence of cheating: and that means contracts are well defined and observed by all. Now the principal reason domination[2] exists is that the labor contract is not costlessly enforceable, nor can it be perfectly delineated. This point is usually put more graphically when Marxists speak of the problems of extracting the labor from the labor power. Indeed, the contemporary labor process literature addresses the methods capitalism (and perhaps socialism) has developed to solve this problem.[20] But for our thought experiment, we are entitled to assume the delivery of *labor* (not simply labor power) for the wage is as simple and enforceable a transaction as the delivery of an apple for a dime. In such a world, exploitation continues to exist, but domination[2] does not. And I claim Marxists would be almost as critical of such a perfect capitalism as they are of existing capitalism, replete as the real thing is with domination[2] due to the contract enforcement problem. Indeed, Marxists consider sharecroppers and borrowers to be *exploited* (unjustly so, that is), even when domination[2] is absent from those contracts. The Isomorphism Theorem I quoted was an attempt to develop this point formally, that in a world absenting deleterious domination[2] effects, the exploitation observed in labor markets would be indistinguishable from that observed in credit or sharecropping arrangements.[21]

A criticism of the Isomorphism Theorem can be made as follows. If one wishes to study the relationship between domination[2] and exploitation, then the model of the Class Exploitation Correspondence Theorem and the Iso-morphism Theorem is inappropriate, because it is there assumed that domi-nation[2] is not an issue to the people involved. In reply to this point, I have worked out a revised model (which is available in detail from the author) where domination[2] effects exist. These are captured as follows: Each agent has an initial endowment of means of production, which takes on a value as finance capital at given prices. He seeks to maximize a utility function of income and work performed. It matters to him whether the work is per-formed in his own shop, or under a boss. Thus, the utility function has three arguments: income, labor performed on one's own account, and wage labor performed for others. Subject to his capital constraint, determined by initial asset holdings and prices, each agent maximizes utility. The domina-tion[2] postulate is that every agent would rather work on his own account than for a boss, and this is reflected in the utility function. At equilibrium, agents sort themselves into five classes:

Class 1: those who only hire others
Class 2: those who hire others and work on their own account
Class 3: those who only work on their own account
Class 4: those who work on their own account and sell wage labor
Class 5: those who only sell wage labor

I say an agent is *dominated* if he maximizes utility subject to constraint by placing himself in classes 4 or 5, and he is *dominating* if he optimizes by being in classes 1 or 2. The theorem, which can be called the Exploitation-Domination Correspondence, states that any dominated agent is exploited and any dominating agent is an exploiter. The converse, however, does not hold. In particular, agents in class position 3 will often be either exploited or exploiting, but they are neither dominated nor dominating.

It is therefore difficult to justify an interest in exploitation if our real concern is domination[2], for two reasons. First, domination[2] is directly ob-servable (simply look at who hires whom) and exploitation is not. Hence, calculating whether an agent is exploited (a difficult calculation, necessitat-ing all sorts of technological information to compute socially necessary labor times) would be a strangely circuitous route to concluding he is dominated[2]. Second, it is not true that an exploited agent is necessarily dominated or that an exploiter is necessarily dominating; the Exploitation-Domination Correspondence states the converse. Exploited (exploiting) agents who are not dominated (dominating) would have a confused ethical status if our judgment about them is made on the basis of exploitation, but our interest in exploitation is as a proxy for domination. The hardworking shopkeeper or sharecropper would have our ethical sympathy on grounds of exploita-tion but not domination[2]. This does not help us provide independent reason for an interest in exploitation theory, of course, which is the task at hand. Thus exploitation is a poor statistic for domination[2] on several counts.

My conclusions concerning domination[2] are: (a) Our interest in exploitation theory cannot be justified on grounds that it is indicative of or a proxy for domination[2], either logically, or on pragmatic grounds; (b) although domination[2] is prevalent in existing capitalism, it is arguably a phenomenon of second order in a *Marxist* condemnation of capitalism, being associated with the imperfections in writing and enforcing contracts, while Marxist arguments should apply to a capitalism with frictionless contracts. In addition, although not argued here (as my concern is not with the evils of domination[2] but with the evils of exploitation), I think the analogy between domination[2] and slavery is ill founded. It is arguable that the life of the small independent producer is not so marvelous compared to that of the factory worker, that the transition from poor peasant to urban proletarian is one made willingly, even gladly, and with reasonably good information, where the erstwhile independent producer is knowledgeable about the trade-offs. I say arguable, not obvious: but it is more than arguable that no population ever voluntarily committed itself to slavery willingly and gladly.

5. THE ALIENATION THEORY

To discuss properly a possible justification of an interest in exploitation theory on grounds that it is indicative of different degrees of alienation, we must separate alienation from, on the one hand, domination and on the other hand differential ownership of the means of production, as those issues are discussed separately under (2) and (4). An interest in differential alienation must be defended per se, even in the absence of domination and differential ownership of the means of production. Perhaps the most graphic vision of exploitation is as the extraction of surplus labor from the worker: the extraction, that is, of more labor from him than he receives back as social labor in what he consumes or can purchase with his wages. His labor is alienated from him not because he performs it for another (under conditions of domination[2]) but because it is labor performed to produce goods for exchange, not for use. More precisely, the goods produced are traded to an anonymous final recipient on a market, and thus labor becomes alienated in a way it would not have been were there a social division of labor but the final disposition of goods was in one's "community." (See B. Traven's marvelous story "Assembly Line" for a discussion of alienation.)[22] Now if everyone started off with the same endowment of means of production and had the same skills and preferences, but all agents produced goods for a market, there would be alienation of labor in this sense, but not differential alienation, since it can be shown everyone would receive back as much social labor in goods as he alienated in production for the market. Exploitation can be said to exist in a market economy when some people alienate more labor than they receive from others, and some alienate less labor than they receive back. Why might alienation be a bad thing? Perhaps because one's time is the only really valuable asset one has, and production for the market is considered to be a waste of time. Perhaps because productive labor for oneself or one's community is what constitutes the good life, but the use of labor to earn revenues solely to survive, not to produce for others directly, is a prostitution of a deep aspect of the self. Thus alienation might be bad, and differential alienation might be unjust or *exploitative*. (There are certainly other forms of alienation in Marx, but this kind of differential alienation appears to be the only kind for which exploitation as the unequal exchange of labor is an indicator.)

Any ethical condemnation of differential alienation cannot be a welfarist one, in the sense of Amartya Sen,[23] based only on the preferences of individuals. For I will outline a situation where agents with different preferences start with equal endowments of resources and voluntarily enter into relations of differential alienation (i.e., exploitation) as the way to maximize their utilities. Consider two agents, Adam and Karl, who each start off with the same amount of corn, which is the only good in the economy and can be used both as capital (seed corn) and as the consumption good. We have the same technological possibilities as in the model of section 2.

Farm: 3 days labor produces 1 bushel corn
Factory: 1 day labor plus 1 bushel seed corn produces 2 bushels corn

Adam and Karl each start with ½ bushel of corn, and each will live and must consume for many weeks. (Recall, a week is the time period required in each case to bring corn to fruition, although the amount of labor expended during the week differs in the two processes.) Karl is highly averse to performing work in the present: He desires only to consume 1 bushel of corn per week, subject to the requirement that he not run down his seed stock. In the first week, he therefore works ½ day in the Factory (fully utilizing his seed corn) and 1½ days on the Farm, producing a total of 1½ bushels, one of which he consumes at harvest time, leaving him with ½ bushel to start with in week 2. Adam accumulates; he works ½ day in the Factory, utilizing his seed, and 4½ days on the Farm, producing 2½ bushels gross. After consuming 1 bushel, he has 1½ bushels left to start week 2. In week 2, Karl works up his own seed stock in ½ day in the Factory producing 1 bushel; then, instead of going to the Farm, Karl borrows or rents Adam's 1½ bushels of seed and works it up in the Factory. This takes Karl precisely 1½ days, and he produces 3 bushels gross in the factory. Of the 3 bushels he keeps ½ bushel, and returns 2½ bushels to Adam (Adam's principal of 1½ bushels plus interest of 1 bushel.) Indeed, Karl is quite content with this arrangement, for he has worked for a total of 2 days and received 1½ bushels, just as in week 1, when he had to use the inferior Farm technology. Adam, on the other hand, receives a profit of 1 bushel from Karl's labor, which he consumes, and is left again to begin week 3 with 1½ bushels. He has not worked at all in week 2. This arrangement can continue forever, with Karl working 2 days each week and consuming 1 bushel, and Adam working 5 days during the first week, and zero days thereafter. Clearly there is exploitation in the sense of differential alienation in this story, in all weeks after the first, but its genesis is in the differential preferences Karl and Adam have for the consumption of corn and leisure over their lives. Thus exploitation cannot be blamed, in this story, on differential initial ownership of the means of production, nor can the situation be condemned on Paretian grounds, as no other arrangement would suit Karl and Adam more. They chose this path of consumption/leisure streams. Indeed during any week Karl could decide to work on the Farm and accumulate more seed corn, thus enabling him to cut his working hours in future weeks. (I am assuming he is *able* to do so; if he is not, then Karl is handicapped, and the ethical verdict is certainly more complicated.) But he does not.

Actually the above example does not quite rigorously make the point that differential alienation cannot be condemned on Paretian grounds: because if alienation is to be so condemned, then the agents themselves should distinguish between the performance of alienated and nonalienated labor in their utility functions. That is, each agent should prefer to perform nonalienated labor to alienated labor. If we now modify the story to include such a preference, then the above example fails, since Karl could have achieved the same outcome of 2 days labor and 1 bushel corn, each week, by continuing his autarchic program of working partly in the factory on his *own* seed corn, and then moving to the farm and working for his *own* consumption. Karl would perform no alienated labor (producing goods only for himself) and would hence be better off. Were this to occur, then Adam would have to work some in the Factory each period, since Karl refused to borrow seed capital from him. But this failure of the example can easily be fixed: simply note that Adam could work a little longer in the first week, producing a little more seed capital, and then in future weeks he could lend his seed to Karl at a sufficiently low interest rate that Karl would be compensated for his distaste in performing alienated labor by the savings in overall labor he achieves by borrowing from Adam. Thus both Adam and Karl can strictly benefit from cooperation, even if each has a distaste for performing alienated labor, so long as there is a trade-off between that distaste and the taste for leisure. Hence the claim is true: that even if alienation matters to people, an outcome of differential alienation cannot be condemned on Paretian or welfarist grounds, nor on grounds of inequality in the distribution of assets, since an example has been constructed where agents who start off with identical endowments choose to enter into relations of differential alienation. And if alienation, as I have defined it, seems unrealistic in a society of two people, then replicate the economy one millionfold, so there are a million each of Karls and Adams. Moreover, we can introduce many goods into the economy so that there is a real social division of labor, and some Adams make car fenders all day long and other Adams make pin heads all day long. But the same result can be constructed: Starting from the same endowments, agents with different preferences for the various goods, leisure, and nonalienated labor may well choose to enter into relations of differential alienation.

So if we are to conclude that differential alienation is *exploitative*, in the sense of ethically condemnable, that verdict cannot be arrived at on Paretian grounds. Indeed, the above example enables us to speak of "the impossibility of being a differential-alienation-condemning Paretian" in exactly the sense of "the impossibility of being a Paretian liberal."[24] For, as the last several paragraphs demonstrate, to avoid alienation Karl must produce only for himself (using both the Farm and the Factory), which will require Adam to work each week for himself. But in the example this is not a Pareto optimal allocation of labor. Only by engaging in differentially alienated labor can Karl and Adam take full advantage of the efficient Factory technology. Thus even the mind welfarist requirement of Pareto efficiency comes into conflict with exploitation-as-differential-alienation. There may still be grounds for calling such differential alienation *exploitative*, but it appears such grounds must be based on *rights*, not welfare outcomes as the agents see them.

We are led to ask, then, whether a person has a *right* not to perform more alienated labor than another person. We might be able to argue that one has a right not to be *forced* to perform more alienated labor than another: but that will lead straight into a discussion of differential ownership of the means of production, which is not the issue here.[25] For in our story Karl chooses to perform more alienated labor than Adam from a position of equality of resources and opportunity. Nobody forces him, unless we slide further down the slippery slope of defining the "resources" available to the person and argue that Karl was forced because he had no choice of the personal characteristics that gave rise to his carpe diem preferences. I cannot see a compelling argument for declaiming such a right, in part because I cannot see a compelling argument against the performance of alienated labor, let alone differential alienation. I think moral intuitions on this matter must take their cue from history. It is far from clear that people, in historical reality, have had an aversion to performing alienated labor. Indeed, many (including Marxists) argue that production for the market has been a liberating process for many populations, a process which they enter into willingly. (Recall, we are not concerned here with domination, of choosing to work for others, but only with alienation, of producing for a market.)

I think the argument for postulating that a person has a right not to perform more alienated labor than another person is extremely weak. Hence I cannot defend an interest in exploitation as a proxy for an interest in differentially alienated labor. The problem is that there is not necessarily anything condemnable with differentially alienated labor if it arises from differential preferences which we accept as well formed and not like handicaps. To consider "myopic" preferences to be handicaps, we would have to argue that there is an upper bound on correct rates of time discount, and people who discount time more highly are handicapped. While in some instances the case for such a handicap can be made (typically, when a high rate of time discount is a consequence of having been severely deprived of assets in the past), in the general instance, it cannot be. The last parenthetical aside cues the most important situation where we might view differential alienation, arrived at from differential preferences, as exploitative: when those preferences are in fact learned as a consequence of differential ownership of the means of production in the past. Suppose the rich learn to save, and the poor do not; having learned such rates of time preference from their past environments, formerly rich Adam may end up accumulating and exploiting formerly poor Karl, even when the new state starts them off with clean slates by redistributing the initial endowment to one of equality between them. But in this case our justification for thinking of differential alienation as exploitative is due to the rich background of Adam and the poor one of Karl; we are reduced to an argument for an interest in exploitation as an indicator of inequality in the ownership of assets, to which I soon turn.

The possibility remains that even though nondifferentially alienated outcomes cannot be defended on Paretian grounds, nor on grounds of rights, perhaps they can be defended for perfectionist reasons. I will not attempt here to defend my position against a perfectionist attack, except to say that my defense would amplify on the point of the two previous paragraphs. It seems that differential alienation of labor, from an initial position of equal opportunity and fair division of assets, can vastly increase the welfare and life quality of people, and so a perfectionist defense of nonalienation seems remote.

6. Differential Ownership of Productive Assets

The fourth reason to be interested in exploitation is as an index of the inequality in ownership of productive assets. This approach is represented, for example, in the epigraph from Marx. The Marxist position that socialist revolution entails redistribution or nationalization of the means of production to eliminate exploitation traces to this conception of exploitation. (In contrast, the emphasis of exploitation as domination[2] gives rise to industrial democracy as the key aspect of socialist transformation.) In my recent book and in other articles I have claimed that this is the most compelling reason to be interested in exploitation, by showing in a series of models that the existence of exploitation is equivalent to inequality in distribution of initial assets, and that the rich exploit the poor. Hence exploitation theory can be justified if we accept a presumption that initial inequality in the wealth of agents is unjust, for exploitation (in these models) is essentially equivalent to initial inequality of assets. Nevertheless this may appear to weaken the argument for being interested in exploitation (defined as I have done throughout this article), for it is probably easier to observe inequality in ownership of assets than it is to calculate exploitation accounts. Surprisingly, however, if our ethical interest is really in initial inequality of ownership of assets, the importance of Marxian *class* theory is strengthened. For in the models I investigated, class membership is closely related to wealth: The "higher" one's class position, the wealthier one is in productive assets. In particular, any agent who optimizes by hiring others is wealthy and is an exploiter, and any agent who optimizes by selling labor power is relatively poor and is exploited. Now class relations are still easier to observe than wealth, and so the Class-Wealth Correspondence enables us to conclude a great deal about the initial distribution of productive assets by observing how people relate to the hiring and selling of labor power. Class position provides a convenient proxy for the fundamental inequality in which, I claim, we are interested; but exploitation drops out as an unnecessary detour.

Still, according to this description of the results, exploitation may be thought of as an *innocuous* appendix to our true ethical concerns: innocuous because although unnecessary, surplus value accounts correspond to underlying inequality in ownership of assets in the proper way. I now go further and claim that in the general case, exploitation theory leads to results which may conflict directly with the inequality-of-productive-assets theory. And therefore, finding no other reasons to be interested in exploitation accounts, I must say exploitation theory, in the general case, is misconceived. It does not provide a proper model or account of Marxian moral sentiments; the proper Marxian claim, I think, is for equality in the distribution of productive assets, not for the elimination of exploitation.

The "general case" in which exploitation accounts and inequality accounts diverge occurs when general preferences for agents are admitted. In particular, if preferences for income versus leisure differ across agents, the divergence can occur. Indeed, the two theories can diverge even for cases when preferences are identical for all agents as I will show. In my book, I assumed preferences of all agents were the same, and of certain special forms: Either all agents wanted to accumulate as much as possible, or they wanted just to subsist, two preference profiles that appear to be polar opposites. Indeed, there may be a strong case that the assumption of one of these profiles of preferences is not a bad one, historically, in which case exploitation theory might correspond empirically to Marxian ethical conceptions. But I am concerned here with the logical foundations of exploitation theory, and for that purpose general and abstract formulations with respect to admissable preference profiles are essential.

Before proceeding, it is important to correct a possible misimpression from an earlier article.[26] I argued there that a pure inequality-of-assets definition was better than the Marxian surplus value definition for characterizing exploitation; that claim is weaker than the claim here, for in that article I took the Marxian surplus value definition to mean "the extraction of surplus labor from one agent by another in a production relation." In the present paper, I am taking exploitation to be defined by "unequal exchange of labor," whether or not there is a production relation between the agents in which one "extracts" the labor of another. In the previous article, I did not argue against the "unequal exchange of labor" conception of exploitation, except to say that the inequality-of-property definition was a cleaner but equivalent characterization of the same phenomenon. I now claim that "unequal exchange of labor" is not characterized by the inequality of productive assets when we admit general preferences structures.

I shall show that if the preferences of agents do not satisfy a certain condition, then it can happen that the asset-rich are exploited by the asset-poor: The flow of surplus value goes the "wrong way." This can occur even when all agents have identical preference maps for income and leisure—but what is critical is that the agents' preference for leisure must change rather substantially, and in a particular way, as their wealth changes. Once this example is demonstrated, one can no longer claim that exploitation is a significant index of inequality of initial assets which measures the flow from the asset-poor to the asset-rich.

I will first give a general explanation of why the correspondence between exploitation and wealth can fail. Then, a simple example will be given illustrating the phenomenon. Readers may skip directly to the example on page 144 without undue loss of comprehension.

A brief review of the Class Exploitation Correspondence Principle and the Class-Wealth Correspondence Principle is necessary. The model consists of many agents; agent i begins with a vector of impersonal assets ω^i that can be used in production, plus one unit of labor power. (I assume labor is homogeneous, as I have throughout this article. If labor is hetero-geneous, then poking holes in exploitation theory is almost child's play. Homogeneity of labor at least gives the theory a fighting chance.) There is a common technology which all agents can use. Each agent has a utility function, of goods and leisure. Since we have shown that an interest in exploitation cannot be justified by an interest in domination or alienation, we need not put into the utility function any concerns with where or under whom the labor one expends is performed. *Assume all agents have identical preferences*, although they own different initial bundles ω^i. Facing a vector of commodity prices p, which I normalize by letting the wage be unity, agent i now has finance capital in amount $p\omega^i$. Given his capital constraint, he chooses how much labor to supply and how much income to earn in order to maximize his utility. An equilibrium price vector is of the usual sort, allowing all markets, including the market for labor, to clear. An agent typically has three sources of revenue in the model: wage income from sell-ing some labor power, profit income from hiring others, and proprietary income, from working himself on his own finance capital. If we introduce a capital market, there will also be interest or rental income, but that does not change the story at all. An agent is exploited if his total revenues do not enable him to purchase goods embodying as much social labor as he chose to expend in production. Class position of agents has been discussed before, in section 4 above.

At the equilibrium prices, let us call the wealth of agent i: $W^i = p\omega^i$. Wealth is the valuation at equilibrium prices of his nonlabor assets, his finance capital. We can view the labor he decides to supply in production, by maximizing his utility, as a function, at equilibrium prices p, of this wealth. Call this labor supply function $L(W)$. If agents possessed different utility functions, then we would have to write different labor supply func-tions, $L^i(W)$, but by assumption, all agents have the same preferences. $L(W^i)$ can be thought of as a cross-sectional labor supply function, which tells how much labor any agent will supply at the equilibrium prices, if his wealth is W^i. Now the key lemma is this: Membership in the five classes is monotonically related to the ratio $\gamma^i = W^i/L(W^i)$ and so is exploitation sta-tus.[27] That is, the larger is the ratio γ^i, the higher up the class ladder agent i is, and the more of an exploiter he is. (The class ladder is described in section 4 above.) When do class and exploitation status of agents give us a good proxy for the agent's initial wealth of nonlabor assets? Precisely when the index γ^i is monotonically related to wealth W^i. Thus exploitation and class can be indicators of our interest in wealth inequality precisely when $d\gamma/dW > 0$, that is, when the γ index increases with wealth. Taking the derivative:

$$\frac{d\gamma}{dW} > 0 \quad \text{if and only if} \quad \frac{dL}{dW} < \frac{L}{W} \quad \text{or} \quad \frac{dL}{L} \Big/ \frac{dW}{W} < 1.$$

This last condition is of a familiar type in economics: It says that the labor supplied by the agent is inelastic with respect to his wealth; that is, a 1 percent increase in the agent's wealth will cause him to increase his supply of labor by less than 1 percent. Summarizing:

> *Theorem*: Under identical preferences of agents, class and exploitation status accurately reflect inequality in distribution of finance capital (productive assets other than labor) if and only if the labor supplied by agents is inelastic with respect to their wealth at equilibrium prices. If preferences differ, then class and exploitation status accurately reflect wealth if and only if *cross-sectionally* labor is inelastically supplied as wealth increases.

This elasticity condition is perhaps a reasonable condition on preferences.[28] In particular, we often think of agents supplying *less* labor as their wealth increases, in which case the above condition certainly holds. The condition allows agents to increase the labor they supply with increases in wealth, so long as they do not increase the labor supplied faster than their wealth increases. However, if we allow an "unrestricted domain" of preferences for goods and leisure (even if we constrain all agents to have the same preferences!), then the relation between exploitation and class, on the one hand, and wealth on the other, is lost. It will be possible to design cases where we have an agent Karl who hires labor (and does not sell it), who will be an exploiter by the Class Exploitation Correspondence Principle, and another agent Adam who sells labor and is exploited, *but* Adam is wealthier than Karl, *and* Karl and Adam have the *same preferences* over bundles of goods and leisure. This can only happen when the elasticity condition fails, and that provides the intuition which resolves the apparent paradox. With a wealth-elastic labor supply function, Adam, who is rich, wants to work terribly hard, while Karl who is poor hardly wants to work at all. Indeed Karl does not even want to work hard enough to utilize fully his paltry stock of productive assets, and so he hires Adam to work up the rest of his capital for him, which Adam is willing to do, even after he has worked all he can on his substantial stock of assets. Thus poor Karl hires and, by the Class Exploitation Correspondence Principle, exploits rich Adam.

Noneconomists might think of Karl and Adam in the above example as having different preference orderings, since one wants to supply a lot of labor and the other a little. But preference orderings are defined for an individual over all bundles of labor (or leisure) and goods he might consume, and so it is perfectly consistent for Karl and Adam to have the same preference orderings yet to supply labor differentially because of their different wealths. Saying they have the same preference orderings implies they have the same utility function and the same labor supply *function*, not that they supply the same amount of labor.

We have now to consider the case where differential preferences are admitted. Then, a fortiori, the index $\gamma^i = W^i/L^i(W^i)$ will in general not be monotonically correlated with wealth W^i. Now, $L^i(W)$ can vary with i. We cannot say the rich exploit the poor with any degree of rigor. We can only be assured that the rich exploit the poor when the elasticity condition holds cross-sectionally, that an increment in wealth implies a less than proportionate increment in labor supplied. Failing this relation, the poor can be exploiters of the rich.

Notice *cross-sectional* labor supply behavior which is wealth-elastic might be quite common if agents have different preferences for leisure and income. Indeed, it is possible for labor supply cross-sectionally to exhibit elasticity with respect to wealth, while each individual agent has a "well-behaved" wealth-inelastic labor supply schedule. Those who become wealthy (in one of the versions of the neoclassical paradigm) are those who have a low preference for leisure. Hence the individuals we observe as wealthy could have gotten that way by working long hours—although their own labor supply schedules might be inelastic as their wealth increases. We might then very well observe labor supply across the population increasing faster than wealth for some interval of wealths. For an individual's labor supply to be wealth-elastic, leisure must be an inferior good for him; but for the population labor supply to be cross-sectionally wealth-elastic, this is not the case.

For the sake of concreteness, here is a simple example illustrating the divergence between exploitation and inequality of assets. It does not matter, for this example, whether the different amounts of labor which Karl and Adam supply are a consequence of different preferences or the same preferences. All that matters is that given their different initial wealths, they optimize by supplying labor in the pattern indicated. I postulate the same Farm and Factory technologies as before:

> Farm: 3 days labor (and no capital) produces 1 bushel of corn
> Factory: 1 day labor plus 1 bushel seed corn produces 2 bushels corn

This time, however, Karl has an initial endowment of 1 corn and Adam of 3 corn. Denote a bundle of corn and labor as (C,L). Thus $(1,1)$ represents the consumption of 1 corn and the provision of 1 day's labor. I assume, as before, that each agent is not willing to run down his initial stock of corn (because he might die at any time, and he wishes, at least, not to deprive his only child of the same endowment that his parent passed down to him). Suppose we know at least this about Adam's and Karl's preferences:

$(\frac{2}{3},0) \succ_K (1,1)$
$(3\frac{1}{3},4) \succ_A (3,3)$

(To translate, the first line says Karl would strictly prefer to consume $\frac{2}{3}$ bushel of corn and not to work at all than to work 1 day and consume 1 bushel.) Now note that Karl can achieve (1,1) by working up his 1 corn in the Factory in 1 day; he consumes 1 of the bushels produced, and starts week 2 with his initial 1 bushel. Likewise, Adam can achieve (3,3) by working up his 3 bushels in the Factory with 3 days' labor; he consumes 3 of the 6 bushels produced, and replaces his initial stock for week 2. But this solution is not Pareto optimal. For now suppose Karl lends his 1 bushel to Adam. Adam works up the total of 4 bushels in 4 days in the Factory, produces 8 bushels, and pays back Karl his original bushel plus $\frac{2}{3}$ bushel as interest for the loan. This leaves Adam with $3\frac{1}{3}$ bushels, after replacing his 3 bushels of initial stock. Thus Karl can consume $\frac{2}{3}$ bushel and work not at all, which he prefers to (1,1), and Adam consumes the bundle $(3\frac{1}{3},4)$ which he prefers to (3,3). We have a strict Pareto improvement. (The interest rate charged is the competitive one; for if Adam, instead of borrowing from Karl, worked on the Farm for an extra day he would make precisely $\frac{1}{3}$ bushel of corn.) This arrangement may continue forever: Karl never works and lives off the interest from Adam's labor. According to the unequal exchange definition of exploitation, there is no shadow of a doubt that Karl exploits Adam. However, Adam is richer than Karl. On what basis can we condemn this exploitation? Not on the basis of domination or alienation (we have decided), and surely not on the basis of differential ownership of the means of production, since the exploitation is going the "wrong way." Indeed, eliminating inequality in the ownership of the means of production should improve the lot of the exploited at the expense of the exploiters. (That is the property relations definition I formalized in other work.[29]) But in this case an equalization of the initial assets at 2 bushels of corn for each renders the exploiter (Karl) better off, and the exploited (Adam) worse off![30]

It should be remarked that the preferences postulated in this example for Karl and Adam are not perverse in the sense that they can be embedded in a full preference relation which has convex indifference curves of the usual sort, in corn-leisure space. This is the case even when Karl and Adam possess the same (convex) preferences.

If we have reason for calling unjust the postulated inequality in the original distribution of seed-corn assets, then it is Karl who is suffering an injustice in the previous example, and not Adam; but according to exploitation theory, Karl exploits Adam. As I have said, I think the most consistent Marxian ethical position is against inequality in the initial distribution of productive assets; when exploitation accounts reflect the unequal distribution of productive assets in the proper way (that the rich exploit the poor), that is what makes exploitation theory attractive. But if that correlation can fail, as it has, then no foundation remains for a justification of exploitation theory.

It might still be maintained that two injustices are involved when productive assets are unjustly distributed: the injustice of that distribution of stocks, and the injustice of the flows arising from them.[31] Exploitation is a statement concerning the injustice of flows, but I have invoked it only as a proxy for the underlying injustice (more precisely, inequality) of stocks. There remains the necessity for some judgment of the injustice of flows emanating from an unjust distribution of stocks: My point is that flows of labor are an imperfect proxy for that. In the Karl-Adam example, I say that Adam is unjustly gaining from the flows between him and Karl, if the initial distribution of stocks is unjust against Karl, despite the formal exploitation of Adam by Karl. In cases where exploitation does render the correct judgment on the injustice of flows, then perhaps the degree or rate of exploitation is useful in assessing the degree of injustice in the flow. But in the general case counterexamples can be supplied against this claim as well— situations where A is exploited more than B but we would agree B is more unjustly treated. It is beyond my scope here to inquire into a robust measure of the injustice of flows emanating from an unjust stock.

Another point should be made with respect to the argument of this section. It might be argued that so long as exploitation comes about, then the initial distribution of assets was not "equal." An "equal" initial distribution might be defined as one which eliminates exploitation. First, such a position is circular with respect to any attempt to vindicate exploitation theory by claiming it helps to reveal an initial inequality of assets. Second, such a definition of equality of initial endowments is in fact a theory of outcome equality, not a theory of resource equality. We would still be left with the question: What is wrong with exploitation?

A fifth explanation of our interest in exploitation theory, which I have enumerated (4') as I consider it to be convincing only when it paraphrases the inequality theory, might be called the expropriation theory. The expropriation theory is summarized, for example, by G. A. Cohen,[32] as follows:

(i) The laborer is the only person who creates the product, that which has value.
(ii) The capitalist receives some of the value of the product.
Therefore: (iii) The laborer receives less value than the value of what he creates, and
(iv) The capitalist receives some of the value of what the laborer creates.
Therefore: (v) The laborer is exploited by the capitalist.

The expropriation theory (which Cohen calls the Plain Marxian Argument) does not claim an injustice on grounds of alienation or domination, but on grounds of rightful ownership of what one has made. I think the argument is ethically defensible only when it coincides with the inequality-of-resources theory, that is, when the expropriation takes place because the laborer does not have access to the means of production he is entitled to. To see the unreasonableness of the expropriation theory in the general case, substitute "Karl" for "the capitalist" and "Adam" for "the laborer" in the above argument (i)–(v) where Karl and Adam are the dramatis personae of the last example. Statements (ii) through (iv) remain unobjectionable and perhaps statement (i) does as well; but statement (v) certainly does not follow as an *ethically* convincing statement (although *formal* exploitation exists). If we respect the ownership pattern of assets and the preferences of the agents (which, to repeat, can even be uniform preferences), I see no good reason to give exclusive ownership rights of a product to the person who has made the product. Only on grounds of alienation (which I have said is unconvincing) does it seem one's labor could confer special ownership rights over the product. Justly acquired initial resources, which the direct producer might borrow from another, must count as well in ascribing ownership of the final product. What power the expropriation theory appears to have comes from another assumption, not stated, that the capitalist starts out with a monopoly on the ownership of the means of production, unjustly acquired; it is the injustice of that monopoly which leads us to believe he has no just claim to the product of the laborer. As Cohen says, in his own criticism of the expropriation theory: "If it is morally all right that capitalists do and workers do not own the means of production, then capitalist profit is not the fruit of exploitation; and if the pre-contractual distributive position is morally wrong, then the case for exploitation is made."[33]

7. MOLLIFYING THE VERDICT

Many writers have shown the indefensibility of the labor theory of *value*, the claim that Marxian analysis gains special insight from deducing a relationship between embodied labor values and prices.[34] There is no theory of price formation, special to Marxism, with a rigorous foundation. With the demise of the labor theory of value, various writers in the Marxian tradition have shown that the theory of exploitation can be reconstructed on a foundation which does not utilize the labor theory of value.[35] (Marx's logic derived the theory of exploitation from the labor theory of price formation.) I have now argued there is no logically compelling reason to be interested in exploitation theory. This claim is not so destructive as might appear to the Marxian enterprise, however, for I think the reasons Marxists have been interested in exploitation theory are important and, to a large extent, distinguish Marxism from other kinds of social science: It is just that these reasons do not justify an interest in exploitation theory which is an unnecessary detour to the other concerns. First, within ethics, Marxism lays emphasis on the importance of equal access to the means of production. It regards with suspicion any large inequality in access to the means of production, while its foil in social science tends to justify such inequality on grounds of differential rates of time preference, skill, or even luck.[36] Having said that equality in the ownership of means of production is desirable as an initial condition, much is left to elaborate concerning inheritance, handicaps, and needs. Libertarian theorists view inheritance as a just means of acquiring resources;[37] Ronald Dworkin, in recent work on equality of resources, does not discuss inheritance;[38] Bruce Ackerman in recent work does attack that problem;[39] I imagine a Marxian theory of inheritance, when elaborated, will circumscribe inheritance rights quite sharply.[40] Second, Marxism calls attention to domination; domination is of interest on its own, even though it provides no reason to be interested in exploitation. Interest in domination has given rise to an important literature on the labor process and technical change under capitalism, which demonstrates how a specifically Marxian question, perhaps motivated by normative concerns, can give rise to new analysis of a positive type. Another example of positive analysis related to domination and exploitation is class theory. Class position is easily observable, and class may be an excellent indicator of alliances in struggles within capitalism, for reasons closer to domination than exploitation.[41] Third, the concern with alienation is related to the interest Marxists have had in the emergence of market economies and the proletarianization of labor forces, both in the past and the present, an interest which again leads to the posing of questions which would not otherwise have been asked. Fourth, the concern with accumulation has given Marxists a view of capitalism as guided by a pursuit of profits which in a deep sense is anarchic and collectively irrational, while the predominant opposing view (neoclassical economics) pictures capitalism as collectively rational, as the price system harnesses profit motives to serve the needs of people.[42] While Marxists have not developed a theory of crisis and disequilibrium which is as well founded and intellectually convincing as neoclassical equilibrium theory, one suspects the Marxian questions will eventually lead to a rigorous theory of uneven development and crisis.

Unlike the labor theory of value, the reasons for a purported interest in exploitation theory have given rise to provocative social theory. There have, on the other hand, been costs to the adherence to exploitation theory, chiefly associated with what might be called the fetishism of labor. The costs are often associated with the inappropriate application of exploitation theory in cases where some underlying deeper phenomenon, which usually coincides with exploitation, ceases to coincide with it. For example, socialist countries have exhibited a reluctant history to use material incentives and decentralizing markets. To some extent, this may result from a confusion concerning the permissibility of "exploitation" when the initial distribution of ownership or control of the means of production is just. A second cost has been the equation claimed by some Marxists between socialism and industrial democracy, the belief that hierarchical forms of production are necessarily nonsocialist. A third example, associated with an overriding concern with alienation, views the final social goal as a moneyless economy, perhaps with no detailed division of labor, in which, somehow, all of society becomes one community.[43] Strictly speaking, the last two examples do not impugn exploitation theory, but rather domination and alienation; but exploitation theory has formalized the concern with labor which reinforces this sort of misapplication.

It should be reiterated that the failure of exploitation to mirror properly the unequal distribution of the means of production is a logical one; as I noted, in what are perhaps the most important actual historical cases, preferences of agents are such that the unequal-exchange-of-labor theory coincides with the inequality-of-productive-assets theory, and so exploitation theory pronounces the "right" ethical verdict.[44]

Parallel to my view on the usefulness of exploitation theory as a proxy for inequality in the ownership of the means of production is George Stigler's observation concerning David Ricardo's use of the labor theory of value. Stigler writes:

> I can find no basis for the belief that Ricardo had an *analytical* labor theory of value, for quantities of labor are *not* the only determinants of relative values. . . . On the other hand, there is no doubt that he held what may be called an *empirical* labor theory of value, that is, a theory that the relative quantities of labor required in production are the dominant determinants of relative values. Such an empirical proposition cannot be interpreted as an analytical theory.

Stigler concludes with a statement which applies to my argument concerning exploitation:

> The failure to distinguish between analytical and empirical propositions has been a source of much misunderstanding in economics. An analytical statement concerns functional relationships; an empirical statement takes account of the quantitative significance of the relationships.[45]

Unlike Stigler's Ricardo, I think the labor theory of value is not a useful empirical theory. While the errors in the labor theory of value are Ptolemaic, the defects in exploitation theory are Newtonian. As an empirical statement,

surplus value accounts mirror inequality in ownership of the means of production pretty well, if it is true that cross-sectional wealth-elastic labor supply behavior is as empirically inconsequential as the precession in the perihelion
of the orbit of Mercury. But for the sake of clarity and consistency, I think
exploitation conceived of as the unequal exchange of labor should be replaced with exploitation conceived of as the distributional consequences of
an unjust inequality in the distribution of productive assets and resources.
Precisely when the asset distribution is unjust becomes the central question
to which Marxian political philosophy should direct its attention.

Notes

I am indebted to the following individuals for many discussions, comments, and
disagreements: G. A. Cohen, Jon Elster, Joseph Ostroy, Amartya Sen, Philippe Van
Parijs, Erik Wright; and to participants in seminars where these ideas were presented, at the University of Oslo, the University of Copenhagen, Yale University,
the University of Chicago, the 1983 Maison des Sciences de l'Homme Colloquium
in London, and the 1984 Colloque Marx in Paris organized by the Ecole des Hautes
Etudes en Sciences Sociales.

1. For a discussion of the gray area of agents, see John E. Roemer, *A General
   Theory of Exploitation and Class* (Cambridge: Harvard University Press, 1982),
   ch. 4.
2. See, for example, Joan Robinson, *An Essay on Marxian Economics* (New York:
   St. Martin's Press, 1966); Michio Morishima, *Marx's Economics* (Cambridge: Cam-
   bridge University Press, 1973); Ian Steedman, *Marx after Sraffa* (London: New
   Left Books, 1977); John E. Roemer, *Analytical Foundations of Marxian Economic
   Theory* (Cambridge: Cambridge University Press, 1981); Paul A. Samuelson,
   "Understanding the Marxian Notion of Exploitation: A summary of the So-
   called Transformation Problem between Marxian Values and Competitive Prices,"
   Journal of Economic Literature 9 (1971): 339–431; Jon Elster, *Making Sense of
   Marx* (Cambridge University Press, 1985).
3. Definitions of "exploitation" are from Webster's Dictionary (1966).
4. Allen Wood, *Karl Marx* (London: Routledge and Kegal Paul, 1981), ch. 9.
5. Morishima, *Marx's Economics*. Many authors have since studied and generalized
   the Fundamental Marxian Theorem.
6. This Generalized Commodity Exploitation Theorem has been proved and/or
   observed by many authors, including Josep Ma. Vegara, *Economia Politica y Modelos
   Multisectoriales* (Madrid: Editorial Tecnos, 1979); Samuel Bowles and Herbert
   Gintis, "Structure and Practice in the Labor Theory of Value," *Review of Radical Political Economics* 12, no. 4 (Winter 1981): 1–26; Robert P. Wolff, "A Critique and Reinterpretation of Marx's Labor Theory of Value," *Philosophy and
   Public Affairs* 10, no. 2 (Spring 1981): 89–120; Roemer, *General Theory*, appendix 6.1; Paul A. Samuelson, "The Normative and Positivistic Inferiority of Marx's
   Values Paradigm," *Southern Economic Journal* 49, no. 1 (1982): 11–18.
7. See J. E. Roemer, "R. P. Wolff's Reinterpretation of Marx's Labor Theory of

Value: Comment," *Philosophy and Public Affairs* 12, no. 1 (Winter 1983): 70–83; J. E. Roemer, "Why Labor Classes?" (U.C. Davis working paper, 1982).

8. R. P. Wolff, "A Critique and Reinterpretation," while recognizing that the exploitation of labor cannot explain profits, offers a reason other than domination and alienation to be interested in exploitation; as I have argued against his proposal elsewhere (Roemer, "R. P. Wolff's Reinterpretation of Marx's Labor Theory of Value"), I will not repeat that discussion.

9. G. A. Cohen, "Freedom, Justice, and Capitalism," *New Left Review*, no. 125 (1981). For an opposite point of view, see Wood, *Karl Marx*.

10. Ellen Meiksins Wood, "The Separation of the Economic and Political in Capitalism," *New Left Review*, no. 127 (May–June 1981); Bowles and Gintis, "Structure and Practice"; Erik Olin Wright, "The Status of the Political in the Concept of Class Structure," *Politics and Society* 11, no. 3 (1982): 321–42.

11. C. B. Macpherson, *Property: Mainstream and Critical Positions* (Toronto: University of Toronto Press, 1978), ch. 1.

12. Samuel Bowles and Herbert Gintis, "The Power of Capital: On the Inadequacy of the Conception of the Capitalist Economy as 'Private,'" *Philosophical Forum* 14, nos. 3–4 (1983), claim that even in perfect competition, if there are multiple equilibria, then property values are not well defined and there is room for domination[1] in determining which set of equilibrium prices will prevail. This is a dubious assertion. If indeed no agent has economic power, in the sense perfect competition postulates, then which of several multiple equilibria will rule is not due to domination[1] but is simply an unanswerable question, given the information in the model.

13. See Richard Edwards, *Contested Terrain: The Transformation of the Workplace in America* (New York: Basic Books, 1979).

14. Samuel Bowles and Herbert Gintis, *Schooling in Capitalist America* (New York: Basic Books, 1976).

15. Adam Przeworski, "Material Interests, Class Compromise, and the Transition to Socialism," *Politics and Society* 10, no. 2 (1980).

16. For a detailed presentation of this material, see Roemer, *General Theory*, parts 1 and 2. For a summary, see J. Roemer, "New Directions in the Marxian Theory of Exploitation and Class," *Politics and Society* 11, no. 3 (1982): 253–88.

17. I am speaking of a pure form of Credit Market Capitalism; in actual credit markets, lenders often supervise debtors if sufficient collateral is not available, or if there would be problems in enforcing collection of collateral.

18. For the details of this economy see *General Theory*, ch. 1; for a simple example, see J. E. Roemer, "Are Socialist Ethics Consistent with Efficiency?" *Philosophical Forum* 14, nos. 3–4 (1983): 369–88.

19. See J. E. Roemer, "Unequal Exchange, Labor Migration, and International Capital Flows: A Theoretical Synthesis," in Padma Desai, ed., *Marxism, the Soviet, Economy and Central Planning: Essays in Honor of Alexander Erlich* (Cambridge: MIT Press, 1983).

20. For example, see Harry Braverman, *Labor and Monopoly Capital* (New York: Monthly Review Press, 1974), and Richard Edwards, *Contested Terrain*.

21. Further discussion of some of these issues can be found in J. E. Roemer, "Reply," *Politics and Society* 11, no. 3 (1982): 375–94.

22. B. Traven, *The Night Visitor and Other Stories* (New York: Hill and Wang, 1973). In the story "Assembly Line," a Mexican Indian has been offered a huge sum of money, more than he has ever dreamed of, to mass-produce little baskets for a

New York department store, which he has formerly made only in small quantities for the local market. The New York buyer is astonished that the Indian is not interested in the proposal. The Indian explains: "Yes, I know that jefecito, my little chief," the Indian answered, entirely unconcerned. "It must be the same price because I cannot make any other one. Besides, señor, there's still another thing which perhaps you don't know. You see, my good lordy and caballero, I've to make these canastitas my own way and with my song in them and with bits of my soul woven into them. If I were to make them in great numbers there would no longer be my soul in each, or my songs. Each would look like the other with no difference whatever and such a thing would slowly eat my heart. Each has to be another song which I hear in the morning when the sun rises and when the birds begin to chirp and the butterflies come and sit down on my baskets so that I may see a new beauty, because, you see, the butterflies like my baskets and the pretty colors in them, that's why they come and sit down, and I can make my canastitas after them. And now, señor jefecito, if you will kindly excuse me, I have wasted much time already, although it was a pleasure and a great honor to hear the talk of such a distinguished caballero like you. But I'm afraid I've to attend to my work now, for day after tomorrow is market day in town and I got to take my baskets there."

23. See, for a definition of welfarism, Amartya Sen, "Utilitarianism and Welfarism," *Journal of Philosophy* 76, no. 9 (1979): 463–89.

24. On the impossibility of being a Paretian liberal, see, for instance, Amartya Sen, *Collective Choice and Social Welfare* (New York: North Holland, 1979), ch. 6.

25. For a discussion of why proletarians can be thought of as forced to alienate their labor, even in a world of voluntary wage contracts, see G. A. Cohen, "The Structure of Proletarian Unfreedom," *Philosophy and Public Affairs* 12, no. 1 (Winter 1983): 3–33.

26. J. Roemer, "Property Relations vs. Surplus Value in Marxian Exploitation," *Philosophy and Public Affairs* 11, no. 4 (Fall 1982): 281–313.

27. For a demonstration of this lemma, see J. Roemer, *General Theory*, 176. A fuller discussion is in J. Roemer, "Why Labor Classes?"

28. In the two special cases I studied in *General Theory*, the correspondence between exploitation and wealth followed because the elasticity condition held. For the subsistence model, the elasticity of labor supply with respect to wealth is negative, and for the accumulation model it is zero. In the subsistence model, agents desire to minimize labor performed subject to consuming a certain subsistence bundle which is independent of wealth; in the accumulation model, they desire only to accumulate, and each works as much as is physically possible (an amount assumed to be the same for all). I believed, falsely, that since these two models posed behavior representing two extremes with respect to leisure preferences that the correspondence between exploitation and wealth would hold for any preferences uniform across agents.

29. Roemer, "Property Relations vs. Surplus Value."

30. Actually, even if there is a unique equilibrium there are some perverse cases in general equilibrium models when an agent can improve his final welfare by giving away some of his initial endowment. This is not such a case.

31. I thank G. A. Cohen for pressing this point.

32. G. A. Cohen, "The Labor Theory of Value and the Concept of Exploitation," *Philosophy and Public Affairs* 8, no. 4 (Summer 1979): 338–60.

33. G. A. Cohen, "More on the Labor Theory of Value," *Inquiry* (Fall 1983).

34. For a summary of the criticism of the labor theory of value see Elster, *Making Sense of Marx*, ch. 3.
35. See Cohen, "The Labor Theory of Value and the Concept of Exploitation"; Roemer, *General Theory*; Morishima, *Marx's Economics*.
36. Robert Nozick, for example, considers luck to be a just method for acquiring assets (*Anarchy, State, and Utopia* [New York: Basic Books, 1974]).
37. Ibid.
38. Ronald Dworkin, "What Is Equality? Part 2: Equality of Resources," *Philosophy and Public Affairs* 10, no. 4 (Fall 1981): 283–345. See 313 n. 9.
39. Bruce Ackerman, *Social Justice in the Liberal State* (New Haven: Yale University Press, 1980).
40. For some very tentative indications, see Roemer, "Are Socialist Ethics Consistent with Efficiency?" part 4.
41. I have not considered in this paper a sixth possible reason to be interested in exploitation: as an explanation of class struggle, that the exploited struggle against the exploiters. I think that if the exploited struggle against the exploiters, that is because the former are dominated, are alienated, or suffer from an unfair allocation in the distribution of assets. The unequal exchange of labor cannot be the cause of class struggle: Rather, that unequal exchange must be the symptom of what must cause class struggle. (People do not calculate surplus value accounts; in fact, one of the classical Marxian points is that the surplus value accounts are masked and veiled by the market, and so the exploited do not see the true nature of the unequal exchange from which they are suffering.) But I have shown, now, that exploitation is not a useful proxy for the various injustices which may, indeed, be at the root of class struggle. Hence, my nondiscussion of exploitation as the cause of class struggle.
42. It is this collective irrationality of capitalism which Elster, *Making Sense of Marx*, sees as the main contribution of Marxian "dialectics."
43. A fine discussion of the costs which dogmatic Marxism has imposed on developing socialist societies is in Alec Nove, *The Economics of Feasible Socialism* (London: George Allen and Unwin, 1983).
44. A striking example which suggests that labor supply may be elastic with respect to wealth, and therefore that exploitation theory is even historically wrong, is presented by Pranab Bardhan, "Agrarian Class Formation in India," *Journal of Peasant Studies* 10, no. 1 (1982): 78. In India, as the wealth of middle-peasant families increases, poor relations come and join the family. Viewing this extended family as the unit, it appears that labor supply increases with wealth. It is not obvious that the family labor supply increases elastically with wealth, but Bardhan's example shows, at least, there is a range of wealths for which labor supply has positive elasticity.
45. George Stigler, "Ricardo and the 93% Labor Theory of Value," *American Economic Review* 48 (June 1958): 361, 366.

Exploitation, Force, and the Moral Assessment of Capitalism: Thoughts on Roemer and Cohen

Jeffrey Reiman

Introduction: The Force-Inclusive Definition of Exploitation

Marxists and non-marxists alike would profit from a common understanding of the meaning of the Marxian concept of exploitation and the angle of vision it provides. Toward this end, I want to discuss and defend the following definition of *exploitation*: "A society is exploitative when its social structure is organized so that unpaid labor is systematically forced out of one class and put at the disposal of another." Note that *both* unpaid labor *and* force are included here in the definition of exploitation.[1] It is not underpaid labor, but unpaid labor; and not only unpaid labor, but forced unpaid labor. On this definition, exploitation (in any economic system, capitalist or other) is a kind of coercive "prying loose" from workers of unpaid labor. I call this the "force-inclusive definition," in order to distinguish it from what I call the "distributive definition," which defines exploitation as some form of maldistribution to which force is an external support.

Defending a definition of exploitation that includes both force and unpaid labor requires showing that it is worthwhile to view social processes characterized by both of these as unitary phenomena. There is nothing unusual about this. We do an analogous thing when we separate out "robbery"—which includes both theft and force—from other forms of theft. One reason that it is worthwhile to view processes that force unpaid labor out of workers as unitary phenomena is that such processes are arguably forms of slavery, and thus worthy of special moral scrutiny.

Marxists hold that workers in capitalism work more hours for their bosses than the number of hours of work it takes to produce the real equivalent of the wages their bosses give them in return, and thus that they work in part without pay. And, with capitalists owning all the means of production, workers must do this in order to get a chance at making a living, and thus a chance at living at all. Therefore, workers are said to be forced to work without pay, and capitalism is said to be a form of slavery. If this sounds odd, it is because the term "slavery" normally refers to a specific historical form of forced extraction of unpaid labor (the "classical slavery" of the ancient world or antebellum America) in which individuals "owned" others—and this is not to be found in the other modes of production which Marxism calls exploitative, namely, feudalism and capitalism. Holding that these systems are forms of slavery requires thinking of the defining feature of slavery as *forced unpaid labor* which can be realized in various forms, one of which is the classical form where individuals are directly owned by other individuals. In what follows, I shall mean by "slavery" this essential core of "forced unpaid labor," and reserve the term "classical slavery" for the particular form it took in the ancient world or antebellum America. On the force-inclusive definition of exploitation, any exploitative society is a form of slavery.

My discussion and defense of the force-inclusive definition of exploitation will take the following shape. In section 1, I explicate the main terms in the definition and suggest how the definition relates to other features of the way Marxism understands societies. In particular, I indicate how exploitation relates to the labor theory of value, and how the force in it is to be understood. In section 2, I argue for the superiority of the force-inclusive definition for Marxian theory by pointing out the shortcomings of the important work of John Roemer that result from his use of the distributive definition.[2] In section 3, I discuss the applicability of the force-inclusive definition to capitalism by showing how it can solve an important problem, posed recently by G. A. Cohen, about the plausibility of the Marxian claim that workers in capitalism are forced to sell their labor power.[3]

One point of this exercise is to set up the issues in a way that enables us to see what follows for the moral assessment of capitalism if Marxian theory

is essentially correct. By this moral assessment, I mean primarily the determination of the justice of capitalism. And by that, I do not mean the determination of what Marx thought about capitalism's justice, but what we
should think, in light of *our* conception of justice, if the Marxian analysis
of capitalism is essentially correct.[4] I shall not try to complete the moral
assessment of capitalism that would determine whether it is just or not.
Rather, I try to spell out the nature of exploitation as a necessary preparation for that assessment, and attempt to show how that assessment is affected
by the determination that capitalism is exploitative.

1. EXPLOITATION, LABOR, STRUCTURAL FORCE, AND MORALITY

In this section, I present an extended gloss on the force-inclusive definition
of exploitation. I argue that it depends on a *general* version of the labor
theory of value, and on a *structural* conception of force, and that establishing that capitalism is exploitative according to this definition leaves open
the question of its justness.

Consider first the notion of "unpaid labor" in the proposed definition.
When Marxists say that workers (in any mode of production) labor without
pay, they take this to follow automatically from the claim that the workers
give more labor than they receive back in the form of compensation. In
capitalism, Marx held that workers work without pay because they give their
bosses more labor time than the amount of labor time they get back in the
form of their wage. A worker works, say, a forty-hour week and receives
back a wage which will purchase some amount of goods that it takes (whoever produces them) less than forty hours of labor to produce. The worker
gives a surplus of labor over the amount he receives in return, and this
surplus labor is held to be unpaid.

But from the fact that I give my boss more labor than I get back from
him, it does not automatically follow that the surplus I give is unpaid. It
only follows automatically if labor is the proper measure of what my boss
and I have exchanged. If, by contrast, the proper measure is, say, marginal
utility, then it is possible that my wage (meaning the goods it will purchase) represents marginal utility for me equivalent to what my work represents for my boss, even if I must work longer to produce his utility than
wage-good workers worked to produce mine. Since the application of the
definition of exploitation to capitalism rests on the assumption that surplus
labor is unpaid because it is surplus, it requires the doctrine that labor is
the proper measure of what bosses and workers trade. That means that it
requires something like "the labor theory of value." And, since the Marxian
charge of exploitation in any mode of production always rests on the no-

tion that surplus labor is ipso facto unpaid labor, I take it that the definition of exploitation generally depends on something like the labor theory of value.

I say "something like" the labor theory of value because I do not mean the whole of the theory by that name which Marx develops in *Capital*. In its specific application to capitalism, this theory holds that the market values of commodities tend to reflect (through various refractions) the relative amounts of time upon which they have been labored. This in turn is taken as implying that the prices of commodities could ultimately be transformed into the amounts of labor time normally expended in their production. And this is widely thought to be impossible, thus rendering the labor theory of value generally vulnerable and many Marxists willing to jettison it. I shall not try to defend the theory as a theory of price formation. But I do think that a more general version of the theory, which makes no claim to account for prices, is defensible and must be defended if the Marxian notion of exploitation is to be applied to capitalism, and to any other social system.

To see this more general version, consider that the labor theory of value might be thought of as a two-storied theory. On the ground floor is the notion that labor time is the sole measure of the real value that produced things have as a result of being produced. On the floor above is the notion that capitalism works (via the market, competition, and so forth) to bring the prices of produced things into some systematic relationship with the amount of time labored on them.[5] Notice that "value" means something different in this upper-floor theory, which we can call the "special labor theory of value," than it means in the ground-floor theory, which we can call the "general labor theory of value." In the former, value means something like "what a product will bring on the market," while in the latter, it means something like "what ultimately matters about a product." Though the two senses are distinct, there is an understandable relationship between them: The special labor theory of value claims that capitalism has built-in mechanisms that bring the prices of things into systematic relationship with what ultimately matters about them in any system of production.

Marx obviously held the special labor theory of value with respect to capitalism, and I think he implicitly held the general labor theory of value for all modes of production.[6] If he didn't, I contend he should have, since it is the minimum necessary to make the concept of surplus labor imply unpaid labor in any mode of production, not just one in which the capitalist price-formation mechanisms are operating. The general theory supports the charge of exploitation in capitalism even when doubts about the special theory are raised; and it can be plausibly defended, even if there are fatal flaws in the special theory.[7] Crudely and by no means completely stated, the defense is this.

An economic system is some organization of the productive labor of society and of the distribution of the products of that labor among the members of society. Such a system works by means of a system of ownership, understood in the broadest sense as any system of recognized claims on parts of the social product (including the resources that went into it). By means of a system of ownership, an economic system works so that different people end up possessing products that others have worked on.

Suppose, now, that we are surveying the various economic systems that have existed in history so that we might assess them morally. We shall surely want a neutral way of characterizing what it is that people give one another in the various systems (where "give" is understood very broadly to refer to any way in which some person undergoes a loss that ends up a gain to another). By neutral, I mean a way of characterizing that does not presuppose the validity of any of the systems of ownership that are under inspection. Accordingly, we cannot say that what people give others is equivalent to "what they give of what they own." The reason is that if ownership is not valid, then in giving what I (invalidly) "own," I may really not be giving anything but only passing on what is actually given by someone else. Indeed, it is precisely such matters that we would want to be able to identify for purposes of our moral assessment. More generally, since an economic system includes its system of ownership, measuring what people give one another in an economic system in terms of what they own in that system effectively builds a bias in favor of that system into our measurement (it allows that system to supply the measure of what is to count as giving). Thus we need a way of characterizing what people give each other in an economic system that is independent of ownership. Then, while remaining neutral on its validity, we will be able to say of any ownership system how it works to get some people to give things to others.

When nothing that presupposes the validity of the system of ownership can be used, all that remains that workers give in production is their time and energy, in a word, their labor, or as Marx had it, their "labor time" (which he understood to include a standard measure of energy exerted).[8] And this labor time is really *given* in the sense that it is "used up"—as finite human beings workers have only finite time and energy, and thus less left over when they have given some up. The same cannot be said, for example, of their talents. First of all, their talents are the result of their natural gifts plus the time and energy they devoted to developing those gifts. This time and energy counts of course, and it must be factored into labor time, so that the talented labor devoted to producing something now must include some measure of the earlier labor that went into producing that level of talent. But the "natural gifts" themselves are, as the word suggests, given to the worker and thus merely passed on by him. What's

more, talents are not used up in exercising them. If anything, they are augmented by use rather than depleted. Outside of ownership, labor, and talent, all that is left in any part of the social product are the natural materials
that went into it. And these (less the labor that went into extracting them
or working them up into usable form) are not given by anyone to anyone
else unless they are owned.

Try the following thought experiment. Suppose that A and B are equal
in their talents, and that C enslaves them both, forcing A to work two
eight-hour days and B to work one eight-hour day at the same level of
intensity (relative to their capacities). I expect that readers will agree that
what happens to A here is worse than what happens to B and that it is
roughly twice as bad (or, equivalently, that what C does to A is worse,
roughly by a factor of two, than what he does to B). Suppose that A and B
are each forced to work one eight-hour day, though A is forced to work at
twice the level of intensity that B is (again relative to their capacities).
Here too, I expect that readers will agree that what happens to (or what C
does to) A is worse than what happens to (or what C does to) B and that
it is roughly twice as bad. Suppose now that X is twice as talented as Y,
though both have devoted the same amount of time and energy to reaching
their respective levels of talent, and that Z enslaves them both, forcing
them each to work at their respective levels of talent for one eight-hour
day at the same level of intensity. Is X's enslavement twice as bad as Y's? Is
it worse at all? I think the reader will agree that their enslavements (thought
of either as their fates or as what Z does) are equally bad. Doesn't it follow
from this that (*ceteris paribus*) taking more time and energy from one person than from another amounts to taking more from the first, while taking
more talented labor from one than from another does not? I think this
reflects the recognition that what people give in laboring is their time and
energy and not their talents.

It might be objected that counting labor as given by workers presupposes
that workers *own* it. But I think that it only presupposes that labor is physically their *own*, in the way that their pains and their deaths are their own.
And this I take to be a natural fact. People give themselves in laboring;
they literally use themselves up. *Labor done, however willingly or even joy-
ously, is life itself spent.* I suspect that it is this natural fact that accounts for
the lingering appeal of the labor theory of value, and for the reluctance of
many Marxists to part with the theory in the face of apparently unanswerable objections to it. In any event no stronger notion of ownership is implied here than is implied in the standard Marxist usage of the term
"alienation."

It might also be objected that the general labor theory of value is itself a
moral theory, in that it seems to give a kind of moral priority to labor time

for purposes of moral assessment of economic systems. I grant this point, but I do not regard it as an objection. We arrive at the general labor theory looking for a way of characterizing what people give in productive arrangements that is neutral, not cosmically neutral, but neutral regarding the validity of systems of ownership. As long as the general theory can be formulated neutrally in this respect, it will do what we want even if it is not morally neutral in some ultimate sense. That we reach it by looking for means to assess economic systems morally already suggests that what we will find is something that matters morally, and that it will have some moral implications about how we determine the validity of ownership systems. But it will do its job as long as it does no more than this while leaving open the final determination of their validity.[9] In fact, rather than an objection, this is a confirmation. As Marx and Marxists use the term exploitation, it is a descriptive notion which carries a strong negative moral presumption with it. The general labor theory accounts for this peculiar quasi-moral nature of the concept of exploitation.

Consider now the term "force" in the proposed definition. The force in capitalism is as elusive as the unpaid nature of surplus labor in capitalism. This is because, unlike the masters of classical slaves, capitalists are normally prohibited from using physical violence against their workers either on the job or at the negotiating table. Consequently, that workers are forced to work in order not to starve (or more recently, in order not to be reduced to surviving minimally on the dole) appears as no more than the natural fact that food doesn't fall from the sky and thus people must work in order to eat. The invisibility of exploitative force in capitalism results from the fact that, in capitalism, overt force is supplanted by force built into the very structure of the system of ownership and the classes defined by that system. Because there is the human institution of private ownership of means of production by a small class of people, the members of the class of nonowners are forced to work *for those people*—though not necessarily forced *by* those people—in order to get a crack at a living at all. Accordingly, I take it that the force in our definition must apply not only to overt violence, but to force that is "structural," both in its effects and in its origins.

Take the effects first: Unlike the usual strongarm stuff that singles out particular individuals as its targets, this force works on people by virtue of their location in the social structure (that is, for example, qua members of some class), and it affects individuals more or less "statistically." By this I mean that *such force affects individuals by imposing an array of fates on some group while leaving it open how particular individuals in that group get sorted, or sort themselves, into those fates.* The term "structural" is appropriate for such force because it works the way that a physical structure such as a bottleneck (in the road) imposes fates on groups, forcing a majority of cars to slow down while leaving it to chance and other factors who makes up that majority and who gets into the minority that slips easily through.

This force is structural in its origin also: Though the force works to transfer labor from one class to another, it is not the benefiting class that forces the losing one—rather the structure of the ownership or class system itself forces the transfer. (Among the roles constituting a structure, some will be assigned the dirty work of administering violence; but I take this to be a tool of structural force, not the thing itself.)

To get a handle on the notion of structural force, picture a large crowd of spectators who must pass through a human bottleneck as they leave a stadium. I mean "human bottleneck" quite literally. Imagine that people are standing shoulder to shoulder in the shape of a bottleneck and that the crowd must pass through this human funnel to get out of the stadium. The people making up the human bottleneck are there with varying degrees of intentionalness, some are there just minding their own business and some are there because they want the crowd to have to pass through just this sort of shape. But all are inclined to stay where they are because they want to, or believe they should or must, or because they are conditioned to, or some combination of these. If people in the crowd try to break through the human bottleneck, they will at least be resisted, and where they succeed in making an opening, people from other points on the bottleneck will move to seal it up and prevent their passing through. And other bottleneckers will at least support this and even offer to lend a hand. The crowd leaving the stadium, then, will find in this bottleneck varying degrees of resistance to their attempts to break through it, but enough so that they will have to adapt their flow to the shape.

It seems to me that we can say here that the crowd is forced into a certain pattern by the structure of the human bottleneck. Note that this force works its effects "statistically." Some people—say, those who move quickly to the head of the crowd—will hardly be slowed or constrained at all; they may follow the same path they would have had there been no one else there. And the force originates structurally. To be sure, the bottleneck structure is manned by real individuals, but they play their roles more or less unthinkingly, and none of those who play their roles thinkingly could succeed in keeping the crowd in the shape were it not for the rest of the people making up the bottleneck. The result of their all generally playing their roles is to force the crowd to take on the shape of the bottleneck, while leaving undetermined which individual will end up in each particular spot inside that shape.

The institution of private property is like the human bottleneck. A large number of people play roles—as judges, lawyers, police officers, laborers, consumers, real estate agents, voters, and so on—in that institution, thinkingly and unthinkingly, more or less actively. And it is the overall shape of those roles that forces a certain pattern of options on the people subject to it, while leaving it open exactly which options are forced on which particular individuals.[10]

I shall not launch a full-scale justification of using the term "force" in this way. Note, however, that the features of standard cases of force are here in recognizable if somewhat altered form. First, in the standard cases we take force to limit people's options by making all their alternatives but one either unacceptable or prohibitively costly (as in "your money or your life"). With structural force, people's options are limited by their social position to a *range* of things they can do, with options outside this range unacceptable or prohibitively costly. So, by virtue of occupying a social position defined, say, by lack of access to means of production, a person will be limited to a range of ways in which he can achieve a living, because alternatives outside this range (such as starvation or begging or crime) are unacceptable or prohibitively costly. Second, in the standard cases of force, it is exercised intentionally by human beings. Structural force is a kind of leverage over people to which they are vulnerable by virtue of their location in the social structure. But the social structure—say, a caste or property system—is nothing but a pattern of human behavior.[11] So, while structural force need not be exercised intentionally, there is no doubt that it is exerted by human beings.[12] And if it is not intentional, it is in principle something that, by making people aware of the effects of their actions, could be made intentional; and in fact, if enough people became aware, they could alter this force or rightly be held to intend it.

More controversial is the following. In the standard cases, the target of force has no real choice over his fate, either because all his alternatives save one are unacceptable, or because he has no alternatives at all (perhaps he has been bound or drugged). In structural force, by contrast, there is some *play*. Structural force works to constrain a group of individuals to some array of situations, leaving it to them or to other factors to determine how they are distributed among those situations. Therefore, between the forcing structure and its effects there can be room for the operation of free and rational choice on the part of individuals affected. That is, while people are constrained to the set of situations in the array (because alternatives outside the array are unacceptable or prohibitively costly), they may be able to exercise real choice among those in the array, selecting the one that they find most desirable. Nonetheless, I contend that, as long as the group is constrained such that its members must end up distributed among all the situations in the array determined by the structure, all the individuals are "forced into" the particular situations in which they end up—even if they exercised some choice on the way. In short, structural force can operate through free choice. And the reason for this is that force need not only take advantage of your fear (say, of dying)—it can also work, indeed often more effectively, by taking advantage of your rationality.

Suppose an outlaw is laying in wait for a stagecoach, in which he knows there will be six passengers each wearing a gold watch worth twenty dollars and each carrying about that amount in cash. Our outlaw wants to emerge with three watches and sixty dollars but is indifferent about who gives which. He resolves then to give the passengers a chance to choose which they will give, although if their choices don't arrive at his desired outcome he will rescind the privilege and just take three watches and sixty dollars. Stopping the coach, gun in hand, he orders the passengers to give him either their watch or their cash. The passengers are utility maximizers who regard their watches and their twenty dollars as comparably desirable, though each has a decided if small preference for one or the other. As luck would have it, their preferences match the outlaw's desired outcome, and three give up their watches and three their cash.

Now, take one passenger at random who, say, has given up his watch. Is it not the case that he was forced to give up the watch? It certainly seems odd to say that he wasn't forced to give up his watch because he had an acceptable alternative. To say that seems to focus excessively on what happens in the last moment just before the passenger handed over his watch and to pay too little attention to the fact that the situation had been set up so that there was a good chance that by allowing him (and the others) to choose (rationally, in light of their preferences), the outlaw would succeed in subordinating their wills to his ends.

Suppose that at the moment our outlaw stops the coach and makes his threat another stranger passes by and offers to protect the three passengers who would have given up their watches. Our protector, however, wants sixty dollars for his trouble. Suppose now that the passengers decide to give up their watches (on the same grounds that they decided this in the first example), and thus turn down the offer of protection. If you held that the passenger in the first example was not forced to give up his watch, mustn't you hold that now? If so, you would have to say that the passenger freely chose to be robbed, or that he was not robbed but gave away his watch freely—which is preposterous. I take it then that a person can be said to be forced to do something even if he has rationally chosen that thing from among other acceptable alternatives, provided that the whole array of alternatives can be said to be forced upon him.

This will be no news to con artists and spy-story authors. They well know that a free choice can be the last link in the chain that ties a person to a forced fate. It is possible to get someone to do your bidding by setting up a situation in which doing your bidding is your victim's most rational choice, even if there are other choices which are acceptable though less rational for him. It is easy to overlook this, since when a person does what is most rational for him because it is most rational, and not just because it is the only thing acceptable, he seems to be acting freely. And, to an extent he is. But rather than showing that he is thus not forced, what that shows is that force can work through his free choice. An intelligent forcer can take advantage of the fact that, left free, people will normally do what is most rational for them. And this is an advantage because when people do another's bidding this way, they are less likely to see (or feel) that they are being forced. Accordingly, force can be more effective because less visible if it can work through people's predictable free choices. For this very reason we must free ourselves from the notion that force occurs only when a person is presented with alternatives all of which are unacceptable but one. Otherwise, we shall miss the way in which social structures force fates on people while appearing to leave their fates up to them.

When Marx wrote that the wage-worker "is compelled to sell himself of his own free will" (C 1:766), he was not being arch or paradoxical. He was telling us both how force works in capitalism *and* why it is unseen. Indeed, I contend that what Marxists call capitalist ideology boils down to little more than the invisibility of structural force. And libertarian capitalism is the theory that results when the love of freedom falls prey to that invisibility.[13]

How much real choice people have over which of the situations they end up in will be a matter of how much play there is in the structural force. I shall say that where people can choose among the situations in the array to which they are constrained, the relative acceptability of the alternative situations one can choose among determines whether one is "tightly" or "loosely" forced into the situation one ends up in. Suppose, then, that a structure imposes on people an array of two situations, A and B, while leaving it to them to choose which they will end up in. If B is considerably less acceptable than A, I would say that those who end up in A have been (relatively) tightly forced (by the structure) into A. If A and B are roughly comparable in acceptability, I would say that those who end up in A have been (relatively) loosely forced there (by the structure)—though still truly forced. And in general, the greater the number of acceptable nonredundant alternatives in an array, the more loosely individuals are forced into the ones in which they end up.

Bear in mind that the array of situations determined by a social structure is not an arbitrary matter. Unless a structure deploys enough of its people in each of the situations necessary to its functioning, that structure will soon break down. Accordingly, we should not be surprised to find that structures normally have play in them up to the point that leaving outcomes to choice will yield the needed distribution of individuals—just as much play as there was in our outlaw's force.

In section 3, we shall have occasion to put this notion of structural force into use, and to consider additional grounds for its plausibility. For the present, if it still sounds strange to speak this way, consider the possibility that our language has been shaped in ways that serve structural force by making us unlikely to label it. What if this is just how we have to be able to talk about societies in order to morally assess them correctly? What if the fact that there is a role for choice blinds us to the force that is at work determining the shape of the larger terrain within which we choose? What if the very salience of the standard forms of direct or violent force blinds us to the less visible indirect ways in which force can work? I contend that all a social structure has to do to count as forcing fates on its members is force them into an array of fates among which they will be distributed or distribute themselves in some manner within the limits of tolerance necessary to the functioning of that structure. This is all that is necessary, because, for the purpose of moral assessment of social structures, what is crucial is how they constrain people's lives, and that is so even if there is enough play in that constraint to allow a role for choice. To insist on more, in determining what should count as force, is to be overly dominated in one's imagination by the image of one person physically forcing or threatening another.[14]

Marx counsels that the illusion about the nature of capitalism "vanishes immediately, if, instead of taking a single capitalist and a single labourer, we take the class of capitalists and the class of labourers as a whole" (C 1:568). Applied to force, this would require us to open ourselves to the possibility of a kind of force that operates from the shape of the social structure itself and on classes as a whole. I contend that something like this is necessary to free ourselves from illusions about how force operates in capitalism. And more generally, it is necessary if we are to give concrete sense to claims such as Rawls's that "unjust social arrangements are themselves a kind of extortion, even violence."[15]

Note that, as the force in exploitation is structural, so is the exploitation itself. Unpaid labor is extracted from the class of laborers as a whole and put at the disposal of the other class as a whole, rather than individual laborers each dumping their quantum of unpaid labor into the hands of individuals in the receiving class. Thus, even if some highly paid workers in fact receive more labor time in their wage than they give on the job, it can still be said that the working class is exploited as long as the total time it labors is more than the labor time it gets back in wages. Here too, the structure affects individuals in a statistical way.

The final feature of the definition on which I shall comment (briefly) is its relation to morality. I contend that the claim that capitalism is exploitative is compatible with its being just, or at least being the most just system actually possible. In defense of this, I shall make three points. The first, and most obvious, is that the fact that a system is exploitative and thus slavery creates a presumption against its justice, but no more. In principle that presumption could be overridden. Even those who think that slavery is invariably evil generally allow that there are conceivable conditions under which it could be just.[16] And this is given added support by the fact that, since capitalist slavery is not classical slavery, it is possible that some of the features that make the latter particularly awful are absent or can be moderated in the former. Second, social systems must be assessed as systems, not piecemeal. That it is exploitative is only one feature of capitalism. Capitalism is also a system (as Marx well saw) that dramatically increases the productivity of labor, and thus that has the capacity to raise the standard of material well-being while reducing the amount of labor needed to produce it. Marx understood this as capitalism's historical mission (C 3:441, 819–20). Moreover, advanced capitalist societies have been characterized by an undeniably large range of personal and political freedom, which materialists at least must suspect is somehow linked to the structure of the capitalist mode of production. I shall have more to say about this at the end of this article. For the present, it suffices to say that if capitalism is judged as a whole system, and if its productivity and freedom are in some way inextricably linked to its mode of extracting unpaid labor, the overall judgment of capitalism's justice cannot be determined exclusively by the fact of its exploitativeness.

Third, social systems must be assessed in terms of what is really possible in history, not just what is in principle desirable. Marx actually said very little about the socialism and communism he hoped or expected would replace capitalism. In his writings, these appear as little more than theoretical constructs arrived at by negating the troublesome features of capitalism. If capitalism is exploitative because of private ownership of the means of production, then we can project in theory the remedy for this in the form of collective ownership, first via the state in socialism, and then directly in communism. But judgments about capitalism cannot fairly be made by comparing its reality with some ideal system. It must be compared with what is actually possible. And here it is an open question whether systems of collective ownership can actually be made to function in a way which overall is superior to the way in which capitalism does function. Thus, even if capitalism is exploitative, it might, as a matter of historical fact, be the most just system actually possible. My point here is not to assert this, but to make clear that it is not foreclosed by finding capitalism exploitative.

2. EXPLOITATION, FORCE, AND ROEMER

Capitalism, wrote Marx, is a system of "forced labour—no matter how much it may seem to result from free contractual agreement" (C 3:819). Thus, once the surface appearances are penetrated, capitalism is revealed to share the essential feature that characterized feudalism and classical slavery. All three modes of production are systems of forced labor, though the mechanism by means of which the force operates is different, and sometimes different enough to obscure the underlying likeness. In classical slavery, labor is extracted by overt violence wielded by masters, and in feudalism, by overt violence wielded by landlords or their henchmen. In capitalism, by contrast, the "dull compulsion of economic relations" enforces the extraction and "direct force, outside economic conditions is used only . . . exceptionally" (C, 1:737, 3:791–92). Thus Marx characterizes the "transformation of feudal exploitation into capitalist exploitation" as a "change of form" of the laborer's servitude (C 1:715). And in a letter to P. V. Annenkov, Marx contrasts the "indirect . . . slavery of the proletariat" to the "direct slavery . . . of the black races in . . . the Southern States of North America."[17]

In my view, the theory called "historical materialism" is the conjunction of two hypotheses. The *materialist* hypothesis is that the decisive feature (the one that predominantly though not exclusively shapes all the other features) of a social structure is the way in which it channels the productive activities by means of which the material conditions of existence are secured. Accordingly, social structures are identified by their dominant "mode of production" and other social arrangements are in general understood by the functions they serve in promoting, defending, and reproducing the mode of production. The *historical* hypothesis is that all modes of production (after primitive communism if it really existed, and until socialism if it is really possible) are forms of exploitation of producers by nonproducers, and that history moves from one such form of exploitation to another pushed by the growing ability to wring a living from nature (growth in the forces of production) as this interacts with the tensions inevitable in arrangements (relations of production) in which part of the human species is forced, one way or another, to produce the means of existence for another part.[18] In short, the Marxian claim is that history is the succession of social systems which, each in its own way, work to force some to produce without compensation for others, and thus each is a form of slavery (until of course socialism arrives to end this). This centrality of concern with force is why Marxism is a theory of *political* economy, not just of economy.

In this section, I want to show that the force-inclusive definition of exploitation is superior to the distributive definition for Marxian theory. I do not think that it is possible to prove definitively that Marx *meant* the force-inclusive definition rather than the distributive, by reference to Marxian scriptural sources.[19] Marx was not consistent enough in his use of terms to support such a proof, and more important, it is Marxian theory that ought to be our concern, not what went on in the mind of Marx the person. My claim can be understood as urging that the force-inclusive definition is the one that Marx should have put forth, and that Marxists should subscribe to, to give the theory its sharpest cutting edge.

Perhaps the best argument for adopting the force-inclusive definition is the work of John Roemer. Roemer has written a series of closely argued essays on the Marxian concept of exploitation, in which this concept is defined strictly distributively, "as the unequal exchange of labor for goods: the exchange is unequal when the amount of labor embodied in the goods which the worker can purchase with his income (which usually consists only of wage income) is less than the amount of labor he expended to earn that income" (SM, 30). This is from the opening line of an article entitled "Should Marxists Be Interested in Exploitation?" in which Roemer tries to prove they should not. In my view, what he actually proves is that Marxists should not be interested in exploitation defined as the unequal transfer of labor *without reference to the fact that the transfer is forced.* All Roemer's conclusions about the uninterestingness of exploitation follow from his distributive definition of it, and thus prove the uninterestingness of exploitation defined distributively. Roemer's work shows the danger of treating Marxism as a theory of economy rather than as a theory of *political* economy.

Roemer's attack on exploitation is in two stages, the second of which is reflected in the negative answer he argues for in "Should Marxists Be Interested in Exploitation?" The first stage is Roemer's proposal—defended in "Property Relations vs. Surplus Value in Marxian Exploitation"—for replacing (what he took to be) the standard Marxian "surplus-value" definition of exploitation with a "property-relations" definition. "Marxian exploitation," writes Roemer, "is defined as the expropriation of surplus labor . . . at the point of production" (PR, 281). The "property-relations" definition which is to supplant this "surplus-value" definition is rather elaborate and technical (PR, 285), but nicely paraphrased by Roemer (in a subsequent article) as: "a group of economic agents [is] exploited if they would be better off under a redistribution of assets in which everyone in the society were endowed with exactly the same amount of alienable assets, and if their complement [the group with whom they interact economically] in society would be worse off (in terms of income) under this distribution" (WR, 81). On this definition, then, workers are exploited when they are economically disadvantaged as a result of an unequal distribution of property.

Note that both the "surplus value" and the "property relations" definitions are distributive definitions of exploitation; they make no reference to force. Moreover, while "unequal exchange of labor" is the core of the surplus-value definition, it still plays a role in the property-relations definition. In the property-relations definition, unequal exchange of labor is exploitation insofar as the unequal exchange results from the suspect property relations. Thus, in the first stage of his attack, Roemer replaces one distributive definition with another. And if anything, that other is even more distributive than the first, since the "property relations approach implies that exploitation takes place because of the distribution of the means of production, not at the point of production" (PR, 284). Exploitation then can occur simply in exchange, even between different countries (PR, 298–300). With exploitation stripped both of force and reference to production, it is indeed not very interesting. And so the ground is prepared for the final stage of the assault in "Should Marxists Be Interested in Exploitation?" However, both stages are marked by what I take to be Roemer's characteristic mistake: Having defined exploitation distributively, he is able to show the weakness of the concept so defined. From this, he infers that the problem is with the concept of exploitation. But this doesn't follow, since the problem might be with his definition of it.

For example, in the first stage of his attack, Roemer sets up a comparison of two hypothetical cases, which is supposed to prove the superiority of the property-relations over the surplus-value definition (PR, 286–90). In both hypothetical cases, there are two technologies for producing corn, a "farm technology" in which corn is produced using only labor (presumably through the harvesting of wild corn), and a "factory technology" in which corn is produced with labor and seed (capital). In both cases, people desire only to subsist, which requires b bushels of corn per day. It takes sixteen hours to produce b on the farm and eight hours to produce b in the factory. And, finally, society possesses *half* the seed corn necessary to produce b for everyone, and this seed corn is distributed to everyone in equal shares.

In the first hypothetical case, everyone works four hours in the factory using his share of seed corn to produce $1/2\ b$ for himself, and then eight hours on the farm to produce the other $1/2\ b$ he needs to subsist. Everyone here works twelve hours, and, says Roemer, "there is no exploitation." In the second hypothetical case, with the same equal distribution of seed corn, two-thirds of the society (called H) offer their seed for members of the remaining third (called S) to work on. Here each S works four hours on one H's seed producing $1/2\ b$ of which the S gets $1/4\ b$ as his wage and the H keeps $1/4\ b$ as his profit; then that same S does the same thing for a second H (remember there are twice as many Hs as Ss). At this point Ss will have earned $1/2\ b$, without using any of their seed capital, and Hs will have each earned 1/4 *b* and used up all their capital. Accordingly, Ss will have to work an additional four hours in the factory using their own seed to produce their remaining 1/2 *b*, and Hs will have to work on the farm for twelve hours to produce their remaining 3/4 *b*. Thus, everyone in the society (S or H) starts with an equal share of seed, works twelve hours, and ends up with his *b*—the same as in the first case.

Roemer takes these two cases to show the superiority of the property-relations over the surplus-value definition of exploitation because the property relations definition yields "correct" judgments about the existence of exploitation in the two cases, and the surplus-value definition does not. According to the surplus value definition, while there is no exploitation in the first case, there is in the second case, because "each producer in S does produce 1/2 *b* of surplus product, which is expropriated by two agents in H." But Roemer claims "it is incorrect, intuitively, to view S as exploited by H [in the second case], for the outcome of each producer working twelve hours is identical [to the first case], where clearly there is no exploitation" (PR, 289). He then goes on to show that the "property relations definition renders the intuitively correct judgment," namely, that no exploitation occurs in either case.

But victory for the property relations definition results from the fact that Roemer only tests it against another distributive definition. In the two cases, the force-inclusive definition yields the same judgments as the property-relations definition. The second case is not exploitation according to the force-inclusive definition, since the Ss have the choice of working the way they did in the first case, and thus are not forced to work for the Hs. Moreover, consider what happens when we try to alter the second case to introduce force into it without altering either the egalitarian distributions of original endowments, of hours worked, and corn realized. This is no easy feat, but it might be done if we think of the Hs getting out and working their twelve hours on the farm just before a tornado wipes out the remaining wild corn, and before the Ss have decided what they are going to do. In this third case, the Ss have no choice but to work for the Hs as they did (voluntarily) in the second case. Everything else remains the same, so that everyone starts out with his equal share of seed, everyone works twelve hours, and everyone ends up with his *b*. Are the Ss exploited by the Hs? I don't think one can put terribly much stock in intuitions about such cooked-up cases, but it seems to me at least intuitively plausible to say that the Ss are exploited here. And if that is so, then the force-inclusive definition yields the "intuitively correct judgment" while the property-relations definition does not.

As I indicated earlier, the upshot of Roemer's first stage is that exploitation is still unequal labor exchange, but only insofar as such exchange is the outcome of inequality in original productive assets. That is, exploita-

tion occurs when those rich in assets are able (because of their greater assets) to get more labor from the asset-poor than they give to the asset-poor.
Roemer's second stage builds on this first stage in the following way. Having (supposedly) proven, in the article just discussed and elsewhere, "that
the existence of exploitation is equivalent to inequality in distribution of
initial assets . . . ," Roemer continues, "I now go further and claim that in
the general case, exploitation theory leads to results which may conflict
directly with the inequality-of-productive-assets theory" (SM, 52–53). That
is, having argued that the heart of exploitation lies in the unequal exchange
of labor that occurs between the asset-poor and the asset-rich to the benefit
of the latter, he will now cut that heart out by showing that "it can happen
that the asset-rich are exploited by the asset-poor: the flow of surplus value
goes the 'wrong way'" (SM, 54).

Roemer argues that, given their preferences for leisure versus goods, an
owner of small productive assets who would prefer no work at a small income can exploit an owner of large productive assets who is willing to work
to get a larger income. This is possible because the first might lend his
assets to the second for just enough to amount to what is called in Jane
Austen's novels "a small living," and not work at all. Then the two would
be living off of the labor of the second, which, since the first wasn't laboring
at all, would constitute an unequal labor exchange in favor of the first. The
poor would be exploiting the rich (SM, 58–59). Based on this, Roemer
writes, "When exploitation accounts reflect the unequal distribution of productive assets in the proper way (that the rich exploit the poor), that is
what makes exploitation theory attractive. But if that correlation can fail,
as it has, then no foundation remains for a justification of exploitation theory"
(SM, 59). Adios, exploitation.

We see here another example of what I have called Roemer's characteristic mistake. Having defined exploitation distributively, he shows its weakness, and then concludes that the problem is with exploitation, not with
his definition. And as in the earlier example, the defect that Roemer claims
to have found with exploitation is a defect in the distributive definition,
and it can be easily rectified with the force-inclusive definition. To wit:
The unequal labor exchange from the asset-rich borrower to the asset-poor
lender is not exploitation since the asset-rich individual, being rich in assets, did not have to borrow to live (or even to live modestly well), and
thus was not forced to labor for the asset-poor individual.

So far I have shown that Roemer's conclusions about exploitation stem
from, and only apply to, exploitation defined distributively. Exploitation as
the forced extraction of unpaid labor is untouched by his argument. I now
want to point out the ways in which the distributive definition is costly to
Marxism. First of all, taking the crucial feature of the relationship between

capitalists and workers to lie in the inequality of the productive assets they own takes the teeth out of the Marxian critique. While it is true that inequality is one way of characterizing the difference between owning some means of production and owning none, it is surely not strong enough to support the claim that the owners of none are indirect slaves—anymore than claiming that classical masters and slaves have unequal freedom, while true, is strong enough to support the charge that the latter are direct slaves. It is not inequality in productive assets per se that makes the difference, but a particular inequality, that between owning some means of production and owning none. And what is crucial about this is not simply that it leads to unequal labor exchanges, since it would lead to that among people who owned means of production even if no one owned none. What is crucial must be a way in which those who own none are disadvantaged even compared to those who own some but little. And this must be the particular way in which owning none makes one wholly dependent on those who own some for one's very existence. And that is morally interesting even if a few poor rentiers live off the labor of wealthy petit bourgeois businessmen.

In addition to weakening the Marxian critique, the distributive definition of exploitation is costly to Marxian theory in other ways. If it is possible for owners of small capital to exploit owners of large capital, then the class relation, which is presumably central to Marxian accounts of capitalism (and of other modes of production as well), is only contingently related to exploitation. For Marx, the class relation is the axis along which capitalist exploitation runs, so to speak, from owners of means of production to nonowners. But with exploitation defined distributively, it is possible—as Roemer has shown—for owners of means of production to exploit one another.[20] Striking confirmation of this displacement of class from center stage is found in Roemer's use of "rich" and "poor" as important defining features of economic agents. Rich and poor do not define class positions; they refer to distributive outcomes. Not surprisingly these terms play no theoretical role for Marx.

Equally telling is the fact that defining exploitation as unequal transfer of labor renders the selection of labor for this role arbitrary. Among its other roles, exploitation of labor functions in Marxian theory to account for the production of capitalists' profits. A certain amount of labor time expended on a certain amount of raw material, say, wood, produces a commodity with more value than the value of the labor and of the wood that went into it. Marx explains this by holding that of all the inputs it is labor that can produce more than its own value. But strictly speaking, we could posit any input as the expanding one. We might say that the resulting commodity embodied the same value of labor as went into it, but that the wood had expanded in value (SM, 36). Then if we insist on labor we seem to be making a selection that cannot be justified by reference to the facts, and this must reflect a prior moral preference.

And at least before he gave up entirely on exploitation, Roemer seemed prepared to embrace such a preference: "As Marxists, we look at history and see poor workers fighting rich capitalists. To explain this, or to justify it, or to direct it and provide it with ideological ammunition, we construct a theory of exploitation in which the two antagonistic sides become classified as the exploiters and exploited. . . . Labor power is uniquely suited . . . for this task" (*ND*, 274–75). Even aside from the fact that we only rarely see workers fighting capitalists, and hardly more frequently than we see workers and capitalists fighting among themselves, this argument cannot work.

There are many ways to *explain* fighting between poor workers and rich capitalists, including, say, the poor's inveterate cantankerousness, or displaced frustration, or their envy of and resentment for their natural superiors, and so on. If we omit these possibilities in favor of an explanation that *justifies* the struggles of the poor, then we must *already* believe that the poor are poor as a result of some unfairness. If we think that the theory that the poor are exploited can justify their struggles, then we must believe that exploitation is the unfairness that results in their poverty. And since this belief is the basis upon which we believe that the struggles of the poor can be justified, the belief that the poor are exploited is already presupposed if we think that it can justify their struggles. What's more, to believe that the poor are exploited we must already have some theory of what constitutes (not just what causes) exploitation. And if that theory is that labor is uncompensated, we must *already* believe in something like the labor theory of exploitation if we think that the struggles of the poor are justifiable. It follows that we cannot select the labor theory of exploitation *in order to* explain and justify the struggles of the poor, since the notion that this theory can justify those struggles presupposes that we already believe that the theory is true. Nor could we select the theory to guide the poor in their struggles, since if it is not true independently, then it is likely to *misguide* the poor.[21]

Roemer's argument here is tantamount to assuming that tobacco is the cause of cancer in order to explain and justify the struggles of anticancer groups against tobacco companies. Since the justifiability of their struggles depends on the (prior) truth of the claim that tobacco causes cancer, we can't assume that truth in order to justify their struggles. Nor, of course, can we assume it to guide their struggles, since unless it is true, struggle against tobacco companies is unlikely to improve people's chances of avoiding cancer.

By contrast, if exploitation is defined as including force, then taking labor as the substance of what is forced is not arbitrary. Only human beings can be forced, and—with belief in the validity of property systems suspended—

the only thing that can be forced out of them in production is their time and energy, that is, their labor time. If exploitation is defined strictly distributively, it is arbitrary whether it is labor that gets exploitatively distributed. However, if exploitation is defined as including force, then it is only labor that can be exploited. *This shows that force and labor are a natural pair, and thus it exhibits the inner coherence of including both in the definition of exploitation.*

Moreover, I contend that including force in the definition of exploitation supplies us with precisely what Roemer's property-relations theory of exploitation does not supply him—the reason for thinking that exploitation is morally important. Replying to some criticisms of his argument about the grounds for selecting labor as the substance of exploitation, Roemer links that argument to his belief that it is inequality in the ownership of productive assets that is the villain: "The reason we consider workers to be exploited is because they do not have access to their share of the means of production; that is why we call their labor expropriated" (R, 387). But immediately thereafter, Roemer confesses that "what I have not defended— nor to my knowledge, has anyone else very successfully defended—is *why* Marxists consider relations based on inegalitarian distribution of the means of production to be exploitative" (R, 388). But this is because he has ignored the answer to this question that Marx and Engels already gave in *The Communist Manifesto*. There, they say that it is not all property or even all private appropriation that communists aim to abolish. They aim only to abolish private ownership of means of production because it gives owners "the power to subjugate the labour of others."[22] And while this is not (for reasons I have already mentioned) definitive grounds for moral condemnation, neither is it an arbitrary or dubious moral preference (particularly in light of the arguments given earlier in defense of the general labor theory of value). Indeed, I suspect that what nondubious or nonarbitrary moral import Roemer's property-relations definition of exploitation has, it gets in the form of light reflected from the Marxian force-inclusive definition.

Roemer does not ignore force entirely. He takes up the question of the relationship between exploitation and force in the form of what he calls the domination of workers by capitalists. Since he has already defined exploitation distributively, he poses the question as that of whether "exploitation can be shown to imply domination of workers by capitalists" (SM, 38–39). It should be clear from the fact that he has already shown that exploitation can occur between owners of productive assets, that he will show that it does not imply this domination. More interesting is how Roemer defines domination. He distinguishes two forms. The first is the use of force to maintain private property in means of production (essentially "police power protecting assets, preventing their expropriation by those not owning them" [SM, 40]), and the second is domination in the workplace ("the hierarchical and autocratic structure of work" [SM, 39]).

In my view, neither of these is *the* force that ought to be included in the definition of exploitation. That force is strictly the leverage that ownership of means of production gives owners over nonowners, in a social structure that has these two social positions. This leverage is likely to be supported by police enforcement—but it need not be in principle. Owners would have the leverage if all the workers believed (correctly or incorrectly) that ownership were just and thus acceded to it voluntarily. Or, if you will, owners would have it if they were the only ones tall enough to reach the switches that start up the means of production, or if the means of production could only be operated with a secret password known only to capitalists. On the other hand, given this leverage, it is likely that workplaces will be organized hierarchically and autocratically—but they need not be in principle. Owners might successfully use their power by encouraging spontaneity and democratic decision making among workers. Or, as Roemer himself points out, labor unions may effectively control the workplace, without challenging capitalists' ownership of it (R, 377–78). This suggests that Roemer's exclusion of force from exploitation is connected to missing generally the way force operates in capitalism. It is to this that we now turn.

3. CAPITALISM, FORCE, AND COHEN

G. A. Cohen has argued, first, that workers in capitalism are *individually free* to stop selling their labor power, and thus none is forced to sell his labor power; and second, that all workers cannot stop selling their labor power together, and thus that workers in capitalism are *collectively unfree* to stop selling their labor power. The argument for the first of the two conclusions is that there exist in (at least some) capitalist societies more possibilities of escape into the petit bourgeoisie than workers who attempt to escape. "One thinks," Cohen writes,

> of those [members of certain immigrant groups] who are willing to work very long hours in shops bought from native British bourgeois, shops which used to close early. Their initial capital is typically an amalgam of savings, which they accumulated, perhaps painfully, while still in the proletarian condition, and some form of external finance. *Objectively speaking*, most British proletarians are in a position to obtain these. Therefore most British proletarians are not forced to sell their labor power. (SP, 7).

To this, Cohen adds that capitalism cannot tolerate too many defections from the industrial working force, so that if very many workers took this escape route, it would be closed off. Then, as might be said of a group of people in a room from which one and only one might escape but no one tries, each is free to escape—until someone tries. "If enough workers were to exercise their freedom to escape, then the rest would lose it. The freedom each has is conditional on very few using it. That shows that, as well as being individually free to leave the working class, they are collectively unfree to do so" (AW, 102; see also SP, 14).

By the time he finishes, Cohen expresses some reservations about the first part of this conclusion. He considers that workers may not try for the available escapes into the petit bourgeoisie because they have personal deficiencies (lack of skills or appropriate attitudes) which, if caused by capitalism, might count as "forcing" them not to escape (SP, 27). He entertains the possibility that, with its risks and costs of failure, trying to become a petit bourgeois might be bad enough to count as an unacceptable alternative, and thus render the worker "forced" to stay where he is (SP, 31). And he allows that there may be some capitalist countries where in fact enough workers are trying to get into the petit bourgeoisie so that the escape routes are clogged, "forcing" the remaining individuals to stay where they are (SP, 32). Of these three reservations, the first and third tend to cancel each other out, and the second is intuitively implausible. If the escape routes might be clogged, that suggests that capitalism cannot be imposing enough deficiencies to account for why they are not being used where they are not clogged. And to say that trying to become a petit bourgeois is unacceptable in the sense that would render a worker forced to stay where he was requires believing not only that its risks are greater than, say, those of being a coal miner, but so much greater as to count as forcing coal miners to stay where they are. In any event, I take it that Cohen is not so tempted by any of these reservations to doubt that the argument and its conclusion are worth considering as they stand. I shall follow suit. Noting that the argument and conclusion are not Cohen's final work on the matter, I shall take them up in their unreserved form.

While I think that Cohen is on to something here, I think he has not correctly understood the Marxian claim that workers in capitalism are forced to sell their labor power. Consequently, he has misinterpreted the implications for Marxian theory of the argument under consideration. To show this, I shall make three points. First, I shall argue that there are two senses of the Marxian claim about force, of which one sense is more important to the theory than the other, and that Cohen's argument that workers are individually free but collectively unfree to stop selling their labor power concerns only the less important. Second, I shall argue that if my account of structural force is accepted, then even the less important sense of the Marxian claim withstands Cohen's attack. And third, I shall try to show that Cohen's argument does have important implications for the moral assessment of capitalism even if my first two points against it are established.

The Marxian claim that workers in capitalism are forced to sell their labor power is really two claims, which we might distinguish as "synchronic" and "diachronic," since the first is a claim about capitalism at any given moment and the second a claim about capitalism over time: The synchronic claim is that the structure of capitalism—meaning the fact that it is characterized by owners and nonowners of means of production—works "to force nonowners to sell their labor power to owners of means of production." The diachronic claim is that the structure of capitalism works "to force nonowners to have to *continue* to sell their labor power to owners of means of production."

Note a few features of these claims. First, the diachronic claim includes the synchronic. Fully stated, the diachronic claim is that "*the structure of capitalism works to force nonowners of means of production to remain nonowners of means of production* and thus (via the synchronic claim) to continue to have to sell their labor power." The emphasized words in the last sentence also constitute a diachronic claim, not about sale of labor power, but about the way members of the working class are forced to remain members of the working class. Let's call this embedded diachronic claim the "class-diachronic" claim. Then the diachronic claim (by which I shall always mean the full statement given at the beginning of this paragraph, or its briefer equivalent given at the end of the previous paragraph) is the sum of the class-diachronic claim plus the synchronic claim. This rather clumsy terminology will come in handy when we need to distinguish the diachronic claim from the synchronic claim, since the class-diachronic claim is what distinguishes the diachronic from the synchronic claim.

Second, while the synchronic claim makes no reference to any time span, it refers to something longer than an instantaneous time slice. A person who owns means of production would not be compelled to sell his labor power if he were deprived of them for just a second. Rather the synchronic claim refers to what we might think of as the economic form of what James called "the specious present," that slightly extended duration we commonly call "now."[23] The economic form of the specious present is something like the time it takes from satiety to the onset of the pains of starvation (or some other pressing need), since that is the time by which, deprived of means of production (and of savings produced from them), one will be compelled to sell his labor power.

Third, I shall for reasons of simplicity refer to the force described in the synchronic claim as synchronic force, and speak similarly of diachronic and class-diachronic force. Diachronic force is the cooperation of class-diachronic and synchronic force. And while these are all cases of structural force, I am not in using the terms "synchronic" and "diachronic" volunteering to be saddled with all the shortcomings of the structuralism which has been their recent home. Nonetheless, I do think that the structuralists have identified some valuable ways of looking at societies which can be separated from the unfortunately obscurantist way they write about them.

Cohen only questions the diachronic claim. He takes it as the whole of the Marxian assertion. He writes that "when Marxists say that proletarians are forced to sell their labor power, they do not mean: 'X is a proletarian at time t only if X is at t forced to sell his labor power at t' for that would be compatible with his not being forced at time $t + n$, no matter how small n is" (SP, 8). Ignoring the possibility of there being a separate point to the synchronic claim (in which n is the economic specious present), Cohen writes:

> The manifest intent of the Marxist claim is that the proletarian is forced at t to *continue* to sell his labor power, throughout a period from t to $t + n$, for some considerable n. It follows that because there is a route out of the proletariat, which our counterexamples travelled, reaching their destination in, as I would argue, an amount of time less than n, they were, though proletarians, not forced to sell their labor power in the *required* Marxist sense (SP, 8; last emphasis mine).

Needless to say, Cohen's counterexamples (the struggling immigrants and their like) do not reach their destination in the time it would take to go from full to hungry. He recognizes, for instance, (as the first quotation above shows) that they must put in a stint as proletarians in order to save at least that part of the initial capital that they will have to put down in order to get the rest lent. In fact, Cohen holds that the Marxian claim is unseated if proletarians could get themselves out of the working class within *five years* after they had decided to do so (SP, 14)! I think this is rather generous, I should be inclined to say that a system that forced its nonowners of means of production to sell their labor power for as much as five years—a period longer than most prison sentences—actually forced them in the diachronic sense. But let us grant Cohen's claim here for the moment, noting that it applies only to the diachronic form of the Marxian assertion. Note also that even if it is thought that the synchronic claim must apply to a period longer than the economic specious present, it is in any event far shorter than that to which the diachronic applies, and thus the distinction will survive quibbles about the precise lengths of time at stake.

Cohen is wrong to think that the diachronic claim is the sum total of the *required* Marxist sense of the assertion. Actually the synchronic and diachronic claims play distinct roles in Marxian theory. I shall point out four roles (numbered below for ease of identification) played by the synchronic claim in Marxian theory, which do not depend on the truth of the diachronic claim; and I shall argue that of the two claims, the synchronic is the more important.

(1) The synchronic claim runs against the common illusion that the sale of labor power is a free choice like the sale of any other commodity—or, to use the contemporary argot, that labor is just another factor of production that one may or may not offer on the market depending on opportunity costs.

(2) The synchronic claim runs against the notion that lack of ownership of means of production is a natural condition. If it were natural, the fact that nonowners have to work would not qualify as force in any socially relevant sense. It would be of a piece with the fact that nature doesn't provide us a living without some human effort. Thus the synchronic claim is connected to Marx's criticism of political economists at the end of his discussion of commodity fetishism, where he takes them to task for failing to see that the division of the world into owners of means of production and nonowners is a particular social arrangement, and for failing to ask what sort of social relations make labor time into the measure of value (C 1:80–83). It is because this division of the world is a social arrangement, sustained by an alterable pattern of human behavior, that it amounts to forcing nonowners to sell their labor power, even if for a short period of time.

(3) Assuming the validity of the other features of Marx's analysis, the synchronic claim is all that is needed to make the Marxian charge that capitalism is a form of slavery. Insofar as workers sell their labor power, they must give some extra amount of it above the amount they get in compensation, and thus they must work in some degree gratis. To the extent that they are forced to do this, they are enslaved. And this is true irrespective of the period for which they are enslaved. Short-term slavery may be less odious than lifelong slavery, but it is no less slavery, any more than a sentence of five years of forced labor is not forced labor because only five years. This claim is obviously based on the distinction, introduced earlier, between slavery per se and classical slavery. The shorter-lasting capitalist slavery is, the less like classical slavery it is, and consequently, other things equal, the less our moral judgment about capitalist slavery will be like our moral judgment about the classical variety. Accordingly, the severity of our judgment of capitalism will depend in important ways on the truth of the diachronic claim. This notwithstanding, it remains the case that, whatever its moral implications, the charge that capitalism is slavery of some sort can stand on the synchronic claim independent of the diachronic.

Incidentally, the synchronic claim's independence of the diachronic works backwards in time as well. It represents a claim about capitalism that is independent of how capitalism arose historically. Even if a generation of humanity voluntarily handed over the means of production to a few of their contemporaries, the owners would still have the same power over the nonowners as the synchronic claim asserts. And this would be all the more clear of the relation between the descendants of the two groups. Thus, to the extent that the synchronic claim is true, capitalism would count as slavery whether it arose by violence as Marx thought or in the peaceful way it does in Nozick's fantasy.

(4) Finally, the synchronic claim is enough for Marx's analysis of the way capitalism works economically. The various tendencies that Marx found in capitalism, the push for technological development, the falling rate of profit, crises, and the rest, would work (if they work in capitalism at all) in a system in which workers exchanged places with owners every so often, and certainly in one in which workers were drafted for periods of, say, five years.

By contrast, the diachronic claim belongs primarily to Marxist sociology rather than to Marxist economics. Put more precisely, the class-diachronic claim (wherein the diachronic differs from the synchronic claim) belongs primarily to Marxist sociology. It is a claim about how the working class is reproduced over time, and about how individuals get deployed into that and other classes. It is a claim about the permeability of the barriers around and between those classes, not a claim about whether there are classes or whether one of those classes is forced to labor for the other.

So far, I think I have established the fact that the synchronic claim is independent of the diachronic and independently important. But I also contend that the synchronic claim is more important to Marxism than the diachronic one is. It is more important because the falsity of the synchronic claim would essentially refute the Marxian analysis of the capitalist mode of production, while the falsity of the diachronic claim (if the synchronic claim remains true, this means the falsity of the class-diachronic claim) merely modifies Marxism's understanding of how the capitalist mode of production reproduces itself socially. And the synchronic claim is also more important because the moral significance of the diachronic claim is parasitic on the truth of the synchronic, rather than vice versa. We care about workers being forced to sell their labor power, because we understand this as forcing them to work without pay. And we care about how long workers are forced to work without pay, because of how we feel about people being forced to work without pay for any period of time. Thus, if the synchronic claim is true, the falsity of the diachronic claim only reduces moral antipathy to capitalism; while the falsity of the synchronic claim (leaving the class-diachronic claim true) would render moral antipathy to capitalism (for forcing unpaid labor) groundless.

I take it, then, that if Cohen's argument succeeds, it does so only against the less important part of the Marxian claim about forced labor; the diachronic part. However, I shall now argue that even the diachronic claim survives Cohen's argument if my account of structural force in section 1 is accepted.

Cohen considers an objection to his argument which he attributes to

Chaim Tannenbaum. Tannenbaum does not deny that there are more exits into the petit bourgeoisie than are tried, nor "does he deny that petty bourgeois existence is relevantly superior to proletarian. His objection is that for most workers the existence of petty bourgeois exits does not . . . generate an acceptable alternative course to remaining a worker. For one must consider . . . the risk attached to the attempt to occupy a petty bourgeois position, which, to judge by the rate at which fledgling enterprises fail, is very high; and also the costs of failure, since often a worker who has tried and failed to become a petty bourgeois is worse off than if he had not tried at all. . . . Accordingly, the expected utility of attempting the petty bourgeois alternative is normally too low to justify the statement that most workers are not forced to sell their labor power" (SP, 28).

Cohen responds that Tannenbaum's objection mistakenly assumes that the fact that attempting the petit bourgeois alternative has a lower expected utility than remaining a worker suffices to render the alternative unacceptable in the way that is needed to say that the worker is forced to remain a worker. "An alternative to a given course can be acceptable even if it has less expected utility than the given course" (SP, 30). Thus the Tannenbaum objection will only work if attempting the petit bourgeois alternative is so much lower in expected utility as to constitute "a particularly bad thing to do" (SP, 31). As I indicated at the outset of this section, Cohen leaves open the possibility that this is so, but is not sufficiently moved by it to give up his argument. Accordingly, he contends that simply showing that trying for the petit bourgeoisie has a lower expected utility than remaining a worker does not show that the worker is forced to be a worker.

Now, I think that attempting to escape into the petit bourgeoisie has for most workers an even lower expected utility than the Tannenbaum objection suggests, but I agree with Cohen in doubting that this amounts to rendering the attempt unacceptable in the relevant sense. The attempt is worse than the Tannenbaum objection paints it because it has other costs, in addition to the risks and costs of failure.[24] There is first, as Cohen recognizes, the fact that attempters will have to work for some time in order to save up at least part of their initial capital, and he is not fazed by the prospect of this taking as much as five years. When you consider that workers are not generally overpaid and that it is hard for them to save even for some needed consumer items, reducing consumption for five years—to a level below that normal for workers—to save up in hope of becoming a petit bourgeois is a rather considerable sacrifice for an attempt whose success is far from assured.

What's more, the worker who aims to become a petit bourgeois will not only have to sell his labor power for awhile to earn part of his initial capital, once he opens his little business he will also have to submit to the conditions of those from whom he borrows the rest. And this submission will be something like selling his labor power to them at least until he is on his own feet. This is not to suggest that a capitalist who borrows money is selling his labor power to his banker, since qua capitalist, he need not work at all to pay off his loans. A capitalist may pay off his loans with profit produced by his workers. A petit bourgeois is different. His distinguishing feature is that, while he may hire wage laborers, he must himself work as well. And then, at least until he has accumulated a sufficient amount of capital to give him some independence (even if not enough to free him from working entirely, particularly in light of the standard of living to which he has in the interim become accustomed), he will be forced to sell his labor power to owners of means of production in the sense that part of the work that he does while self-employed will have to be translated into profits for them. (Financiers are members of the class of owners of means of production, even if what they own is fictitious, "paper" capital).[25] The new petit bourgeois is then like a worker who, instead of selling his labor to a capitalist who will sell its products to a consumer for cash, sells his labor directly to a consumer and passes the cash on to the capitalist. Cohen allows that when workers form producer cooperatives and, in return for finance, give their creditors some say in the operation, they sell their labor power "in effect if not in form" (SP, 24–25). But, once we can speak of selling one's labor power "in effect," this must apply to the beginning years of any small business started up on loans. And then to Cohen's five years of proletarian saving, must be added how many more years of petit bourgeois repaying before we have full-fledged freedom from selling one's labor power? It can hardly be less than another five years.

This is not to deny that there are advantages to petit bourgeois existence not available to workers. There is, even in the first years of struggle, a kind of autonomy available to the former which Marxists at least cannot help but regard as valuable (SP, 28n). All things considered, it is probably better to be hounded by creditors than bossed around by employers. I grant then that trying for the petit bourgeoisie is not "a particularly bad thing to do," it is not *unacceptable*. My point, rather, is that when to the risks and costs of failure cited by Tannenbaum are added the costs of trying even if one succeeds, it is bad enough, so that for most workers, it is more rational to stay workers than to try to become petit bourgeois. *And, if my account of structural force is accepted, this is enough to warrant saying that workers are forced to stay workers, even if they have the acceptable alternative of trying to become petit bourgeois. And then the diachronic claim is saved.*

Diachronic force is structural force. Not every nonowner of means of production is forced by that fact into selling his labor power. Some can join religious orders, some can become successful criminals, and some can become full-time homemakers married to sellers of labor power.[26] And some others can scrimp and save and try for the petit bourgeoisie. In short, nonownership of means of production forces upon people an array of fates, of which, for most of them, selling labor power is the most rational course. And if it is allowed that force can operate through people's free and rational choices, then those who take this course can be said to be forced to do so, albeit more loosely forced than if there were no acceptable alternatives to it at all.

The situation of nonowners of means of production facing the array of choices that includes selling labor power and attempting to be a petit bourgeois is analogous to that of our stagecoach passengers facing the choice between giving up their watches or their cash. In both cases the parties are forced to choose among an array of alternatives and their own choices are links in the chain that ties them to their fates. But further, in both cases they are allowed only so much choice as is compatible with their deploying themselves among the fates before them in roughly the way their forcer wants. In the case of capitalism, this happens impersonally, but it happens nonetheless. This is the significance of what Cohen calls the workers' collective unfreedom. Though he is not very specific about why only a limited number can become petit bourgeois, the explanation is not far to find. Without capitalism's industrial plant adequately manned, there would be neither products for small business owners to sell nor paying customers to sell them to. Once too many workers went for the exits into the petit bourgeoisie, the exits would automatically close up. With such a mechanism in place, and given the general unattractiveness of going for the exits anyway, capitalism needs no tighter force than its structure currently exerts to deploy people in a satisfactory way. It is this piece of good fortune for capitalism that leads to workers not seeing that they are forced to continue to sell their labor power. But once force is understood structurally, Marxist philosophers should be able to see otherwise.

I think that I have shown how the diachronic form of the Marxian claim can survive Cohen's assault. I do believe, however, that Cohen is on to something important. Its importance comes up when we turn to morally assessing capitalism. My comments here should be read in conjunction with those at the end of section 1.

Even if we grant that capitalism is exploitative according to the force-inclusive definition, and that workers are forced to continue to sell their labor power in line with the structural nature of synchronic and diachronic force, it remains significant *that they have a choice* and *that they pass it up*. I want to emphasize the separate significance of these two facts. The first signifies that capitalist slavery is freer than classical slavery, and the second signifies that capitalist slavery is less awful than classical slavery. The capitalist variety is imposed by looser force than the classical variety. It cannot be denied that a society that allows its workers to choose its slavery from among acceptable alternatives constrains their freedom less than one that does not. And to that extent, the freedom that Cohen has identified counts in the positive column in any moral assessment of capitalism. Moreover, that workers pass up acceptable alternatives to selling their labor power suggests that, whatever the disabilities of selling labor power may be, they are not intolerable. It would be hard to imagine many classical slaves passing up a similar way of escaping from their situation. Thus the freedom that Cohen has identified must also count to reduce the sum in the negative column in any moral assessment of capitalism.

As I see it, the implication of Cohen's argument, then, is that capitalist slavery is a substantially milder thing than classical slavery, and no Marxist can rightly call capitalism slavery with the intention of conveying that it is as bad as the classical variety. Capitalism might be, or might be made into, a relatively mild form of slavery. But this possibility must be viewed alongside another. No one who is aware of the power conferred by ownership of means of production can ignore the potential danger involved in handing ownership of the means of production over to the state. Capitalist slavery might be mild in part because in it ownership of means of production is private and thus power is decentralized. This could be the material condition of the looseness in capitalist structural force. The space between a plurality of centers of power may be just the space in which freedom occurs, and conflicts between the centers may work to keep that space open. State ownership, by contrast, might not be slavery at all, in that, by means of the state, the people themselves would own the means of production, and people cannot be slaves to themselves. But as a material fact, state ownership might still represent a condition in which people were more vulnerable to, or less able to resist or escape from, force than they are in capitalism. It follows that, even if socialism ends capitalist slavery, it remains possible, on materialist grounds, that some achievable form of capitalism will be morally superior to any achievable form of socialism. And this remains possible even if capitalism is exploitative according to the force-inclusive definition.

Notes

I am grateful to G. A. Cohen for his generous and helpful comments on an earlier draft of this essay. I thank also the Editors of Philosophy and Public Affairs for many thought-provoking suggestions.

1. I claim no particular originality for this definition. Nancy Holmstrom, for example, takes the "features common to exploitation" to be "that it involves forced,

surplus, and unpaid labor, the product of which is not under the producers' control" (Nancy Holmstrom, "Exploitation," *Canadian Journal of Philosophy* 7, no. 2 [June 1977]: 359 [this volume, selection 5, p. 81]). She presents arguments to support the claim that the force-inclusive definition is the best interpretation of what Marx seems to have meant by exploitation. Though I agree with many of Holmstrom's points, my defense of this definition and of the conditions of its application to capitalism takes a substantially different form than hers does. This is due to the fact that Marxist writers have recently posed questions about exploitation and force that raise doubts about whether the concept of exploitation ought to be kept irrespective of "what Marx meant." I want to defend the force-inclusive definition in a way that shows that these doubts can be dealt with. I hope also to convince non-Marxists that the concept of exploitation is a valuable and usable tool of social analysis. See note 19, below.

2. I shall draw on the following articles by John Roemer—the letters in brackets are the initials by which I shall cite these articles in the text: [PR] "Property Relations vs. Surplus Value in Marxian Exploitation," *Philosophy and Public Affairs* 11, no. 4 (Fall 1982): 281–313; [ND] "New Directions in the Marxian Theory of Exploitation and Class," *Politics and Society* 11, no. 3 (1982): 253–87; [R] "Reply," *Politics and Society* 11, no. 3 (1982): 375–94; [WR] "R. P. Wolff's Reinterpretation of Marx's Labor Theory of Value: Comment," *Philosophy and Public Affairs* 12, no. 1 (Winter 1983): 70–83; [SM] "Should Marxists Be Interested in Exploitation?" *Philosophy and Public Affairs* 14, no. 1 (Winter 1985): 30–65 [this volume, selection 7].

3. I shall draw on the following articles by G. A. Cohen—the letters in brackets are the initials by which I shall cite these articles in the text: [LT] "The Labor Theory of Value and the Concept of Exploitation," *Philosophy and Public Affairs* 8, no. 4 (Summer 1979): 338–60; [SP] "The Structure of Proletarian Unfreedom," *Philosophy and Public Affairs* 12, no. 1 (Winter 1983): 3–33; [AW] "Are Workers Forced to Sell Their Labor Power?" *Philosophy and Public Affairs* 14, no. 1 (Winter 1985): 99–105.

4. There is a substantial literature on the question of whether capitalism is unjust according to Marxism. See articles in M. Cohen, T. Nagel, and T. Scanlon, eds., *Marx, Justice, and History* (Princeton: Princeton University Press, 1980); K. Nielsen and S. Patten, eds., *Marx and Morality* (*Canadian Journal of Philosophy*, suppl. vol. 7, 1981), and J. Pennock and J. Chapman, eds., *Marxism: Nomos XXVI* (New York: New York University Press, 1983); as well as G. A. Cohen, "Freedom, Justice, and Capitalism," *New Left Review* 126 (March/April 1981): 3–16; and more recently, Norman Geras's review of the whole discussion, "The Controversy about Marx and Justice," *New Left Review* 150 (March/April 1985): 47–85. Geras concludes, quite wisely I think, that "Marx did think that capitalism was unjust but he did not think he thought so" (70). As the convoluted nature of this answer should suggest, this literature is dogged by unclarity about what question it should be asking. Allan Wood, for example, presents convincing textual evidence showing at least that Marx calls capitalism just, and then Wood goes on to conclude that Marx's problem with capitalism was not a problem about its injustice at all, but about the fact that it is a form of servitude (Allen Wood, "The Marxian Critique of Justice," in Cohen, Nagel, and Scanlon, eds., *Marx, Justice, and History*, 1–41). In my view, it is of little more than historical interest whether Marx called capitalism just. And saying that Marx's problem with capitalism was its servitude, not its injustice, assumes that justice

is distributive justice and that servitude is not an issue of justice, neither of which assumptions seems true or helpful. As recent arguments about the injustice of slavery have evidenced, contemporary conceptions of justice cover issues of servitude. In my view, the relevant question is whether capitalism is unjust *according to our conception of justice* if *the Marxian analysis of capitalism is essentially correct*. This is the question we must answer to determine our stance toward capitalism. See my "The Possibility of a Marxian Theory of Justice," in Nielsen and Patten, eds., *Marx and Morality*, 307–22.

5. By "some systematic relationship" I include the fact that Marx held the value of a commodity to be determined by "socially necessary labor time" (the average amount necessary to produce such a commodity at the time it comes on the market) rather than by the actual amount labored on it, and that Marx showed in great detail the structural reasons why prices deviate from socially necessary labor time. Karl Marx, *Capital* (New York: International Publishers, 1967), 1:39 and 3:142 ff. Hereafter, references to *Capital* will be cited in the text as "C" followed by the volume number and the page number.

6. Marx writes that "however varied the useful kinds of labour . . . may be, it is a physiological fact, that they are functions of the human organism, and that each such function, whatever may be its nature or form, is essentially the *expenditure* of human brain, nerves, muscles, & c. . . . In all states of society, the labour-time that it costs to produce the means of subsistence, must *necessarily be an object of interest to mankind*. . . . And lastly, from the moment that men in any way work for one another, their labour assumes a *social* form" (C 1:71; emphasis mine). This does not of course amount to a statement of the general theory, but the emphasized terms do represent most of its basic elements.

7. This is an important dividend of separating out the general from the special labor theory of value. Cohen has argued for separating the concept of exploitation from the labor theory of value because the socially necessary labor constituting value is not the same as the actual labor that went into products, and thus appropriation of surplus value is not appropriation of actual labor. And Roemer has taken as one reason for suspicion about the Marxian concept of exploitation the fact that the labor theory, with which it is linked, seems subject to insuperable theoretical objections. Without commenting on the validity of these points, note that in both cases the difficulties are with the special and not the general labor theory of value. Separating out the general labor theory allows the concept of exploitation to stay tied to the labor theory of value even if Cohen and Roemer are right about the liabilities of the special theory. See Cohen, *LT*, passim; and Roemer, *PR*, 283.

8. "The labour-time socially necessary is that required to produce an article under the normal conditions of production, and with the average degree of skill and *intensity* prevalent at the time" (C 1:39; emphasis mine).

9. Rather than determine the validity of ownership systems, what the general theory does is strip away the halo of legitimacy that normally surrounds titles of ownership, and allow us to see any economic system in terms of what ultimately matters, that is, as a distribution of the labor time that goes into the products produced. And this means that any economic distribution is a system of relations in which people can be said to be *laboring for* others in varying proportions—irrespective of whether they are *forced to*, or whether they are laboring for others *without compensation*. I contend that this gives us the appropriate neutral standpoint from which to evaluate property systems morally. I have

developed the implications of this approach to evaluating distributions in "The Labor Theory of the Difference Principle," *Philosophy and Public Affairs* 12, no. 2 (Spring 1983): 133–59.

10. There is no logical problem with people playing roles in the structures that limit their freedom. A military command structure, for example, forces obedience on every soldier by the general likelihood that other soldiers will obey orders to punish disobedients, and these others are forced (and thus likely) to obey because of yet others, and so on. Each individual soldier is among the "other soldiers" for everyone else. It follows that every soldier plays a role in the structure that limits every soldier's freedom. Insofar as workers pay taxes, respect "No Trespassing" signs, and the like, they play roles in the structure of private ownership that in turn constrains their freedom.

11. "The social system is not an unchangeable order beyond human control but a pattern of human action" (John Rawls, *A Theory of Justice* [Cambridge: Harvard University Press, 1971], 102).

12. Cohen writes, "Where relations of production force people to do things, people force people to do things" (*SP*, 6). Cohen, by the way, allows that people can also be forced without being forced by people, but adopts, for the present argument, the narrower view that they can only be forced by people. I do the same.

13. See my "The Fallacy of Libertarian Capitalism," *Ethics* 92 (Oct. 1981): 85–95.

14. I have explored the way this domination of our imaginations limits our conception of crime to the kinds of things that poor people do, in *The Rich Get Richer and the Poor Get Prison: Ideology, Class, and Criminal Justice*, 2d ed. (New York: John Wiley, 1984), 45–76. See also my "The Marxian Critique of Criminal Justice," *Criminal Justice* 6, no. 1 (Winter/Spring 1987).

15. Rawls, *A Theory of Justice*, 343.

16. See, for example, ibid., 248.

17. Karl Marx, *The Poverty of Philosophy* (Moscow: Progress Publishers, 1955), appendix, 163.

18. I am deeply sympathetic to Cohen's attempt to state this in precise terms in *Karl Marx's Theory of History* (Princeton: Princeton University Press, 1978), and broadly sympathetic to the picture that results.

19. For a valuable attempt, see Holmstrom, "Exploitation." Perhaps the chief textual source against the claim that Marx *meant* the force-inclusive definition is *Capital*, vol. 1, ch. 9, sec. 1, "The Degree of Exploitation of Labour-Power" (*C* 1:212–20). Here, where Marx first discusses exploitation in *Capital*, there is no reference made to force. Also troubling are such passages as: "And exploitation, the appropriation of the unpaid labour of others, has quite as often been represented as . . ." (*C* 3:385).

20. The same displacement of the class relation from center stage follows if one takes alienation to be the crux of the Marxian indictment of capitalism, since owners of means of production can be alienated from one another as easily as from workers, and vice versa. I think this applies to Allan Buchanan's *Marx and Justice: The Radical Critique of Liberalism* (Totowa, NJ: Rowman and Littlefield, 1982).

21. This same criticism applies to those who, like Paul Hirst, believe that "Marxism is not a 'science' but a 'political theory,' a medium of political calculation. That is, it is one of the means by which political situations of action are constructed and definite actions in relation to those situations determined" (Paul Hirst, *On Law and Ideology* [Atlantic Highlands, NJ: Humanities Press, 1979], 3).

The belief in the effectiveness of a cure cannot precede belief in the validity of the diagnosis, nor can the diagnosis be selected on the basis of one's preference for some cure—if one cares about the patient.

22. Karl Marx and Friedrich Engels, *The Communist Manifesto* (Harmondsworth: Penguin Books, 1967), 99.

23. William James, *The Principles of Psychology* (New York: Henry Holt, 1890), 1:631: "The original paragon and prototype of all conceived times is the specious present, the short duration of which we are immediately and incessantly sensible."

24. The risk of business failure is indeed quite substantial. In the United States between 1980 and 1983, the number of new businesses formed each year ranged between 90,757 and 100,868, while the number of bankruptcies each year ranged between 43,374 and 65,807. These are not of course all the same businesses. But the fact that the number of bankruptcies hovers around half the number of business starts suggests a very high level of risk. See *The State of Small Business: A Report of the President* (Washington, D.C.: U.S. Government Printing Office, 1985), 11 and 13. Moreover, during that same period of 1980 to 1983, approximately half of all business failures occurred in businesses no more than five years old. See *The Business Failure Record* (New York: Dun and Bradstreet, 1985), 12.

25. Just as the class of nonowners of means of production is larger than the number of persons who sell their labor power, so the class of owners is larger than the number of those who have legal title to factories and the like. Some are financiers, others are retailers, and still others are just married to factory owners. The structure of capitalism deploys members of the class of owners of means of production into an array of situations no less than it does nonowners. However, since the owners have the alternative of becoming nonowners (more or less effortlessly), they choose their situations from a much wider range of acceptable situations than workers do and are thus forced more loosely into their ultimate situations. Moreover, it is a condition of structural force that the array among which a person must choose must itself be forced upon him. If among those choices are ones he might have sought out voluntarily, that weakens generally the claim that he has been forced into the situation he eventually chooses. To the extent that the positions available to the class of owners are substantially superior to those available to the nonowners, it becomes increasingly likely that owners might have chosen their fates independently of the structure's constraints, and thus increasingly doubtful that they are forced.

26. "In the case of labor power, its value includes the necessities of life not only for the worker, but also for the worker's family, so as to ensure the future supply of labor power" (Holmstrom, "Exploitation," 78–79).

What Is Exploitation? Reply to Jeffrey Reiman

JOHN E. ROEMER

IN A RECENT ARTICLE, Jeffrey Reiman criticizes me for defanging Marx's concept of exploitation by replacing its classic definition with a "distributive" one.[1] Reiman writes that "a society is exploitative when its social structure is organized so that unpaid labor is systematically forced out of one class and put at the disposal of another" (3). I have written that a group[2] of people S is exploited by its complement S' in a society with private ownership of the means of production if S would benefit, and S' would suffer, by a redistribution of ownership in the means of production in which each owned his per capita share. Call this the property-relations (PR) definition of exploitation.[3] A third definition of exploitation, the unequal-exchange (UE) definition, states that an agent who expends in production more hours of labor than are embodied in the goods he can purchase with his revenues from production (which may come from wages, profits, or the sale of commodities) is exploited, while one who can purchase goods embodying more social labor than he expended in production is an exploiter.

In my book *A General Theory of Exploitation and Class*, I took the UE definition to be a generalization of Marx's. I showed that by using this definition, one could rigorously construct a theory of exploitation and class formation that captured many classic Marxist insights, and had the virtue of deriving as theorems what had been, classically, assumed as postulates. I

From John E. Roemer, "What Is Exploitation? Reply to Jeffrey Reiman," *Philosophy and Public Affairs* 18, no. 1: 90–97, copyright 1989 by Princeton University Press. Reprinted by permission of Princeton University Press.

located, however, certain cases in which the UE definition gave intuitively incorrect verdicts about who was exploited.[4] I argued that the PR definition was superior to the UE definition, in that it rendered the intuitively right verdict in these strange cases and agreed with the UE definition whenever the UE definition seemed to work. I further claimed that the PR definition was superior in placing property relations at the center of exploitation, rather than unequal labor exchange, since the latter is a rather abstract idea (because socially embodied labor time is an abstract idea) whose moral associations come from the property relations that bring about the phenomenon. Reiman argues that I weakened the concept of exploitation by representing it as either UE or PR: Both these definitions are "distributive," and gloss over the central fact of the forced extraction of unpaid labor, which is the heart of exploitation. The various hard cases I propose are hard, he claims, only because I am comparing two definitions of exploitation both of which are wrong.

There is difficulty in distinguishing among these definitions of exploitation because each of them suffices to diagnose exploitation in the standard case of capitalism with proletarians who own no means of production. I find Reiman's definition of exploitation inadequate, however, for several reasons. First, the notion of "unpaid labor" is undefined; I believe that identifying some labor as unpaid often requires a prior diagnosis of exploitation, and so Reiman's use of it in a definition of exploitation is circular. There are also problems with defining "forced," of course, but I will accept Reiman's intuitions on that here, as that is not the focus of my objections. Second, I think that being forced to provide unpaid labor (assuming that we agree what that means in some standard cases) is neither necessary nor sufficient for exploitation.

Consider example 1, which I have discussed elsewhere.[5] There are a number of agents each of whom possesses an endowment consisting of some labor and some produced commodities, which are inputs into the production of commodities. All agents have access to the same technology. There is no labor market or capital market. Each agent wants to consume the same "subsistence" bundle of commodities, subject to the constraint that he not deplete his initial endowment in value terms. Suppose that there is enough endowment in aggregate so that, were it divided equally among the people, each person could produce his subsistence needs in six hours. In the private ownership economy, prices established in a market for commodities allow agents to trade inputs, before production begins, and to trade outputs, after production has occurred. Each agent is a producer of commodities. He decides upon a production plan that minimizes the labor he must expend, subject to producing an output whose value, at the current prices, is sufficient to enable him to purchase his subsistence bundle. He is constrained by the value of his initial holdings: A producer can choose only a production plan whose inputs he already has or can purchase by cashing in his initial holdings. A price vector p is an equilibrium for this economy if, when each agent chooses his optimal production plan subject to p, the market for production inputs clears, and the market for trade in produced commodities after production clears: Each agent ends up with his desired subsistence bundle. It can be proved that at an equilibrium, some agents (the ones whose initial endowments are small) work more than six hours, and others (the ones whose initial endowments are large) work less than six hours. Exploitation, in the unequal exchange sense, occurs *although there is no labor exchange of any kind*; the labor transfer occurs entirely through the trade of produced commodities. It is bizarre to speak, as Reiman apparently would, of unpaid labor in this example, when there is no institution for paying labor. Every agent is an independent producer who works only for himself. The only rationale for speaking of unpaid labor would be, circularly, if one already had concluded that the labor transfer that occurs is exploitative, and then designated the labor performed beyond labor embodied in the subsistence bundle as unpaid.

Marxists almost universally agree (in my experience) that there is exploitation in example 1, although there is neither a labor market nor a class structure. (A class structure comes into being when some agents work as independent producers, some agents hire others to work on their capital, and some agents sell labor power to those who hire.) The example is meant, of course, to point out that Marxian exploitation is a general phenomenon that can occur even without labor markets, if there is trade from an unequal initial distribution. While Reiman's definition fails in this case to diagnose exploitation, because of its reliance on the existence of unpaid labor, both the UE and the PR definitions work. If the endowments of produced commodities are redistributed so that each producer owns a per capita share, there will be no exploitation in the unequal exchange sense at equilibrium: Each producer will work just the socially necessary labor time (six hours). Thus, PR and UE lead to the same verdict.

In example 1 the asset-poor[6] producers are "forced," by the distribution of property, to work more hours than are socially embodied in the subsistence bundle in order to produce commodities sufficient in value, at market prices, to exchange for their subsistence needs. But why is the forcing a bad thing, a cause for calling the outcome exploitative? I claim it is so only because, or if, we view the initial unequal distribution of ownership of inputs (the means of production in this case) as unjust. We require knowledge of the justice of property relations to pass judgment on whether the forcing is bad. To see this, consider example 2, an economy with two agents, Karl and Adam, who have different preferences regarding consumption over time.[7] Initially, each begins with the same amount of capital, which can also be consumed. There are two time periods. During the first period, and only during that period, it is possible for each agent to augment his capital stock. Karl prefers to work very little during the first period, when he is young; he is willing to trade future leisure for present leisure. Adam has the opposite preference; he prefers to take leisure during the second period, and is willing to work hard during the first in order to do so. Consequently, Adam works hard during period one and builds up a large capital stock. Karl consumes his capital stock in period one. In period two, Adam hires Karl to work on Adam's capital stock; using Adam's capital, Karl produces enough consumption goods for both of them. Now Karl *is* forced to work for Adam during the second period, for there is no other way for him to receive his consumption (for Adam will not just give it to him). There is exploitation according to the UE definition, because Karl works in period two for more hours than are embodied in the consumption goods he receives. According to Reiman's definition, there is exploitation (assuming that the "unpaid labor" is the labor embodied in Adam's consumption in period two). But, if Karl knew what the consequences of his leisure taking in period one would be, and if his preferences were autonomously formed under conditions of equal opportunity, then I think we cannot call this outcome exploitative.[8] Adam and Karl are lucky that they are in a society together, where it is possible for both of them to achieve their preferred intertemporal streams of leisure and consumption by arranging the trade described. The PR definition of exploitation renders the correct verdict in this example: There is no exploitation because Karl and Adam each began with the same capital endowment. To make the example more dramatic, imagine that there are ten time periods, and in every one after the first, Karl is forced to work for Adam because only Adam has accumulated capital. I reach a verdict of no exploitation, as long as Karl chose willingly, and the initial distribution of capital was fair.

Thus, I claim that forcing is not sufficient for exploitation. Karl prefers taking a course of action in which he will later be forced to work for Adam to avoiding such a course of action. (Reiman could respond that, in fact, Karl is not forced to work for Adam in example 2, because he was free to choose a different course of action in the initial period. I think it is more natural to say, however, that Karl is forced to work for Adam in later periods, but that forcing is not a bad thing because of the justice of the initial distribution and the autonomous formation of preferences.) Neither, I think, is forcing necessary for exploitation. Consider example 3, in which Andrea is endowed with a big machine, Bob with a small one, and we are told that his inequality is unfair. Bob can produce his subsistence needs using his small machine, but Andrea offers to hire him to work her machine at a wage that permits him to earn his subsistence needs by expending less labor than he would require using his own machine, and at which her profits from his labor finance her subsistence as well. Thus Bob is not forced to work for Andrea, but Andrea lives off Bob's labor. I think that Bob is exploited in this case, even though there is no forcing, because the initial distribution of property rights was unfair. If rights were distributed so that Andrea and Bob each owned one-half of (the stock in) each machine, there would be no exploitation, regardless of their respective preferences for leisure and consumption (that is, regardless of who hires whom). The PR definition renders the correct verdict, and the UE definition happens to do so as well, while Reiman's definition does not.

A more delicate issue is the distinction between the PR and the UE definitions. In example 4, which Reiman reproduces (25), Maggie owns a big machine and Ron[9] a small one, and this distribution is unfair (the means of production should be equally distributed). Their preferences differ. Ron wants to take leisure, and is willing to consume just a small amount of the consumption good in order to do so. Maggie wants a lot of consumption good, and is willing to work very hard in order to maximize her consumption of it. Preferences have been autonomously formed. Maggie uses her own machine to capacity, but wants still more consumption, and so sells her labor power to Ron, who pays her a small wage to operate his machine, taking the profits therefrom for his consumption. Now there is an unequal labor exchange (Maggie expends more hours of labor than are embodied in her consumption, and Ron expends fewer than are embodied in his),[10] which implies, according to the UE definition, that Maggie is exploited. But I believe Maggie is not exploited, because the unequal exchange does not result from her lack of equal access to the means of production. In fact, she owns the big machine. The PR definition renders this verdict, while the UE definition does not. Reiman agrees that Maggie is not exploited, but says that is because she is not forced to work for Ron. I agree that she is not forced, but don't agree that explains why she is not exploited. (For in example 3, Bob was exploited by Andrea even though he was not forced to work for her.) What distinguishes the situations of Bob and Maggie is that, although both suffer from an unequal exchange, and neither is forced, the unequal exchange that Bob suffers is a consequence of his less-than-equal ownership of the means of production, while Maggie suffers from unequal exchange even though she is better endowed than she should be.

In the article in which I originally proposed example 4, I concluded that Ron was exploited, because he would benefit and Maggie would suffer from a redistribution of property ownership in which each owned one-half of society's capital stock. I am now less willing to conclude that, and more apt to believe that neither Ron nor Maggie is exploited in example 4. I therefore think that the PR definition is insufficient as a definition of exploitation, and would now prefer to say that an agent is exploited in the Marxist sense, or capitalistically exploited, *if and only if PR holds and the exploiter gains by virtue of the labor of the exploited* (that is, the exploiter would be worse off if the exploited ceased working).[11] In example 4, I think Ron suffers an injustice by virtue of the unequal ownership of the means of production, although he is not exploited by Maggie according to the amended definition because she does not gain by virtue of his labor.

Reiman gets carried away with the forced aspect of the labor exchange between proletarians and capitalists when he writes that slavery is equivalent to "forced unpaid labor," and that therefore "any exploitative society is a form of slavery" (4). Calling capitalism a form of slavery is a bad mistake. My principal concern, however, is not that Reiman mischaracterizes the social relations of capitalism in history, but that getting the definition of exploitation right is important for the analysis of contemporary socialism. The most important economic innovations in socialist societies during the coming years will apparently be their experiments with markets and private accumulation. Class relations (that is, relations of selling and hiring of labor and borrowing and lending of capital among agents) will develop. Our views about whether these relations are instances of exploitation will depend upon which definition we adopt. Socialist planners have, I think, unfortunately shied away from using markets, because of an incorrect belief that class relations among private agents are necessarily the mark of exploitation.[12] I think these socialist theorists hold a conception of exploitation that is, essentially, Reiman's. In judging whether a relation is exploitative, this conception does not consider the moral status of the property relations that give rise to it. I maintain that our focus must be on the "initial" distribution of capital, what caused the class relations to emerge, and what opportunities exist for new generations and latecomers to the scene. Exploitation can occur without the buying and selling of labor power; and conversely, such buying and selling can occur, resulting in an unequal labor exchange, without exploitation.[13]

Notes

1. Jeffrey Reiman, "Exploitation, Force, and the Moral Assessment of Capitalism: Thoughts on Roemer and Cohen," *Philosophy and Public Affairs* 16, no. 1 (Winter 1987): 3–41 [this volume, selection 8]. Page references to this article are given in parentheses.
2. I say "group" instead of "class," not in order to further defang Marxism, but because, for me, "class" has a precise definition, and whether classes are exploited as such should be a theorem, not an assumption, of a definition of exploitation.

3. I have used both a "withdrawal" criterion and the "redistributive" criterion, proposed here, for the property-relations definition of exploitation. For the former, see J. Roemer, *A General Theory of Exploitation and Class* (Cambridge: Harvard University Press, 1982), ch. 7; for the latter, see J. Roemer, *Free to Lose: An Introduction to Marxist Economic Philosophy* (Cambridge: Harvard University Press, 1988), ch. 9. There are some defects in each approach, which I will not comment on here, as they are irrelevant to my disagreements with Reiman.

4. See J. Roemer, "Should Marxists Be Interested in Exploitation?" *Philosophy and Public Affairs* 14, no. 1 (Winter 1985): 30–65 [this volume, selection 7].

5. Roemer, *A General Theory*, 33–43.

6. Reiman takes it as "striking confirmation" of my having displaced class from center stage, and replaced it with distribution, that I define agents as "rich" and "poor" (26). I *define* agents by their initial endowments and preferences, and the class position they will occupy as a consequence of rational and constrained economic behavior. It may be an agent's class position that will determine his social behavior, and indeed the preferences of his children, but it is more revealing to deduce class position from prior causes than to take it as a defining characteristic of agents. (For a discussion of how it is consistent to take preferences as a defining characteristic of an agent and yet to argue that class membership forms preferences, see my "Rational Choice Marxism," in *Analytical Marxism*, ed. J. Roemer [Cambridge: Cambridge University Press, 1986].)

7. See J. Roemer, "Are Socialist Ethics Consistent with Efficiency?" *Philosophical Forum* 14 (1983): 369–88.

8. Surely, there are some deals that Adam and Karl might strike in which we might say that Adam had unfairly taken advantage of Karl's preference for leisure in youth. But any deal that allows Karl to not work during his youth will involve an "unequal exchange exploitation" of him by Adam in period 2, and not all such deals are, in my opinion, exploitative.

9. When I initially introduced the present example 4, in Roemer, "Should Marxists Be Interested in Exploitation?" the names of the characters were not Maggie and Ron. They have been so named here to distinguish them from the other dramatis personae.

10. Because Ron does not work, but consumes some of Maggie's output.

11. The suggestion to include the "labor" clause is Erik Wright's. I do not defend the idea that gaining by virtue of another's labor is morally worse than gaining through some other channel by virtue of another's unjustly having a small endowment; but the expending of effort is characteristically associated with exploitation, as opposed to other means by which unfair advantage might be taken of the poorly endowed. Imagine the case of two agents, one poorly endowed with several goods and one well endowed. They have different tastes, and they are able to trade with each other to achieve an equilibrium that strictly Pareto dominates the initial allocation. With an equal per capita redistribution of the original endowments, the erstwhile poor one would gain and the erstwhile rich one would lose in the final equilibrium. The labor clause saves me from calling the first equilibrium exploitative, because no labor is performed by the poor agent.

Instead of appending the labor clause, a slightly different tack would be to append the UE condition—that is, to say that a group is exploited if and only if both the PR and the UE characterizations hold. The upshot for the present example is the same; neither Ron nor Maggie is exploited. These two tacks are not equivalent, for note that, with the labor clause, the unemployed who receive some transfer payments are not exploited, but they are exploited under the PR + UE characterization of exploitation. I prefer appending the labor clause.

12. They have also not used markets because the power of the bureaucracy is enhanced by its control of the allocation of resources. But I think theoretical views about exploitation have been important as well in giving market socialism a bad name among Marxists.

13. I have not discussed in this reply all my differences with Reiman, in particular those concerning the labor theory of value. But I should remark that I accept his criticism of a paragraph I wrote that is unrelated to the present discussion (27–28).

Roemer versus Marx: Alternative Perspectives on Exploitation

Gary A. Dymski and John E. Elliott

Introduction

THIS PAPER ARGUES THAT exploitation is a central and nonredundant concept in Marx's understanding of capitalism. This finding runs counter to John Roemer's conclusion in his writings on exploitation (Roemer 1985, 1988). Given settings of static or long-run equilibria in perfectly competitive markets, Roemer shows that exploitation is a property of agents which derives from unequal wealth endowments, that is, differential ownership of productive assets (DOPA), not a social relation between capitalists and workers. Further, DOPA suffices in this setting to explain domination and inequality without reference to an independent notion of exploitation. Because his model is *general*, Roemer concludes that DOPA is the central analytical category in Marxian theory, and exploitation a redundant, indeed incorrect concept therein.[1]

We reject these conclusions. DOPA fully encompasses exploitation only under a narrow conception of the character of exploitation and domination in capitalist production. This narrow conception rests on assumptions about

From Gary A. Dymski and John E. Elliott, "Roemer versus Marx: Alternative Perspectives on Exploitation," *Review of Radical Political Economics* 20 (1988): 25–33, with the permission of Blackwell Publishers.

worker's choice sets and about the technological and contractual basis of production which are unwarranted for capitalism. Roemer assumes labor is unforced and the labor/labor-power distinction analytically inconsequential. But if labor is forced or if labor exceeds labor power by an indeterminate amount, exploitation no longer simply reduces to DOPA, reversing Roemer's conclusion that exploitation is superfluous.[2]

ROEMER'S APPROACH TO EXPLOITATION

Roemer's conceptualization of exploitation (hereafter, E) has evolved rapidly. In a major work published in 1981, Roemer (1981, ch. 7) accepted both E as a significant concept in Marxian theory and a labor theory of exploitation (though not of exchange). He moved a step away from this position a year later. In his "general theory" E remains center stage, but is rooted expressly in DOPA (Roemer 1982a). The labor theory of exploitation is relegated to the task of providing linkages with Marxian theories of class struggle and historical materialism. Although either a surplus labor or a DOPA approach may be used to characterize exploitation, the latter is superior because of its generality: It allows for such anomalies as the possibility that asset-rich workers may exploit capitalists.

More recently, Roemer (1985, 1988) has argued that E is superfluous in Marxian discourse. This surprising conclusion derives from his definitions of central terms in this discourse. E is an "unequal exchange of labor for goods"; exploiters "command with their income more labor embodied in goods than the labor they performed." So E emerges in the "pattern of the redistribution of labor" as individual agents exchange "their current productive labor for social labor congealed in goods received." Unlike his earlier formulations, E is defined without reference to surplus labor or production relations; it is not a relationship between capital and labor, but between "a person and society," measured by the reciprocal transfer of an individual's labor to society and society's labor to an individual, "as embodied in goods the person claims" (1985, 30–31, 36).

Roemer's 1985 paper focuses on the relationships among E, inequality, and domination. In his model, DOPA causes inequality in income and consumption: asset-rich (-poor) individuals receive more (less) social labor embodied in goods than the current productive labor they provide. In short, the rich exploit the poor. This hypothesis, Roemer suggests, is the very epitome of Marxian thought: The link between inequality and E is the "most compelling reason" for interest in the latter (1985, 52).

Now under some assumptions, E is, indeed, "essentially equivalent" to "inequality in distribution of initial assets." Thus, in the (special) case where the rich are capitalist employers and the poor are workers, the (rich) capitalists may be said to exploit the (poor) workers. In this event, the test for capitalist exploitation is whether a "coalition of agents," if it withdrew from the capitalist system "with its per capita share of society's alienable assets," could increase its income. This contrast between unequal and egalitarian distributions of the means of production "captures precisely what Marxists mean by exploitation in terms of surplus-value transfer" (Roemer 1984, 203–4). Anyone who is Marxian exploited in terms of surplus-value transfer is capitalist exploited, in that income could be increased by withdrawing per capita alienable assets. Conversely, anyone who is capitalist exploited is Marxian exploited. Thus, although causation runs from DOPA to inequality in income, the equivalence (in this special case) of Marxian exploitation and DOPA make it possible to use the exploitation theory as a rough proxy.

But Marxian exploitation theory, Roemer contends, exhibits several major deficiencies. First, even when the results from DOPA and surplus-value transfer are equivalent, the Marxian mode of argument is at best redundant and innocuous. To say that "(poor) workers are exploited by (rich) capitalists" adds no information to the statement that DOPA causes inequality if (as Roemer supposes) there are no other means, in perfectly competitive, full-employment equilibrium, to generate unequal economic outcomes for individuals than DOPA. Next, DOPA is superior to the traditional surplus-value interpretation because it "makes clear the ethical imperative when one speaks of exploitation," namely, that "initial inequality in the wealth of agents is unjust" (Roemer 1984, 204; 1985, 52).

Last, Roemer argues that DOPA is superior to the Marxian exploitation concept because the former handles properly a perverse case which the latter misinterprets. Suppose individuals have the same preference orderings, but the labor supply function is wealth-elastic. Then an asset-rich individual will want to work harder than an asset-poor individual. In an extreme case, the rich individual may still want to work even after fully utilizing his extensive assets, while the work effort of the poor individual may not fully utilize even her small stock of assets. In this event, the rich individual will work for the poor one. The perspective of the "unequal exchange of labor" describes the (poor) employer as exploiting the (rich) worker. But the perspective of the "distributional consequences of an unjust inequality in the distribution of productive assets and resources" allows the intuitively more attractive conclusion that the rich with a high propensity to work exploit the poor with a low propensity to work (Roemer 1985, 54, 65).

Roemer similarly rejects domination as providing persuasive grounds for retaining the category of *E*. Roemer distinguishes two types of domination (*D*): the enforcement of private property in the means of production, and domination in the production process, that is, autocratic and hierarchical work structures. Following Roemer, we designate, these two instances as domination[1] (D^1) and domination[2] (D^2). D^1 involves two forms of enforcement: one, the protection of property through police powers; second, the use of extramarket means, such as public education and the minimum wage, to affect the market values of services and assets.

Because D^1 entails the protection and enhancement of private property, it collapses into DOPA. D^1 implies E, but this is a reason for interest in D^1, and thereby DOPA, not E. E typically implies the police-powers sense of D^1, but only for the purpose of maintaining inequality in DOPA. And while E may also, in practice, imply D^1 in the sense of extramarket means of enhancing property value, such instances constitute departures from perfect competition and hence from pure capitalism.

D^2, or hierarchical and undemocratic processes in the workplace, is not similarly reducible to DOPA. But it also raises problems, according to Roemer, as a defense of a Marxian interest in E. It can be shown that D^2 elicits profits beyond those attributable to DOPA per se and thereby implies E. But, again, this provides reason for concern with D^2 in its own right, not E. Precisely because D^2 is largely independent of DOPA, E does not necessarily imply D^2. Financial and landed capitalists, for example, may exploit sharecroppers and borrowers without D^2. In addition, D^2 is a second-order phenomenon arising from imperfections in making and enforcing contracts. It diverges from Marx's desire to show "the economic viability of capitalism in the absence of cheating: and that means that contracts are well-defined and observed by all" (Roemer 1985, 44). In short, a model consistent with Marx's intent must be perfectly competitive. Moreover, the paramount focus in a Marxian critique must be DOPA. Subduing the despotism of the boss is an important, but subsidiary, goal. Overturning DOPA is the primary Marxist socialist aspiration.

ROEMER'S UNDERLYING ASSUMPTIONS

Roemer's conclusions that DOPA is the fundamental Marxian analytical category and D^2 inessential rest on assumptions about individual choice and production processes.

In Roemer's view of individual choice, patterns of labor-power exchange choice result from agents' utility maximization. Identically endowed agents may, given different preferences, opt to sell or withhold their labor power, and/or to buy other agents' labor power. The key is that the agents' choice is unforced (see note 2): Withholding labor power is a relevant and rational option for all agents. This guarantees the empirical relevance of the technical conception of production. If *some* production processes are characterized by indeterminate productivity, as per D^2, the presence of technically determined production processes will drive forcible extraction in such industries to a minimum. If *all* production processes are characterized by indeterminacy and forcible extraction, worker's exit option—their ability to choose not to labor for capitalist firms—will reduce forcible extraction to a uniform level.

In turn, the technical or effectively technical nature of production, policed by labor-market choice, allows a narrow, technical conception of E. Because no person can be made to perform an act without consent, E is just an accounting calculation, *not* a social relation between capitalists and workers. The terms of any relation between two agents are spelled out contractually—extraneous or extraeconomic E occurs only in disequilibrium.

The role of these two assumptions in Roemer's argument for the irrelevance of E is illustrated by his factory/farm parable (Roemer 1985, 34–36; 1988, ch. 2). Suppose agents have identical, finite preferences for a composite output good. Two fixed-coefficient technologies can produce this good; the more efficient technology (the "factory") requires scarce capital, while any agent can operate the less efficient technology (the "farm") with no start-up capital. Agents unequally endowed with the scarce capital good obtain some of the net product of the agents they hire.

There are several noteworthy aspects of this scenario. D^2 is absent. There is no reason to suppose the "exploited" agents working in the factory are coerced; no coercion is required, since these agents are at least as well off in utility terms as the nonexploited agents on the farm. Complete contracts preclude any coercive extraction of additional surplus labor time through D^2. Because all workers can opt for undominated labor on the farm, D (in the weak sense of D^1) is freely chosen. D^1 operates exclusively through market processes, which are perfectly competitive. Thus, on the one hand, all forms of extramarket power (other than DOPA), including collective/societal bargains over the length of the working day, are excluded. On the other, market processes work perfectly, and full employment equilibrium is assured. With D^2, extramarket aspects of D^1, and unemployment all excluded, DOPA remains the sole source of E.

The redundancy of E in this intentionally simple scenario implies that more involved models guarantee that same result. The appearance of nonreductive simplicity, however, is misleading. Roemer's conclusion that D^2 is absent rests on (1) the presence of the farm and (2) the assumption of determinate ex ante relationship between labor and labor power. The first assumption guarantees that the intensity of the production process is compensated by an additional increment (decrement) of net output which just offsets the disutility (utility) of a more (less) work process than on the farm. The second assumption guarantees that the deal struck between capital owner and laborer results in delivery of agreed-upon levels of net output. Jointly, these assumptions make the production process analytically peripheral.

In effect, the existence of the farm assures that labor is not forced, and the assumption about production implies that markets are complete. Roemer's conclusion about E hinges on these features. Without the farm, the unemployed would bid down the factory wage to the subsistence level. And even then no "equilibrium" exists, since poor agents unable to find work will starve. And if effort per unit of labor in production were indeterminate ex ante, the threat of starvation would allow capital owners to forcibly extract extraordinary effort from workers. Under such circumstances, exploitation must be defined differently. Denote exploitation under unforced conditions with ex ante determination labor/labor-power relations, Roemer's case, as E^1. Then observed exploitation, E, exceeds E^1 when forced labor or incomplete markets lead to additional exploitation, E^2, where $E^2 = f(D^2)$ and $f^1 > 0$. So, in general, $E = E^1 + E^2 = E^1 + f(D^2)$; Roemer has identified the special case in which $E = E^1$.

The existence of some surplus labor not transferred pursuant to unforced market transactions makes Roemer's scenario incomplete. E^2 derives from a relation, not a state (DOPA). Thus, preferences, technology, and endowments no longer suffice to characterize economic outcomes: Assumptions about information structures, conflict in production, etc., are required to ascertain the extent of D^2 and hence the magnitude of E.

MARX'S CATEGORY OF EXPLOITATION

Roemer defends his approach by drawing explicitly on Marx's authority; he claims that Marx derives his conclusions in a context of fair exchanges and no "cheating," requirements which Roemer associates with pure capitalism operating under perfect competition (Roemer 1985, 41, 44). Roemer claims Marx's mantle, but does not cite Marx. Marx's works, however, employ a different approach from Roemer's.[3]

On the crucial issue of the primary versus secondary nature of E^1 and E^2, Marx's approach is the opposite of Roemer's. Marx occasionally uses the term E to denote efficacious use of resources in production; labor is assigned to pride of place in this meaning of E, as shown by Marx's discussions of the "exploitation" of nature and machines as well as labor (Marx 1963, 49; 1967a, 605; 1967b, 795; 1973, 700; 1975, 89). The bourgeois economist, he states, apparently cannot distinguish between the human and social process of "exploitation of the workman by the machine" under capitalist control and technical and natural process of the "exploitation of the machine by the workman" (1967a, 443). Marx gives no name to this latter, nonsocial E; we term it "basic exploitation."

Marx also uses the term "exploitation" in the sense of "human and social exploitation." The definition of exploitation in the Oxford Dictionary of the English Language as, inter alia, a regime of "mastery of advantage" provides a working approximation of Marx's meaning here. Marx discusses social relations of "mastery or advantage" in two kinds of circumstances. In one, basic and human and social E comingle. Marx calls this "primary exploitation taking place in the production process itself." In effect, Marx posits mastery over and advantage of a working class by a capitalist class through productive and profitable use of resources. A less familiar but significant use of the term "exploitation" posits mastery or advantage without productive or profitable use. Marx calls this purely distributive phenomenon "secondary exploitation" (1967b, 609).

Under capitalism, the industrial capitalist engages in primary exploitation on the basis of a class monopoly over the physical means of production and a regime of alienated labor and domination both inside and outside the enterprise. When successful, such primary exploitation yields its "golden fruits": surplus values which are translated into profits through competition. Secondary exploitation, based purely on property ownership and facilitated by markets for credit and land, is conducted by the financial and landed capitalist; in effect, rentier capitalists extract a portion of society's total surplus value as interest and rent. Roemer and Marx then present opposing views: What is primary for Marx is secondary for Roemer, and vice versa. Prima facie, Roemer's secondary claim that his argument is consistent with, indeed "precisely captures," the preeminent theme in Marx's original project is plainly discordant with the textual evidence.

In fact, Roemer's argument concerning Marx is primarily inferential rather than textual. To achieve Marx's aspiration of a modeling of capitalist economy unencumbered by "swindling and cheating," Roemer claims, "perfect" competition is necessary. But differentiation between labor and labor power, unemployment, and control over length of the working day or wages by extramarket power are excluded by definition from this kind of equilibrium, although not from robust but less than "perfect" competitive equilibria. Therefore, Roemer ignores Marx's own rich textual argument and imports into Marx's dynamic and historical system the narrow methodology of Walrasian general equilibrium. This methodological foundation underlies Roemer's conclusion that "labor can be just as exploited if it hires capital as if it is hired by capital. The key question is the wealth position of the laborer and not which market is used" (Roemer 1982, 196).

In Marx's dynamic argument, by contrast, tastes, technologies, and endowments are subject to change as a result of D within production. Consequently, contemplating the E which would remain once perfectly competitive equilibrium eliminated all D based on extramarket power would be highly speculative, because even temporary D creates new opportunities for E and for new social powers which thereby re-create both D^1 and D^2. Second, according to Marx, capitalist institutions profoundly affect the motivations which undergird competition. Because exchange values dominate under capitalism and capitalist industrialists dominate production and labor processes, a "boundless thirst for surplus-labor arises from the nature of the production process itself." Because E takes the "value form" capital's "blind unrestrainable passion," its "vampire-like" thirst and "werewolf hunger" for surplus labor is translated into a "mania" for surplus value and a "boundless greed after riches" (Marx 1967a, 152–253, 233, 235, 264–65). These motivations generate powerful pressures for the expansion of D, as capitalists use the state to increase the length of the working day (D^1) and carry out various measures increasing the intensity of labor (D^2). Third, Marx's own category of competition is rich with social class and historical content. The most important kind of competition, for Marx, concerns who will hold wealth and power in society. Once that division is established historically, competition is shaped by capitalist power and works within its framework (Marx 1973, 649–52). If capitalism's competition were truly "perfect," would this not entail perfect class mobility? Last, the notion of a tendency toward full employment is at odds with Marx's theory of the industrial reserve army and the role of unemployment in keeping the "pretensions [of labor] in check" (Marx 1967a, 639). In short, Roemer's notion of competition pales against Marx's, which incorporates a dynamic and historical perspective.

For Marx, each dimension of alienated labor has a corollary element of capitalist D. Thus, the alienation of workers from ownership and control over means of production and subsistence is accompanied by capitalist ownership and control. This, for Marx, is "the real foundation, in fact, and the starting point of capitalist production" (1967a, 570). Indeed, in the case of "secondary exploitation," it is a sufficient cause of exploitation by financial and landed capital. Given this basic property relation, economic circumstances impel workers to engage in the sale or "alienation of labor-power" (1967a, 174). The corollary is industrial employers' purchase of this labor power, the first step in the process of capitalist D^2, which lays the foundation for E beyond that entailed in property relations per se.[4] But then the laborer, Marx observes, "works under the control of the capitalist to whom his labour belongs." Consequently, the work process falls under the domination of the capitalist, the product becomes his "property" (Marx 1967a, 184–86),[5] workers experience alienation both from the work process and from the products they have made, the regime of capitalist "mastery and advantage" is extended,[6] and additional opportunities for E and profits are thereby created.

Moreover, Marx insists on mutual causation and nonredundancy among DOPA, D, and E. Consequently, although capitalist property relations are the "means by which labour is alienated," they are also the "product, the necessary result, of alienated labour" (1964, 131). Marx claims the same kind of interaction between DOPA, on the one hand, and *D* and *E*, on the other: "The capitalist system presupposes the complete separation of the labourers from all property in the means by which they can realize their labour. As soon as capitalist production is on its own legs, it not only maintains this separation, but produces it on a continually extending scale" (1967a, 712). Capitalism reproduces itself in the process of producing and distributing products. At the end of the production cycle, the worker produces products in the form of capital, "an alien power that dominates and exploits him," while the capitalist "produces" labor power itself, separated from the products needed for its sustenance. "This incessant reproduction is the sine qua non of capitalist production" (1967, 571).

Finally, interactions among property, *D*, and *E* in Marx's writings reveal a chasm between mere DOPA and Marx's more powerful presupposition of capitalist class monopoly of the instruments of production and subsistence. For Marx, the difference between a mildly unequal DOPA and the extreme DOPA entailed in the capitalists' class position is clearly qualitative, not just quantitative. Thus, Marx's case cannot be subsumed as a special variant of Roemer's more general argument. First, Roemer sees *E* as based on pure exchange, without the necessity of a capital/labor relation. Marx, by contrast, typically refrains from designating simple exchanges as exploitative despite inequalities in wealth, income, and labor: The mild inequalities resulting therefrom are qualitatively different from those under capitalism because they are unconnected to the social relation between exchangers "as such" (Marx 1973, 247). Second, it is doubtful that mild differences in DOPA could establish capitalist relations of exploitation. For Marx, capitalism's historical genesis required a "primitive accumulation" sufficient to create a large working class, bereft of property and dependent on capitalist authority for its livelihood.

CONCLUSION

Roemer's modeling of capitalism requires that we be able to meaningfully distinguish between an "observed" reality, in which social imperfections appear, and an unobserved, "perfectly competitive" reality, in which social processes are automatic, in their essence technical, and fully consonant with coordination through a price-auction system. But granting this distinction conflates conclusions drawn from a restricted model with conclusions appropriate for capitalism as a whole. The perceived redundancy of exploitation derives from unwarranted assumptions about the scope of worker choice and the nature of production; and Roemer's allegation that it is an incorrect analytical category results from an ahistorical theoretical schema characterizing DOPA, in effect, as a deus ex machina rather than as an organic link in capitalism's emergence and development. Restoring the autonomy of exploitation through an enriched conception suggests a richer terrain for Marxian theory than Roemer allows. Production relations cannot be ignored in favor of property relations. Together, DOPA and exploitation constitute economic relations, complementing and reinforcing one another in any social formation.

Notes

1. This paper is an abridged and revised version of Dymski and Elliott (1989). The range of topics considered herein has been restricted due to considerations of length. In particular, the relationship of exploitation and domination to alienation is not addressed in this essay.
2. The term "forced" is used herein as in Elster's work. Elster (1985, 211–12) defines "force" as implying the presence of constraints that leave no room for choice; coercion is a stronger condition requiring the presence of an intentional agent. Elster states (214–15) that the most reasonable way of interpreting Marx's claim that the worker is forced to sell his labor power is to say that although "the worker can survive without selling his labor power, he can do so only under conditions so bad that the only acceptable course of action is to sell his labor power." The forced sale of labor power is discussed at length in Cohen (1983).
3. In addition to the differences explored in the text, Marx and Roemer differ methodologically. Roemer's exposition of E presupposes what has been called "methodological individualism." According to this view, collective entities or activities are invariably reducible to the actions of their individual units (such as individual demanders and suppliers in Walrasian economics). By contrast, Marx's view of exploitation is rooted in a theory of social class (notably capitalists versus workers) and collective entities such as class are not entirely reducible to the actions of individual agents.
4. Although grounded in DOPA and the economic necessity for most workers to sell labor power "voluntarily," the de facto servitude of labor under capitalist domination, according to Marx, rests on additional factors, namely, "a working-class, which by education, tradition, habit looks upon the conditions of that [capitalist] mode of production as self-evident laws of Nature," a despotic capitalist organization of production which "breaks down all resistance," the constant creation of an industrial reserve army which keeps wages "in a rut that corresponds with the wants of capital," and the "dull compulsion of economic relations [which] completes the subjection of the labourer to the capitalist" (Marx 1967a, 737).
5. Elsewhere, Marx makes clear, however, that the capitalist's dominion is imperfect. Workers fight back, and capitalists must impose supervisory costs to reduce shirking (1967a, 330–32).
6. If the worker is related to the product of his labor as an alien, powerful object, then "an alien, hostile, powerful and independent man is the lord of this object." If work activity is alienated and unfree, then "it is under the domination, coercion, and yoke of another man," namely, "the capitalist (or whatever one likes to call the lord of labour)" (Marx 1964, 130–31).

References

Cohen, G. A. 1983. "The Structure of Proletarian Unfreedom." *Philosophy and Public Affairs* 12:3–33.

Dymski, Gary A., and John E. Elliott. 1989. "Should *Anyone* Be Interested in Exploitation?" *Canadian Journal of Philosophy*, supp. vol. 15. Calgary, Canada: University of Calgary Press.

Elster, Jon. 1985. *Making Sense of Marx*. Cambridge: Cambridge University Press.

Marx, Karl. 1964. Economic and Philosophical Manuscripts. In, *Karl Marx: Early Writings*. Tom Bottomore (ed.). New York: McGraw-Hill.

———. 1967a. *Capital*, vol. 1. New York: International Publishers.

———. 1967b. *Capital*, vol. 3. New York: International Publishers.

———. 1973. *Grundrisse*. New York: Random House.

———. 1975. "Wage Labor and Capital." In *Marx and Engels on Economics, Politics, and Society*, ed. John E. Elliott. Santa Monica: Scott Foresman.

McLellan, David. 1970. *Marx before Marxism*. New York: Harper and Row.

Roemer, John E. 1981. *Analytical Foundations of Marxian Economic Theory*. Cambridge: Cambridge University Press.

———. 1982a. *A General Theory of Exploitation and Class*. Cambridge: Harvard University Press.

———. 1982b. "Property Relations versus Surplus Value in Marxian Exploitation." *Philosophy and Public Affairs* 11 4:281–13.

———. 1984. Exploitation, Class, and Property Relations. In *After Marx*, ed. Terence Ball and James Farr. Cambridge: Cambridge University Press.

———. 1985. "Should Marxists Be Interested in Exploitation?" *Philosophy and Public Affairs* 14:30–65 [this volume, selection 7].

———. 1988. *Free to Lose*. Cambridge: Harvard University Press.

Ne Hic Saltaveris:
The Marxian Theory of
Exploitation after Roemer

GILBERT L. SKILLMAN

1. INTRODUCTION

IN HIS BOOK A *General Theory of Exploitation and Class* (1982) (hereafter
GT), John Roemer employs the tools of mainstream general equilibrium
and game-theoretic analysis to develop a fundamental critique and broad-
based reformulation of Marxian economic theory. Perhaps Roemer's most
striking departure from traditional Marxian tenets lies in his explanation of
the material basis of exploitation in capitalist economies. Roemer argues
that capitalist exploitation must be understood as essentially the consequence
of exchange given differential ownership of relatively scarce productive assets (DORSPA). In particular, Roemer concludes that capitalist exploitation does not fundamentally depend on capitalist domination of production,
or what Marx termed the subsumption of labor under capital.[1]

Roemer's alternative account, as developed in GT and its less technical
counterpart *Free to Lose* (FL, 1988), has been subjected to extensive critical
attack on methodological and substantive grounds (see, for example,
Anderson and Thompson 1988; Devine and Dymski 1989, 1991; Dymski
and Elliott 1989; Foley 1989; Houston 1989; Howard and King 1992,
ch. 17; Lebowitz 1988). The methodological critique suggests that Roemer's

From Gilbert Skillman, "*Ne Hic Saltaveris*: The Marxian Theory of Exploitation after Roemer,"
Economics and Philosophy (October 1995), with the permission of Cambridge University Press
and the consent of the author.

individualistic, ahistorical, and nondialectical mode of analysis is necessarily irrelevant to Marx's theoretical project. In Lebowitz's verdict (1988, 193), analytical Marxism, as embodied in Roemer's formalisms, "is not Marxism . . . indeed, it is in essence *anti*-Marxist."

The substantive critique is that Roemer has ignored key structural features of the reality Marx intended to explore. The chief objection along these lines concerns Roemer's neglect of Marx's distinction between labor and labor power, particularly in terms of the conditions under which profitable quantities of the former might be obtained from suppliers of the latter. Specifically, Roemer's critics understand Marx to insist that surplus labor cannot simply be *contracted for* in the context of exchange, but must be coercively *extracted* in the process of capitalist production. In Anderson and Thompson's representative assessment (1988, 218), "Evidently . . . coercive social relations in the workplace are necessary ingredients of exploitation, and competition and unequal distribution are not sufficient."

My purpose here is to provide a targeted defense of Roemer's theory of exploitation against criticisms along the foregoing lines. Specifically, I argue that the objections to Roemer's conceptual framework and analytical method are insufficient to deny the relevance of his analysis to Marx's account of capitalist exploitation, and that Roemer's treatment of the issue, whatever its limitations in scope, is at least adequate to force a severe qualification of the claim that capitalist exploitation requires capitalist domination.

Marx presents two arguments, which I term *value-theoretic* and *historical-strategic*, in support of this claim. The former, developed in volume 1, part 2 of *Capital*, deduces from premises built upon Marx's value theory that exploitation cannot be explained solely on the basis of commodity exchange relations. Close investigation of this argument reveals that two key premises are incorrect, and Roemer's analysis demonstrates by way of counterexample the consequent illegitimacy of Marx's value-theoretic conclusions.

Roemer's central results in this connection are derived under the assumption that market transactions are governed by fully specified and costlessly enforceable contracts. Since Marx's value-theoretic analysis does not address this *completeness* assumption, criticisms of the latter have no bearing on Roemer's disqualification of that analysis.

Roemer's completeness assumption is instead the implicit target of Marx's historical-strategic argument concerning the necessity of labor's subsumption for capitalist exploitation, developed in *Capital*, and *Resultate* (R, 1990b), the *Grundrisse* (G, 1993), and volume 3 of *Theories of Surplus Value* (TSV, 1971). Here Marx argues that as a practical and historical matter the class antagonisms engendered by capitalism dictate that exploitation must be accomplished via direct supervision and control of the labor process by capitalists or their proxies. This is the line of argument typically emphasized by

Roemer's critics (e.g., Anderson and Thompson 1988, 217–18; Devine and Dymski 1991, 260–64; Dymski and Elliott 1989, 360–64; Lebowitz 1988, 208–9, and Houston 1989, 180).

But again, a close reading of Marx's argument does not support the conclusion that such strategic considerations establish the necessity of direct capitalist control of production for the exploitation of labor under capitalism. This assessment is not contradicted by theoretical and empirical developments since the publication of *Capital*. A large and growing literature on the strategic nature of capitalist production relations supports the weaker conclusion that the latter are germane to the *intensity* rather than the *existence* of capitalist exploitation.

Subsumption of labor under capital is thus seen to be at most necessary for realizing the *maximal* rate of exploitation relative to given market and production conditions. Such conditions may vary significantly across industries, and technical innovations might plausibly be expected to render subsumption progressively less important for capitalist exploitation, a possibility Marx explicitly acknowledges.

Finally, circuits of capital which do not presume the subsumption of labor are in Marx's view inherently unable to transform the conditions of production so as to increase profit in the form of *relative* surplus value. Granting that this is the case, however, does not imply that capitalists must oversee production in order to exploit labor. The main argument closes by considering the viability of a scenario in which capital suppliers may dictate the choice of production technique but do not supervise the labor process.

The overarching conclusion which emerges from these considerations is that Roemer is substantially correct to insist that capitalist exploitation does not fundamentally require direct capitalist control of production. Some implications of this insight for the future development of Marxian economic theory are considered in the closing section of the paper.

2. ROEMER'S WALRASIAN ACCOUNT OF CAPITALIST EXPLOITATION

At issue is Roemer's *positive* theory of Marxian exploitation as it arises in capitalist economies. I am thus not concerned here with Roemer's treatment of the normative implications of exploitation (GT, ch. 9; FL, ch. 5). Consequently, I do not address Roemer's recasting of exploitation in terms of the structure of property relations (GT, part 3). One justification for the limited scope of this inquiry is that the legitimacy of Roemer's reformulation depends in large part on the validity of his claims concerning the role of DORSPA in capitalist exploitation.

I begin by restating those of Roemer's definitions and results which are central to this issue, and then consider the force of methodological and substantive criticisms of Roemer's account of capitalist exploitation.

2.1 SUMMARY OF ROEMER'S ACCOUNT

Roemer understands *exploitation in the Marxian sense* to exist when an individual expends more labor in production than is embodied in any consumption bundle which that person can afford. Correspondingly, those who can afford commodity bundles which embody more labor than they expend in production are deemed exploiters (GT, 122).

In Roemer's framework, *capitalism* denotes an exchange economy in which both consumption goods and productive assets are privately owned. This definition clearly covers Marx's specification in *Capital* (vol. 1, ch. 6) (in which workers are understood to be "free in the double sense," legally able and economically bound to lease their productive capacities), but also allows that workers may own other productive assets or hire inputs to use in their own productive efforts. In this view, the Roemerian scenarios of *Capital Market Island* (CMI) (characterized by product markets and a market for producer credit) and *Labor Market Island* (LMI) (an exchange economy with product markets and a market for labor power) are two polar manifestations of a capitalist economy (FL, ch. 7).

Combining the preceding definitions implies a conception of *capitalist exploitation* (understood in a value-theoretic sense) as Marxian exploitation which arises in an economy with credit or labor markets. In Marx's terms, Roemer understands capitalist exploitation as the appropriation of surplus value on the basis of some circuit of capital.

The fullest picture of Roemer's account of capitalist exploitation emerges from a comparison of his results for a capitalist economy (as defined above) and for a simple exchange economy, that is, a market economy without labor or credit markets, presented in GT and Roemer 1983 (hereafter UE). The latter I term *Product Market Island* (PMI), and its characteristic mode of exploitation, following Roemer, *unequal-exchange* exploitation. Roemer's conclusions rest on three sets of assumptions:

(A1) (*Preferences*) Individuals value commodities and leisure. (This assumption is for some results strengthened to include *the nonbenevolence of capitalists*; see GT, 65).

(A2) (*Production conditions*) Capital and labor are imperfect substitutes in time-consuming production processes characterized by constant returns to scale. There are at least two alternative processes which differ in labor intensity.

(A3) (*Market conditions*) Where they exist, markets are *competitive* and *perfectly complete*; that is, they are characterized by price-taking behavior governed by fully specified and costlessly enforceable contracts.

Roemer derives the following results based on these assumptions.

(R1) (*Basis of exploitation*) DORSPA implies the existence of unequal-exchange exploitation on PMI (*UE*, theorem 1) and capitalist exploitation on LMI (*GT*, theorem 2.4). The former is equivalent to the condition that product prices are not proportional to their respective labor values (*GT*, theorem 1.5), and the latter is equivalent to the existence of positive profits (*GT*, theorem 2.2, the Fundamental Marxian Theorem).

(R2) (*Correspondence of Unequal-Exchange Exploitation and Capitalist Exploitation*) Individuals who are unequal-exchange-exploited in PMI correspond to those who are subject to capitalist exploitation in LMI under identical preference, production, and market conditions (*GT*, theorems 2.5, 2.7; *UE*, theorems 2, 3). Similarly, the identities of exploiters in PMI and LMI coincide in the two scenarios.

(R3) (*Isomorphism between Interest Capital and Industrial Capital*) Equilibria in LMI are isomorphic to equilibria in CMI (*GT*, theorem 3.4; *UE*, theorem 4) under identical preference, production, and market conditions. In particular, patterns and rates of exploitation are identical under the isomorphic equilibria.

These arguments recast the traditional Marxian account of exploitation in at least three ways. First, and most important, Roemer identifies DORSPA as the essential basis of exploitation in exchange economies. Workers would consequently be exploited through credit market transactions even if capital suppliers did not supervise production. Furthermore, the same groups would exploit and be exploited through simple commodity exchange even if labor and credit markets did not exist.

Second, Roemer shows that the presence of exploitation in exchange economies generically corresponds to a disproportionality of commodity prices and labor values. This is clearly the basis of unequal-exchange exploitation in PMI. Furthermore, in CMI the price of the money commodity in the circuit of capital diverges from its labor value in proportion to the rate of interest.

An apparent exception to this result arises in the LMI scenario, if one assumes, following Marx's canonical account, that workers are paid the value of their labor power. However, this is not a necessary characterization of equilibria in LMI. Under the assumption of perfectly complete contracts, LMI is equivalent to a scenario which I label *Service Market Island* (SMI). In this scenario capital suppliers engage workers to perform specific tasks involving the transformation of input commodities into goods of higher net market value.

The putting-out system is a historical case of this scenario.[2] Profits are realized on SMI by paying service providers less than the value they add to commodities; prices and values diverge because production is based on exchange in labor services rather than labor power.[3]

Finally, Roemer's analysis of exploitation corresponds to Marx's accounts of *usury*, or interest-bearing capital prior to the era of capitalist production, and *ground rent*. With respect to these phenomena Marx, like Roemer, explains exploitation on the basis of class monopolization of relatively scarce productive resources (3:737–38, 762–63, 772). This correspondence figures in the argument to follow for three reasons. First, it illustrates that diverse surface forms of exploitation may derive from the same material basis.

Second, the correspondence hints at the problematic status of domination in Marx's theory of exploitation. Marx nowhere suggests that domination of production by usurers or landlords is necessary for the latter to exploit labor. Furthermore, Marx does not argue that industrial capitalists must be subsumed under interest capital or landed capital in order for the latter to extract their respective shares of surplus value.

Third, a comparison of interest capital and ground rent prompts questions about the robustness of Roemer's account when extended to a dynamic context. It is presumably easier to expand the capital stock than the stock of productive land, and thus there is greater scope for eliminating the relative scarcity (and thus profitability) of capital through processes of accumulation essential to capitalism. This possibility informs one of the two major substantive indictments of Roemer's analysis, to be discussed in the next section.

2.2   THE CRITIQUE OF ROEMER'S WALRASIAN ACCOUNT

Marxian critics have attacked every aspect of Roemer's alternative account of capitalist exploitation save the validity of his mathematical reasoning. The major targets of censure are Roemer's formulation of core concepts, his axiomatic characterization of economic conditions, and his reliance on an individualistic, ahistorical, nondialectical methodology.

Two broad conclusions have been drawn in these critiques. The first is that Roemer's brand of "analytical Marxism" cannot be considered Marxist analysis. The second conclusion is that Roemer's account of capitalist exploitation is fundamentally inconsistent with the reality Marx sought to explain. Put in Devine and Dymski's terms, this second level of critique suggests that Roemer's analysis is only a special and historically limited case of phenomena for which Marx has provided the *general* theory. As damaging as Roemer's conclusions (RI)–(R3) may at first appear to the traditional account, the latter view dismisses them as based on postulates which are for the most part incommensurate with the territory Marx sought to chart.

I maintain that grounds for the second conclusion have not been established by Roemer's critics, whatever their success in demonstrating the un-Marxian nature of his analysis. This is most clearly the case with respect to the value-theoretic argument Marx develops in volume 1, part 2 of *Capital*, to the effect that exploitation cannot be accounted for on the sole basis of commodity exchange relations. Roemer's results, which manifestly contradict this claim, are based on premises which Marx does not contest (and in some cases explicitly embraces) in his value-theoretic analysis.

Two lacunae in Roemer's analysis render it less apparently responsive to Marx's historical-strategic account of capitalist exploitation. First, Roemer does not assess the effects of market imperfections, evidently central to Marx's account, which may impede the translation of labor power into labor. Such imperfections challenge the legitimacy of Roemer's assumption of perfectly complete markets. Second, it is not evident from Roemer's account how DORSPA can be sustained in a dynamic setting.

The central question is thus whether incorporating such considerations within Roemer's "rational-choice" framework would fundamentally alter his conclusion that DORSPA provides a sufficient basis for the existence of exploitation in private ownership economies. I argue in this section that Roemer's critics have not successfully affirmed this question, and that DORSPA is in fact sufficient to account for the persistence of exploitation in a dynamic capitalist economy. In section 4 I argue further that there are neither theoretical nor empirical grounds for the general claim that the form of market failure implicit in *Capital* implies the necessity of capitalist domination for the existence of capitalist exploitation.

Let's focus the argument by making clear what is *not* at issue concerning Roemer's relevance to either the value-theoretic or the historical-strategic accounts:

1. *Definitions of core concepts.* Several critics have taken issue with Roemer's definition of exploitation (e.g., Foley 1989) on the grounds that it obscures important aspects of its social context such as the role of force (Reiman 1987, 1990; Dymski and Elliott 1989). Such objections do not deny that for most applications of interest, Roemer's and Marx's conceptions of exploitation effectively coincide. Roemer clearly affirms that wage labor is exploited if it produces a profit. Reciprocally, Marx understands exploitation to arise from the interest-bearing form of capital which prevails in Roemer's CMI scenario: "Usurer's capital has capital's mode of exploitation without its mode of production" (3:732; also see G, 853). Moreover, Marx affirms that exploitation arises from the putting-out system and other modes of production and exchange which do not presume the subsumption of labor under capital (R, 1023; G, 851–52).[4]

Where objections along these lines matter, they do so with respect to possible implications of contractual incompleteness. For example, Foley suggests that Roemer "misses Marx's central point that the specific relations that underlie exploitation are the critical factors shaping society and social consciousness" (1989, 192), but he does not show that Marx's "central point" contradicts Roemer's claim that capitalist domination is unnecessary for the *existence* of capitalist exploitation, whatever form it might take.

Similarly, Lebowitz's objection to Roemer's definition of *capitalism* hinges on his claim that capitalist domination is necessary for the result that "the capitalist—but not the worker—will gain by increasing the intensity of labor . . . [and] be the direct recipient of gains resulting from increased productivity" (1988, 207). These and related claims can be shown to depend on the nature and degree of contractual incompleteness. Who controls production is irrelevant if contracts are perfectly complete (Milgrom and Roberts 1990, 289), but the converse does not necessarily hold (see section 4).

2. *Ahistorical, individualistic method.* Roemer is often criticized for his reliance on an ahistorical, atomistic mode of argument. Concerning the issue of historical analysis, it is demonstrably the case (see sections 3 and 4) that in both his value-theoretic and historical-strategic accounts, Marx deduces claims of possibility and necessity from premises which are no more historically specific than the conditions of commodity exchange and class antagonism, which is the same terrain mapped by Roemer. Marx also makes use of counterfactual argument to indicate the robustness of his conclusions (e.g., 3:501).

Whatever the general failings of methodological individualism (see, for example, Foley 1989, 196–97; Howard and King 1992, 344–48; Lebowitz 1988, 193–204), they are not shown to void Roemer's relevance to Marx. Exploitation in Marx's account is clearly consistent with optimizing behavior in a sense similar to Roemer's (see, e.g., 1:280, 342–43).

3. *Exogenously given preferences, endowments, and technology.* Critics of "rational-choice Marxism" argue that preferences are socially determined and thus cannot be taken as given in the manner of Roemer's Walrasian methodology (Foley 1989, 196–97, Howard and King 1992, 344–45). But issues concerning the derivation of preferences pertain to the realm of use value, which Marx insists is irrelevant to the logic of determining exchange value (1:127–28), and thus exploitation. In particular, no important aspect of Marx's account of capitalist exploitation turns on the endogeneity of preferences.

Roemer concludes that DORSPA is the fundamental basis of exploitation in private ownership economies, but does not formally account for its existence in his model. Foley argues that this procedure inverts Marx's understanding of the ground of exploitation, in that DORSPA itself "is a consequence of the fact that one class appropriates the social surplus product through specific social relations" (1989, 193).

This is a legitimate point, but it does not invalidate Roemer's argument. Roemer's analysis challenges the claim that *capitalist* domination is necessary for capitalist exploitation, no matter what the historical basis of DORSPA. Moreover, Roemer's account gains credibility if as an empirical matter preexisting wealth inequalities were intensified by circuits of capital which did not require subsumption, as Marx suggests in volume 3, chapter 36 of *Capital*.

Finally, Roemer's specification of exogenously given constant returns to scale technology is formally at odds with Marx's analysis of capitalist technological development in chapters 13–15 of *Capital*, volume 1. But as Devine and Dymski's criticism of Roemer's analysis on this score suggests (1991, 260), this condition matters only insofar as it relates to the strategic problem of extracting surplus labor from labor power, which depends in turn on the nature and degree of contractual imperfections to be considered below.

4. *Competitive equilibrium.* It is not evident that Roemer runs afoul of Marx's understanding of capitalist exploitation by studying the phenomenon in the context of competitive equilibrium. Marx takes issue with neither the assumption of price-taking behavior nor the presumed absence of mobility barriers (R, 1014, 1032). Moreover, Marx correlates equalization of commodity prices and values to a market-clearing equilibrium condition (3:477–78).

Devine and Dymski (1991), however, question the coherence of Roemer's Walrasian account of exploitation when extended to a dynamic context. Specifically, they see a necessary conflict between conditions which support persistent capital scarcity and the existence of a market-clearing equilibrium (1991, 252–54).

Central to their argument is the claim that persistence of relative capital scarcity *rules out* the possibility of a "subsistence" sector (i.e., autarkic production, a welfare sector, or an underground economy). But this is not the case. Under their conditions, persistent capital scarcity is consistent with a scenario in which labor demand intersects labor supply strictly within a region which is infinitely elastic at a subsistence-level wage. The result is a competitive equilibrium in which some workers aren't hired at the going wage, as Roemer's theory requires if DORSPA is to be sustained in the presence of significant capital accumulation. Furthermore, capital suppliers in this scenario are price takers, so there is no "coercion" in Devine and Dymski's sense. There is also no involuntary unemployment in the Keynesian, nonmarket-clearing sense, but Roemer's account does not require it. For that matter, it is not evident that Marx's corresponding account of the "general law of capitalist accumulation" (vol. 1, ch. 25) requires the existence of Keynesian unemployment.

Let's now consider the consequences of contractual incompleteness and capital accumulation for Roemer's account of capitalist exploitation.

DORSPA and Contractual Incompleteness
The central point of contention in the critical response to Roemer's substantive argument concerns his assumption of perfectly complete contracts.

As suggested in the introduction, most of Roemer's critics contest the assumption on the ground of Marx's qualitative distinction between labor power and labor performed. Others raise the issue in the context of criticizing Roemer's terminology or analytical methods. While some critics go so far as to claim that prevalent forms of contractual incompleteness imply the necessity of capitalist domination for capitalist exploitation (Anderson and Thompson 1988, 218; Devine and Dymski 1991, 262), all who raise the issue insist that the prevalence of incomplete contracting compromises the validity of Roemer's claim that DORSPA is sufficient for the *existence* of exploitation in private ownership economies.

It is remarkable, then, that none of these critics offers explicit grounds for such a claim, or references to the necessary argument in the literature, or even the outline of what such an argument might entail. It is clear that an argument is needed; as will be discussed in section 4, Marx himself acknowledges that exploitation may under some conditions arise from circuits of capital which do not presume the subsumption of labor under capital, and neither theoretical nor empirical developments since Marx wrote support the unqualified assertion that capitalist exploitation requires capitalist domination. Even the growing radical literature on class relations in production focuses on the legitimate but weaker claim that capitalist control of production promotes the *maximal* degree of exploitation relative to given technical and market conditions (see, for example, Marglin 1974; Braverman 1974; Bowles and Gintis 1975; Edwards 1979; Reich and Devine 1981; Bowles 1985).

Among Roemer's critics, the completeness issue is addressed in greatest detail by Anderson and Thompson (1988) and Devine and Dymski (1991). Anderson and Thompson premise their argument on the assumption that workers must be coerced by capitalists at the point of production to provide surplus labor, but this claim seems to overlook the potential efficacy of other forms of inducement based on contingent contract renewal or bonuses and penalties based on output. Devine and Dymski carefully analyze the ways in which factor complementarities in production translate into monitoring and incentive problems, but then assert without argument (or refutation of contrary results in the literature) that such problems cannot be addressed even partially through contractual means (1991, 261–62).

In short, Roemer's critics establish grounds for the belief that capitalist domination is relevant to the magnitude of exploitation, but not for the stronger claim necessary to contradict Roemer's qualitative results.

DORSPA and Capital Accumulation

As noted in section 2.1, Roemer's analysis prompts legitimate questions about the persistence of capitalist exploitation given capital accumulation. Devine and Dymski (1991) argue correctly that given Roemer's assumptions, extension of his results to a dynamic context is problematic. They charge that Roemer's analytical framework, unlike Marx's, cannot provide coherent grounds for the persistence of DORSPA given accumulation.

This line of criticism, while certainly relevant, does not invalidate Roemer's Walrasian approach. To the contrary, in a sense one can more directly account for persistent exploitation on Walrasian than on traditional Marxian grounds, in that the former embraces notions of time preference which the latter disparages (1:298–99, 314n).

In particular, one can extend Roemer's static results in a manner consistent with both his methodology and his economic philosophy (as outlined, e.g., in FL, 60–63) by postulating that intensity of time preference or "impatience" is inversely proportional to initial income or wealth. Employing this assumption, Ryder (1985) derives competitive equilibria characterized by persistently positive rates of interest and progressive immiseration of borrowers. Lawrance (1990) provides empirical support for this postulate.

Thus, Devine and Dymski's critique implies at most that Roemer's analytical edifice is incomplete rather than fundamentally misconceived. DORSPA is an essentially static condition which is necessarily threatened by the process of capital accumulation, as Marx clearly understood. However, Roemer's analytical framework is adequate to account for the persistence of profits in the face of such accumulation.

3. MARX'S VALUE-THEORETIC ACCOUNT OF CAPITALIST EXPLOITATION

In the words of Howard and King, "Roemer attacks other Marxists, not Marx" (1992, 340). As the foregoing discussion indicates, this focus has permitted lingering uncertainty about the relevance of Roemer's account to Marx's analytical concerns. In an effort to address this uncertainty, I summarize and assess Marx's arguments in light of Roemer's conclusions, beginning with Marx's value-theoretic account in volume 1, part 2 of *Capital*.

3.1 SUMMARY OF MARX'S ACCOUNT

Marx's argument in chapters 4 and 5 of volume 1 can be summarized as follows:

(V1) The primary basis of surplus value appropriation in private ownership economies is the circuit of capital M–C–M', where M' > C = M in value terms. That is, M–C–M' is the "general formula of capital" (1:257).

(V2) Appropriation of surplus value cannot be accomplished on the basis of commodity exchange relations alone, whether or not commodity prices are proportional to their respective labor values.

(V3) However, surplus value must be realized through commodity exchange. (V4) Therefore, appropriation of surplus value in the general case requires commodity exchange consistent with the circuit M–C–M', plus some condition S.[5]

In chapters 6 and 7, Marx identifies condition S as the subsumption of labor under capital, such that capitalists hire the commodity labor power and in the process of production extract a quantity of its use value, labor, in excess of its exchange value.

Roemer's analysis indicates that premises (V1) and (V2) are in general false, rendering the conclusion (V4) incorrect whatever the validity of Marx's reasoning from these premises. I consider in turn Marx's arguments in support of these premises.

3.2 THE GENERAL FORMULA OF CAPITAL

Marx argues in chapter 4 that M–C–M' is the "general formula of capital" but does not explain why it should be considered any more "general" than other formulas such as M–M', the circuit of interest-bearing capital. He suggests that the latter is simply the "abridged form" of the former circuit, but in the absence of argument one could as readily insist that M–C–M' is simply the "expanded form" of the historically antecedent circuit M–M'.

On what grounds does Marx insist on the former conclusion? Arguments he presents elsewhere (3:515–17, TSV, 455–56, 461) suggest that Marx's construction here is motivated by his critique of the political economy of his day, according to which capital was understood to have the innate power of yielding interest. In Marx's view, positing M–M' as a primary basis for the appropriation of surplus value begs the question of how simple money-lending could possibly support this appropriation.

This is not a necessary consequence of admitting M–M' as a vehicle for accruing surplus value. In particular, Roemer's account does not suffer from this defect. In his analysis interest derives from the class monopolization of relatively scarce productive assets, not from some inherent fructuousness of capital. In light of Roemer's results there are no compelling grounds, even given Marx's implicit polemical concerns, to dismiss this form of capital as an elemental mode of appropriating surplus value.

This conclusion is not voided on the grounds that the expression M–M' obscures auxiliary exchanges and production activity which must take place if loan capital is to yield interest in the manner suggested by Roemer. An identical objection could be lodged with respect to Marx's candidate for the "general formula of capital." Specifically, both circuits of capital necessarily correspond to the expanded schematic M–C ... P ... C'–M' (2:109), where " ... P ..." represents production which takes place outside of exchange.

Moreover, this schematic is also consistent with the circuit M–C′–M′, where M′ = C′ > M in value terms, corresponding to the putting-out system and other forms of exchange in SMI. Marx's neglect of this alternative version of his "general formula" hinges on the legitimacy of premise (V2), which I examine next. In any case, premise (V1) is baseless.

3.3   COMMODITY EXCHANGE AND SURPLUS VALUE

Marx interprets the task of explaining surplus value as one of determining whether the "simple circulation of commodities . . . might permit the valorization of the values entering into it" (1:259), that is, whether value can be augmented in the process of exchange. This characterization is strictly speaking inaccurate, in that surplus value also results from exchange if some class L of traders thereby transfers a given quantity of value to a different class K of traders. Thus the total quantity of value need not be expanded in the process of exchange; it need only be redistributed. The class L will of necessity lose that quantity of value, but this is irrelevant from the standpoint of the circuit Marx seeks to explain.

Hindsight suggests that Marx intends the more stringent condition for explaining surplus value as a postulate; that is, in anticipation of subsequent analytical concerns he is interested primarily in accounting for the surplus value which arises from an expansion of value subsequent to the initiation of a given circuit of capital. However, exchanges on CMI and SMI are consistent with this more stringent condition, contradicting Marx's ensuing claim that capitalists must purchase labor power in order to realize surplus value.

Marx's first argument with respect to the problem as posed addresses the case in which all commodity prices are equal to their respective values, which Marx terms the "pure form" of commodity exchange (1:259–61). This characterization is suspect at best. As Roemer confirms (GT, theorem 1.5), this scenario begets no surplus value, but it is also inessential to the economic reality Marx seeks to explain. As Marx reveals in chapter 6, DORSPA is fundamental to that reality, and Roemer shows that DORSPA generically results in the disproportionality of prices and values. The circuit of capital based on wage labor permits an exception, but it enjoys no special explanatory status unless Marx's characterization of the case in which commodity prices and values are unequal is correct.

Marx addresses this case in three ways. His first argument (1:262–64) concerns the scenario in which prices diverge proportionately from their respective values, which Roemer demonstrates to be formally equivalent to the case in which prices equal values. The analytically relevant case is instead one in which the prices of certain goods, for example, those supplied by a given class K, diverge from their respective values. Marx dismisses this case on the grounds that it assumes the existence of "a class of buyers who do not sell, i.e. a class of consumers who do not produce."

Neither clause of this assertion is valid, as is illustrated, for example, by Roemer's analysis of CMI. Existence of surplus value in the latter need only presume "a class of buyers who do not sell" a *particular* set of commodities, that is, those associated with the provision of means of production on credit (whether or not this credit is extended in the form of money is immaterial). This scenario also exposes Marx's second characterization as a non sequitur: the exploited class does indeed produce, using the wherewithal provided by the lenders of capital. Consequently there is no need to presume, contrary to Marx's claim, that "the money with which such a class is constantly making purchases must constantly flow into its coffers" from the pockets of the exploiting class itself. Surplus value, as Roemer shows, is drawn from the surplus product created by the exploited class using the wherewithal provided by capital suppliers on CMI.

Similar advantages are enjoyed by those relatively well endowed with alienable productive assets on PMI and SMI. In both cases, DORSPA supports the appropriation of value through unequal exchange. Thus, contrary to Marx, there is no sense in which such results are "inexplicable from the standpoint of simple circulation."

Marx's last argument with respect to this case is based on treating traders as individuals rather than "personified categories." Here he argues that any price-value disparity in exchange between A and B merely redistributes value without augmenting the sum of values in circulation. Here the fallacy introduced in the opening argument of chapter 5 returns to haunt Marx's analysis: His conclusion is manifestly true, but irrelevant. The existence of surplus value is adequately explained so long as one class of traders systematically reaps the benefit of such price-value disparities. Marx thus commits a fallacy of division when he suggests that the capitalist class would have to "defraud itself" (1:266) in this scenario.

In sum, Marx's exclusive focus in volume 1 of *Capital* on wage labor as the vehicle of capitalist exploitation can be justified on value-theoretic grounds only if one *assumes* that the canonical form of exploitation is one in which commodity prices are proportional to their respective labor values and that surplus value must derive from an augmentation of value subsequent to the initiation of a given circuit of capital. Discarding the first condition admits exploitation via circuits of capital which prevail on CMI and SMI. Discarding both conditions, one can also account for transfers of value in terms of the unequal exchanges which characterize PMI.

4. MARX'S HISTORICAL-STRATEGIC ACCOUNT OF CAPITALIST EXPLOITATION

The argument I refer to as Marx's historical-strategic account of capitalist exploitation is spread across the working notebooks which contain his mature economic thinking. Reflecting the fact that Marx did not live to edit any of this material for publication save that in volume 1 of *Capital*, the account is less fully developed and linearly presented than Marx's value-theoretic analysis, appearing instead as a series of partially overlapping segments connected by a common set of themes. I summarize the form and substance of this account and then consider its two primary components.

4.1 EXPLOITATION AND SUBSUMPTION

Marx's historical-strategic account chronicles the development of capitalist production relations in response to capital's "boundless thirst" for surplus labor. In terms of the present discussion the central problematic of this account stems from Marx's insistence that capitalist production relations became necessary for the existence of exploitation once such relations prevailed, but not before.

Marx's analysis of the relationship between capitalist domination and capitalist exploitation is based on his parallel distinctions between *absolute* versus *relative* surplus value on one hand and *formal* versus *real* subsumption of labor on the other. The former terms characterize the manner in which surplus value is created: Absolute value is that which is produced by extending the working day beyond the duration necessary to reproduce labor power, while relative surplus value is that which arises from reducing the magnitude of necessary labor time (1:432).

The latter terms refer to the degree to which capitalists control the labor process. Formal subsumption denotes the coercive supervision of labor under given conditions of production: "The capitalist intervenes in the [labor] process as its director, manager. For him it also represents the direct exploitation of the labor of others. It is this that I refer to as the *formal subsumption of labor under capital*" (R, 1019). In contrast, real subsumption refers to the transformation of the conditions of the labor process itself by capitalist firm owners (R, 1034–35).

In Marx's historical-strategic account of capitalist exploitation, production of absolute surplus value is held to require formal subsumption, while production of relative surplus value is understood to depend on the real subsumption of labor under capital (R, 1025). I consider in turn Marx's arguments with respect to these linkages.

4.2 FORMAL SUBSUMPTION AND ABSOLUTE SURPLUS VALUE

Marx repeatedly identifies conditions of exploitation arising from circuits of capital, corresponding to the characteristic forms of exchange in CMI and SMI, which antedate the subsumption of labor under capital (1:645; 3:732; R, 1023; G, 851–53; TSV, 487). Consistent with Roemer's analysis, Marx understands these forms of exploitation to derive from class monopolization of productive assets (3:737–38, 762–63).

However, Marx apparently also insists that exploitation *requires* formal subsumption of labor once capitalist production relations predominate (2:135–36; 3:524), a condition he correlates to the subordination of interest capital to industrial capital. Subsumption of this form requires the *active* intervention of capitalists in the labor process, Marx asserts, because "the exploitation of productive labor takes effort, whether [the capitalist] does this himself or has it done in his name by others" (3:503). Thus if there were no industrial capitalists, "the result would be a tremendous devaluation of money capital and a tremendous fall in the rate of interest," with the result that many would be "compelled to turn themselves back into industrial capitalists" (3:501).

Why might this be the case? The proximate reason given by Marx is the *class antagonism* between capital and labor (1:450; 3:507–08; TSV, 505). But this is manifestly insufficient to explain the necessity of formal subsumption for capitalist exploitation. For example, the evidently antagonistic interests of usurers and their victims did not prevent the extortion of "exorbitant interest" by the former (R, 1023).

As argued in section 2, antagonistic class relations in exchange can be mediated by the state if they are governed by sufficiently complete contracts. Thus an adequate explanation for the necessity of labor's subsumption for capitalist exploitation must begin with an analysis of market or production conditions which preclude exchange based on fully specified and externally enforceable terms. Marx suggests the basis for such an explanation when he argues that "leaving aside certain extremely elastic restrictions, the nature of commodity exchange itself imposes no limit to the working day" (1:344).[6]

However, the absence of perfectly complete contracting conditions does not of itself establish the necessity of formal subsumption for maximal rates of exploitation, much less for its existence. As I'll discuss in more detail below, magnitudes of surplus labor attainable with perfectly complete contracts can in some cases be induced by market-based incentives such as payment by the piece, bonuses and commissions, penalties, and contingent threats of nonrenewal. Thus, given the structure of Marx's historical account, any argument on strategic grounds as to the necessity of capitalist domination for capitalist exploitation must fulfill a double burden: It must explain why such market-based incentives necessarily fail to achieve *any* level of exploitation once capitalist production relations predominate, *despite* the fact that they evidently succeeded prior to the general diffusion of such relations.

Two separate arguments in Marx's historical-strategic account, only one of which is explicitly drawn, address this double burden. The implicit argument, which emerges in contrasting Marx's discussions of usury (vol. 3, ch. 36) and wage labor (vol. 1, ch. 6), suggests that the historically contingent role of capitalist domination in the exploitation of labor turns on the extent to which loans to producers could be secured by collateral.

In Marx's view, a central characteristic of "pre-capitalist" credit markets is that borrowers typically owned productive assets with which they could secure loans (3:729); indeed, in Marx's account the limited transformative effect of usury capital derived in part from its absorption of collateralized assets when borrowers defaulted (3:729–32). In contrast, Marx sees the canonical form of capitalism as one in which workers own no productive assets (1:272–73). Thus, unlike in the earlier epoch of interest capital, workers cannot be spurred to provide surplus labor by the fear of losing their collateral.

This argument certainly establishes the basis for a historical distinction between usury and credit markets under modern capitalism, but it provides neither theoretical nor empirical grounds for the claim that capitalist production relations are required to exploit labor if and only if such relations predominate. In terms of the theoretical account, collateral is not in general required to secure surplus labor, and it may not even be necessary in order to secure the maximal level of surplus labor consistent with perfectly complete contracts.

The modern theoretical literature on the economics of information and incentives has identified a number of conditions under which capital suppliers might more or less closely approximate outcomes achieved with perfectly complete contracts, using familiar forms of compensation based on externally verifiable aspects of performance or production. For example, capital suppliers may achieve the desired outcomes through the use of appropriate penalties or rewards (Grossman and Hart 1980, 16) or payment by the piece (Stiglitz 1975, 560). These mechanisms for yielding surplus labor may be more effective in long-term relationships (Radner 1985, 1986). Under conditions of collective or "team" production, in which workers' productivity levels are interdependent, capitalists may accrue complete-market profit levels through "divide and conquer" compensation strategies (Holmström, 1982, 327–30; Ma, Moore, and Turnbull 1988).

Moreover, even if conditions most favorable to capital suppliers do not obtain, the existence of consequential market incompleteness does not in general imply the necessity of subsuming labor under capital for the *exis-*

tence of capitalist exploitation. Rather, the theoretical literature on effort and incentives suggests that in the absence of subsumption capitalists may achieve positive but "second-best" levels of return (see, for example, Grossman and Hart 1980; Holmström 1979, 1982; Sappington 1980).

The empirical case for the necessity of collateral in exploiting workers via credit exchanges is undermined by the historical persistence of forms of production which do not depend on the formal subsumption of labor. This point has been argued forcefully by historian Maxine Berg (1983, 1986), who states that "the ubiquity and comparative success of domestic and workshop manufacture in the 18th century, and its continuation alongside the factory system well into the 19th, were based on the intensive exploitation of labour . . . at least equal to that suffered under the factory system" (1986, 19).

Marx's second and explicit argument with respect to the historically contingent role of labor subsumption in capitalist exploitation suggests that the progressive attainment of relative surplus value via capitalist development of the labor process creates increasing difficulties in extracting absolute surplus value. Exploring this development in volume 1, part 4 of *Capital*, Marx writes, "As the number of co-operating workers increases, so too does their resistance to the domination of capital, and, necessarily, the pressure put on by capital to overcome this resistance" (1:449).

But again, this tendency does not establish the necessity of formal subsumption for the *existence* of capitalist exploitation of labor working co-operatively. As discussed above, capitalists may effectively use team payment schemes which for given conditions of production induce non-cooperative behavior among workers, thus promoting the extraction of surplus labor. Furthermore, the process of real subsumption may also *reduce* the need for direct capitalist oversight of production, either by expanding the scope for inducing performance by contractual means (Holmström and Milgrom 1991) or by habituating workers to a certain rate of labor extraction. Marx explicitly affirms the latter possibility: "The organization of the capitalist process of production, once it is fully developed, breaks down all resistance. . . . Direct extra-economic force is still of course used, *but only in exceptional cases*. In the ordinary run of things, the worker can be left to the 'natural laws of production' " . . . (1:899; emphasis added). Thus the process of capitalist development may virtually eliminate the need for capitalist oversight of the labor process.

4.3   REAL SUBSUMPTION AND RELATIVE SURPLUS VALUE

To Marx, usurer's capital was a powerful engine for reaping *absolute* surplus value, capable of appropriating "everything in excess of the producers' most essential means of subsistence" (3:730). In his view usury also played a critical role in establishing the preconditions for capitalism by separating workers from their means of production while concentrating wealth in the hands of capital suppliers (3:729–32; TSV, 529–30).

In Marx's account the chief weakness of this primitive circuit of capital lay in its failure to generate *relative* surplus value via transformation of the existing conditions of production (3:730–31, 745; TSV, 531). Furthermore, Marx understands this failure to transform the labor process as an *intrinsic* feature of capital which does not seize control of production (G, 853). In short, Marx insists that systematic appropriation of relative surplus value requires the real subsumption of labor under capital (R, 1037).

Why might this be the case? In hindsight, Marx is making implicit assumptions about market conditions which parallel those he invokes in arguing for the contingent necessity of formal subsumption in reaping absolute surplus value. If capital markets were governed by perfectly complete contracts, capitalists could mimic the gains Marx understands to flow from real subsumption by contractually stipulating the choice of production technique.

This is most easily seen in the context of SMI (corresponding, for example, to sharecropping or the putting-out system). Here capitalists have the same direct interest in reducing necessary labor time as they do in the case of production characterized by wage labor. If transactions with labor service providers were governed by fully specifiable and costlessly enforceable contracts, capitalists could simply dictate production techniques of the type analyzed by Marx in volume 1, chapters 13–15 of *Capital.*

Of course, exchanges such as those associated with the putting-out system were clearly not characterized by ideal contracting conditions. Historical accounts focusing on problems of embezzlement, quality control, and nonresponsiveness to changing market conditions suggest the dimensions of contractual incompleteness which triggered the general demise of this mode of production (Kriedte 1983, 141–42; Marglin 1974).

However, such accounts do not establish that this mode was genetically incapable of reaping *any* gains in the form of relative surplus value, only that they did not achieve *maximal* levels of profit in this form. Berg, Hudson, and Sonenscher (1983, 10–11), for example, point to a pattern of labor-saving innovations which preceded the era of capitalist production relations and yet anticipated the technical developments discussed by Marx.

Moreover, contractual incompleteness with respect to the choice of production technique does not imply the necessity of direct capitalist oversight of the labor process in order to exploit labor, despite suggestions to the contrary by Roemer's critics. Imperfect contracting may require that capitalists personally dictate rather than contractually stipulate the technical conditions under which workers produce, without requiring capitalists to supervise the labor process itself. Berg, Hudson, and Sonenscher's (1983, 31) suggestion that improvements in numerical control and computer technology permit dispersion of the labor process away from the factory center appears to be borne out by recent trends in U.S. industry toward out-sourcing work (Lohr 1992; Ansberry 1993).

In short, there is no doubt that capitalist domination of the labor process greatly accelerated the pace of labor-saving innovations which Marx links to the generation of relative surplus value. But there are not strong theoretical or empirical grounds for the claim that capitalist domination is necessary for the existence of relative surplus value, or that achievement of the latter requires direct capitalist oversight of the labor process.

5. CONCLUSION

In light of the foregoing arguments, I conclude that Roemer's identification of DORSPA as the essential basis of Marxian exploitation in capitalist economies must be considered substantially correct. This conclusion is consistent with Marx's analysis of exchange-based exploitation prior to capitalist domination of production. Roemer's critics are right to insist that direct oversight of production provided capital suppliers with new weapons in their quest for surplus labor, but it does not follow that these weapons became necessary for the exploitation of labor once capitalist domination prevailed.

The arguments presented here bear additional implications for the agenda of Marxian political economy. First, it is evident that Marxian value theory provides a poor basis for comprehending the economic logic of capitalist exploitation. In particular, Marx's allegiance in *Capital* to the conception of price-value equivalence as the "pure" and thus analytically primary case of commodity exchange leads him to significant errors of emphasis and interpretation. It is telling in this regard that criticism of Roemer's neglect of the labor/labor-power distinction has in no case been based on Marx's value-theoretic account.

The significance of Marx's distinction between labor power and labor is thus best understood in strategic terms. A large mainstream literature has developed in the last twenty-five years which explores the strategic consequences of incomplete contracts and asymmetric information in production, the phenomena typically invoked by Roemer's critics. However, as suggested by the argument in sections 2 and 4 above, Marxian economists have harvested this literature in somewhat haphazard fashion. Important work remains to be done in developing critical and institutionally specific alternatives to abstract and ahistorical mainstream analysis. Promising steps in this direction include Bowles and Gintis (1990) and Hahnel and Albert (1990). Complementary approaches suggest the conclusion that struggle over the extraction of labor from labor power is but one important aspect of strategic

conflict in production (see, for example, Bowles, Gintis, and Gustafsson 1993), but this broader critical understanding is far from being fully worked out.
These are the conditions of the problem. *Hic Rhodus* ...

Notes

I thank Mike Lebowitz, Jim Devine, Peter Kilby, Alex Dupuy, three anonymous referees, and especially Frank Thompson for comments on earlier versions of the argument presented here. I would also like to acknowledge Bo Gustafsson for arranging generous research support through the Swedish Collegium for Advanced Study in the Social Sciences in the fall of 1992. Finally, thanks to David Konstan for help with the Latin in the title (a negation of the imperative which concludes volume 1, chapter 5 of *Capital*).

1. I follow the Fowkes/Fernbach rendering of the German term *Subsumtion* in their recent translation of *Capital* (1990a, 1991, 1992, hereafter cited by volume number).
2. Transactions in the putting-out system differed from pure credit exchanges in that capital suppliers owned both the inputs supplied and the resulting output (Kriedte 1983, 36).
3. A labor service is a commodity insofar as it is produced and exchanged. Marx's dismissal of labor services as unproductive of value (G, 272) refers only to *personal* services, the results of which are not intended for sale, and is thus irrelevant to this discussion.
4. According to Dymski and Elliott (1989, 347–48), Marx understands usury and ground rent as "secondary" forms of exploitation, in contrast to the "primary" form realized through subsumption of labor under capital. This assessment does not clearly follow from the passage they cite (3:745 in the Penguin edition), which refers to exchanges involving means of subsistence rather than means of production. Moreover, their construction is counterintuitive to the extent it suggests that exploitation would become somehow less significant were a technical innovation to enable capitalists to discard indirect strategic methods in favor of direct contractual means of extracting surplus labor (cf. the discussion in section 4.2).
5. Marx additionally stipulates that an adequate account of this phenomenon must proceed from the assumption of price-value equivalence in exchange, since "it cannot be explained by referring to any divergence between price and value" (1:269n). I argue in section 3.3 that this claim is incorrect, but Marx's inference here is invalid in any case, since his argument establishes at most that surplus value cannot be explained on the basis of price-value disparities *taken alone*.
6. Marx's subsequent argument suggests that this indeterminacy arises only at the political, or collective, level of class conflict (1:344). In an economy without significant mobility barriers (cf. R, 1014), it is clear that no one firm can impose more strenuous working conditions than its competitors.

References

Anderson, W. H. Locke, and Frank Thompson. 1988. "Neoclassical Marxism." *Science and Society* 52:215–28.

Ansberry, Clare. 1993. "Workers Are Forced to Take More Jobs with Few Benefits." *Wall Street Journal*, March 11.

Berg, Maxine. 1986. *The Age of Manufactures: Industry, Innovation, and Work in Britain, 1700–1820.* Oxford University Press.

Berg, Maxine, Pat Hudson, and Michael Sonenscher. 1983. "Manufacture in Town and Country before the Factory." In Maxine Berg, Pat Hudson, and Michael Sonenscher, eds., *Manufacture in Town and Country before the Factory.* Cambridge University Press.

Bowles, Samuel. 1985. "The Production Process in a Competitive Economy: Walrasian, Neo-Hobbesian, and Marxian Models." *American Economic Review* 75:16–36.

Bowles, Samuel, and Herbert Gintis. 1975. *Schooling in Capitalist America: Educational Reform and the Contradictions of Economic Life.* Basic Books.

————.1990. "Contested Exchange: New Microfoundations of the Political Economy of Capitalism." *Politics and Society* 18:165–222.

Bowles, Samuel, Herbert Gintis, and Bo Gustafsson. 1993. *Markets and Democracy: Participation, Accountability, and Efficiency.* Cambridge University Press.

Braverman, Harry. 1974. *Labor and Monopoly Capital: The Degradation of Work in the Twentieth Century.* Monthly Review Press.

Devine, James, and Gary Dymski. 1989. "Roemer's Theory of Capitalist Exploitation: The Contradictions of Walrasian Marxism." *Review of Radical Political Economics* 21:13–17.

————. 1991. "Roemer's 'General' Theory of Exploitation Is a Special Case." *Economics and Philosophy* 7:235–75.

————. 1992. "Walrasian Marxism Once Again." *Economics and Philosophy* 8:157–62.

Dymski, Gary, and John Elliott. 1989. "Roemer vs. Marx: Should *Anyone* Be Interested in Exploitation?" In Robert Ware and Kai Nielsen, eds., *Analyzing Marxism: New Essays on Analytical Marxism.* University of Calgary Press.

Edwards, Richard. 1979. *Contested Terrain: The Transformation of the Workplace in the Twentieth Century.* Basic Books.

Foley, Duncan. 1989. "Roemer on Marx on Exploitation." *Economics and Politics* 1:187–99.

Grossman, Sanford, and Oliver Hart. 1980. "An Analysis of the Principal-Agent Problem." *Econometrica* 51:7–45.

Hahnel, Robin, and Michael Albert. 1990. *Quiet Revolution in Welfare Economics.* Princeton University Press.

Holmström, Bengt. 1979. "Moral Hazard and Observability." *Bell Journal of Economics* 10:74–91.

————. 1982. "Moral Hazard in Teams." *Bell Journal of Economics* 13:324–40.

Holmström, Bengt, and Paul Milgrom. 1991. "Multitask Principal-Agent Analyses: Incentive Contracts, Asset Ownership, and Job Design." *Journal of Law, Economics, and Organization* 7:24–52.

Houston, David. 1989. "Roemer on Exploitation and Class." *Review of Radical Political Economics* 21:175–87.

Howard, M., and J. King. 1992. *A History of Marxian Economics*, vol. 2, *1929–1990.* Princeton University Press.

Kriedte, Peter. 1983. *Peasants, Landlords, and Merchant Capitalists: Empire and the World Economy, 1500–1800.* Berg Publishers.

Lawrance, Emily. 1991. "Poverty and the Rate of Time Preference: Evidence from Panel Data." *Journal of Political Economy* 99:54–77.

Lebowitz, Michael A. 1988. "Is 'Analytical Marxism' Marxism?" *Science and Society* 52:191–214.

Lohr, Steve. 1992. "More Workers in the U.S. Are Becoming Hired Guns." *New York Times*, Aug. 14.

Ma, Chin-to, John Moore, and Steven Turnbull. 1988. "Stopping Agents from 'Cheating.'" *Journal of Economic Theory* 46:355–72.

Marglin, Stephen A. 1974. "What Do Bosses Do?" *Review of Radical Political Economics* 6:1–60.

Marx, Karl. 1971. *Theories of Surplus Value*, part 3. Progress Publishers.

———. 1990a. *Capital*, vol. 1 [1867]. Penguin.

———. 1990b. "Results of the Immediate Process of Production (*Resultate*)." In *Capital* 1:948–1084. Penguin.

———. 1991. *Capital*, vol. 3 [1894]. Penguin.

———. 1992. *Capital*, vol. 2 [1885]. Penguin.

———. 1993. *Grundrisse* [1973]. Penguin.

Milgrom, Paul, and John Roberts. 1992. *Economics, Organization, and Management*. Prentice-Hall.

Radner, Roy. 1985. "Repeated Principal-Agent Games with Discounting." *Econometrica* 53:1173–98.

———. 1986. "Repeated Moral Hazard with Low Discount Rates." In Walter Heller, Ross Starr, and David Starrett, eds., *Uncertainty, Information, and Communication: Essays in Honor of Kenneth J. Arrow, Volume 3*. Cambridge University Press.

Reich, Michael, and James Devine. 1981. "The Microeconomics of Conflict and Hierarchy in Capitalist Production." *Review of Radical Political Economics* 12:27–45.

Reiman, Jeffrey. 1987. "Exploitation, Force, and the Moral Assessment of Capitalism: Thoughts on Roemer and Cohen." *Philosophy and Public Affairs* 16:2–41 [this volume, selection 8].

———. 1990. "Why Worry about How Exploitation Is Defined? Reply to John Roemer." *Social Theory and Practice* 16:101–13.

Roemer, John. 1982. *A General Theory of Exploitation and Class*. Harvard University Press.

———. 1983. "Unequal Exchange, Labor Migration, and International Capital Flows: A Theoretical Synthesis." In Padma Desai, ed., *Marxism, Central Planning, and the Soviet Economy: Economic Essays in Honor of Alexander Erlich*. MIT Press.

———. 1988. *Free to Lose: An Introduction to Marxist Economic Philosophy*. Harvard University Press.

Ryder, Harl E. 1985. "Heterogeneous Time Preferences and the Distribution of Wealth." *Mathematical Social Sciences* 9:63–76.

Sappington, David. 1983. "Limited Liability Contracts between Principal and Agent." *Journal of Economic Theory* 29:1–21.

Stiglitz, Joseph. 1975. "Incentives, Risk, and Information: Notes toward a Theory of Hierarchy." *Bell Journal of Economics* 6:552–79.

PART IV

Exploitation and Feminism

The One-Sidedness of Wage Labor

MICHAEL A. LEBOWITZ

NONWAGE LABORER

THROUGH THE OWNERSHIP OF a *slave*, it is possible to secure necessary use values without either working to produce them or exchanging for them. In this case, the use values required as inputs for the process of production of labor power are obtained through a process of exploitation—defined simply as compelling the performance of surplus labor.

In the slave relation, a dependent producer "belongs to the *individual, particular* owner, and is his labouring machine." Labor power here does not "belong" to the dependent producer, and the disposition of its expenditure (as well as the enjoyment of the fruits of its activity) are the right of the owner.[1] In this case, rather than economic compulsion, it is "*direct compulsion*" which maintains the slave in his position. He works under the spur of fear—although "not for *his existence* which is *guaranteed* even though it does not belong to him."[2]

Exploitation means that the slave "must add to the labour-time necessary for his own maintenance an extra quantity of labour-time in order to produce the means of subsistence for the owner of the means of production."[3] It means that the master benefits by receiving surplus products and/or "free time"—the reduced requirement to perform that labor "absolutely necessary

From Michael A. Lebowitz, "Wage-Labourers and Non-Wage-Labourers," in *Beyond Capital: Marx's Political Economy of the Working Class* (New York: St. Martin's Press, 1992), 112–24, with the permission of the author.

in order to consume things." Of course, the very benefits of the slave relation to the wage laborer may be captured by capital in the form of an increased intensity of the capitalist workday or reduced wage requirements. Yet, this no more alters the character of slave exploitation than the character of capitalist exploitation is changed in the case where a capitalist is unable to realize all the surplus value generated in the process of production.

Again, we may note that, while the slave's labor is indeed productive for the slaveowner, *in itself* it remains private and unproductive with respect to capital. Only insofar as the wage laborer is successful in securing the money requirements for the slave's means of subsistence which take a commodity form will there be any representation under the heading of "social" labor. Similarly, the ability of the master to secure these money requirements through wage labor will be a condition for the maintenance of the slave relation. However, the value of labor power will not include provision for the necessities consumed by the slave *because capital wants wage labourers to have slaves!* (This would be yet another absurdity consistent with the one-sided concept of the value of labor power. . . .) Rather, the value of labor power includes such provisions insofar as the wage laborer has been successful in struggling for them.

Although it is possible to explore this particular relation and its inherent dynamics further, the obvious question is—*why even raise the specter of slave ownership in the context of our discussion of the production of the wage laborer?* Of course, the answer is that it is precisely the way in which Marx described relations within the family at the time. In the *German Ideology*, he spoke of the "latent slavery in the family," where "wife and children are the slaves of the husband"; the latter in this case had "the power of disposing of the labour-power of others."[4] Similarly, in the *Communist Manifesto*, Marx and Engels emphasized that the program of the Communists would do away with both the "exploitation of children by their parents" and "the status of women as mere instruments of production."[5]

Marx explicitly returned to this theme in his note for *Capital*. "In private property of every type," he indicated, "the *slavery* of the members of the family at least is always implicit since they are made use of and exploited by the head of the family."[6] As well, Engels would subsequently note that "the modern individual family is based on the open or disguised domestic enslavement of the woman."[7]

In defining the relationship within the family as one of slavery, Marx was clearly stating that "the family labour necessary for consumption," that "independent labour at home, within customary limits, for the family itself" (including the exercise of "economy and judgement in the consumption and preparation of the means of subsistence") occurs in a situation where the producer in the household is exploited within a slave relation.[8] *How could it be denied that this is what Marx was arguing?*

Yet, this is a point that Marxists have resisted. As Nancy Folbre comments, there has been a "reluctance to consider the possibility of exploitation within the realm of reproduction" with the result that such exploitation was "largely defined out of existence in the domestic labor debates."[9] Further, the very designation of the relation by Marx and Engels as one of slavery has been described "as more metaphorical than scientific"—and, indeed, as evoking "dangerous metaphors."[10] Yet, not only does this assertion display a curious selectivity in drawing upon Marx but it also ignores the *consistency* in his argument.

Consider what happens to this "old family relationship" characterized by patriarchal authority ("*patria potestas*") when the degree of immiseration increases—either because of a fall in real wages or because of a growth in social needs.[11] One option is an increase in exploitation within the household—i.e., an increase in the extra quantity of labor performed by wife and children. An increased expenditure of labor in the house, we know, will be accompanied by a reduced expenditure of money outside. Referring to the exploitation of children, Marx noted that "this exploitation always existed to a certain extent among the peasants, and was the more developed, the heavier the yoke pressing on the countryman."[12]

Yet, there is another possible response when wages are too low to satisfy requirements (one likely to occur when increased domestic labor is inadequate to satisfy needs)—an extension of the labor time performed directly for capital. Just as for the individual worker there is a backward-sloping supply of labor such that the supply of labor is "to a certain extent independent of the supply of workers," so also do we find this in the case of the worker's family "when the quantity of labour provided by the head of the family is augmented by the labour of the members of the family."[13] More labor can be furnished to capital (and more money thereby secured) "by enrolling, under the direct sway of capital, every member of the worker's family, without distinction of age or sex."[14]

In itself, this development does not change the nature of the relation between "the head of the family" and those whom he exploits—any more than the slaveowner of antiquity ceased to be the owner of the person of others when he rented his slaves out. From slaves within the household, the chattels of the head of the family become income-earning slaves as the result of the need for additional money. And this is exactly how Marx described this development. Working-class parents, he argued, "have assumed characteristics that are truly revolting and thoroughly like slave-dealing." Not only did the male wage laborer sell his own labor power. "Now he sells wife and child. He has become a slave dealer."[15]

Of course, Marx did propose that this very process in which capital assigned "an important part in socially organized processes of production, outside the sphere of the domestic economy, to women, young persons and children of both sexes, does nevertheless create a new economic foundation for a higher form of the family and of relations between the sexes."[16] It is not at all contradictory, however, that something undertaken for short-term benefits may have quite different long-term implications.[17] In any event, it is not difficult to see *why* Marx considered this development to be a basis for the potential alteration of social relations within the household. The seller of labor power is "formally posited as a person," as one who has labor power as her own property.[18] Accordingly, with the entry of women into wage labor, there is the potential for the end of the "old family relationships":

> With the slave's awareness that he *cannot be the property of another*, with his consciousness of himself as a person, the existence of slavery becomes a merely artificial, vegetative existence, and ceases to be able to prevail as the basis of production.[19]

In the same manner, Engels commented that the shift of women from the household to the labor market removed "all foundation" for male domination in the proletarian home. "The first premise for the emancipation of women is the reintroduction of the entire female sex into public industry."[20] Of course, that is only the *first* premise, and "a new economic foundation for a higher form of the family" is not equivalent to the *realization* of that form.

Now, how critical is the precise designation of this relation as one of slavery? Many feminists would be uncomfortable with this term, and certainly not all of the attributes of property in people (such as the right to buy and sell people) were present at the time that Marx wrote. On the other hand, it is well to recall that, as a student of the classics, Marx's primary reference point would have been to slavery in antiquity (rather than in the New World) and that in the former case slavery displayed a variety of characteristics (including that of individuals entering into that state voluntarily because of the unacceptability of their available options).

Nevertheless, the central issue is not the precise term but the essential characteristic—exploitation. What Marx described is entirely consistent with the argument that, in addition to capitalist relations, wage laborers *also* existed within a "patriarchal mode of production," defined by Nancy Folbre as "a distinctive set of social relations, including but by no means limited to control over the means of production, that structures the exploitation of women and/or children by men."[21]

For our purpose here, which is to explore Marx's consideration of the determinateness of the worker, we need say no more. Whatever the potential future implication of the entry of women and children into wage labor, it is evident that Marx viewed the male wage laborer *at the time* as existing within two relationships, two class relationships: as wage laborer in relation to capital and as slaveowner. In this respect, the worker we have been considering until now is really not an abstract wage laborer at all but, rather, the *patriarchal* wage laborer!

Similarly, wife and children, insofar as they became wage laborers, also existed in two class relations. *In short, to speak of wage laborers is to describe people who are in no way identical in their relations.* They are identical only insofar as they are wage laborers for capital. As long as our subject is capital, it may be appropriate to consider these human beings only in their characteristic as wage laborer. Yet, as soon as the subject becomes wage labor, it is necessary to consider the *other* relations in which people exist.

In positing the existence of male and female wage laborers who exist within patriarchal relations, we are considering workers with differing goals and differing hierarchies of needs. For the patriarchal wage laborer, the struggle for higher wages is in part a struggle to permit the reproduction of patriarchy; his increased wages, all other things equal, will allow for an increased expenditure of labor in the house for him by his wife (and children). (The "family wage" is the condition for reproduction of both relations in which he exists.) For the female wage laborer, on the other hand, the struggle for higher wages is in part the struggle to *escape* that set of relations in which men control the means of production within the household and exploit women and/or children.

Certainly, there is here the basis for a divergence of interests between wage laborers of differing age and sex. When we recognize that our subject has been the patriarchal wage laborer, it places our discussion in chapter 4 ["The Political Economy of Wage Labor"] of the struggles of wage laborers in a somewhat different light. For example, any individual patriarchal wage laborer ("head of the family") gains, all other things equal, "by enrolling under the direct sway of capital, every member of the worker's family, without distinction of age or sex." Yet, patriarchal wage laborers *as a whole* lose as the result of the increased competition (and lower wages) which occur when *all* patriarchal wage laborers act in this way. In this context, restrictions (through a form "possessing general, socially coercive force") upon the ability of individual patriarchal wage laborers to sell their wives and children by voluntary contract to capital appear as the result of the political movement of patriarchal wage labor as a whole.[22]

The implications of patriarchy, however, go further. Within this patriarchal (or slave) relation, men and women are produced *differently*. Since, as we have noted, "their *needs*, consequently their nature, and the method of satisfying their needs, connected them with one another (relations between the sexes, exchange, division of labor), they *had to* enter into relations with one another." Yet, the nature of the people produced is not independent of the precise relations into which they have entered. As Marx and Engels continued:

> Since this intercourse, in its turn, determined production and needs, it was, therefore, precisely the personal, individual behaviour of individuals, their behaviour to one another as individuals, that created the existing relations and daily produces them anew. . . . Hence it certainly follows that the development of an individual is determined by the development of all others with whom he is directly or indirectly associated.[23]

Not only do men and women produce themselves differently in the course of the labor "absolutely necessary to consume things" as it is carried out under patriarchal relations, but they also produce themselves differently *through the consumption of the output of that process.* For, although the specific material use values produced may be independent of relations of production, the *content* of those use values is not. Marx touched upon this question in considering the difference between purchasing a coat from a "jobbing tailor" who performs the work in the buyer's home and having a domestic servant. In both cases, there was a relation of buyers and sellers. But there was a critical difference in these two exchanges. In the case of the domestic servant, he noted:

> But the way in which the use-value is enjoyed in this case *in addition* bears a patriarchal form of relation, a relation of master and servant, *which modifies the relation in its content,* though not in its economic form, and makes it distasteful.[24]

In the course of producing ourselves, in short, *we consume not only specific use values but also the social relations under which those use values are produced.* There is a difference between consuming a use value produced by the independent owner of labor power and one produced in a patriarchal form of relation. Just as the object of art creates "a public which is sensitive to art and enjoys beauty," so also do human beings who consume patriarchal relations produce themselves in a particular way. "The development of an individual is determined by the development of all others with whom he is directly or indirectly associated."

Thus, from the time of their birth, males and females produce themselves by consuming not only the use values provided under a gendered division of labor but also the patriarchal relations that determine that division. Implicit in this process, then, is the production of different persons, different personalities, differing natures with respect to domination and nurturance. As Sandra Harding has emphasized, "the kinds of persons infants become are greatly influenced by the particular social relations the infant experiences as it is transformed, and transforms itself, from a biological infant into a social person.[25]

We are here considering a subject upon which Marxist feminists have made and continue to make major contributions. At this point, therefore, it seems appropriate to comment upon the limitations of Marx's discussion. Despite Marx's description of the existing relationship within the working-class household as slave in nature, there is no consideration of this class relation as one of struggle (now open, now hidden) nor of the wives (and children) as subjects and actors.[26] All of this is precluded, of course, by Marx's subject in *Capital*. Yet, it would be naive to think that any of this would have appeared in the missing book on wage labor if Marx had ever written it.

True, Marx hoped for a "higher form of the family and of relations between the sexes." And, certainly, he found the existing arrangement personally "distasteful" and repugnant (as he did slavery in the New World). Yet, there is little reason to assume that he would have explored these questions in any detail. There is no indication that he was able to go beyond Victorian conventions in a manner similar to his contemporary John Stuart Mill, who specifically criticized the Factory Acts' restriction of women's labor "in order that they might have time to labour for the husband, in what is called by the advocates of restriction, *his* home."[27]

In raising these questions, therefore, it is not my goal to present Marx, the historical individual, as having been adequate. That would be rewriting history. *Rather, it is to demonstrate that within the Marxian framework there is the theoretical space to develop these questions.* In short, one does not have to add alien elements onto Marxian theory in an eclectic manner in order to create a "usable" Marx. It certainly is also not my intention to suggest that the questions raised here constitute an adequate treatment; that is a project that many feminist Marxists are currently undertaking with important results.[28] So, the issues raised here are not what would have been in *Wage Labor* but, rather, point to what *belongs* in it.

It may appear as if we have gone somewhat far afield in our discussion of the wage laborer as nonwage laborer. Yet, consideration of these issues is essential if we are to explore the determinateness of the wage laborers who face capital. It similarly underlines the significance of a missing book on wage labor. For certainly the specific exploitation of women will always remain peripheral and nonessential for one-sided Marxism so long as the implications of that missing book are not recognized. Patriarchy is necessarily secondary as long as workers are stripped "of all determinateness" and regarded only as abstract wage laborers.

Of course, the wage laborers who face capital are not only distinguished as men and women. Once we acknowledge that "every kind of consumption . . . in one way or another produces human beings in some particular aspect," then it is not a great leap to extend the discussion of differently produced wage laborers to differences based on age, race, ethnicity, religion, nationality, historical circumstances and, indeed, on "*all* human relations and functions, however and in whatever form they may appear."

Marx did not take this step. He limited his comments to the matter immediately at hand—the question of the value of labor power. Thus, he acknowledged that "historical tradition and social habitude" played an important part in generating different standards of necessity for different groups of workers.[29] Not only do necessary needs vary over time; they also vary among individuals and groups of workers at any given time. An obvious example was the situation of the Irish worker, for whom "the most animal minimum of needs and subsistence appears to him as the sole object and purpose of his exchange with capital."[30] Marx argued that their low necessary needs (compared to those of the English male worker) reflected the historical conditions under which Irish workers entered wage labor, conditions which drove the standard of necessity to which they became accustomed to the level of physiological needs.[31]

Yet, differences in the value of labor power reflect *more* than differences in "the social conditions in which people are placed and reared up." These are merely the "historical" premises; and, on this basis, we could never explain alterations in relative wages—for example, the equalization (upward or downward) of the value of labor power of differing groups of workers. Limited to these historical premises as an explanation, "the more or less favourable conditions" under which various groups of workers "emerged from the state of serfdom" would appear as original sin.[32]

In short, just as in the case of changes in the standard of necessity over time, differences in that standard for different groups of workers are the result of class struggle—the result of capitalist and worker pressing in opposite directions. The historical premises (insofar as they have affected the level of social needs) may explain why particular workers do not press very hard against capital; however, it is what workers accept in the present, rather than the historical premises, which determines the level of their necessary needs.

The principle, of course, goes beyond the case of Irish and English workers. It encompasses not only workers of differing ethnic and national background but also male and female workers. Unless, for example, we recognize the central place of class struggle in the determination of the value of labor power, we are left with an explanation of male/female wage differentials which rests on the assumption of lower subsitence requirements for women. Just as it is absurd, however, to assume that Marx believed that the value of labor power of Irish workers would *always* be below that of English workers, it is equally absurd to retain a flawed concept of the value of labor power (which ignores the "peculiarity" of that commodity)—one which must imply that lower wages for women reflect their lower subsistence requirements (requirements given once and for all by the social conditions in which they are placed and reared up).

Rather than believing that all workers were identical, Marx's conception was that every individual is an ensemble of the social relations in which he or she acts. That has its implications. Given that workers produce themselves as heterogeneous human beings (with differing hierarchies of needs) and that the needs they are normally able to satisfy reflect the results of struggle, it is clear that at any given point there exist differing degrees and dimensions of immiseration.[33] Although the point was not developed in *Capital*, once we begin to explore workers insofar as they are nonwage laborers, we see that, rather than abstract wage laborers, the workers in question are human beings in all their determinateness.

THE PRODUCTION OF THE WORKER AS A WHOLE

It would be wrong, however, to view the process of production of the worker as occurring *only* outside wage labor. If we think of the household as *the* site in which the production of the worker takes place, then there remains an implicit view of the process as natural and physical rather than as social. If every activity of the worker produces her in some particular aspect, however, then this must include as well the process of capitalist production.

. . . A certain type of human being is produced under the alienating conditions of capitalist production—one with the need of possess alien commodities. And, as noted, those needs are generated not only by production proper but also through capital's sales efforts to expand the sphere of circulation. Those needs are needs which, within capitalist relations, can only be secured by the sale of labor power. Capital, thus, necessarily appears as the mediator for the wage laborer.

The worker, accordingly, is produced as one conscious of his dependence upon capital. And everything about capitalist production contributes not only to the relation of dependence but also to the "feeling of dependence."[34] The very nature of capital is mystified—"all the productive forces of social labour appear attributable to it, and not to labour as such, as a power springing forth from its own womb." Having surrendered the right to his "*creative power*, like Esau his birthright for a mess of pottage," capital, thus, becomes "a very mystical being" for the worker because it appears as the source of all productivity.[35]

Fixed capital, machinery, technology, science—all necessarily appear only as capital, are known only in their capitalist form:

The accumulation of knowledge and of skill, of the general productive forces of the social brain, is thus absorbed into capital, as opposed to labour, and hence appears as an attribute of capital.[36]

Thus, as Marx noted, this transposition of "the social productivity of labour into the material attributes of capital is so firmly entrenched in people's minds that the advantages of machinery, the use of science, invention, etc., are *necessarily* conceived in this *alienated* form, so that all these things are deemed to be the *attributes of capital.*"[37] *In short, wage labor assigns its own attributes to capital in its mind because the very nature of the capital/wage-labour relation is one in which it has already done so in reality.*

In the normal course of things, thus, capital can rely upon the worker's dependence upon capital. The very process of capitalist production produces and reproduces workers who view the necessity for capital as self-evident:

The advance of capitalist production develops a working class which by education, tradition and habit looks upon the requirements of that mode as self-evident natural laws. The organization of the capitalist process of production, once it is fully developed, breaks down all resistance.[38]

Capital, however, does more than simply produce workers for whom the very thought of going beyond capital appears contrary to natural law. It also produces workers who are separated. In part, this is the result of the conscious effort of capital to divide and separate workers—both in the labor market and in the process of production. (Both moments of the circuit of capital are characterized by the struggle of capital to divide workers and to equalize their conditions downward versus the struggle of workers to unite and to equalize their conditions upward.) Yet, the separation of workers is produced as well by the form of existence of capital as a whole.

The very existence of capital as "many capitals" (i.e., as individual capitals competing against each other) separates workers insofar as they feel dependent not only upon capital as a whole but on *particular* capitals. In the battle of competition of capitals, there is thus a basis for groups of workers to link their ability to satisfy their needs to the success of the particular capitals which employ them. Thus, there is a classic inversion in competition—rather than the competition among workers being recognized as a form of the competition of capitals and as a condition of capital securing its goals, the competition of capitals spontaneously appears as a form of the competition of workers and as a means for them to satisfy *their* goals. In the real existence of capital as many capitals, there exists a basis for separation between workers in different firms (within and without a country) and for "concessions" to capital in the battle of competition.[39]

Even if *outside of wage labor* workers were produced perfectly homogeneously, there thus would still be a basis for divisions among them given by the normal workings of capitalist production. . . . Capital's ownership of the products of social labor serves to hide from both mental and manual labourer their unity as differing limbs of the collective worker. Similarly, . . . the very struggle wherein the worker "measures his demands against the capitalist's profit and demands a certain share of the surplus value created by him" tends to the reproduction of capital's concept of productive labor and to the maintenance of the separation between those who work for capital and those workers who constitute the other limbs of the collective worker. Thus, that unity of workers which is a condition for going beyond capital is precisely what is not produced by capital.

Yet, the breaking down of resistance to the rule of capital and the separation of workers occur not only because capital itself produces the workers who face it. Capital faces workers who have been produced outside of their relation to capital, and that as well contributes to the education, tradition, and habit which makes the requirements of capital appear as self-evident. "All human relations and functions," in short, "influence material production and have a more or less decisive influence on it." Thus, drawing upon this very point by Marx, Wilhelm Reich stressed the relationship between patriarchy and the acceptance of the rule of the authoritarian state and capital:

> The authoritarian position of the father reflects his political role and discloses the relation of the family to the authoritarian state. Within the family the father holds the same position that his boss holds toward him in the production process. And he reproduces his subservient attitude toward authority in his children, particularly in his sons.[40]

Capital is strengthened in many ways by the production of workers as nonwage laborers. We have seen that a condition of existence of capital is its ability to divide and separate workers. Yet, the very process by which workers are produced outside of their relation to capital ensures that they approach capital as heterogeneous human beings—i.e., as wage laborers who are *already divided* by (among other aspects) sex, age, race, and nationality. If we add this to the inherent tendency in capital itself to foster competition among workers, it appears that the conditions for the maintenance of capitalist hegemony are easily satisfied.

Consider the case of Irish workers. Their historically given standard of necessity meant that they were prepared to work for lower wages than those to which English workers were accustomed. The tendency was to drive down the wages of the latter; and the result, Marx saw, was one which clearly strengthened the rule of capital. There was *far more* to the matter, however, than a general competition among workers which weakened them in relation to capital:

Every industrial and commercial centre in England now possesses a working class *divided* into two *hostile* camps, English proletarians and Irish proletarians. The ordinary English worker hates the Irish worker as a competitor who lowers his standard of life. In relation to the Irish worker he feels himself a member of the *ruling* nation and so turns himself into a tool of the aristocrats and capitalists of his country *against* Ireland, thus strengthening their domination over *himself*. He cherishes religious, social and national prejudices against the Irish worker. . . . The Irishman pays him back with interest in his own money. He sees in the English worker at once the accomplice and the stupid tool of the *English rule in Ireland*.

Thus, there was not merely the division between competing sellers of labor power but an "*antagonism*" which drew for its strength upon all those characteristics (religious, social, and national) which formed the Irish and English workers as differing human beings. *Difference became, under the normal workings of capitalism, hostility.* In this antagonism, Marx saw "the *secret of the impotence of the English working class*, despite its organization. It is the secret by which the capitalist class maintains its power. And that class is fully aware of it."[41]

When one recalls, however, all of the ways in which the hegemony of capital is reinforced, it is uncertain that this particular separation of workers *by itself* can be seen as the single "secret" by which capital maintains its power. And that is the question which comes to the fore once we consider workers as the subject and move away from the concept of an abstract wage laborer. Once we think about the workers who face capital in all their determinateness, the question before us is—*why did Marx ever think that workers could go beyond capital?*

Notes

1. *Grundrisse*, 464.
2. *Capital* 1:1031. Although all use values produced by the slave are themselves the property of the master, a portion of these must be allocated to his "laboring machine" in order to preserve the natural conditions of his existence as master.
3. *Capital* 1:344.
4. *German Ideology*, in Marx and Engels, *Collected Works* 5:46.
5. *Communist Manifesto*, in Marx and Engels, *Collected Works* 6:501–2.
6. *Capital* 1:1083.
7. Frederick Engels, *The Origin of the Family, Private Property, and the State*, in Marx and Engels, *Selected Works* 2:232.
8. *Capital* 1:517–18, 518n.
9. Nancy R. Folbre, "A Patriarchal Mode of Production," in Randy Albelda, Christopher Gunn, and William Waller, eds., *Alternatives to Economic Orthodoxy: A Reader in Political Economy*, 326.

10. Lise Vogel, *Marxism and the Oppression of Women: Toward a Unitary Theory,* 61, 130.
11. *Capital* 1:620. The following discussion draws upon a tentative exploration in an unpublished manuscript, "Notes on Immiseration and Household Labour" (Dec. 1976).
12. *Capital* 1:385n.
13. *Capital* 1:684, 687–88, 793.
14. *Capital* 1:517.
15. *Capital* 1:519–20, 519n. In this context, Marx includes "the premium that the exploitation of the workers' children sets on their production" as a reason for high population growth among the industrial proletariat. Ibid., 795. Quite consistently, Nancy Folbre has stressed the relation between child labor laws and the decline in average family size within capitalism. See, for example, Ann Ferguson and Nancy Folbre, "The Unhappy Marriage of Patriarchy and Capitalism," in Lydia Sargent, ed., *Women and Revolution: A Discussion of the Unhappy Marriage of Marxism and Feminism,* 323.
16. *Capital* 1:620–21.
17. Consider, for example, the long-term effects of the release by manorial lords of peasants from labor service requirements in return for money payments.
18. *Grundrisse,* 289, 465.
19. Ibid., 463.
20. *Origin of the Family, Private Property, and the State,* 231, 233.
21. Folbre, "Patriarchal Mode," 330.
22. This does not, of course, mean that such state legislation as child labor laws and restrictions on the workday for women and children were not in the interests of workers as a whole.
23. *German Ideology,* 437–38.
24. *Theories of Surplus Value* 1:287. Emphasis added.
25. Sandra Harding, "What Is the Real Material Base of Patriarchy and Capital?" in Sargent, *Women and Revolution,* p. 147. The pathbreaking work on the relationship between patriarchy and the social construction of gender personality is Nancy Chodorow, *The Reproduction of Mothering: Psychoanalysis and the Sociology of Gender.*
26. Vogel points out that, in all Marx's comments about slavery, women and children are portrayed "as passive victims rather than historical actors." Vogel, *Marxism and the Oppression of Women,* 61.
27. John Stuart Mill, quoted in Michele Pujol, *Economic Efficiency or Economic Chivalry? Women's Status and Women's Work in Early Neo-Classical Economics.*
28. In particular, it is important to stress that consideration of patriarchy goes far beyond matters explored here and must properly include issues which cannot be addressed here such as the place of rape and violence against women and children.
29. *Value, Price, and Profit,* 145. Marx also noted the role of differences in the "extent of the prime necessities of life in their natural and historical development" in explaining national differences in wages. *Capital* 1:701.
30. *Grundrisse,* 285.
31. *Capital* 1:854–70.
32. *Value, Price, and Profit,* 145.
33. Differing hierarchies of needs—even with identical "necessary needs" (considered broadly)—will yield differing degrees of immiseration. Alternatively, since

the particular needs normally satisfied by workers will differ depending on their success in struggles (and their individual ranking of needs), there will be different degrees of immiseration even if hierarchies of need are identical. . . .

34. *Capital* 1:936.
35. *Capital* 3:966.
36. *Grundrisse*, 694.
37. *Capital* 1:1058.
38. *Capital* 1:899. Marx also notes that "the severe discipline of capital, acting on succeeding generations, has developed general industriousness as the general property of the new species." *Grundrisse*, 325.
39. Insofar as workers in competing firms cannot co-operate, they are placed in a "Prisoners' Dilemma." In this context, see Michael A. Lebowitz, "Trade and Class: Labour Strategies in a World of Strong Capital."
40. Wilhelm Reich, *The Mass Psychology of Fascism*, 49. See also 14–15.
41. Marx to S. Meyer and A. Vogt, 9 April 1870, in Marx and Engels, *On Colonialism*, 334.

References

Albelda, Randy, Christopher Gunn, and William Waller, eds. 1986. *Alternatives to Economic Orthodoxy: A Reader in Political Economy*. Armonk NY: M. E. Sharpe.

Chodorow, Nancy. 1978. *The Reproduction of Mothering: Psychoanalysis and the Sociology of Gender*. Berkeley: University of California Press.

Lebowitz, Michael A. 1988. "Trade and Class: Labour Strategies in a World of Strong Capital." *Studies in Political Economy* 27 (Autumn).

Marx, Karl. 1865. *Value, Price, and Profit*. In Marx and Engels 1985.

——. 1973. *Grundrisse*. New York: Vintage Books.

——. 1977. *Capital*, vol. 1. New York: Vintage Books.

——. 1981. *Capital*, vol. 3. New York: Vintage Books.

——. n.d. *Theories of Surplus Value*, vol. 1. Moscow: Foreign Languages Publishing House.

——. Marx, Karl, and Frederick Engels 1848. *Communist Manifesto*. In Marx and Engels 1976b.

——. 1962. *Selected Works*. 2 vols. Moscow: Foreign Languages Publishing House.

——. 1976a. *Collected Works*, vol. 5. New York: International Publishers.

——. 1976b. *Collected Works*, vol. 6. New York: International Publishers.

——. 1985. *Collected Works*, vol. 20. New York: International Publishers.

——. n.d. *On Colonialism*. Moscow: Foreign Languages Publishing House.

Pujol, Michele. 1989. *Economic Efficiency or Economic Chivalry? Women's Status and Women's Work in Early Neo-Classical Economics*. Diss. Simon Fraser University.

Reich, Wilhelm. 1976. *The Mass Psychology of Fascism*. New York: Pocket Books.

Sargent, Lydia, ed. 1981. *Women and Revolution: A Discussion of the Unhappy Marriage of Marxism and Feminism*. Montreal: Black Rose Books.

Vogel, Lise. 1983. *Marxism and the Oppression of Women: Toward a Unitary Theory*. New Brunswick: Rutgers University Press.

Exploitation Comes Home:
A Critique of the Marxian
Theory of Family Labor

NANCY FOLBRE

SOCIAL SCIENTISTS, DEMOGRAPHERS AMONG them, are slowly beginning to acknowledge that inequalities based on age and sex may have a
significant impact on household behavior. Yet the influence of what is now
commonly termed "patriarchy" on household decisions is almost always pic-
tured in political or ideological terms. The *economic* consequences of patriarchy are often overlooked, despite the fact that they clearly hold important
implications for the analysis of production and distribution within the family.

Neglect of this particular issue may be partially attributed to the influence of neoclassical economic theory, a theory which not only excludes the
possibility of exploitation in any voluntary exchange, but also ignores the
way in which individual tastes and preferences are presumably merged into
a joint utility function. Yet Marxian theory is equally deserving of blame.
While many Marxists are sympathetic to the political perspective of socialist feminism, most cling to an interpretation of Marxian theory which effectively excludes the very possibility that exploitation could take place
within the family.

This common interpretation grows out of Marx's exposition of the labor
theory of value. Marx was convinced that the labor theory of value could
not operate outside the realm of capitalist commodity production because

From Nancy Folbre, "Exploitation Comes Home: A Critique of the Marxian Theory of
Family Labour," *Cambridge Journal of Economics* 6 (1982): 317–29, with the permission of
Academic Press Ltd.

the labor embodied in one good might vary arbitrarily between producers. The actual amount of labor time devoted to production could not be used as a standard of value, because some workers might work more or less efficiently than others. Labor value, he reasoned, should be determined by "socially necessary" labor time, and the concept of socially necessary labor time is relevant only if some social forces operate in such a way as to eliminate inefficient producers. Without socially necessary labor time, there can be no analysis of labor value, and without an analysis of labor value, there can be no analysis of exploitation.

The logic of this argument is impeccable. The logic, however, conceals an assumption that seems somewhat inconsistent with the spirit of Marx's theory: the assumption that capitalist competition is the only force that can lead to the systematic elimination of inefficient producers. This assumption unnecessarily forecloses the possibility that other forces, or independent motives, might lead noncapitalist producers systematically to adopt efficient strategies of production.

Exploration of this prospect of efficient allocation within the household leads me to argue, in the following pages, that the labor theory of value can be sensibly reinterpreted in such a way as to provide important insights into both production and distribution in the family. This reinterpretation paves the way for the development of a theoretical framework which can describe the cooperative dimension of family production, the way in which collective decisions are made in response to economic factors such as prices and incomes. It also sets the stage for consideration of the potential antagonism implicit in family production, the way in which differences in bargaining power may lead to unequal distribution of consumption goods and leisure time within the family. While this theoretical framework raises the possibility of exploitation within the family, it leads far beyond a discussion of exploitation per se, providing important insights into a fundamental historical change in the reproduction of labor power—the demographic transition to lower fertility.

This analysis moves from a consideration of the general issue of production and reproduction in the household to a specific focus on factors affecting family size decisions. In part 1, I argue that failure to define adequately the cost of reproduction of labor power represents a serious problem within the Marxian theory of exploitation, a problem as yet unresolved by discussions of the value of domestic labor. In part 2, I explain how the cost of reproduction of labor power may be redefined to include family labor, and lay out the conditions under which transfers of surplus labor time within the family may constitute exploitation. In part 3, I argue that historical changes in relative rates of exploitation in the family play an important role in fertility decline.

1. THE THEORY OF EXPLOITATION

In Marxian theory exploitation is explicitly described as the expropriation of surplus value. The description carries both political and economic meaning (Bowles and Gintis 1981). "Expropriation" must be differentiated from voluntary exchange. "Surplus value" must be conceptualized as value produced, but not consumed, by the worker. The distinction between these two aspects of exploitation is crucial to any discussion of Marxian theory. It is particularly crucial to any assessment of the Marxian theory of patriarchy, because it explains why Marxists seldom if ever apply the term "exploitation" to the forms of involuntary inequality which they observe within the family.

The concept of surplus value is normally applied to the analysis of the capitalist mode of production. In this context, it is seen to be equivalent to the difference between the value of a wage worker's labor power and the value which he transfers to the product through wage labor. The value of labor power is embodied in the goods which the worker consumes in order to "reproduce" his capacity to work. The labor embodied in the goods consumed is set equal, by assumption, to the labor embodied in the wage bundle.

In volume 1 of *Capital*, Marx briefly mentioned two other factors which might enter into the determination of the value of labor power, "the cost of developing that power" and the "difference between the labour power of men and women, children and adults." "Both these factors," he wrote, "are excluded in the following investigation" (Marx 1977, 685). With this brief caveat, he dismissed the possibility that household labor might have a significant or even noticeable effect on the reproduction of labor power.

But, to quote Marx again, "This peculiar commodity, labor power, must now be examined more closely" (Marx 1977, 274). Wage workers do not normally consume their entire wage bundle, but share it with their family. Families, in turn, provide their wage-worker members with important and valuable goods and services. If the portion of wage goods transferred to the family were exactly equivalent in value to the portion of family-produced goods and services the wage worker consumed, the wage bundle would in fact be an accurate reflection of the actual amount of socially necessary labor time devoted to the reproduction of labor power. But there is absolutely no reason to assume that the exchange between wage worker and family *is* equivalent in value terms. This assumption merely circumvents a serious problem. If family labor cannot be analyzed in value terms, the *condition* of equivalent exchange cannot even be defined, much less satisfied.

It is hardly surprising, then, that consideration of women's domestic labor initiated a heated debate beginning with Maria Dalla Costa and Selma James's bold assertion that women's unpaid labor serves to lower the value of labor power, cheapening real wages (Dalla Costa and James 1970). The controversy has been intensified by radical feminists, who argue that individual men, as well as capitalists as a class, benefit directly from women's domestic labor (Delphy 1976). A number of ways of addressing these issues have been suggested. Harrison argues that household labor constitutes a separate mode of production which does not produce value, but is capable of producing a surplus (Harrison 1973). Seccombe suggests that the reproduction of labor power may be analyzed in value terms because labor power is a commodity, but denies that it can produce a surplus (Seccombe 1974). Many Marxists, however, accept Himmelweit and Mohun's argument that work performed in the household is simply incommensurate with wage labor because it is not subject to the law of value (Himmelweit and Mohun 1977.)[1] Thus the debate has ended where it started, excluding non-wage labor, by definition, from the value of labor power.

Some issues have been clarified along the way. Others have been obscured. The categories of age and gender have been subsumed into the undifferentiated term "domestic labour," and the domestic laborer/wage worker dichotomy has deflected attention from differences between the economic position of husbands and wives, parents and children, differences that often exist independently of the wage-worker status of one or more family members. The distinction between different types of domestic labor has also been glossed over. Intrahousehold exchanges between parents and children clearly have different implications than do exchanges between husbands and wives, but these have not been explored in any detail (Molyneux 1979).

Virtually no attention has been devoted to the social organization of human reproduction, reinforcing a Marxist tendency to analyze demographic dynamics exclusively in terms of their effect on relationships between capitalists and workers. Meillasoux's work is a case in point. Locating the reproduction of labor power in what he terms the "domestic community," Meillasoux does not explore its internal logic or its internal division of labor (Meillasoux 1977). While he correctly observes that the Third World provides an enormous reserve army of labor for capital accumulation, he offers no insights into the causes of the decline in fertility which is diminishing the size of this reserve army.

Himmelweit and Mohun are also seemingly incognizant of the demographic transition to lower fertility rates. Stressing the fact that the living laborer cannot be produced as a commodity under capitalism, they argue that this imposes limits on the proletarianization of housewives (Himmelweit and Mohun 1977, 30). They entirely overlook the fact that increases in female labor-force participation rates in the developed capitalist countries have in fact been associated with a steady decline in average family size. Decreases in the total fertility rate among whites in the United States between 1800 and 1975, for instance, reduced the average number of children born per woman from seven to 1.7 (Coale and Zelnick 1963; *Statistical Abstract* 1978, table 80). Child care remains a very demanding responsibility for women in the United States, but the percentage of women's life cycle devoted to the care and nurture of young children has been substantially reduced.

If the reproduction of labor power were a static, unchanging process which had no real effect on the dynamics of capital accumulation, existing analyses of domestic labor would perhaps suffice. But the process of fertility decline clearly affects the size of the reserve army of labor, the proletarianization of women, and the social policies of the capitalist state. Marx himself wrote in a period in which family size may have been determined by the "labourer's instincts of self preservation and propagation" (Marx 1977, 718). But contemporary Marxists must confront a serious dilemma: If overwhelmingly significant changes in the reproduction of labor power leave the value of labor power unaffected, then the concept of value of labor power may lose much of its contempory relevance.[2] Even more important, a theory which cannot explain changes in the reproduction of labor power may be unable to provide a satisfactory account of the transition to capitalism.

The fact that Marxian theory offers no ready-made tools with which to analyze the reproduction of labor power does not mean that it should be ignored. It means, rather, that a new set of tools should be fashioned. The labor theory of value can serve, in this instance, as a useful template.

2. THE ECONOMICS OF THE HOUSEHOLD

PRODUCTION

Every process of production involves some intangible inputs and some intangible outputs. Attitudes toward work, the organization of the work process, and the nature of the product inevitably affect production itself. Such intangibles obviously play a particularly important role in household production. There are two different ways of addressing this issue: either using a catch-all concept similar to the neoclassical concept of "utility," or simply restricting the analysis to those aspects of production which can be described in material terms, such as physical inputs and labor time.

The distinctive advantage of an economic analysis based on physical inputs and labor time is that it does not normally exclude the possibility that a worker produces more than he or she consumes. While the materialist approach restricts the purview of analysis, it does so in an explicit way, bracketing the nonmaterial aspects of household production but leaving them open to separate consideration.

While neoclassical economists have devoted considerable attention to the analysis of the household as a cooperative unit, they tend to sidestep the prob-lem of potential conflict of interest.[3] They base their approach on the as-sumption of a joint utility function which is ostensibly shared by all families, and constant over time. This assumption effectively precludes the possibil-ity that changes in family behavior are motivated by anything *but* changes in prices and incomes.

While neoclassical economists define the family's objective function too narrowly, Marxists tend to deny that families follow any decision rule at all. Likely to concede that individual families may pursue certain economic goals, Marxists are nonetheless resistant to the claim that groups or classes or families may have a common objective function. This resistance finds expression in the claim that the labor theory of value cannot be applied to household production because production may be organized in "arbitrary", "idiosyncratic" or "inefficient" ways.

Ironically, however, an implicit objective function lies embedded in the Marxian notion that the primary goal of working-class families is to survive and to subsist. If the survival constraint were truly binding, there would be a process which would eliminate inefficient households—they would not successfully survive and reproduce themselves unless they adopted the most efficient household production technology. In this context, the concept of socially necessary labor time clearly *could* be applied.

The notion that household behavior is dictated purely by survival is credible only in a context in which wages are set at a subsistence level. But Marx never intended to limit the scope of his theory to a subsistence economy. He consistently argued that the value of labor power had a "moral and historical" element. It could be increased as workers successfully bargained for an increase in the size of their wage bundle.

It seems logical, then, to argue that a "moral and historical" element may also govern the amount of household labor that is devoted to the reproduc-tion of labor power. Households that earn more than their subsistence may still pursue some economic objectives. They may, for instance, seek to minimize the cost of meeting the households' collectively defined needs. The full cost of the reproduction of labor power, specific to a given cultural and class context, may be affected by traditions and social norms.

The particular form of the household's objective function is less impor-tant than the hypothesis that households do in fact pursue some specific economic objectives, objectives which may motivate rational economic choices. This hypothesis is quite distinct from the neoclassical presumption that all households seek to maximize the same implicit joint utility function, un-changing over time. In fact, it directs attention toward the possibility that the household's objective may vary across classes and change over time.

The claim that households do in fact concern themselves with the efficiency of household production represents a radical departure from the analysis presented by Himmelweit and Mohun (1977). It differs from the perspectives outlined by Harrison (1973) and Seccombe (1974) because it suggests that both surplus and value may be generated within the household. This fundamental theoretical reorientation makes it possible to analyze transfers of goods and labor time between family members, and formally to redefine the value of labor power.

HOUSEHOLD DISTRIBUTION

The cost of reproduction of labor power is the key to any analysis of exploitation, for it provides a basis for comparing what a worker produces with what he or she consumes in the form of embodied labor. The claim that family members cooperate in making certain rational decisions regarding production does not imply that the products of family labor are distributed equally. But it does provide a framework for *asking* whether they are distributed equally.

Moving beyond the simplistic model in which the worker essentially "reproduces himself" by exchanging a share of his wage for an equivalent value of family labor, consider a model in which family members pool their labor, their income, and/or their product to "reproduce" each other. Limiting the model to the case in which there is, at most, one wage earner, the role of family nonwage labor can be accommodated by adding a new term to the traditional formulation. Let us assume that each family member consumes some share of the products of both waged and unwaged labor, and what he or she consumes is embodied in the value of his or her labor power:

$$E_i = \gamma_i lw + a_i U \tag{1}$$

where E_i = value of an individual family member's labor power
γ_i = individual share of wage goods consumed by family as a whole
a_i = individual share of nonwage labor produced goods or services consumed by family as a whole
l = number of hours of wage labor performed by family as a whole
w = value embodied in the hourly wage bundle
U = value embodied in nonwage labor produced goods and services consumed by family as a whole

If none of the family members engages in wage labor, $l = 0$. If none of the family members engages in nonwage labor, $U = 0$.

If at least one worker is engaged in wage labor, and surplus value is being expropriated from him, the total number of hours worked by family members will necessarily be greater than the total hours embodied in their total consumption bundle, because the wage worker is bringing home a contribution which embodies fewer hours than his work. Exploitation, in other words, comes home. But the burden of exploitation is not necessarily shared equally.

In exploring the possibility of economic inequality within the family, it is important to note that neither the work day nor the work year is a meaningful time period of analysis. In the first place, age is a very important determinant of both production and consumption. Young children will clearly consume more value relative to what they produce than will parents, but, as they mature, they may "repay" their parents by contributing to parental income or providing support in old age. And, on the more general level, all family members may enjoy a certain amount of reciprocity, agreeing to help out others for a certain period of time, in return for assistance at a later date. If genuine reciprocity prevails, then, exchanges should be approximately equal over the life cycle of family members.

Families may, of course, define reciprocity in nonmaterial terms: "to each according to his or her need." But for the purpose of this economic analysis it is interesting to ask whether or not they observe a distinct principle of equality: to each according to his work. If they do, the ratio between labor hours worked and labor hours consumed over the life cycle will be equal.

The difference between labor hours worked and labor hours consumed can be described as a form of surplus value.

$$S_f = L_f - E_f$$
$$S_m = L_m - E_m \qquad (2)$$
$$S_c = L_c - E_c$$

where S = surplus value
$\quad L$ = total socially necessary labor hours worked in wage labor and/
$\qquad$ or nonwage labor
$\quad E$ = value of labor power
Subscripts f, m, c designate fathers, mothers, children, respectively.

A set of intrafamily equality conditions can now be expressed in terms directly analogous to the Marxian rate of exploitation.

$$\frac{S_f}{E_f} = \frac{S_m}{E_m} = \frac{S_c}{E_c} \text{ or equivalently, } \frac{L_f}{E_f} = \frac{L_m}{E_m} = \frac{L_c}{E_c} \qquad (3)$$

If one family member is exploited outside the home as a wage worker, three distinct possibilities emerge. The wage worker may exchange labor equally with family members, in which case he is exploited, but they are not. The wage worker may recoup the surplus value relinquished to the capitalist through unequal exchange with the family, in which case family members may be exploited but he is not. Alternatively, if equation 3 is satisfied the burden of exploitation is shared equally.

Which of these possibilities, or combination of possibilities, actually holds in reality cannot be determined unless hours worked in household labor are commensurable with wage work in terms of abstract labor. I have argued that this commensurability is made possible by the socially necessary character of household production. Despite the fact that household workers do not produce for the market, they choose the most efficient means possible to perform their tasks. Their work may differ in skill and intensity, their fixed capital may differ in cost and depreciation, and they may engage in joint production, but none of these factors significantly distinguishes their work from that of wage workers.[4]

The model outlined here makes it possible to test the hypothesis that unequal exchange takes place within the family.[5] Data are widely available in the form of household surveys and time budget studies which describe relative hours worked and relative quantities of items consumed. Szalai, for instance, summarizes a large body of international data showing that women tend to work much longer hours overall than men (Szalai 1975). In their analysis of household data from the Philippines, Evenson, Popkin, and King-Quizon (1979) show that female children receive a much smaller share of food and clothing than male children despite the fact that they work longer hours (see also Folbre, 1984). Empirical studies based on such sources of data often suffer from the lack of any explicit theoretical framework, and there is clearly a great deal to be gained from some formalization of the economics of inequality in the household.

EXPLOITATION

The formalization laid out above applies the concept of a "rate of exploitation" to nonwage workers, but it does not necessarily imply that differences in this rate are attributable to exploitation arising within the family itself. A transfer of surplus value is not necessarily an expropriation of surplus value, and the question of exploitation can only be resolved by reference to the political dimension of the Marxian theory of distribution. Inequality of rates of exploitation in the family may reflect purely voluntary material sacrifices, sacrifices related, perhaps, to the intangible and emotional aspects of family life.[6] But one of the most important lessons of Marxian theory is that inequality is often disguised and obscured by ideology, and the material context of "free choice" requires careful scrutiny.

As has often been pointed out in discussions of the process of proletarianization, the wage worker may benefit from the exchange of his labor even if he receives a wage that is less than its true value. If the worker has no independent access to means of production, while the capitalist owns and controls substantial capital, the worker's "choice" to sell his labor power is essentially predetermined. Neoclassical economists ignore the historical and political conditions which set the stage for market transactions. They also overlook the positive consequences, for the exploited and discriminated-against, of nonmarket processes which may work to equalize endowments of capital.

Stressing inequality in access to capital within the context of capitalist social relations, Marxists tend to be less aware of differences in access to the means of production due to age or sex. Yet a large body of scholarship describes peasant and petty commodity modes of production, both outside and within capitalist social formations, in which legal and practical control over the family's land and capital resides in the hands of older males.[7] Even where a large part of the labor force has been proletarianized, control over home and hearth often rests with men. Furthermore, social sanctions and laws which prohibit contraception and abortion sometimes give men substantial control over women's own biological means of reproduction (Delphy 1976; Ferguson and Folbre 1981; Kuhn 1978; Mernissi 1975; Saadawi 1980; Shersey 1973).

Many women enter new households through marriage on a purely voluntary basis, and many children, after reaching their age of majority, may voluntarily leave home. But if women or children lack access to some independent means of livelihood, they are likely to continue to cooperate within a patriarchal family despite its inequalities. They seldom face an either-or situation. If the economic consequences of independence, largely defined by social institutions and practices outside the individual family, are quite gloomy, their bargaining power within the family is quite limited. On the other hand, as economic independence becomes more viable, they may choose to exercise their enhanced bargaining power to *change* the pattern of distribution within the family, rather than simply deserting the family altogether.

In a given historical context, patriarchs may or may not actively seek to exploit other family members. Their motives and their inclinations are unobservable to both economists and historians. But where men participate in the formation and the enforcement of laws, institutions, and social practices which weaken women's and children's potential for economic independence, where men enjoy substantially greater bargaining power than women and children, and where men's rate of exploitation is much lower than that of other family members, one can make a strong case that they are indeed exploiters.[8]

The possibility that exploitation of this type does take place has serious implications, not only for the analysis of patriarchy, but also for the analysis of capitalism itself. It suggests that women and children may in some instance "compensate" the male worker for his exploitation in the market. It suggests that class lines between families are likely to be cross-cut and weakened by nonclass forms of conflict. And it also suggests that changes in relations between mothers, fathers, and children may fundamentally modify family-size decisions.

3. THE DEMOGRAPHIC TRANSITION AND THE TRANSITION TO CAPITALISM

Exchanges of direct and indirect labor time take place between parents and children as well as between husbands and wives. Decisions regarding the bearing and rearing of children cannot be reduced to purely economic considerations. But neither can they be romanticized as decisions completely independent of material constraints. There are many possible motives for rearing children, but only the very rich can ignore the possible economic consequences.

A very large body of literature documents the fact that the growth and expansion of capitalist social relations of production is associated with a gradual but consistent reduction in family size (Kirk 1971; Beaver 1975). The causal relationships underlying this demographic transition to lower fertility are the subject of considerable debate. Many sociologists insist that changes in desired family size are but one aspect of a global process of "modernization" of ideas and attitudes, a process which may precede or even stimulate economic transformation (Goode 1970; Shorter 1975). Economists, on the other hand, tend to argue that economic transformation itself may be the motivating force behind demographic change.

There is a growing consensus that increases in the cost of children have had a significant influence upon fertility rates. A number of empirical studies have shown that children in many agrarian societies make a substantial contribution to family income (Nag 1972; Nag et al. 1978; Tienda 1979; Bulatao 1978). Most neoclassical economic analyses of changes in the "demand" for children emphasize the fact that the "price" of children tends to rise as increasing schooling diminishes their labor-force participation and as increased female labor-force participation increases the opportunity cost of time devoted to child care. A number of econometric studies of differences in family size have generated empirical results consistent with these predictions (Rosenzweig and Evenson, 1977; Rosenzweig 1977).

Despite the fact that many economists are highly critical of the neoclassical approach to fertility decisions, their criticisms have seldom taken a very explicit form. Rejecting out of hand the restrictive assumptions built into household utility and production functions, few critics have articulated an alternative framework for analyzing the costs and benefits of children.

This is not surprising, since an alternative economic framework for analyzing fertility decline must grow out of a larger economic approach to analyzing production as a whole. Once the basic concepts of Marxian theory are extended to the household, however, the Marxian critique of the neoclassical approach to commodity production can be extended, by analogy, to the "new home economics." The basis of this critique is quite simple: The neoclassical approach confines its analysis to changes in prices and incomes, ignoring the possibility that changing social relations of production may modify the nature of the household as a decision-making unit.

Changes in relative bargaining power of women and children, for instance, may lead to a decrease in the ratio of hours worked to embodied labor hours "consumed" (their rate of surplus value, as defined in equation 3). Contrary to neoclassical theory, children are not consumer durables. Though they may not play an active role in family decisions while young, they clearly play an increasingly important role as they mature. Adult children can exercise considerable control over their own economic reciprocity vis-à-vis their parents. It is the extent of this reciprocity, not technological change, that determines their "cost." The common argument that education reduces children's productive contribution to the household is specious. It reduces their contribution as young children, but increases their potential contribution as adults.

Children who are in a strong bargaining position may choose to make the exchange of labor between themselves and their parents even more unequal than parents anticipated, thus increasing their cost to the household. Changes in the bargaining power of women may have a similar but less direct effect. The opportunity cost of time which mothers devote to children is determined not only by what they could earn or produce in the absence of children, but also by the number of hours actually withdrawn from other productive activities. If, for instance, time spent in child care encroaches upon mothers' leisure time, rather than their work hours, the cost of children to the family as a whole is reduced (see, for instance, Ho 1979).

The crucial point is that family members, be they men, women, or children, do not receive a "wage" that is necessarily equivalent to either their marginal or their average product. They receive a *share* of the family's total product which may or may not be commensurate with the number of hours worked. If differences in bargaining power affect the size of this share, the relative prices of family members' work time are affected. Just as an increase in real wages raises the relative price of labor-intensive goods more than that of capital-intensive goods in a conventional Marxian model, decreases in the ratio of hours worked to hours consumed for one set of family members will increase their "price" to the family.

Factors such as education and technological change which affect the relative productivity of men, women, and children clearly do affect the cost of children. But even if their relative productivity remained the same, changes in family members' relative rates of surplus value would also affect those costs. Once this is established as a logical possibility, a more interesting question can be posed: Is there reason to believe that the expansion of capitalist social relations of production might change relative rates of exploitation within the family in such a way as to raise the costs of children and motivate fertility decline?

The answer is yes. The expansion of commodity production may diminish parental power over children in two ways. In the first place, the importance of parental assets such as land and wealth tends to be reduced, partly because many parents with small agricultural holdings or small businesses are unable to compete with capitalist firms and are forced to join the wage labor force. Those who remain in control of a family business which they can pass on to their children may find it difficult to compete with capitalist employers for their children's labor. Second, the increased importance of education forces parents to confer larger benefits on children at a relatively early age. This change in the timing of intergenerational transfer is crucial. While parents directly control young children's economic activities, older, educated children have considerably more control over their earnings and their product. In many instances, older children *do* continue to support their parents—but their contribution becomes increasingly *voluntary* in nature.

One of the most striking and least explored findings of the International Value of Children survey conducted by the East-West Institute is that many respondents agreed that children are less willing to support their parents in old age and are less willing to give part of their wages to their parents when they start working. In Hawaii, 41 percent of respondents felt this way; in Thailand, 63 percent, in Japan, 64 percent. In all cases, a majority of respondents disapproved of these changes (Burpakdi 1978; Arnold and Fawcett 1978; Lon 1978; Initani 1978).

Children do not abruptly abandon their responsibilities to their parents, but they play an increasingly important role in redefining those responsibilities. They may seek to legitimate their new independence by transferring a part of their traditional responsibility to the state. Charles Hohm (1975) has shown that government-implemented social security programs are associated with lower levels of fertility. Hohm and others tend to treat the advent of such programs as exogenous to the process of economic development. Yet social security programs may represent a response to the decline in intergenerational transfers as well as a rationale for continued decline.

The transformation of class structure also has an impact on bargaining power between the sexes. Differences in sons' and daughters' access to inherited land or wealth becomes less important as fewer children choose to pursue traditional ways of life. The expansion of wage labor provides a young woman with an alternative to marriage which is at least slightly more viable than continued residence in her father's household.

Women's employment outside the home may not have an immediate effect on their bargaining power, because patterns of market employment are influenced by patriarchal forms of inequality. Women often receive lower levels of education (or human capital) and are willing to accept relatively poorly paid jobs precisely because the household defines their primary commitment as household production and child care. Employers may perceive certain advantages to forms of discrimination which segment the labor force and impede the development of class consciousness (Gordon 1972). Male-dominated trade unions may restrict women's access to more lucrative forms of employment (Hartmann 1978).

Some development theorists have convincingly argued that the introduction of capitalist relations of production into some countries actually worsened women's position (Boserup 1970; Cheney and Schmink 1976). But the initial effects of new economic institutions imposed by imperialist domination must be distinguished from the long-run effects of the decline in household production. Although the forces described above may work to maintain or even worsen women's wages relative to men's, other forces come into play which modify the traditional sexual division of labor.

Primary among these are changes in desired family size brought about as the net benefits of children are reduced. When women invest a great deal of time in childrearing, part of the productivity of their work lies in expected returns from their adult children's labor. As these returns diminish, a sexual division of labor which channels women into childbearing and childrearing becomes increasingly costly to individual families. While men actively resist changes which reduce their bargaining power in the home, they cannot support wives who find it increasingly difficult to perform productive labor in the home. Women are increasingly forced to seek forms of employment outside the home which are more directly productive. As they do so, they may enhance their relative bargaining power within the family and shift some of the costs of children to other family members who are less willing to pay the price.

CONCLUSION

The family is obviously distinct from the capitalist firm. Its collective goal is not profit maximization, and its internal divisions are not simply based on class. But however distinctive the form which economic rationality takes in the family, economic rationality does operate there. Household production is not governed by market forces, but it is governed by material constraints which motivate households to use the most efficient means possible to accomplish their ends. The applicability of the concept of socially necessary labor time to the household makes it possible to describe intrahousehold allocation in value terms.

The labor theory of value is crucial to an accurate conceptualization of household production. It provides an economic methodology which can describe exchanges between family members in material terms and provide the criteria for equal exchange. It also provides political insights which make it possible to distinguish between voluntary forms of unequal exchange and exploitative forms of unequal exchange.

It has been suggested, in what is clearly intended as a reductio ad absurdum, that if men exploit women, children must exploit them also. The only absurd aspect of this statement is the conflation of unequal exchange and exploitation. In fact, the equality or inequality of economic exchange between parents and children helps determine the cost of children and therefore exercises a major influence on fertility rates.

The last section of this paper has outlined a number of ways in which the transition to capitalism may affect the relative bargaining power of men, women, and children, modify the distribution of surplus value within the family, and undercut the economic supports for high fertility. This outline clearly needs to be filled out in more detail. Changes in class structure associated with the transition to capitalism vary considerably between countries and are affected by dynamics of global capital accumulation.

But while the specific arguments presented here require further elaboration, the general point is quite clear. Marxists must devote more attention to the economics of the family. The production of commodities does not take place by means of commodities. Commodities are produced by labor, labor comes from laborers, and laborers are themselves produced. The production of commodities takes place by means of the reproduction of labor power. And the reproduction of labor power is fundamentally altered by expansion of capitalism itself.

Notes

Much of the labor time embodied in this paper originated with Sam Bowles, Ann Ferguson, and Jane Humphries. Although transfers of labor time between us have, I hope, never been exploitative, they have not yet become reciprocal, and I owe them much. Thanks also to my anonymous reviewers at the *Cambridge Journal of Economics*, whose comments and criticisms were quite helpful.

1. Bowles and Gintis explain this incommensurability in slightly different terms, arguing that "household labour cannot be described as abstract labour, for its allocation is not governed by the same considerations (market regulation) which govern the allocation of labour at the site of capitalist production" (Bowles and Gintis 1981, 11).
2. Bowles and Gintis (1981) make this point very clearly.
3. For a more complete discussion see Folbre 1980. It is important to note some

recent efforts by neoclassical economists to introduce the possibility of conflict with the family by using Nash bargaining models (see Manser and Brown 1978).

4. See Steedman 1977 and Morishima 1973 for a discussion of these problems as they apply to wage labor.

5. In other words, to ask if $\dfrac{L_f}{E_f} = \dfrac{L_m}{E_m} = \dfrac{L_c}{E_c}$

6. The family may, for instance, engage in class struggle as a unified group (see Humphries 1977).

7. For a summary of this literature, see Folbre 1980. See also Cain et al. 1978; Caldwell 1978; Cheung 1972; Greven 1970; Mbilinyi 1972; Newland 1980; Tilly and Scott 1978; Wolf 1972.

8. A good example of research describing men's activities outside the home is Heidi Hartmann's analysis of the role of trade unions (Hartmann 1979).

References

Arnold, F., and J. T. Fawcett. 1978. *The Value of Children: Hawaii*. Honolulu: East-West Population Institute.

Beaver, S. 1975. *Demographic Transition Theory Reinterpreted*. Lexington, MA: Lexington Books.

Boserup, E. 1970. *Women in Economic Development*. New York: St. Martin's Press.

Bowles, S., and H. Gintis. 1981. "Structure and Practice in the Labor Theory of Value." *Review of Radical Political Economics* 12, no. 4 (Winter).

Bulatao, R. A. 1978. *The Value of Children: A Cross-National Study: The Philippines*. Honolulu: East-West Population Institute.

Burpakdi, U. 1978. *The Value of Children: Thailand*. Honolulu: East-West Population Institute.

Cain, M., et al. 1978. "The Household Life Cycle and Economic Mobility in Rural Bangladesh." *Population and Development Review* 4, no. 3.

Caldwell, J. 1978. "A Theory of Fertility: From High Plateau to Stabilization." *Population and Development Review* 4, no. 4 (Dec.).

Cheney, E. M., and M. Schmink. 1976. "Women and Modernization: Access to Tools." In J. Nash and H. I. Safa, eds., *Sex and Class in Latin America*. New York: Praeger.

Cheung, S. 1972. "The Enforcement of Property Rights in Children, and the Marriage Contract." *Economic Journal*. June.

Coale, A., and M. Zelnick. 1963. *New Estimates of Fertility and Population in the U.S.* Princeton: Princeton University Press.

Dalla Costa, M., and James S. Dalla Costa. 1970. *The Power of Women and the Subversion of the Community*. Bristol: Falling Wall Press.

Delphy, C. 1976. *The Main Enemy*. London: Women's Research and Resource Centre.

Evenson, R. E., P. Popkin, and E. King-Quizon. "Nutrition, Work, and Demographic Behavior in Rural Philippine Households." Yale University, Economic Growth Center Discussion Paper 308. Jan.

Ferguson, A., and N. Folbre. 1981. "The Unhappy Marriage of Patriarchy and Capitalism." In L. Sargent, ed., *Women and Revolution*. Boston: South End Press.

Folbre, N. 1983. "Of Patriarchy Born: The Political Economy of Fertility Decisions." *Feminist Studies* 9, no. 2: 261–84.

———. 1984. "Household Production in the Philippines: A Non-Neoclassical Approach." *Economic Development and Cultural Change*, 32, no. 2: 303–330.

Goode, W. J. 1970. *World Revolution and Family Patterns*. New York: Free Press.

Gordon, D. 1972. *Theories of Poverty and Underemployment*. Toronto: Lexington Publishers.

Greven, P. 1970. *Four Generations: Population, Land, and Family in Colonial Andover, Massachusetts*. New York: Cornell University Press.

Harrison, J. 1973. "The Political Economy of Housework." *Bulletin of the Conference of Socialist Economists* 4, no. 4.

Hartmann, H. 1979. "Capitalism, Patriarchy, and Job Segregation by Sex." In Z. Eisenstein, ed., *Capitalist Patriarchy and the Case for Socialist Feminism*. New York: Monthly Review Press.

Himmelweit, S., and S. Mohun. 1977. "Domestic Labour and Capital." *Cambridge Journal of Economics* 1, no. 1 (March).

Ho, T. 1979. "Time Costs of Child Rearing in the Philippines." *Population and Development Review* 5, no. 4 (Dec.).

Hohm, C. 1975. "Social Security and Fertility: An International Perspective." *Demography* 12, no. 5 (Nov.).

Humphries, J. 1977. "Class Struggle and the Persistence of the Working-Class Family." *Cambridge Journal of Economics* 1, no. 3 (Sept.).

Intani, T. 1978. *The Value of Children: Japan*. Honolulu: East-West Population Institute.

Kirk, D. 1971. "Towards a New Demographic Transition." In *Rapid Population Growth*. Washington, DC: National Academy of Sciences.

Kuhn, A. 1978. "Structures of Patriarchy and Capital in the Family." In A. Kuhn and A. M. Wolpe, eds., *Feminism and Materialism*. London: Routledge and Kegan Paul.

Lon, T. S. 1978. *The Value of Children: Taiwan*. Honolulu: East-West Population Institute.

Manser, M., and M. Brown. 1978. "Marriage and Household Decision-Making: A Bargaining Analysis." State University of New York at Buffalo, Discussion Paper 376. Jan.

Marx, K. 1977. *Capital*, vol. 1. New York: Vintage Books.

Mbilinyi, M. 1972. "The State of Women in Tanzania." *Canadian Journal of African Studies* 2.

Meillasoux, C. 1977. *Mujeres, granero, y capitales*. Spanish tr. Mexico: D.V. Sigloveintiuno.

Mernissi, F. 1975. *Beyond the Veil*. New York: John Wiley and Sons.

Molyneux, M. 1979. "Beyond the Domestic Labour Debate." *New Left Review* 116.

Morishima, M. 1973. *Marx's Economics*. London: CUP

Nag, M. 1972. "Economic Value of Children in Agricultural Societies: Evaluation of Existing Knowledge and an Anthropological Approach." In J. T. Fawcett, ed., *The Satisfaction and Cost of Children: Theories, Concepts, Methods*. Honolulu: East-West Center.

Nag, M., R. C. Peet, and B. White. 1972. "An Anthropological Approach to the Study of the Economic Value of Children in Java and Nepal." *Current Anthropology* 19, no. 2.

Newland, K. 1980. "Righting Ancient Wrongs." *People* 7, no. 3.

Rosenzweig, M. 1977. "The Demand for Children in Farm Households." *Journal of Political Economics* 85, no. 1.

Rosenzweig, M., and R. Evenson. 1977. "Fertility, Schooling, and the Economic Contribution of Children in Rural India: An Econometric Analysis." *Econometrica* 45, no. 5.

Saadawi, N. H. 1980. *The Hidden Face of Eve*. London: Zed Press.

Seccombe, W. 1974. "The Housewife and Her Labour under Capitalism." *New Left Review* 83.

Shorter, E. 1975. *The Making of the Modern Family*. New York: Basic Books.

Shersey, M. J. 1973. *The Nature and Evolution of Female Sexuality*. New York: Vintage Books.

Statistical Abstract of the United States. 1978.

Steedman, I. 1977. *Marx after Sraffa*. London: New Left Books.

Szalai, A. 1975. "Women's Time: Women in the Light of Contemporary Time Budget Research." *Futures*. Oct.

Tienda, M. 1979. "The Economic Activity of Children in Peru." *Rural Sociology* 44, no. 2.

Tilly, L., and J. Scott. 1978. *Women, Work, and Family*. New York: Holt, Rinehart, and Winston.

Wolf, M. 1972. *Women and the Family in Rural Taiwan*. Stanford: Stanford University Press.

Social Origins of the Sexual Division of Labor

Maria Mies

The Search for Origins Within a Feminist Perspective

Since the rise of positivism and functionalism as the dominant schools of thought among Western social scientists in the 1920s, the search for the origins of unequal and hierarchical relationships in society in general, and the asymmetric division of labor between men and women in particular, has been taboo. The neglect, and even systematic suppression, of this question has been part of an overall campaign against Marxist thinking and theorizing in the academic world, particularly in the Anglo-Saxon world (Martin and Voorhies 1975, 155 ff). It is only now that this question is being asked again. Significantly, it was not first asked by academics, but by women actively involved in the women's movement. Whatever the ideological differences between the various feminist groups, they are united in their rebellion against this hierarchical relationship, which is no longer accepted as biological destiny, but seen as something to be abolished. Their search for the social foundations of this asymmetry is the necessary consequence of their rebellion. Women who are committed to struggle against the age-old oppression and exploitation of women cannot rest content with the indifferent conclusion put forward by many academics, that the question of origins should not be raised because we know so little about them.

From Maria Mies, "Social Origins of the Sexual Division of Labour," in *Patriarchy and Accumulation on a World Scale* (London: Zed Books, 1986), 44–49, with the permission of Zed Books.

The search for the social origins of this relationship is part of the political strategy of women's emancipation (Reiter 1977). Without understanding the foundation and the functioning of the asymmetric relationship between men and women, it is not possible to overcome it.

This political and strategic motivation fundamentally differentiates this new quest for the origins from other academic speculation and research endeavors. Its aim is not merely to analyze or to find an interpretation of an old problem, the purpose is rather to solve it.

The following discussion should, therefore, be understood as a contribution to "spreading the consciousness of the existence of gender hierarchy and collective action aimed at dismantling it" (Reiter 1977, 5).

BIASED CONCEPTS

When we began to ask about the origins of the oppressive relationship between the sexes, we soon discovered that none of the old explanations put forward by social scientists since the last century was satisfactory. For in all explanations, whether they stem from an evolutionist, a positivist-functionalist, or even a Marxist approach, the problem which needs explanation is, in the last analysis, seen as biologically determined and hence beyond the scope of social change. Therefore, before discussing the origins of an asymmetric division of labor between the sexes, it is useful to identify the biological biases in some of the concepts we commonly use in our debates.

This covert or overt biological determinism, paraphrased in Freud's statement that anatomy is destiny, is perhaps the most deep-rooted obstacle to the analysis of the causes of women's oppression and exploitation. Although women who struggle for their emancipation have rejected biological determinism, they find it very difficult to establish that the unequal, hierarchical, and exploitative relationship between men and women is caused by social, that is, historical, factors. One of our main problems is the fact that not only the analysis as such, but also the tools of the analysis, the basic concepts and definitions, are affected—or rather infected—by biological determinism.

This is largely true of the basic concepts which are central to our analysis, such as the concepts of *nature*, of *labor*, of *the sexual division of labor*, of the *family*, and of *productivity*. If these concepts are used without a critique of their implicit ideological biases, they tend to obscure rather than to clarify the issues. This is above all true for the concept of *nature*.

Too often this concept has been used to explain social inequalities or exploitative relations as inborn, and, hence, beyond the scope of social change. Women should be particularly suspicious when this term is used to explain their status in society. Their share in the production and reproduction of life is usually defined as a function of their biology or "nature." Thus, women's household and child-care work are seen as an extension of their physiology, of the fact that they give birth to children, of the fact that "nature" has provided them with a uterus. All the labor that goes into the production of life, including the labor of giving birth to a child, is not seen as the conscious interaction of a human being *with* nature, that is, a truly human activity, but rather as an activity *of* nature, which produces plants and animals unconsciously and has no control over this process. This definition of women's interaction with nature—including her own nature—as an act *of* nature has had and still has far-reaching consequences.

What is mystified by a biologistically infected concept of nature is a relationship of dominance and exploitation, dominance of the (male) human being over (female) nature. This dominance relationship is also implicit in the other concepts mentioned above when applied to women. Take the concept of *labor*! Due to the biologistic definition of women's interaction with her nature, her work both in giving birth and raising children as well as the rest of domestic work does not appear as work or labor. The concept of labor is usually reserved for men's productive work under capitalist conditions, which means work for the production of surplus value.

Though women also perform such surplus-value-generating labor, under capitalism the concept of labor is generally used with a male or patriarchal bias, because under capitalism, women are typically defined as housewives, which means as nonworkers.

The instruments of this labor, or the bodily means of production implicitly referred to in this concept, are the hands and the head, but never the womb or the breasts of a woman. Thus, not only are men and women differently defined in their interaction with nature, but the human body itself is divided into truly "human" parts (head and hand), and "natural" or purely "animal" parts (genitalia, womb, etc.).

This division cannot be attributed to some universal sexism of men as such, but is a consequence of the capitalist mode of production which is only interested in those parts of the human body which can be directly used as instruments of labor or which can become an extension of the machine.

The same hidden asymmetry and biologistic bias, which we could observe in the concept of labor, also prevails in the concept of *sexual division of labor* itself. Though overtly this concept seems to suggest that men and women simply divide different tasks between themselves, it hides the fact that men's tasks are usually considered as truly human ones (that is, conscious, rational, planned, productive, etc.), whereas women's tasks are again seen as basically determined by their "nature." The sexual division of labor, according to this definition, could be paraphrased as one between "human labor" and "natural activity." What is more, however, this concept also obscures the fact that the relationship between male (that is, "human"), and female ("natural") laborers or workers is a relationship of dominance and even of exploitation. The term "exploitation" is used here in the sense that a more or less permanent separation and hierarchization has taken place between producers and consumers, and that the latter can appropriate products and services of the former without themselves producing. The original situation in an egalitarian community, that is, one in which those who produce something are also—in an intergenerational sense—its consumers, has been disrupted. Exploitative social relations exist when nonproducers are able to appropriate and consume (or invest) products and services of actual producers (Sohn-Rethel 1978; Luxemburg 1925). This concept of exploitation can be used to characterize the man-woman relationship over large periods of history, including our own.

Yet, when we try to analyze the social origins of this division of labor, we have to make clear that we mean this asymmetric, hierarchical, and exploitative relationship, and not a simple division of tasks between equal partners.

The same obfuscating biologistic logic prevails with regard to the concept of *family*. Not only is this concept used and universalized in a rather Eurocentric and ahistoric way, presenting the nuclear family as the basic and timeless structure of all institutionalization of men-women relations, it also hides the fact that the structure of this institution is a hierarchical, unegalitarian one. Phrases like "partnership or democracy within the family" only serve to veil the true nature of this institution.

Concepts like the "biological" or "natural" family are linked to this particular ahistorical concept of the family which is based on the compulsory combination of heterosexual intercourse and the procreation of consanguine children.

This brief discussion of the biologistic biases inherent in some of the important concepts has made clear that it is necessary systematically to expose the ideological function of these biases, which is to obscure and mystify asymmetric and exploitative social relations, particularly those between men and women.

This means with regard to the problem before us, namely, the analysis of the social origins of the sexual division of labor, that we are *not* asking: When did a division of labor between men and women arise? Our question is rather: What are the reasons why this division of labor became a relationship of dominance and exploitation, an asymmetric, hierarchical relationship? This question still looms large in all discussions on women's liberation.

SUGGESTED APPROACH

What can we do to eliminate the biases in the abovementioned concepts? Not use the concepts at all, as some women suggest? But then we would be without a language to express our ideas. Or invent new ones? But concepts summarize historical practice and theory and cannot voluntaristically be invented. We have to accept that the basic concepts we use in our analysis have already been "occupied"—like territories or colonies—by dominant sexist ideology. Though we cannot abandon them, we can look at them "from below," not from the point of view of the dominant ideology, but from the point of view of the historical experiences of the oppressed, exploited, and subordinated and their struggle for emancipation.

It is thus necessary, regarding the concept of the *productivity of labor*, to reject its narrow definition and to show that labor can only be productive in the sense of producing surplus value as long as it can tap, extract, exploit, and appropriate labor which is spent in the *production of life*, or *subsistence production* (Mies 1980) which is largely nonwage labor mainly done by women. As this *production of life* is the perennial precondition of all other historical forms of productive labor, including that under conditions of capitalist accumulation, it has to be defined as *work* and not as unconscious "natural" activity.

In what follows, I will call the labor that goes into the production of life *productive labor* in the broad sense of producing use values for the satisfaction of human needs. The separation from and the superimposition of surplus-producing labor over life-producing labor is an abstraction which leads to the fact that women and their work are being "defined into nature."

In his discussion of the labor process in *Capital*, volume 1, Marx first uses a broad definition of "productive labor" which, by a change of natural matter, produces a product for human use, that is, for the satisfaction of human needs (Marx 1974a, vol. 1). But in a footnote he already warns that this definition, correct for the simple labor process, is not at all adequate for the capitalist production process, where the concept of "productive labor" is narrowed down to mean only the *production of surplus value*: "Only that labourer is productive who produces surplus for the realization of capital." Marx uses here the narrow concept of productivity of labor which was developed by Adam Smith and other political economists (see Marx 1974b, 212). He still criticizes this concept in the sense that he states that to be a "productive labourer under capitalism is not good luck but bad luck" (532) because the worker becomes a direct instrument of valuation of capital. But by focusing only on this capitalist concept of productive labor and by universalizing it to the virtual eclipse of the more general and fundamental concept of productive labor—which could include women's production of life—Marx himself has theoretically contributed to the removal of all "nonproductive" labor (that is, nonwage labor, including most of women's labor) from public visibility. The concept of "productive labour," used henceforth both by bourgeois as well as by Marxist theoreticians, has maintained this capitalist connotation, and the critique which Marx had still attached to it is long forgotten. I consider this narrow, capitalist concept of "productive labor" the most formidable hurdle in our struggle to come to an understanding of women's labor both under capitalism and actually existing socialism.

It is my thesis that this general production of life, or subsistence production—mainly performed through the nonwage labor of women and other nonwage laborers as slaves, contract workers, and peasants in the colonies—constitutes the perennial basis upon which "capitalist productive labor" can be built up and exploited. Without the ongoing subsistence production of nonwage laborers (mainly women), wage labor would not be "productive." In contrast to Marx, I consider the capitalist production process as one which comprises both: the *superexploitation* of nonwage laborers (women, colonies, peasants) upon which wage-labor exploitation then is possible. I define their exploitation as superexploitation because it is not based on the appropriation (by the capitalist) of the time and labor over and above the "necessary" labor time, the *surplus* labor, but of the time and labor *necessary* for people's own survival or subsistence production. It is not compensated for by a wage, the size of which is calculated on the "necessary" reproduction costs of the laborer, but is mainly determined by force or coercive institutions. This is the main reason for the growing poverty and starvation of Third World producers. In their case, the principle of an exchange of equivalents underlying the wage negotiations of workers in the West is not applied.

The search for the origins of the hierarchical sexual division of labor should not be limited to the search for the moment in history or prehistory when the "world-historic defeat of the female sex" (Engels) took place. Though studies in primatology, prehistory, and archaeology are useful and necessary for our search, we cannot expect them to give an answer to this question unless we are able to develop materialist, historical, nonbiologistic concepts of men and women and their relations to nature and history. As Roswitha Leukert puts it: "The beginning of human history is primarily not a problem of fixing a certain date, but rather that of finding a materialist concept of man [the human being] and history" (Leukert 1976, 18, tr. M. M.).

If we use this approach, which is closely linked to the strategic motivation mentioned earlier, we shall see that the development of vertical, unequal relationships between women and men is not a matter of the past only.

We can learn a lot about the actual formation of sex-hierarchies if we look at "history in the making," that is, if we study what is happening to women under the impact of capitalism both at its centers and at its periphery, where poor peasant and tribal societies are now being "integrated" into a so-called new national and international division of labor under the dictates of capital accumulation. Both in the capitalist metropoles and in the peripheries, a distinct sexist policy was and is used to subsume whole societies and classes under capitalist production relations.

This strategy usually appears in the guise of "progressive" or liberal *family laws* (for example, the prohibition of polygamy), of family planning and development policies. The demand to "integrate women into development," first voiced at the International Women's Conference in Mexico (1975), is largely used in Third World countries to recruit women as the cheapest, most docile, and manipulable labor force for capitalist production processes, both in agrobusiness and industry, as well as in the unorganized sector (Fröbel, Kreye, and Heinrichs 1977; Mies 1982; Grossman 1979; Elson and Pearson 1980; Safa 1980).

This also means that we should no longer look at the sexual division of labor as a problem related to the family only, but rather as a structural problem of a whole society. The hierarchical division of labor between men and women and its dynamics form an integral part of the dominant production relations, that is, the class relations of a particular epoch and society, and of the broader national and international divisions of labor.

Note

This chapter is the result of a longer collective process of reflection among women in the years 1975–77, when I conducted courses on the history of the women's movement at Frankfurt University. Many of the ideas discussed here emerged in a course on "Work and Sexuality in Matristic Societies." The thesis of one of my students, Roswitha Leukert, on "Female Sensuality" (1976), helped to clarify many of our ideas. I want to thank her and all women who took part in these discussions.

The chapter is the revised version of a paper which was first given at the conference "Underdevelopment and Subsistence Reproduction," University of Bielefeld, 1979. It was published as an occasional paper in 1981 by the Institute of Social Studies, The Hague.

References

Elson, D., and R. Pearson. 1980. "The Latest Phase of the Internationalisation of Capital and Its Implications for Women in the Third World." Discussion paper 150, Institute of Development Studies, Sussex University.

Fröbel, F., J. Kreye, and O. Heinrichs. 1980. *The New International Division of Labour.* Cambridge: Cambridge University Press.

Grossman, R. 1978–79. "Women's Place in the Integrated Circuit." *South East Asian Chronicle* 66 (1979) and *Pacific Research* 9, nos. 5–6 (1978).

Leukert, R. 1976. "Weibliche Sinnlichkeit." Diploma thesis, University of Frankfurt.

Luxemburg, R. 1925. *Einführung in die Nationalökonomie.* Ed. P. Levi. Berlin.

Martin, M. K., and B. Voorhies. 1975. *Female of the Species.* New York: Columbia University Press.

Marx, K. 1974a. *Capital: A Critique of Political Economy.* London: Lawrence and Wishart.

———. 1974b. *Grundrisse.* Berlin: Dietz Verlag.

Mies, M. 1980. "Capitalist Development and Subsistence Reproduction: Rural Women in India." *Bulletin of Concerned Asian Scholars* 12, no. 1: 2–14.

———. 1982. *The Lacemakers of Narsapur: Indian Housewives Produce for the Worldmarket.* London: Zed Books.

Reiter, R. R. 1977. "The Search for Origins." *Critique of Anthropology, Women's Issue* 3, nos. 9, 10.

Safa, H. I. 1980. "Export Processing and Female Employment: The Search for Cheap Labour." Paper prepared for Wenner Gren Foundation Symposium on the Sex Division of Labor, Development, and Women's Status, Burg Wartenstein, 2–10 Aug.

Sohn-Rethel, A. 1978. *Warenform und Denkform.* Frankfurt: Suhrkamp.

Sex and Work

ANN FERGUSON

SEX/AFFECTIVE PRODUCTION

IF WOMEN AND MEN belong to oppositional sex classes, in addition to having different relations to capitalist production as individuals and as members of their specific races and families, what system of production so divides them? My theory holds that sexism is based in a semiautonomous system of social domination that persists throughout different modes of economic production. There are historically various ways of organizing, shaping, and molding the human desires connected to sexuality and love, and, consequently, parenting and social bonding. These systems, which I call modes of "sex/ affective production," have also been called "desiring production" by Deleuze and Guattari (1977) and "sex/gender systems" by Gayle Rubin (1975). It is in part through these systems, which socially construct and produce the specific forms of the more general human material need for social union and physical sexual satisfaction I call "sex/affective energy," that different forms of male dominance as well as other types of social domination (e.g., racism, ethnicism, capitalism, and other class-divided systems of social domination) are reproduced.

My approach to understanding sexuality, social bonding, and nurturance is that these are all material needs that, since they have no specific biologically given objects, must be socially organized and produced. In this respect sex/affective energy is like the material need for hunger and shelter: Though

From Ann Ferguson, "Sex and Work: Women as a New Revolutionary Class in the United States," in *Sexual Democracy* (Boulder, CO: Westview Press, 1991), 38–44 (originally in Roger Gottlieb, ed., *An Anthology of Western Marxism* [Oxford: Oxford University Press, 1989]), reprinted with the permission of the author.

they have a biological base, their specific objects (e.g., particular food and shelter preferences) must be culturally produced. Furthermore, the by-product of heterosexual sexuality, children, not only is functionally connected to the reproduction of the economy of any society but also generates new sex/affective needs for, and objects of, nurturant energy.

Thus sex/affective productive systems are both *like* economic modes of production and *functionally part* of such systems in that they are human modes of organizing that both create the social objects of the material needs connected to sex/affective energy and then organize human labor to achieve them. Like economic modes of production, they can also contain dialectical aspects: That is, there may be opposing tendencies in the system that undermine its ability to reproduce itself. Just as Marx thought that the dialectical instabilities in the capitalist system were bound to create a revolutionary movement for social change in the hitherto oppressed working class, the instabilities in our present form of patriarchal sex/affective production present the possibilities for a radical movement for social change in the oppressed sex class of women.

Every society must have one or more historically developed modes of sex/affective production to meet key human needs whose satisfaction is just as basic to the functioning of human society as is the satisfaction of the material needs of hunger and physical security. The satisfaction of these other key human needs—sexuality, nurturance, and children—has been based in the family household in the earlier phases of capitalism. And though our contemporary mode of sex/affective production, racist public patriarchal capitalism, has involved a shift in the *material base* of patriarchy (it is now jointly reproduced by sex/affective relations in the public spheres of wage labor and the welfare state, as well as those in the family), a complete understanding of the power and class relations in capitalism still must include an analysis of the sex/class relations of *family production*.

One way to characterize the interdependence between relations of sex/affective production and the economic system as a whole is to use the concept of a *social formation*. A social formation is a system of production in use in a particular society at a specific time that may contain within it several different historically developed modes of production. A historical example of a social formation is the combined U.S. capitalist/slave modes of production before the Civil War. Our present U.S. economic system can be thought of as a social formation consisting in part of capitalist and patriarchal modes of production. It has a codominant set of relations: (1) those between capital and wage labor and (2) those between men and women in patriarchal sex/affective production. It also has a subordinate set of class relations characteristic of welfare state capitalism—the existence of a class of institutionalized poor, that is, those subsidized by the state on welfare or unemployment. Its radical divisions of wage labor and its general separation of races into different living communities create a set of economic and sex/affective domination relations between the white dominant race and subordinate nonwhite races. Finally, the dominant mode of capitalist production is that controlled by multinational corporations, while a small subordinate sector of capitalist production involves small family businesses (the traditional petite bourgeoisie).

"Patriarchy" I define as a system of social relations in a society such that those who perform what is regarded as the "male" role (e.g., do "male" work) have more social power than, exploit, and control those who perform what is regarded as the "female" role (i.e., do women's work).[1] This use of the concept of patriarchy is somewhat broader than its original use, to mean "control by the father." I use the term "patriarchy" rather than the vaguer concept of "male dominance" as my technical term because in my view the origin, persistence, and potential undermining of male power and domination of women in all the institutions of society stems from the relative strength or weakness of male dominance and exploitation of women in the family and/or associated kin networks.

An argument for the claim that male/female social relations are codominant with other social relations of production is the universal presence in all societies of what Gayle Rubin calls "sex/gender" systems (Rubin 1975), that is, culturally defined male and female roles children learn as part of their social identity.[2] The sex/gender system organizes material work and services, by defining what is culturally acceptable as man's and woman's work. It also organizes nurturance, sexuality, and procreation by directing sexual urges (in most societies toward heterosexual relations and nonincestuous ties), by indicating possible friendships, and by defining parenthood roles and/or kinship ties and responsibilities.[3]

Patriarchal relations have persisted through many different modes of economic production, including socialist modes of production such as those in the Soviet Union, China, and Cuba. The articulation of different modes of patriarchal sex/affective production with different economic modes of production has meant that the content of the sexual division of labor varies (e.g., in some modes of sex/affective production and some social formations men work for wage labor and women do not; in others, e.g., feudal production, neither men nor women work for wages). Other relations of exploitation vary as well (e.g., whether it is a feudal lord, the male head of the family, or a capitalist who benefits from the reproduction of labor power in a family).

Patriarchal family production involves unequal and exploitative relations between men and women in domestic maintenance and sex/affective work. However, the amount of power the man has in relation to the woman in the family varies with their relation to the dominant mode of production. So if the woman has an individual economic class (e.g., if she is working for wage labor or has an independent income) and if she is making equal wages, it will be harder for the man to appropriate the surplus in wages after basic family needs are met. In general the typical nuclear family in the United States is less patriarchal than those in earlier periods, and a substantial minority of households are woman-headed. Nonetheless, the historical prevalence of the patriarchal family and a sexual division of labor has created a male-dominated sexual division of wage labor in which women's work is paid less, is usually part time, and has less job security than men's (Davies 1979; Hartmann 1981). Those women-headed households cannot be said to be matriarchal: That the majority live below the poverty line and that more than a third must depend on the federal government for welfare payments (whose size and availability depend on the changing largesse of a male-dominated government) suggests that the *fact* of male domination has not changed as much as the mechanisms by which it is reinforced.

WOMEN AS SEX CLASS IN THE PATRIARCHAL NUCLEAR FAMILY

Men and women are in *sex classes* in capitalist society today, classes defined by the sexual division of labor in the family (in both the male-headed nuclear family and the mother-headed family) and reinforced by the sexual division of wage labor. In this section I present my arguments to show that women are exploited relative to men in most contemporary forms of the family, that they are dominated and have little autonomy.

By the capitalist patriarchal nuclear family (CPNF) I mean an economic unit of man, woman, and possibly children, in which the man works full time in wage labor (is thus the main breadwinner), while the woman works as the primary domestic and child-care worker in the home.[4] If she is employed in wage labor, she is not employed more than part time.

How then do men exploit women in the CPNF? Four goods are produced in sex/affective production in the family: domestic maintenance, children, nurturance, and sexuality. Since a sex/affective productive system is a system of exchange of goods and labor, we can classify it in terms of the power relations involved; that is, is there an equal exchange between producers? If not, who controls the exchange? Patriarchal sex/affective production is characterized by unequal exchange between men and women: Women receive less of the goods produced than men, and typically work harder, that is, spend more time producing them. The relations between men and women can be considered *exploitative* because the man is able to appropriate more of the woman's labor time for his own use than she is of his, and he also gets more of the goods produced (see also Delphy 1984; Folbre 1982, 1983).[5] It is *oppressive* because the sex/gender roles taught to boys and girls to perpetuate the sexual division of labor develop a female personality structure that internalizes the goal to produce more for men and to accept less for herself (see also Barrett 1980).

The points made here about the exploitation and control by men of women in the CPNF apply as well to most other types of family household in the United States today. Although many families are not of the CPNF structure (e.g., female-headed households, or families in which both husband and wife work full time), most other families with children involve exploitation of the mother's work by the father. This result is partly structural and partly due to social pressure on the mother to accept an unequal sexual division of labor. After all, the CPNF is the legitimized arrangement to which schools, wage-labor jobs, and many social services (e.g., welfare, social security) are coordinated (Barrett and McIntosh 1982). Those who do not live in a patriarchal nuclear family are not only inconvenienced but suffer a loss of status. Schools and older kin make full-time wage-earning mothers feel guilty for time not spent with their children. The absence of affordable child care and the relatively better pay of husbands make it reasonable for mothers rather than fathers to work low-pay jobs whose flexible hours allow mothers to do child care. Thus mothers, not fathers, tend to suffer the second-shift problem of a full shift of wage work added to another shift of child care and housework at home.

Many female-headed households suffer a loss of family class: Their new individual economic class is lower than their family class was (when this is defined by their father or former husband's relations to production) (Sidel 1986). As Delphy (1984) has pointed out, women in such families continue to be exploited by the absent fathers, for women now must perform two full-time jobs without much help: being the breadwinner and doing the housework and child care.

Let me sum up the points presented about the inequalities between men and women in patriarchal capitalism in relation to the criteria for class identity to show why I maintain that women and men form sex classes.

Use of the first criterion, exploitation relations, usually assumes that exploitation involves ownership and/or control of production. I have argued here that men in capitalist patriarchies (whether or not they are actually present in the family household) own the wage and thus control sex/affective production in such a way as to be able to expropriate the surplus: surplus wages, surplus nurturance, and sexuality. Though the CPNF is no longer the dominant site of domestic maintenance and sex/affective production, its historical impact on the sexual division of wage labor, welfare state provisions, and the legal structures of child support continues to create a situation of exploitative sex/affective exchange between men and women, whether in other family households, in wage labor, in politics, or in the courts.

The fourth and fifth criteria, domination and autonomy relations, can be shown to apply to men and women as sex classes, both in the family and in other spheres of social life. If we remember that we are comparing power relations not only in the spheres of housework versus wage work but also the sex/affective work of sexuality and nurturance, it becomes clearer how the analogy holds. After all, the type of work women do in wage labor is primarily gendered sex/affective labor, that is, it involves women doing physical maintenance (nursing, health care), providing nurturance and sexuality (waitressing and other service work with sexual overtones) in which men as clients, bosses, and customers control the exchange.

Men dominate and control women in sexual activity and in nurturance (see Deming 1973; Tax 1970). It can be argued further that men are more autonomous in their sexual activities because they do them as consumers and not as part of their gender-defined work in the family. Here is a quote from a worker at Fisher Body Plant about the connections between his sexuality and his wife's:

> Because my need to be sexually re-vitalized each day is so great, it becomes the first and most basic part of a contract I need to make in order to ensure it.
>
> The goal of this contract is stability, and it includes whatever I need to consume: sex, food, clothes, a house, perhaps children. My partner in this contract is in most cases a woman; by now she is as much a slave to my need to consume as I am a slave to Fisher Body's need to consume me. What does she produce? Again, sex, food, clothes, a house, babies. What does she consume for all this effort?—all the material wealth I can offer plus a life outside of a brutal and uncompromising labor market. Within this picture, it's easy to see why many women get bored with sex. They get bored for the same reason I get bored with stacking bucket seats in cars. (Lippert 1977)

If sex is work for women and play for men, nurturance is as well. This is why those men who have picked up some nurturance skills tend to be more autonomous in their use. That is, since men's sense of gender success is not bound up with being a good nurturer, they are freer not to use nurturance skills in ways that may be self-destructive of their other needs (as in the self-sacrifice in which women often engage).

Notes

1. This definition has an important caveat: Technically it should include the restriction that those who perform the male role have more power than those who perform the female role *only if* all other social factors are equal, viz., provided the "male" actors involved are not from individual economic or family classes (or oppressed race or ethnic groups) that are subordinate to those of the "female" actors.

2. One of the important aspects of gender roles is the fact that they are *socially*, not biologically, defined. Although it is almost always men who occupy the male role and women the female role, this is not always so: There are societies like the Mohave Indians in which homosexuals are accepted as male or female regardless of biological sex, depending only on the gender role they decide to play.

3. The universal sexual division of labor, and societies with communal modes of production in which the sexual division of labor nonetheless gives men more power than women, suggests that Engels's historical theory of the origins of patriarchy (that the oppression of women occurs because of the need of men to control heirs and amass private property) is mistaken (Engels 1972). A counterhypothesis is offered by Lévi-Strauss, who argues that women are the first property, traded to cement bonds between tribes before the development of other types of private property and economic classes (Lévi-Strauss 1969). Gerda Lerner (1986) adds to this hypothesis the view that women are the first slaves, more valuable than male slaves because of their reproductive capacity (see also Meillassoux 1981) and their closer bonds to their offspring, which make them easier to discipline and retain.

   Another origin thesis compatible with Lévi-Strauss, Lerner, and Meillassoux is that societies developed matriarchal, egalitarian, or patriarchal kinship arrangements fairly haphazardly through the period of human prehistory when tribes were isolated from each other. When societies began to overlap, however, and to compete for hunting areas and land, those that were organized patriarchally were able to overcome matriarchal and egalitarian societies, and to impose their form of male-female patterns on those conquered.

   Patriarchal forms of organizing society have two advantages, in survival terms, when they compete with nonpatriarchal societies: (1) They can create very efficient armies. (2) They can generate a high population rate to replace fallen soldiers and/or to provide laborers for production. We can find a direct correlation between high birthrate and high degree of male control over women in historical societies, which suggests that when women have the power to determine their own pregnancies, they tend to keep the birthrate low. If we extrapolate this information to prehistoric societies, we can surmise that many egalitarian or matriarchal societies were not able to compete with militaristic, high-population-producing patriarchal societies. (I owe this line of thought to Nancy Folbre.)

4. It should be noted that this characterization excludes most capitalist-class families, for the male breadwinner is usually not working full time because of his unearned income from capital investments. Indeed, male-female relations are sufficiently different that they have no material base for patriarchy. Neither men nor women have to work: They can hire nannies for the children and maintain separate houses for their lovers, so it seems false that women in the capitalist

class should be thought of as part of an exploited sex class. Divorced women from this class never lose their family class status because of alimony and child support, income from trust funds, and so on. The men, on the other hand, are still members of the exploiter sex class, for their relation to the material means of reproduction allows them the power to exploit women from subordinate family and economic class positions.

5. What evidence is there for the view that men exploit women in sex/affective production? There is clear evidence that women spend more time on housework than men do on wage labor. The figure given by the Chase Manhattan Bank survey is that a full-time housewife puts in an average 99.6 hours of housework a week (Girard 1968). We also know that the inequality in relation to hours of work a week put in by husband and wife persists even when the wife is working in wage labor as well, for in that situation, studies have shown that the wife still puts in roughly forty-four hours of housework a week in addition to her wage work, while the husband only puts in eleven hours of work in addition to his wage work (Ryan 1975).

Because family production is not commodity production, there is no exact quantitative way to measure and compare the values of goods produced for use. Nor does it make sense to speak of the man "building up capital" with his human goods. Nonetheless, we can approximate quantitative measurements of the inequalities involved in the exchange by comparing the market commodity costs of the equivalent amounts of sexuality, child care, maintenance, and nurturance done by men and women. For an economic model of this, see Folbre 1982.

References

Barrett, Michelle. 1980. *Women's Oppression Today*. London: Verso.

Barrett, Michelle, and Mary McIntosh. 1982. *The Anti-Social Family*. London: Verso.

Davies, Margery. 1979. "Woman's Place Is at the Typewriter: The Feminization of the Clerical Labor Force." In Zillah Eisenstein, ed., *Capitalist Patriarchy and the Case for Socialist-Feminism*. New York: Monthly Review.

Deleuze, Giles, and Felix Guattari. 1977. *Anti-Oedipus*. New York: Viking.

Delphy, Christine. 1984. *Close to Home: A Materialist Analysis of Women's Oppression*. Amherst: University of Massachusetts Press.

Deming, Barbara. 1973. "Love Has Been Exploited Labor." *Liberation*. May.

Engels, Friedrich. 1972. *The Origin of the Family, Private Property, and the State*. New York: International Publishers.

Folbre, Nancy. 1982. "Exploitation Comes Home: A Critique of the Marxian Theory of Family Labour." *Cambridge Journal of Economics* 6:317–29 [this volume, selection 13].

———. 1983. "Of Patriarchy Born: The Political Economy of Fertility Decisions." *Feminist Studies* 9, no. 2: 261–84.

Girard, Alain. 1968. "The Time Budget of Married Women in Urban Centers." *Population*.

Hartmann, Heidi. 1981. "The Unhappy Marriage of Marxism and Feminism." In Lydia Sargent, ed., *Women and Revolution*. Boston: South End Press.

Lerner, Gerda. 1986. *The Creation of Patriarchy*. New York: Oxford University Press.

Lévi-Strauss, Claude. 1969. *The Elementary Structures of Kinship*. Boston: Beacon.

Lippert, Jon. 1977. "Sexuality as Consumption." In Jon Snodgrass, ed., *For Men against Sexism*. New York: Times Change Press.

Meillassoux, Claude. 1981. *Maidens, Meal, and Money: Capitalism and the Domestic Economy*. New York: Cambridge University Press.

Rubin, Gayle. 1975. "The Traffic in Women." In Rayna Reiter, ed., *Toward a New Anthropology of Women*. New York: Monthly Review.

Ryan, Mary. 1975. *Womanhood in America*. New York: Watts.

Sidel, Ruth. 1986. *Women and Children Last: The Plight of Poor Women in Affluent America*. New York: Viking/Penguin.

Tax, Meredith. 1970. "Woman and Her Mind: The Story of Everyday Life." Boston: New England Free Press.

Feeding Egos and
Tending Wounds

SANDRA LEE BARTKY

FEMINIST THEORISTS... HAVE NOTED the gendered imbalance in the provision of emotional support. Ann Ferguson, for example, has maintained that men's appropriation of women's emotional labor is a species of exploitation akin in important respects to the exploitation of workers under capitalism. Ferguson posits a sphere of "sex/affective production," parallel in certain respects to commodity production in the waged sector. Four goods are produced in this system: domestic maintenance, children, nurturance (of both men and children), and sexuality.[1]

According to Ferguson, economic domination of the household by men is analogous to capitalist ownership of the means of production. The relations of sex/affective production in a male-dominated society put women in a position of unequal exchange. Just as control of the means of production by capitalists allows them to appropriate "surplus value" from workers, i.e., the difference between the total value of the workers' output and that fraction of value produced the workers get in return—so men's privileged position in the sphere of sex/affective production allows them to appropriate "surplus nurturance" from women.[2] So, for example, the sexual division of labor whereby women are the primary childrearers requires a "'woman as nurturer' sex gender ideal." Girls learn "to find satisfaction in the satisfaction of others, and to place their needs second in the case of a conflict."[3]

Reprinted from Sandra Lee Bartky, "Feeding Egos and Tending Wounds," in *Femininity and Domination* (New York: Routledge, 1990), 100–102, 109–11, 114–19, with the permission of Routledge and the consent of the author.

Men, on the other hand, "learn such skills are women's work, learn to demand nurturance from women yet don't know how to nurture themselves."[4] Women, like workers, are caught within a particular division of labor which requires that they produce more of a good—here, nurturance—than they receive in return.

There is a clear allegation of harm to women in Ferguson's account—the harm of exploitation. Joel Feinberg characterizes exploitation generally as an interpersonal relationship that "involves one party (A) profiting from his relation to another party (B) by somehow 'taking advantage' of some characteristic of B's, or some feature of B's circumstances."[5] In most cases of exploitation, B's interests suffer or her rights are violated, but this need not be the case. Feinberg cites a number of examples in which A exploits B but "B is neither harmed nor benefited in the process."[6] Harmless parasitism is a case in point: Consider the sponger who exploits the generosity of a rich and good-natured patron or the gossip columnist who panders to the vulgar curiosity of the public by reporting the daily activities of some celebrity. The patron may be so rich that he neither minds nor misses the handouts; the celebrity may be utterly indifferent to the publicity.[7]

Now the specific kind of exploitation for which Marxists indict capitalism, and Ferguson patriarchy, is exploitation of the first variety, i.e., a taking advantage in which A's profiting from his relation to B involves substantial damage to B's interests. It is important to understand that for the Marxist, capitalist exploitation involves more than the unequal transfer of value from worker to capitalist. Oftentimes we give more to others than they give us in return—perhaps because we *have* more to give—without feeling ourselves aggrieved or naming ourselves exploited. Indeed, to require an exchange of equivalents in all our dealings with other people reduces the richness and variety of human relationship to the aridity of mere contract.

But, so it is charged, the appropriation of surplus value under capitalism involves an unequal exchange that is not at all benign, for the character of this exchange is such as to bring about the systematic disempowerment of one party to the exchange—the direct producers. The appropriation of surplus value is at the root of the workers' alienation, where by "alienation" is meant the loss of control both of the product of labor and of the productive process itself; the loss of autonomy in production brings with it a diminution in the workers' powers, for example, the atrophy of human capacity that attends a lifetime of repetitive or uncreative work. The appropriation of surplus value forms the basis, as well, of the social, political, and cultural preeminence of the appropriating classes.[8]

Ferguson's argument does not require that the two sets of relationships—workers under capitalism, women in the contemporary household—be identical, as clearly they are not. Her claim, as I understand it, is that both are exploited in the same *sense*, i.e., that both are involved in relationships of unequal exchange in which the character of the exchange is itself disempowering. Now this claim is problematical. First, there is some question whether the imbalance in the provision of emotional sustenance is a relationship of unequal exchange at all. Does it, in other words, satisfy the Marxist's first condition for exploitation? Under capitalism, so Marxists claim, workers receive less of the same kind of thing—value—than they give. Moreover, since the value of the worker's wage can be calculated in the same terms as the value of the worker's product, the difference between the two can be quantified and the exploitative character of the relationship just displayed for all to see. Nor, according to Marxists, is there anything else, i.e., anything other than what can be calculated as "value" in Marxist theory, that the capitalist gives the worker that might balance the books. Now in order for "surplus nurturance" to be parallel to "surplus value," the intimate exchanges of men and women will have to be shown not only to involve an imbalance in the provision of one *kind* of thing—here, nurturance—but not to involve an exchange of equivalents of any sort. But this is just what conservatives deny. The emotional contributions of men and women to intimacy certainly differ, they admit, but their contributions to one another, looked at on a larger canvas, *balance*: He shows his love for her by bringing home the bacon, *she* by securing for him a certain quality of nurturance and concern. Might they be right?[9]

Second, even if women's provision of emotional care to men can be shown not to be embedded within a larger exchange of equivalents, is it clear that women are really harmed by providing such care? Are the men who take more than they give in return anything worse than Feinberg's mere harmless parasites whose exploitation fails to issue in any genuine damage? Differently put, does the situation of women in intimacy satisfy the Marxist's second condition for exploitation, i.e., that there be not only an unequal transfer of powers but a genuine disempowerment in consequence of this transfer? Many feminists have condemned the classic bargain between man and woman (economic support in return for domestic labor and emotional caregiving) on the grounds that economic dependency itself is disempowering. But is it possible to argue that the unreciprocated provision of emotional sustenance—"female tenderness"—is disempowering *in and of itself*? And if it is, in what, precisely, does this disempowerment consist? . . .

Love, affection, and the affectionate dispensing of emotional sustenance may seem to be purely private transactions that have nothing to do with the macrosocial domain of status. But this is false. Sociologist Theodore Kemper maintains that "a love relationship is one in which at least one actor gives (or is prepared to give) extremely high status to another actor."[10] "Status accord" he defines as "the voluntary compliance with the needs, wishes or interests of the other."[11] Now insofar as women's provision of emotional sustenance is a species of compliance with the needs, wishes, and interests of men, such provision can be understood as a conferral of status, a paying of homage by the female to the male. Consider once again the bodily displays that are typical of women's intimate caregiving: the sympathetic cocking of the head; the forward inclination of the body; the frequent smiling; the urging, through appropriate vocalizations, that the man continue his recital, hence, that he may continue to commandeer the woman's time and attention. I find it suggestive that these behaviors are identical to common forms of deference display in hierarchies of status.[12] But status is not accorded mutually: Insofar as the emotional exchanges in question are contained within a gendered division of emotional labor that does not require of men what it requires of women, our caregiving, in effect, is a collective genuflection by women to men, an affirmation of male importance that is unreciprocated. The consistent giving of what we don't get in return is a performative acknowledgement of male supremacy and thus a contribution to our own social demotion. The implications of this collective bending of the knee, however, rarely enter consciousness. The very sincerity and quality of heartfelt concern that the woman brings to her man's emotional needs serves to reinforce in her own mind the importance of his little dramas of daily life. But he receives her attention as a kind of entitlement; by failing to attend to her in the same way she attends to him, he confirms for her and, just as important, for himself, her inferior position in the hierarchy of gender.

Women do not expect mutual recognition from the children we nurture, especially when these children are very young, but given the companionate ideal that now holds sway, we yearn for such recognition from the men with whom we are intimate. Its withholding is painful, especially so since in the larger society it is men and not women who have the power to give or to withhold social recognition generally. Wishing that he would notice; waiting for him to ask: How familiar this is to women, how like waiting for a sovereign to notice a subject, or a rich man, a beggar. Indeed, we sometimes find ourselves begging for his attention—and few things are as disempowering as having to beg.

Women have responded in a number of ways to men's refusal of recognition. A woman may merge with her man psychologically to such an extent that she just claims as her own the joys and sorrows he narrates on occasions of caretaking. She now no longer needs to resent his indifference to her doings, for his doings have just *become* her doings. After eight years of seeing it, we recall the picture easily: Ronald Reagan at the podium, Nancy, a bit behind her husband, fixing upon him a trancelike gaze of total admiration and utter absorption. Here is the perfect visual icon of the attempt to merge one's consciousness with the consciousness of the Other.

Psychologists such as Nancy Chodorow and Dorothy Dinnerstein have maintained that the relational style of women in matters of feeling and our more "permeable ego boundaries" are due to the fact that girls, unlike boys, are not required to sever in the same way their original identification with the maternal caretaker.[13] If this is true, the phenomenon that I am describing may be "overdetermined" by psychological factors. Nevertheless, it is worth asking to what extent the merging of the consciousness of the woman with the object of her emotional care may be a strategy adopted in adult life to avoid anger and the disruption of relationship, effects that might otherwise follow upon the refusal of recognition. Moreover, the successful provision of intimate caregiving itself requires a certain loss of oneself in the Other, whatever the infantile determinants of such merger and whatever the utility such merging may have in the management of anger or resentment. I shall return to this point later.

Women sometimes demand the performance of ritualized gestures of concern from men—the remembering of a birthday or anniversary, a Valentine's Day card—as signs of a male caring that appears to be absent from the transactions of everyday life. The ferocity with which women insist on these ritual observances is a measure, I believe, of our sense of deprivation. If the man forgets, and his forgetting issues in the absence of some object— a present, a Valentine—that cultural rituals have defined as visible and material symbols of esteem, a lack felt privately may be turned into a public affront. Women's preoccupation with such things, in the absence of an understanding of what this preoccupation means, has gained us a reputation for capriciousness and superficiality, a reputation that in itself is disempowering. "Why can't a woman be more like a man?" sings the exasperated Prof. Henry Higgins. "If I forgot your silly birthday, would you fuss? / . . . Why can't a woman be like us?"

Neither of these strategies—minimalism or merger—really works. The woman who accepts a ritualized gesture, performed at most a few times a year and often very perfunctorily, in exchange for the devoted caregiving she provides her man all the time, has made a bad bargain indeed, while the psychological overidentification I describe here is grounded in a self-deceived attempt to deny pain and to avoid the consequences of anger. To attempt such merger is to practice magic or to have a try at self-hypnosis. A woman who is economically dependent on a man may find it natural to identify with his interests; in addition to the kind of merging I have described, such dependency itself feeds a tendency to overidentification. But given the generally fragile character of relationships today, the frequency of divorce, and the conflicts that arise even within ongoing relationships, prudence requires that a woman regard the coincidence of her interests with those of her partner as if they were merely temporary. . . .

Disempowerment, then, may be inscribed in the more prominent features of women's unreciprocated caregiving: in the accord of status and the paying of homage; in the scarcely perceptible ethical and epistemic "leaning" into the reality of one who stands higher in the hierarchy of gender. But this is only part of the story. In this section I want to identify some countertendencies, ways in which women's provision of emotional sustenance to men may *feel* empowering and hence contradict, on a purely phenomenal level, what may be its objectively disempowering character.

Tending to wounds: This is a large part of what it is to provide someone with emotional support. But this means that in one standard scenario of heterosexual intimacy, the man appears to his female caregiver as vulnerable and injured. Fear and insecurity: For many men, these are the offstage companions of competitive displays of masculinity, and they are aspects of men's lives that women know well. To the woman who tends him, this fellow is not only no colossus who bestrides the world, but he may bear little resemblance to the patriarchal oppressor of feminist theory. The man may indeed belong to a more powerful caste; no matter, this isn't what he *seems* to her at the moment.

Why isn't every woman a feminist?... Feminism tells a tale of female injury, but the average woman in heterosexual intimacy knows that men are injured too, as indeed they are. She may be willing to grant, this average woman, that men in general have more power than women in general. This undoubted fact is merely a fact; it is *abstract*, while the man of flesh and blood who stands before her is *concrete*: His hurts are real, his fears palpable. And like those heroic doctors on the late show who work tirelessly through the epidemic even though they may be fainting from fatigue, the woman in intimacy may set her own needs to one side in order better to attend to his. She does this not because she is "chauvinized" or has "false consciousness," but because *this is what the work requires*. Indeed, she may even excuse the man's abuse of her, having glimpsed the great reservoir of pain and rage from which it issues. Here is a further gloss on the ethical disempowerment attendant upon women's caregiving: In such a situation, a woman may be tempted to collude in her own ill-treatment.[14]

Foucault has claimed that the practice of confession is disempowering to the one who confesses. Confession, as it is practiced in psychoanalysis or religion, is designed to lead the one confessing into the heart of a presumed "true" or "real" self, which he is ever after obligated to claim as his own. But there is no such self: The idea of such a self, says Foucault, is an illusion, a mere device whereby norms are inscribed in the one confessing that secure his subordination to the locus of power represented by the confessor.[15] But here is a counterexample to Foucault's claim: In the case of heterosexual intimacy, confession is disempowering not to the man who confesses but to the woman who hears this confession. How so? The woman is not the agent of any institutional power. She has no authority either to exact penance or to interpret the situation according to norms that could, in effect, increase the prestige of the institution she represents, hence her own prestige. Indeed, the exigencies of female tenderness are such as virtually to guarantee the man's absolution by the woman—not on her terms, but on his. Moreover, the man's confession of fear or failure tends to mystify the woman's understanding not only of the power dimensions of the relationship between herself and this particular man, but of the relations of power between men and women in general.

An apparent reversal has taken place: The man, her superior in the hierarchy of gender, now appears before the woman as the weaker before the stronger, the patient before his nurse. A source within the woman has been tapped and she feels flowing outward from herself a great power of healing and making whole. She imagines herself to be a great reservoir of restorative power. This feeling of power gives her a sense of agency and of personal efficacy that she may get nowhere else. We read that one of Kafka's mistresses, Milena Jesenka, "believed she could cure Kafka of all his ills and give him a sense of well-being simply by her presence—if only he wanted it."[16]

While women suffer from our relative lack of power in the world and often resent it, certain dimensions of this powerlessness may seem abstract and remote. We know, for example, that we rarely get to make the laws or direct the major financial institutions. But Wall Street and the U.S. Congress seem very far away. The power a woman feels in herself to heal and sustain, on the other hand—"the power of love"—is, once again, concrete and very near: It is like a field of force emanating from within herself, a great river flowing outward from her very person.

Thus, a complex and contradictory female subjectivity is constructed within the relations of caregiving. Here, as elsewhere, women are affirmed in some ways and diminished in others . . . this within the unity of a single act. The woman who provides a man with largely unreciprocated emotional sustenance accords him status and pays him homage; she agrees to the unspoken proposition that his doings are important enough to deserve substantially more attention than her own. But even as the man's supremacy in the relationship is tacitly assumed by both parties to the transaction, the man reveals himself to his caregiver as vulnerable and insecure. And while she may well be ethically and epistemically disempowered by the care she gives, this caregiving affords her the feeling that a mighty power resides within her being.

The situation of those men in the hierarchy of gender who avail themselves of female tenderness is not thereby altered: Their superordinate position is neither abandoned, nor their male privilege relinquished. The vulnerability these men exhibit is not a prelude in any way to their loss of male privilege or to an elevation in the status of women. Similarly, the feeling that one's love is a mighty force for good in the life of the beloved doesn't make it so, as Milena Jesenka found, to her sorrow. The *feeling* of outflowing personal power so characteristic of the caregiving woman is quite different from the *having* of any actual power in the world. There is no doubt that this sense of personal efficacy provides some compensation for the extradomestic power women are typically denied: If one cannot be a king oneself, being a confidante of kings may be the next best thing. But just as we make a bad bargain in accepting an occasional Valentine in lieu of the sustained attention we deserve, we are ill advised to settle for a mere feeling of power, however heady and intoxicating it may be, in place of the effective power we have every right to exercise in the world.

Finally, a footnote to this discussion of the subjective gratifications of caregiving: In the tending of wounds, is there sometimes an unacknowledged *Schadenfreude*—a pleasure in the contemplation of another's distress—in the sight of the master laid so low? It may or may not be *this* man to whom she is forced to submit, but his vulnerability and dependency may in some sense represent for her the demotion of all men and she may find this symbolic demotion gratifying. Since there is no requirement that our emotional lives exhibit consistency, a mild, quite compensatory *Schadenfreude* may coexist with the most beneficent of motives. But the pleasures of revenge, like the pleasures of merger and self-loss, need to be foregone.

In the provision of emotional sustenance, then, as in the processes of narcissistic self-intoxication, conventional femininity reveals itself as profoundly seductive.... Here, as in other aspects of our lives, we are offered real and gratifying feminine satisfactions in return for what this same femininity requires that we renounce. Until alternative sources of gratification can be found, such pleasures may be indeed difficult to renounce.

Some concluding observations are now in order. We may think of relationships of emotional support as lying along a continuum. At one end are the perfunctory and routinized relationships of commercial caregiving in which the caregiver feels no genuine concern for the object of her attention and where, in the worst case, the doing of her job requires that she manipulate, suppress and falsify her own feeling life. At the other end of the continuum lies the caregiving of absolute sincerity; here there is neither an awareness of ulterior motive on the part of the caregiver nor any inner reservation that might compromise the total partisanship and wholehearted acceptance she directs toward the object of her solicitude. Most provisions of emotional support fall somewhere in between. I have chosen to focus on caregiving of the latter kind because I think that its risks have not been fully appreciated and because in most kinds of noncommercial caregiving we take *this* kind as a norm; we measure ourselves by it and blame ourselves when we fall short.[17] It is sobering to consider the extent to which the Victorian ideal of woman as "angel in the house" has survived even into the era of so-called postfeminism. The dispensing of "female tenderness"—by no means coupled with "unadulterated power"—is still seen, even by writers who declare themselves sympathetic to the aims of the women's movement, as crucial to the manifestation and enactment of femininity.

In regard to the dispensing of female tenderness, the claims of feminist theorists such as Ferguson have been vindicated.[18] Women run real risks of exploitation in the transactions of heterosexual caregiving, indeed, of exploitation in the Marxist sense that Ferguson intends. All too frequently, women's caregiving involves an unequal exchange in which one party to this exchange is disempowered by the particular inequalities that characterize the exchange itself. This disempowerment, I have argued, lies in women's active and affective assimilation of the world according to men; it lies too in certain satisfactions of caregiving that serve to mystify our situation still further. Such disempowerment, like the disempowerment of the wage worker, may be described as a species of alienation, i.e., as a prohibition on the development and exercise of capacities, the exercise of which is thought essential to a fully human existence. . . . The capacity most at risk here is not, as in the traditional Marxist theory of alienation, the capacity for creative labor; rather, it is the capacity, free from the subtle manipulation of consent, to construct an ethical and epistemic standpoint of one's own. Hence, Marxist categories of analysis—categories that have to do with exploitation, alienation, and the organization of the labor process—are by no means irrelevant to women's experience or, as some postmodernist feminists have maintained, do they invariably distort the nature of this experience.[19] Quite the contrary: Marxist questions, if we know how to follow out their answers, can lead us into the heart of female subjectivity.

Many feminist theorists have characterized this disempowerment in metaphors of filling and emptying: Women fill men with their energies, thereby strengthening them and depleting ourselves. I have argued not that there is no depletion, but that this depletion is to be measured not only in an increase of male energies, or—as the safety-valve theory maintains—in a reduction in male tensions, but in subtle affective and ideational changes in women ourselves that, taken in toto, tend to keep us in a position of subservience.

Conservatives argue, in essence, that women's caregiving may be properly exchanged for men's economic support. This view is not defensible. The classic bargain so lauded by conservatives—economic support in return for domestic and emotional labor—has broken down under the weight of economic necessity. Many millions of women must work outside the home.

The continuing need of these women for men's economic patronage is a measure of the undervaluation of women's labor in the waged sector. To their superexploitation at work is added a disproportionate share of domestic labor, child care, and emotional labor; women in this situation are quadruply exploited. Nor should we forget the growing number of single women, some single mothers as well, who give emotional support to men in relationships of shorter or longer duration, but receive absolutely no economic recompense at all. But even in the dwindling number of cases in which men are willing and able to offer economic patronage to women, it would be difficult to show how such support could compensate a woman for the epistemic decentering, ethical damage, and general mystification that put us at risk in unreciprocated caregiving.

Recently, conservatives have been joined by a number of feminist theorists in the celebration of female nurturance. The motives of these thinkers differ: Conservatives extol traditional female virtues in the context of a larger defense of the sexual status quo; feminist theorists, especially those who are drawn to the idea of an "ethics of care" based on women's traditional nurturant activities, want to raise women's status by properly valuing our emotional work and to see this quality of caring extended to the formal domains of commerce and politics. I applaud these aims. However, many feminist thinkers who extol women's nurturance, like most conservatives, have just ignored the possibility that women may suffer moral damage in the doing of emotional labor.[20] Clearly, the development of any ethics of care needs to be augmented by a careful analysis of the pitfalls and temptations of caregiving itself.

It may be true, as feminist object relations theorists claim, that in the course of individuation, women have less need than men to sever our primary attachment to the maternal caretaker; this may account for our more "permeable" ego boundaries and the relatively greater importance of attachment and relationship in our lives. But this is only part of the story. The exigencies of female psychological development alone are not responsible for our greater propensity to offer succor and support. Feminist object-relations theory, like a feminist ethics of care, stands in need of an analysis of the subjective effects of the labor we perform on a daily basis—including our emotional labor—and of the ways in which this labor structures the subjectivity both of those who perform it and of those whom it serves.

Female subjectivity is constructed through a continuous process, a personal "engagement in the practices, discourses, and institutions that lend significance (value, meaning, and affect) to the events of the world":[21] A case in point is the discourse and practice of caregiving in heterosexual intimacy and the institution of domesticity (or its equivalent) that contains it. Insofar as we want to change ourselves and our lives, it is far easier to imagine, indeed, to enact changes in the way we accord status and in the kind of labor we perform on a daily basis than to undertake the restructuring of our basic patterns of psychological response. I am not suggesting that such a restructuring is impossible or that we should not support radical changes in the organization of early infant care, such as coparenting, that might help to develop similar patterns of relationality in men and women.[22] My point is a familiar one: In order to develop an effective politics of everyday life, we need to understand better than we do now not only the processes of personality development, but the "micropolitics" of our most ordinary transactions, the ways in which we inscribe and reinscribe our subjection in the fabric of the ordinary. The most prominent features and many of the subjective effects of this inscription can be grasped independently of any particular theory of personality formation. We need to locate our subordination not only in the hidden recesses of the psyche but in the duties we are happy to perform and in what we thought were the innocent pleasures of everyday life.

Notes

1. Ann Ferguson, *Blood at the Root: Motherhood, Sexuality, and Male Dominance* (London: Unwin Hyman, Pandora Press, 1989), ch. 4. See also Ferguson's earlier essay "Women as a New Revolutionary Class in the U.S," in Pat Walker, ed., *Between Labor and Management* (Boston: South End Press, 1979), p. 18. [See this volume, selection 15.]
2. Ferguson, "Women as a New Revolutionary Class," 23; see also *Blood at the Root*, 130–36.
3. Ibid., 133.
4. "Women as a New Revolutionary Class," 20–21.
5. Joel Feinberg, *Harm to Others* (New York: Oxford University Press, 1984), 178.
6. Ibid., 194.
7. Ibid., 209.
8. For an excellent discussion of the connection in Marxist theory between unequal exchange and disempowerment, see Iris Young, "Five Faces of Oppression," *Philosophical Forum* 19, no. 4 (Summer 1988), esp. 277.
9. An example of this kind of thinking can be found in Marabel Morgan, *The Total Woman* (Old Tappan, NJ: F. H. Revell, 1973).
10. Theodore Kemper, *A Social Interactional Theory of Emotions* (New York: John Wiley and Sons, 1978), 285.
11. Ibid., 96. "Since giving and according status are, by definition, at the heart of love relationships and only one sex is particularly expected to be competent in the performance of this attribute—*although both sexes require it* if the mutuality of the relationship is to be maintained—it is likely that the deficit of affection and love given by men to women will have devastating effects on the relationship. Wives in troubled marriages do in fact report more often than their husbands a lack of demonstrated affection, tenderness and love.... This is precisely what we would have expected from an examination of the sex-linked differential

in standards for status conferral that is an obvious feature of our culture." Ibid., 320.

12. See Arlie Hochschild, *The Managed Heart: The Commercialization of Human Feeling* (Berkeley: University of California Press, 1983), 168. See also Nancy Henley, *Body Politics* (New York: Simon and Schuster, 1977), esp. chs. 6, 9, and 10.

13. Dorothy Dinnerstein, *The Mermaid and the Minotaur* (New York: Harper and Row, 1977), and Nancy Chodorow, *The Reproduction of Mothering: Psychoanalysis and the Sociology of Gender* (Berkeley: University of California Press, 1978).

14. I think that this may be true only for occasional or nonserious abuse. Women stay with chronic abusers either because of the serious emotional injury done them in long-term abusive situations—impairment of judgment, "learned helplessness," disablingly low self-esteem, or fear of worse abuse if they try to leave— or else for largely economic reasons. See Susan Schechter, *Women and Male Violence: The Struggles of the Battered Women's Movement* (Boston: South End Press, 1982).

15. Michel Foucault, *History of Sexuality*, vol. 1 (New York: Random House/Vintage Books, 1980), 58–62.

16. Nahum N. Glatzer, *The Loves of Franz Kafka* (New York: Schocken Books, 1986), x.

17. The risks to women will, of course, vary from one case to the next; they may be a function of a woman's age or her degree of economic or emotional dependency on the man or the presence or absence in her life of resources with which to construct a picture of the world according to herself.

18. See note 1 above.

19. See, for example, Jane Flax, "Postmodernism and Gender Relations in Feminist Theory," in Michelene R. Malson, Jean F. O'Barr, Sarah Westphal-Wihl and Mary Wyer, eds., *Feminist Theory in Practice and Process* (Chicago: University of Chicago Press, 1989), 61.

20. Nell Nodding's otherwise impressive book *Caring: A Feminine Approach to Ethics and Moral Education* (Berkeley: University of California Press, 1984) contains no analysis of the effects on the moral agent of uncompensated caring. Nor is this a significant theme on the part of contributors to *Women and Moral Theory*, ed. Eva Feder Kittay and Diana T. Meyers (Totowa, NJ: Rowman and Littlefield, 1987), a book of essays on the philosophical implications of Carol Gilligan's research on gender differences in moral reasoning—research that has been a central source for theorizing about an ethics of care. Claudia Card's "Gender and Moral Luck" in *Identity, Character, and Morality: Essays in Moral Psychology*, ed. Amelie Rorty and Owen Flanagan (Cambridge: MIT Press, 1990) is a notable exception. Two classic papers on the wrongness of female deference that present approaches somewhat different than my own are Thomas E. Hill Jr., "Servility and Self-Respect," *Monist* 57, no. 1 (Jan. 1973): 87–104; and Marilyn Friedman, "Moral Integrity and the Deferential Wife," *Philosophical Studies* 47 (1985): 141–50.

21. Teresa de Lauretis, *Alice Doesn't* (Bloomington: Indiana University Press, 1983), 159. Cited in Linda Alcoff, "Cultural Feminism versus Post-Structuralism: The Identity Crisis in Feminist Theory," in Malson et al., *Feminist Theory in Practice and Process*, 313.

22. On the necessity for coparenting, see Isaac Balbus, *Marxism and Domination* (Princeton: Princeton University Press, 1982).

PART V

Exploitation Extended

Capitalism, Nature, Peasants, and Women: Contemporary Problems of Marxism

GAIL OMVEDT

INTRODUCTION

INSTEAD OF THE HOPED-FOR crisis of capitalism, we are seeing in the 1990s a crisis of socialism. But this is linked to a crisis of the theory of capitalism. Social processes predictable from the traditional Marxist theory have not occurred. The proletariat has not emerged as a vanguard. Indeed, unless we redefine it drastically, it is becoming difficult to speak of the proletariat as even emerging: "deindustrialization," decline in the proportion of the manufacturing working class, is a fact in advanced capitalist societies, and in the Third World the obvious phenomenon is the growth of the "unorganized" or "informal" sector and, in many countries, the persistence of the peasantry.

Nor is the agrarian class structure behaving as expected. Two decades after the "mode of production" debate we must admit that differentiation is not occurring in India.[1] Numbers of agricultural laborers are increasing, though not drastically by our data, and the largest proportion are impoverished marginal peasants who remain bound to agriculture by the lack of jobs elsewhere, not a "true proletariat" by strict Marxist definitions.[2] Gini coeffi-

---

Reprinted from Gail Omvedt, "Capitalism, Nature, Peasants, and Women: Contemporary Problems of Marxism," *Frontier* (Calcutta) (Autumn 1992), by permission of the author.

cient ratios of landholding do not appear to be widening, and small peasants continue to cling to land. If there is any growing "differentiation," it is between the organized employees and the unorganized sector, between (in particular) agriculture and services (to a lesser extent industry).[3]

In India, as in the rest of the world, "new social movements" have been overtaking traditional trade union organizing (whether of factory workers or agricultural laborers), both in their mass force and in their political salience. Depiction of these movements through the NGO spectacles as small-scale "grassroots," "noneconomic" movements has masked our understanding of them. They have included some very powerful mass movements such as, for example in India, the dalit and anticaste movement and the farmers' movement of peasants fighting for higher crop prices, relief from indebtedness, and similar issues relating to the market and the state—both movements capable of mobilizing in the hundreds of thousands and both seen (as events since the V. P. Singh regime has shown) as threatening by the bourgeois-bureaucratic ruling class. Peasants in other parts of Asia and the Third World seem to be equally mobilizing, not simply against local landlords and moneylenders, but against oppressors of the market and the state. Environmental movements in many countries, based on tribals and peasants, though taking place on smaller territorial localities, have also shown themselves capable of mobilizing significant support and halting major "developmental" projects. The women's movement, finally, diffuse and fractured as it is, has become a significant presence in almost all countries.

Many of the issues of these movements are also being expressed in the form of "ethnic-national" movements. Taken as a whole, they represent a major feature of the day, as much as the concurrent rise, on the right, of religiously based "fundamentalism" and "communalism."

Nor are the movements "noneconomic." Presentation of them as such has done a major disservice. The fundamentalist movements, which try to capture some of their base, are noneconomic. But the movements themselves have been raising issues that not only seek to add new "structures" such as "caste" or "gender" to "class" but directly challenge us to revise and expand our understanding of economic exploitation and capitalism itself.

The women's movement, for example, theorizes the role of household labor and subsistence production as a major factor in accumulation; in the words of Indian feminists it is "redefining exploitation".[4] Interestingly, this line of analysis—going back to Selma James and Mariarossa Dalla Costa and most linked today with a German feminist group with strong Third World contacts[5]—has both linked the exploitation of women and peasants (as nonwage laborers) and developed into an ecofeminist tradition of theorizing. The farmers' movement, in assertions most clearly articulated by Maharashtra's Shara Joshi, has insisted on the importance of the extraction of surplus, via market mechanisms and the use of state power, from exploited peasant labor, for the accumulation of capital. Here, as with the case of women, "class" defined in terms of wage relations and private property does not adequately correlate with "exploitation" defined in terms of the production and appropriation of surplus labor.

Both the farmers' movement and the women's movement have stressed the role of violence and control of the means of violence in exploitation and oppression, thus pointing to the state as central to accumulation. And both the farmers' and the environmental movements have taken both political and economic decentralization as goals and fought for local control of resources and surplus. The environmental movement has been weak in dealing with exploitation as a factor (neglecting not only the exploitation of peasant labor but also the way in which low pricing of nature's products has been related to their destruction) but has instead stressed the destructiveness of contemporary capitalist production. More than other movements, and more than slogans of the traditional left, it has pointed to imperialism itself as a factor in this destructiveness, and has questioned the very nature of development itself. Just as Marx argued that the proletariat could not simply take over the existing state machinery but had to build its own state, so now environmental activists stress that socialism cannot be built on the (industrial) forces of production of capitalism.

Finally all movements raise the question of political forms. They tend to be informal in structure and to emphasize a democratic practice critical of the parties' bureaucracies. Where they have large-scale organizations these are often focused around a charismatic leader, rather than a bureaucratic party structure. They show a suspicion of political parties that is as great as Maoist "anti-revisionism." All political parties, including those of the left, are to them only representatives of alien: upper-caste, patriarchal, urban interests, those of the exploiters. However, rather than aiming like the revolutionary left for the capture of state power through armed struggle, they have organized militant but nonviolent mass movements and campaigns, including *rasta rokos, gavbards, satyagrahas, kisan panchayats*, fasts, marches, and the like. They have sought to exert pressure on parties from without and only occasionally, without great success, have tried to form political platforms or parties themselves. (The dalit movement, which has from the beginning been involved in organizing political parties, is an exception here.)

Yet this has not been terribly successful, and the question of the movements' getting an adequate political representation remains unsolved. This is the obverse side of the weakness of the political parties based on toiling sections. Indian politics for the first time since the 1950s clearly shows the form of two bourgeois-bureaucratic-brahmanic parties (the Congress and the BJP) versus a democratic "third force" representing lower castes and classes and marginalized ethnic groups. But that force remains fragmented and has no program to mobilize its base, aside from the "one-point program" of the Mandal Commission. It has alienated the farmers' movement, has never effectively taken up women's issues, and has from the beginning avoided environmental demands.

The question is one of theory, of an analysis of exploitation based on a theory of capitalism adequate to comprehend the problems of nature, peasants, women, and oppressed communities or ethnic groups today. Let us then look briefly at capitalism itself, beginning from the fundamental analytical issues of wage labor, capital, and commodity production.

THE ANALYSIS OF CAPITALIST PRODUCTION

Theorists such as Samir Amin and Immanuel Wallerstein have in different ways raised the argument that capitalism has to be understood as a system on a world scale that includes the organization of unfree as well as free labor and the extraction of surplus in various forms. Here a slightly different approach will be taken: Before looking at the historically concrete form of capitalism as a world system, let us begin with the theory of capitalist production itself. Let us start, as Marx did, with the commodity, commodity production, capital, and wage labor. I will argue that such a beginning shows that the sphere of capitalist production (capital and wage labor) is of itself incomplete, and that the very process of analyzing it forces us to look to and analyze a wider, more encompassing sphere of capital accumulation.

The question of analyzing *women's labor, domestic labor, or the reproduction of labor power* (primarily performed by women) brings this up immediately. After the long debate on housework it is fairly clear that domestic labor does not produce surplus value, since it is carried on under "private" conditions without a wage; the only labor counted in the value of the worker's labor is the labor embodied in the commodities that have to be bought to reproduce his life.[6] Yet domestic labor does produce surplus, and the performance of this unpaid labor by women (or labor only partially remunerated by a "family wage" controlled by men) makes it possible for capitalists to extract a larger amount of surplus value from their labor force. In the Third World, where workers are more often migrants living singly and much reproduction of their own labor power as well as the maintenance of their families is carried out in a rural, mainly subsistence, economy, the rate of surplus extraction by capitalists is much higher.

In other words, the question of domestic labor immediately confronts us with a type of nonwage labor, carried on outside the sphere of capitalist production, that nevertheless contributes to accumulation. This means that the process of capital accumulation cannot be analyzed only in terms of the dynamic of wage labor and capital, and that we have to admit the existence of, and begin to analyze, a sphere of capital accumulation that encompasses, but is wider than, that of capitalist production, or wage-labor-based commodity production.

The question of nature brings up a similar problem. Here Marx is quite clear: Nature creates use value, but not exchange value. Nature, he tells us, is the source of all wealth; but at the same time natural resources like water are the archtypical "free good," without value except for the labor required for the extraction.

Yet this distinction seems inadequate. The ability of capitalism to treat nature as a "free good" certainly plays a major role in allowing rapid accumulation as well as environmental destruction. In the terms of analysis of James O'Connor and the *Capitalism, Nature, Socialism* group, the ability of capitalism to "externalize" costs allows more rapid accumulation but results in the destruction of the "conditions of production" themselves. But if the products of nature (whether oil, timber, water, soil) have a use value to capitalists, they also do, in a different way, to those inhabitants of the territories from which they are extracted. Capitalists are clearly willing to go to great lengths to secure the use values of natural products at low exchange values (the Gulf War being the latest awesome example of the politics of international pricing), and the fight for control of natural resources is and has always been a momentous question for capital accumulation. What we have here is, again, a situation in which processes not limited to the sphere of capitalist production itself have crucial significance for capital accumulation.

The question of the value of natural resources intersects with another dilemma of the labor theory of value, the question of time. In part of a collection of articles on "the value controversy," G. A. Cohen argues that the statements that "labor produces value" and "value is determined by socially necessary labor time" are mutually incompatible because:

> Suppose a commodity has a certain value at time *t*. Then that value, says the labour theory, is determined by the socially necessary labour-time required to produce a commodity of that kind. Let us now ask: required to produce it *when*? The answer is: at *t*, the time when it has the value to be explained. The amount of time required to produce it in the past and, *a fortiori*, the amount of time actually spent producing it, are magnitudes strictly irrelevant to its value, if the labour theory is true.

The major example he gives:

> Suppose there is a commodity *b* now on the market, and that *b* was not produced by labour, but that a great deal of labour is now required for *b*-like things to appear. (B might be a quantity of clean air bottled before it became necessary to manufacture clean air.) The *b* has a value, even though no labour is 'embodied' in it.[7]

It is not accidental that Cohen's example is one from the environment, since a major correlate of environmental destructiveness is an increase in scarcity of use values. Thus a "full" theory of capitalist accumulation and the workings of the capitalist system requires an analysis of its interaction with environmental dynamics.

The issue of "nature" thus also raises, in a different way, the question of the way in which the system of capitalist production is embedded in a wider system which has its own "laws of motion." In at least one section of *Capital*, in the discussion of "Modern Industry and Agriculture," Marx is eloquent on the destructiveness of capitalist agriculture. "[A]ll progress in capitalistic agriculture is a progress in the art, not only of robbing the laborer, but of robbing the soil; all progress in increasing the fertility of the soil for a given time, is a progress towards ruining the lasting sources of that fertility".[8] He refers to it disturbing "the circulation of matter between man and the soil." Taking the "soil" as the paradigm here for all of nature, Marx has gone a long way to admitting a basic proposition of radical environmentalists. It is worth, then, noting what is missing: the recognition of the existence of a broader environmental system (perhaps comprising the entire earth) such that destructiveness will wreak its vengeance on the destroyers themselves.

Marxists, and Marx himself, have treated nature as primarily an object of capitalism's unlimited expansion, never seeing it as setting limits to expansion or as having a conditioning role on the processes of expansion. They see the destructive aspects of capitalism but retain a faith that, in the end, technology will overcome all obstacles. That nature can be in a sense an "active" component of a wider human-nature system with dynamics and causality working both ways is not admitted. But "the empire strikes back": Soil exhaustion and various forms of environmental destruction have, after all, been responsible for the destruction of civilizations in the past.

Analyzing the possible "laws of motion" of this wider system has hardly been attempted by Marxists, though there is now a flourishing school of "environmental economics." Looking at the system in terms of "energy flows" or energy costs rather than just labor costs, seeing "capital" also as congealed energy as well as congealed labor (or rather than?), would broaden the perspective. While capitalism indeed "views itself" in terms of labor costs and the sphere of capitalist production only, we have to go beyond this appearance and understand the full sphere of the human-nature developmental process in order to understand capitalist accumulation itself.

CAPITALISM AND THE EXPLOITATION OF PEASANT LABOR

The peasantry is not only, as Teodor Shanin has called it, the "awkward class"; it is not admitted to be a class or even a category of the capitalist system by most Marxist scholars. Those gathered around the *Journal of Peasant Studies*, for example, which should be renamed the *Journal of Agrarian Studies* since it does not theoretically recognize the existence of "peasants," see the operative categories for analysis as those of "proletarian" or "capitalist" of one kind or another, or they define the peasantry as "petty commodity producers" who are considered to be not exploited under capitalism. The survival of the peasantry is seen as part of the "articulation" of the capitalist mode of production with still-surviving feudal modes, or as the petty commodity production which is linked to capitalism through historically contingent processes that are part of the "phenomenal" aspect of the capitalist mode of production and not of its "essence."

In India, for pricing agricultural products since independence, the government's Agricultural Price Commission (now the Committee on Agricultural Costs and Prices) has evaluated the labor element of costs at the level of existing agricultural wages: That is, not only is hired labor evaluated at this level, but the labor of the peasant male, performed on his own land, is also evaluated at this level—more specifically at the level of a year-laborer or "bonded laborer," while the labor of the woman of his family has been evaluated at a fraction of this, since censuses regularly show (by vastly undercounting the actual agriculturally connected labor of peasant women) a low level of "work participation" in cultivating households. If the agricultural laborer is exploited, so then is the peasant—and the government's pricing not only "recognizes" the existing low standard of living of the rural producers, but perpetuates it.

If a theory of capitalism cannot analyze these as exploitative relations between the peasants and the state, then it is hard to know how it can be adequate. The question is a central one for analysis, because in one way or another all Third World states seem to have relied upon extracting surplus from their peasantry in the form of low crop prices, whether they have perpetuated the "marketing boards" used from colonial times in order to accumulate funds for industrialization, or whether they have concentrated on providing low-priced wage goods and raw materials to their capitalists.

Peasant labor, then, seems to be exploited via market-state mechanisms. Is this historically contingent or an "essential" part of capitalism? In order to answer this, the questions of the forms of and mechanisms of the exploitation of peasant labor, its degree in the contemporary working of capitalism, and its significance in the historical accumulation of capital have to be dealt with much more than they have been by theories which generally look for only the emergence of a "peasant bourgeoisie" out of processes of "differentiation in agriculture."

Marx himself had little developed analysis of peasant production under capitalism, though in his writings on the French peasantry he stressed the peasantry not only as a "sack of potatoes" but as the indispensable ally of the proletariat, not only as failing to become a "class-for-itself" but as being exploited: "The smallholding of the peasant is now only the pretext that allows the capitalist to draw profits, interest and rent from the soil, while leaving it to the tiller of the soil himself to see how he can extract his wages."[9] It was only his successors, Kautsky, Lenin, and others, who developed a full theory of the differentiation of the peasantry under capitalism. They did not, however, deal with the question of the exploitation of peasant labor as such. Luxembourg spoke of the necessity for existence of noncapitalist sectors (the peasantry, the Third World?) for capitalism to survive as a system—and feminist theorists such as Maria Mies as well as farmers' movement leaders such as Shared Joshi have looked backed to Luxembourg for this—but this was seen by her as necessary only for the realization of surplus value, not so much as a part of its production. Although in fact accumulation of surplus from primarily peasant labor has been central to the historical development of capitalism, it has not been theorized.

This is a crucial gap in research. It is interesting here that feminist theorists have been most ready to see the role of peasant labor in capital accumulation. For instance, in regard to indebtedness, most Marxist studies now understand the role of debt in the colonial period as leading to the "formal subsumption" of the peasantry to capital in being forced to turn over a major share of his product to the moneylender, whether "agriculturist" or "nonagriculturist." However, in the contemporary period, when the major share of debt (at least in India) is to public institutions (banks and cooperatives), radicals are inclined to speak only of the "availability of credit" to the poor peasantry; it has taken Veronica Bennholdt-Thomson, who can make an explicit comparison with women's nonwage labor, to give a critique of the methods (specifically, of the World Bank) in which debt is used to aid the expropriation of peasant labor and generally tie peasants to a particular form of market production.[10] In fact, a serious analysis of the subordination of peasant labor must deal with the way the new system of capitalist agriculture—control by the state, multinational companies, and institutions of inputs and various types of conditions of production—not only allows the extraction of surplus but also changes the labor process itself.

This involves recognizing that Marx's political insights—as expressed in his writings on the French peasantry—did not always have a foundation in his analysis of capitalism. Today, when the development of capitalism has, if anything, meant an intensification of the exploitation of nonwage labor or partially "proletarianized" labor of various kinds in the informal sector, such an analysis is more than ever needed to build up the liberation struggles of the exploited.

"Primitive Accumulation"?

The concept of "primitive accumulation" was the way in which Marx referred to the significance for the historical development of capitalism of some of the processes referred to here—extraction of surplus from Third World peasantry, slavery, loot, and so forth, emphasizing now violence "as the midwife of history" rather than simply control of private property. Processes of colonialism and conquest, the relation of the development of capitalism in Europe to the Third World, seem encompassed here.

But a "midwife" has no essential role in conception; the term is symbolic of the fact that ultimately violence is not determinant for Marx and neither is primitive accumulation. It appears at the point of the establishment of the capitalist mode of production, and then seems to vanish—being after all nonessential. But the problem of time here produces a puzzle: If primitive accumulation is not necessary after the "establishment" of capitalism, why was it necessary at the beginning? Why could not capitalism simply develop on its own momentum, out of processes of accumulation and proletarianization in feudal economy or within a structure of petty commodity production? (Indeed, Marxist theorists have been showing why this should happen.) If in Marx's view loot and extraction of surplus from the Third World played an important role in the early history of capitalism, their necessity has not been shown. But, by the same token, the same factors continue to play a historically important role even if not a necessary one.

It seems time to investigate more systematically the ongoing linkages between the capitalist mode of production and the so-called primitive accumulation. The term encompasses most of what we have been referring to as part of a "sphere of capital accumulation" outside the arena of capitalist production itself: nonwage labor, whether that of slaves, serfs, bonded laborers, apparently independent peasants producing for national and world-level commodity markets and subsistence-producing peasant labor; the nearly unchecked extraction of natural resources; the role of violence in the entire process; and the role of ethnic or community factors in the process and in resistance to it.

Toward a Development of Historical Materialism

Marxist analyses (and much of Communist politics based on them) have so far been mostly confined to the sphere of capitalist production—looked at in terms of the capital/wage relationship, with private property or ownership of the means of production seen as central. Certain other very "material" forces such as violence, sexuality, and natural/environmental processes have been neglected. The focus has been on the "capitalist mode of production," and the existence of other forms of exploitation or other aspects of accumulation has been seen only in terms of the interaction or "articulation" of this with noncapitalist modes ("feudalism" or "semifeudalism" being the main favorite in Asian societies), or as a result of some "phenomenal" or nonessential feature resulting from the historical accident of the concrete "social formations" in which the capitalist mode of production happens to find itself.

This has been inadequate. It has failed drastically in terms of predictive power—either in predicting the rapidity of the "fall of socialism" or in explaining the rise of the new social movements and the issues they have raised. It has left societies in which revolutionary parties have gained power (such as Nicaragua) vulnerable to following statist, bureaucratic, antipeople and antiecological policies of development because the only models they have had before them have been basically versions of the Soviet model based on such assumptions. And it has led a large section of the left—and of radical intelligentsia claiming to speak in the name of the rural proletariat and poor peasantry—to oppose peasant efforts to raise the value of their labor power, thus helping to perpetuate an exploitative and overcentralized developmental policy and the poverty of those they claim to represent.

Clearly there is a need of new theory, new visions of socialism. Most important, there is a need for understanding the way the system of capitalist production is embedded in a wider system that includes the relationship of human society with nature and that has its own dynamics and laws of development determining both the process of capital accumulation and the forms of exploitation of labor power.

The framework that limits the central dynamic of "the capitalist mode of production" to the capital/wage labor relation (and the "class struggle this involves") in effect centers it on the advanced capitalist societies; the Third World, nature, women, and the peasantry are only "objects" of the processes of capitalism's expansion, the "class struggles" they are involved in are inadequately analyzed. This framework has failed to help us understand either capitalism itself—the processes of capital accumulation and the historical unfolding of "class struggle" in the variety of forms of resistance to the exploitation of labor power this involves—or the type of society that can overcome it.

Movements against exploitation in the world today are going beyond the traditional working-class movement which had as its (explicit) goal, if not trade union gains, the capture by the proletariat of the existing, capitalistically developed (and ecologically and humanly destructive) industrial forces of production; they are also, in stressing decentralization and autonomy, going beyond the traditional goal of "national liberation" movements, which was to capture the state and build up for the use of the "nation" the same system. Both goals of traditional "antisystemic movements" represented the project of simply taking over the system of productive forces and the state of the capitalist mode of production; but in a wider system in which this itself was related in exploitative forms to Third World and female laborers and nature in general, this could yield only a state-managed system of exploitation. (The contradictoriness of such a project in "peripheral" societies of the world system gives the "inefficiency" or incapacity in economic terms of such an effort, hence the pressures to open up to full-scale capitalist penetration, hence the "fall of socialism.")

Instead the new movements are dealing, though often in initial and not always adequately articulated ways, with the full range of exploitative processes linked to the development of capitalism. Women's labor, peasant labor, nature, community and ethnicity, and violence are all within their realm of concern. Their campaigns and goals involve a process of "redefining revolution";[11] the need is also for a reinterpretation of Marxism and a reconstruction of the theory of historical materialism to help move out of—not the "end of history" by any means—but the historical cul-de-sac in which the left is getting trapped.

Notes

1. All-India Debt and Investment Survey. *Assets of Rural Households as on June 30, 1971* (Bombay: Reserve Bank of India, 1976); *Assets and Liabilities of Rural and Urban Households as on 30 June 1981* (Bombay: RBI, 1986).
2. V. G. Rastyannikov, *Agrarian Evolution in a Multiform Structure Society* (London: Routledge and Kegan Paul, 1981).
3. Centre for Monitoring the Indian Economy, *Basic Statistics Relating to the Indian Economy, 1987*, volume 1, *All-India* (Bombay, 1987), table and V. M. Dandekar.
4. See Chhaya Datar, *Redefining Exploitation: Towards a Socialist Feminist Critique of Marxist Theory* (Bombay: ISRE, 1981).
5. Maria Mies, *Patriarchy and Accumulation on a World Scale* (London: Zed Press, 1985); *The Lace-Makers of Narsapur: Housewives Produce for the World Market* (London: Zed Books, 1984); Maria Mies, Veronica Bennholdt-Thomson, and Claudia von Werlhof, *Women: The Last Colony* (New Delhi: Kali for Women Press, 1989).
6. Karl Marx, *Capital*, volume 1 (Moscow: Foreign Languages Publishing House), 170–71.
7. G. A. Cohen, "The Labour Theory of Value and the Concept of Exploitation," in Ian Steedman et al., *The Value Controversy*, 209. [See this volume, selection 6.]
8. *Capital* 1:506.
9. Karl Marx, "Peasantry as a Class," excerpted in Teodor Shanin, ed., *Peasants and Peasant Societies* (Penguin: 1975).
10. Veronica Bennholdt-Thomson, "'Investment on the Poor': An Analysis of World Bank Policy," in Mies, Bennholdt-Thomson and von Werlhof, *Women: The Last Colony*.
11. Gail Omvedt, *Redefining Revolution: New Social Movements and the Socialist Tradition in India* (New York: M. E. Sharpe, 1993).

Exploitation in the Periphery

SAMIR AMIN

EXPLANATIONS FOR AFRICA'S AGRICULTURAL failure tend to be partial and contradictory.[1] The remote past—precolonial Africa—is partly to blame. If there is one "special characteristic"—apart from huge variety—of the modes of rural organization in the greater part of Africa, it is perhaps that the still scarcely begun communal or tribute-paying forms implied extensive occupation of the soil. This allowed for much greater food self-sufficiency than is commonly imagined, thanks to relatively high productivity of labor (as a complement to extremely low return to the acre). Higher production per head entails moving to intensive modes requiring a much greater overall quantity of labor in the year. This increase of production per head is accompanied by a reduced productivity of labor (of physical output per working "day") but also by an improved return per acre. This move to intensive agriculture, as a precondition to any development worth the name, is the challenge that the African peoples must take up.[2]

But the challenge has not yet been taken up. Colonization did not only fail to do so; it was not even its aim. Colonialism found it easier to take an immediate superprofit without cost (without investment) by forcing the African peasants into unpaid—or poorly paid—surplus labor through forms of indirect control. Slightly higher output per head at the cost of a greater labor contribution, without equipment or modern inputs (but to the destruction of Africa's land capital), combined with a worsening of peasant living standards, was enough to provide an appreciable margin for capital dominating the

From Samir Amin, "Exploitation in the Periphery," in *Maldevelopment* (Tokyo: United Nations University Press, 1990), 9–17. Copyright 1990 by the United Nations University. All rights reserved. Reprinted with the permission of the United Nations University Press.

global system. Colonization thus continued the ancient tradition of the slave trade: exploitation by pillage that made no provision for reproduction of the labor force over the long term or of the natural conditions for production.

Independence brought no change to this mode of integration in the world capitalist system. Change has come in response to the demands of the new phase in the worldwide expansion of capital (the European construct and United States hegemony) and not in response to the problem of the African peasant. Moreover the prosperity of the 1960s in the West has brought a new enthusiasm in Africa for the "extraverted system." And if René Dumont, always sensitive to the peasant question, has lucidly and courageously denounced the "false start in Africa,"[3] the World Bank, which is nowadays concerned about the peasants' fate (while the IMF forces the most wretched to pay the price of the failure) gave its enthusiastic support to the policies that were to lead, ten years later, to disaster.

The crisis of the 1970s was the result of a conjunction between the superexploitation of land, men, and women, reaching a level difficult to relieve and the crisis striking the capitalist system as a whole. In the face of this crisis the proposals raining down on Africa at an increasing rate are no more than a manifestation of a "quest for palliatives."

If it is no more than a matter of palliatives, then the media's talk "in favor of agriculture" is shown as a contrast to a supposed "preference for industrialization" that was at the origin of the failure. But any meaningful quest for greater output per cultivator is precisely to allow increased urbanization; and urbanization without industrialization can only be parasitic and disastrous. In turn, industry (but not unselectively) is necessary to permit greater output from agriculture for which it must supply equipment and to which it must offer a growing market. Here lies the option for an autocentric popular and national strategy. If this option is rejected in favor of a systematic integration in worldwide expansion, talk of "priority for agriculture" becomes hollow and essentially demagogic. The contradictions in the other "proposals" are manifest: Export industry supposes low salaries and consequently low prices for food crops, at the same time as it urges price rises as an incentive to the peasants to produce more.

The populist garb some have given the proposals does not change their meaning despite talk of basic needs and the strategy of "petty family production." Meanwhile, such rhetoric has never prevented the Western "aid" bodies from showing a preference, in fact, to support for agrobusiness and kulaks—in the name of efficiency. That these policies continue to be advanced is evidence at bottom of the scant seriousness with which Africa is treated. For Africa, in the imperialist view of the world, is above all a source of mineral resources for the West; neither its industrialization nor its agricultural development is genuinely considered.

There is nothing natural about the wretchedness of African agriculture. Undoubtedly underpopulation of tropical Africa, compared with the dense population of tropical Asia, has been an obstacle to intensifying what is described as significant internal migration; and whatever may be said, the Sahel is not irrevocably doomed. There is water there (a group of rivers whose flow matches that of the Nile, extraordinary underground and fossil lakes, if confidential studies are to be believed),[4] sources of energy—what about uranium? and the sun and the oil at less than one thousand metres?—serviceable soils, populations. A social system that claims to be incapable of coordinating these "factors" into a satisfactory plan able to nourish the populations in question can scarcely be regarded as rational, so let us admit that the capitalist system is not rational since it does not necessarily ensure the reproduction of the labor force in each of its segments. Here in the Sahel, for capitalism per se, it is the existence of the Sahelian peoples that is "irrational," since for this capitalism, it would be more appealing if the Sahel had only uranium and not useless Sahelians . . . Such is the logic of this world system for which Africa is still exclusively a source of minerals. By highlighting the campaigns for emergency "relief" distribution, the Western institutions have created a belief that the Sahel was irrevocably doomed. Hence it is accepted as if it were natural that the uranium was not intended for the "natives," and Sahelians must be taught better ways of gathering the blades of grass in the desert and not waste them in their ovens! Africa must adapt to the West's wastage! Is there a better illustration of the vocation as a mineral resource that imperialism consecrates to the continent, and of the subjection of all the so-called development programs to this essential logic, than this ingenuous call to the "imperatives" of the export of the regions's energy resources? But why not the reverse: Let Africa regain control and use of its resources and Europe make the adjustment.

Capitalism's capacity in the abstract to "solve the problem of African development" could be endlessly discussed. Not only has concrete capitalism, as it exists, that is, with worldwide expansion, failed to "solve"—but rather created—the problem over the past 150 years (or even the four centuries since the start of the slave trade) but also has nothing in mind for the next fifty years. The challenge will, therefore, be taken up only by the African peoples, on the day when the necessary popular alliances enable them to delink their development from the demands of transnationalization.

If Africa as a whole has not even begun its agricultural revolution, this is essentially because the entire system in which it is integrated is based on superexploitation of the African peasants' labor, and this is beneficial both to the system of dominant capitalism and to the local classes who act as its relay. The system of superexploitation of the countryside, established by colonialism, has not been challenged by the neocolonial system that faithfully carries on the tradition.

We are inadequately equipped to provide a theoretical analysis of this superexploitation[5] because the great majority of African peasants are petty producers and consequently there are no obvious direct exploiters, such as the great landowners are or have been elsewhere. Conventional economic theory, almost on principle, ignores the phenomenon of labor exploitation. By virtue of its emphasis on market mechanisms it remains a prisoner of the prejudice it feeds on, that of "pure and perfect competition." At most it allows itself to note in passing the gap between this model and the reality of capitalist production. It is particularly the case of Third World peasant production, which far from being independent is subject to this exploitation by capital.

There are varying forms of integration of this peasantry in the world capitalist system: typified in very broad terms, by the integration of petty peasant production in the world commodity market. The essential [thing] here is not as it might at first seem: monopoly of colonial houses, mediated through state bodies in some circumstances, and such monopoly allowing superprofits from circulation, but at a more profound level, namely, direct interference by capital in the organization of production. Obviously such interference will not be perceived if the field of economics is separated from politics, for it operates precisely through political, administrative, and technical incorporation of the petty peasantry. It is through such incorporation that the peasants are obliged to specialize in certain crops, to buy the inputs these need, and finally to rely on the income of their apparent sale. The peasant's formal ownership of the land and the means of production is maintained but emptied of its genuine content: the peasant loses control over economic decision making and organization of the production process and is no longer genuinely a "free petty producer." Thus, behind the apparent sale of the output is concealed a sale of his labor power. Hence the peasant is integrated in capitalist production relations invisible on the scale of the peasant production unit, but perfectly visible at the level of the global system in which he is integrated. It is just as difficult to understand the failure to see the system of exploitation, of which Marx in *Capital* provided a masterly and recognized example, in the system of "putting out" work.

Clearly, forms of exploitation of the peasant economy have themselves evolved in various ways. Sometimes integration in capitalist exchange has provoked appreciable differences in appropriation of the soil and the instruments of production. In such a case, the rich peasants' ("kulak") direct exploitation of agricultural laborers, or of sharecroppers, is superimposed by exploitation of the collective commodity production by monopoly capital. In other cases, administrative, colonial, or neocolonial incorporation is associated with primary native social control that for want of a better term may be described as parastatal, semifeudal. Obviously the class that battens on this "incorporation" does not directly appropriate the soil or the means of production, which is left in the peasants' hands, but it still levies its tithe—the output of the peasant's surplus labor—in one way or another. Here, too, the exploitation of the peasant in these apparently precapitalist systems—apparent only (as they are the product of capitalist integration)— must not obscure the fact that the systems are integrated in global capitalist exploitation. Obviously there are additional forms of superimposing relations of capitalist exploitation on precapitalist relations, whether themselves based on superexploitation or not, just as there is an extremely varied range of forms of articulation between precapitalist and capitalist relations. In the case of Sub-Saharan Africa, we have noted three classifications: the "trading economy," the "reserve economy," and the "concessionary companies economy." All these forms of exploitation must be studied concretely; no abstract theory deduced a priori from some general principles can take the place of concrete analyses.

In analyzing these forms of extraction of surplus it would be helpful to raise in general terms the issue of the law of value, which in the end implicitly governs the validity of the thesis. To make it possible to discuss exploitation the comparison of the values and costs of the labor power of the peasant in question and of the laborer—whose labor is embodied in the goods sold to that peasant—must have some meaning, as obviously the goods exchanged have values and costs that can meaningfully be compared. That is to say that the thesis assumes a worldwide value category of commodities and a worldwide value category of labor power. Even if the first of these theses has won general acceptance, the second has not. The sixth chapter of *Capital* [first published in 1933], however, showed that Marx already had some sense of the problem. Marx suggests in effect how difficult it is to grasp the value at the level of the basic unit of production. He raises consideration of the concept of "collective laborer" and suggests that this tends to include all the workers in an increasingly broader area, comprising various production units. The contents of this chapter, remarkably in advance of its time and not known to Bukharin, were, however, implicitly taken on board by the latter in his view of a capitalist development that taken to its logical conclusion would lead to a "sole ownership" of the means of production: by the state. The value category would then apparently have vanished; although it would still be there . . . Bukharin perhaps had partly in mind a possible evolution of the USSR. But above all he had in mind the profound tendency of capitalism whereby without reaching the stage of "sole ownership" we have by now reached the stage where the dominance of capitalism spreads well beyond the production units that form its base. It is on such theoretical foundations that we have shaped our thesis that labor power tends to have a unique value on a world scale although it retains differential costs, above or below this value. The precise measure of this tendency to a differentiation of the costs of labor power can be gauged, albeit crudely, by "double factorial terms of trade," or the relationship between gross terms of trade and the index of comparative productivities of labor.

An analysis of exploitation in these circumstances calls for a complementary analysis of the overall political economy of the colonial and neocolonial system. In fact the increasing exploitation of peasant labor is the main source of the typical distortions of peripheral capitalist development. To go further in this field it is necessary to make a concrete case-by-case examination of how income distribution and the resulting demand have shaped industrial patterns. It is then necessary to make a concrete examination of how the increasing exploitation integrates the societies of peripheral capitalism in the international division of labor in such a way as to reproduce and intensify the increasing exploitation of labor. Obviously these patterns of development and the increasing contradictions they have provoked are at the origin of the crisis in the imperialist system and of the responses to it by the national liberation movement. The character of the compromises that have invested the independence of Third World states and hence the character of the reforms on which they embarked (such as replacement of the former colonial companies by state bodies) must be considered in this perspective.

We should argue that the current crisis of Third World agriculture reflects the partial character of these reforms, inadequate to free the peasants and the country from imperialist exploitation. We should further argue that peasant superexploitation has reached a degree that endangers not only reproduction of the peasant producers themselves (through famine, rural exodus, and so on) but industrial development too, in the sense that agriculture gradually loses its capability of ensuring acceptable prices for food crops, essential in turn for exploitation of the working class. As is well known, the response of monopoly capital to this crisis is to envisage a series of technical innovations known as the "green revolution." These innovations are certainly intended in part to raise the productivity of peasant labor, but also and principally to integrate in the more intensive relations dominated by agrobusiness transnationals. A counterposing definition must be established as to the social, economic, and technical changes necessary to sustain a national and popular program capable of raising the living standards of the peasants and workers, and broadening the material and social base of the essential development of the forces of production.

The "green revolution" of our day is undoubtedly different from the "agricultural revolution" that preceded the industrial revolution in eighteenth-century Western Europe, but both these "revolutions" lie within the same overall perspective: that of making agriculture capable of supplying the urban proletariat with the means of reproducing their labor power. The "agricultural revolution" of mercantilist and physiocratic Europe fulfilled this essential role by disaggregating feudal relations and transforming them into agrarian capitalist relations. The methods of this transformation are peculiar to their time: There were as yet no industries; the production of inputs for the new agriculture was supplied by the labor of peasants and rural artisans; the surplus food crops sold by the peasants and capitalist farmers to the towns were delivered in their raw states without significant processing.

The "green revolution" of our day surfaced in regions integrated in a global system already dominated by industry: that of the manufacture of agricultural inputs (farm machinery, fertilizers, sprays, for example) and of food industries offering urban consumers processed foods, with a reduction of the artisanal or domestic labor to prepare them in usable form. This "revolution" certainly presupposes the abolition of certain precapitalist relations that had become too serious a handicap to agricultural modernization. Agrarian reforms fulfilled this preliminary role in most of the Third World during the three decades after the Second World War. Once this step had been taken the "green revolution" was on the agenda. It encouraged—peasant or farming capitalist (kulak)—agriculture to integrate in the upstream industries (supplying agricultural inputs) and downstream industries (food processing). Who would control this agroindustrial integration? That was the issue.

Capitalism's "classic" solution is to operate this integration through subjection of the farmers to industry, that is, to the monopolies of the agrobusiness. This evolution, which had its early beginning in the United States and Canada and spread to the whole of Western Europe in the aftermath of the Second World War, is now proposed for the Third World countries. It would have the effect not only of transferring the benefit of peasant surplus labor to the monopolies but also of worsening the overall national dependence of peripherally capitalist societies on these monopolies, and further accentuating the distortions of accumulation in these societies.

In the early 1960s and in the excitement of independence, there began to develop in agriculture a sometimes rather impetuous movement of modern petty commodity producers whenever favorable conditions arose. We have suggested this to be the case where rural population density was "optimum" (of the order of thirty inhabitants to the square kilometer) and where it was possible to attract wage labor by the immigration of outsiders to the ethnic group of the area. This movement encouraged the hope of the launch of an agricultural revolution, reproducing, mutatis mutandis, a model common in nineteenth-century Europe. But the movement was soon smothered and had results only on the scale of limited microregions (in the south of Côte d'Ivoire and in Kenya, for example) to the extent that on a continental scale or even within the beneficiary countries the overall results remained mediocre.[6] The reason for this smothering is related to the fact that this agriculture of "modern farmers" is superexploited by the upstream industries (foreign in this instance) supplying inputs and by the world market imposing real price cuts on these export crops (the World Bank systematically encouraged overproduction for this purpose).

The second solution is to subject agriculture to the state—one whose historical origins and class structure are integrated in various ways in the world system. It might be a Soviet-type state, contemptuous of the peasants, which sees the countryside as no more than a manpower reserve for industrialization and the provider of foodstuffs for the towns. It "collectivizes" and "modernizes" by obliging the peasants to resort to mechanization, while retaining control of the machinery—this was the formula of the Soviet machine and tractor stations—just as it retains ownership and management of the agricultural produce-processing industries. But it might also be a peripherally bourgeois state, one unable (for various particular historical reasons in this or that instance) to base its overall power on an alliance with an agrarian bourgeoisie, that becomes the peasant's "partner," or in fact his master. This form allows exploitation of peasant labor to be subjected to the demands of industrial accumulation.

The third solution, which is still being sought, would entail a genuine popular alliance with the peasants as genuine partners. In this dispensation the sphere of activities controlled by the peasantry could be extended to the upstream and downstream industries. In other words, the "shearing" from prices unfavorable to the rural community could be avoided by collective negotiation of the relative prices of industry and agriculture. Maoism adopted this principle, in intention at least. It was said of the Chinese commune, created in 1957–58, that it was based on equality between the town and countryside. The commune, as is well known, operated on three levels: the team (the natural village) handling simple means of production (draught equipment, hand tools), which—at China's level of development of the forces of production—are still the mainstay of agricultural production; the brigade handling modern equipment utilized by several teams (machinery, transport vehicles, improvements in the irrigation system, and so on); and finally the commune handling some minor upstream industries (for example, tool manufacture, workshops, rural building) and downstream (simple processing: rice mills, shelling, grain mills, among others). Peasant control in principle over these three levels, in marked contrast with the Soviet machine and tractor stations, bore witness to the reliance the authorities claimed to place on the peasantry and reflected the reality of the worker-

and-peasant alliance that gave substance to this authority. The commune, moreover, in integrating social services (health, education, and so on) and administrative powers into its management system paved the way for an eventual integration of political power and economic management. Undoubtedly the "industries" managed by the commune were still, at the current stage of the country's development, rather elementary, and team output accounted for some 80 percent to 85 percent in value of the output of all three levels. In addition, some—the most modern—of the inputs were provided for agriculture by industry properly speaking, that is, collectives of urban workers (or the state).

Obviously the challenge to the system after Mao Zedong's death raises a question mark over the reality of the system as it was operating in the 1960s and 1970s, but this goes beyond the scope of this study. It has been argued that control of the communes really remained in the hands of the party bureaucracy who imposed prices less favorable than supposed. Deng Xiaoping relied on this argument in order to dissolve the communes, "decollectivize" and allow the "market" to operate to the peasants' advantage, and thus correct the terms of trade in a favorable direction, if not for the entire rural community at least for the segments that succeeded in securing a strong foothold in the new market for foodstuffs.[7]

It is impossible to define the exact forms of organization and implementation of economic management and national and popular politics formulated from a priori abstractions divorced from the actual dialectic of relations between state, peasants, and workers. The principles emerging in this schema of the three outline models do, however, merit systematic consideration.

Finally, an analysis of exploitation of peasant labor power inevitably entails the closest examination of the organization of commodity and noncommodity labor within the peasant family. Obviously, the prices paid for peasants' labor decrease as they correspond to an increase in the quantity of "unpaid" labor, that is, the noncommodity labor by the peasant man, and much more often of the peasant woman.

For want of the means, it is rare to find a precise measurement of the quantity and character of the total labor supplied by the entire peasant family. A comparison of this overall quantity of labor and that supplied by the entire family of the worker under capitalist industry would provide a measurement of the real gap between the price of labor power at the periphery and at the center of the system. We argue that this gap would be even more massive than that indicated solely by the double factorial terms of trade, which takes into account only the comparative amounts of direct labor-producing goods.

Notes

1. Mohamed Lamine Gakou, *The Crisis in African Agriculture* (London: Zed, 1988); Hamid Aït Amara and Bernard Founou-Tchuigoua, eds., *Etudes sur la crise des politiques de modernisation en Afrique*, in preparation; and Samir Amin's forewords to these books. Cf. Samir Amin, "Les limites de la révolution verte," *CERES* 3, no. 4 (July 1970), and "Le paradoxe africain le deficit alimentaire de l'Afrique," *CERES* 25 (1973).
2. Ester Boserup, *The Conditions of Agricultural Growth* (London: Allen and Unwin, 1965).
3. René Dumont, *False Start in Africa* (London: Deutsch, 1966).
4. BRGM, *Les eaux souterraines de l'Afrique Sahèlienne* (Paris, 1975).
5. Bernard Founou-Tchuigoua, *Les fondements de l'économies de traite au Sénégal* (Paris: Silex, 1981), and preface by Samir Amin. Cf. Samir Amin, "Underdevelopment and Dependence in Black Africa," *Journal of Modern Africa Studies* 10, no. 4 (1972): 503–24; "The Class Struggle in Africa," *Revolution* 9 (1964): 23–47; introduction to Samir Amin, ed., *Modern Migrations in Western Africa* (Oxford: Oxford University Press for the International African Institute, 1974).
6. Samir Amin, "Le développement du capitalism en Afrique noire," *L'Homme et la Société* 12 (1969).
7. See thesis in preparation by Jean Pierre Leclerc and contributions on China to the MSH–State University of New York Colloquium, Paris, June 1988.

International Oligopoly Capitalism and Superexploitation

GUGLIELMO CARCHEDI

THE QUESTION...IS: Given that oligopolies can restrict competition, and thus the working of the law of value, is this law still valid under oligopoly capitalism? More specifically, can we still assume a tendential equalization of the rates of profit of the different branches into an average rate (and thus the formation of a production price) and its realization by the modal capitals? A few preliminary remarks are needed.

Contrary to what many authors still seem to think, the answer cannot be sought within the boundaries of the individual nation, torn from its international context. Given the international dimension of modern capitalism and thus of capitalist competition, the question as to whether there is competition both within each sector and between the two sectors can only be answered by taking a global view. Thus any attempt to place the law of value within the framework of modern, oligopolistic capitalism must transcend the national boundaries. Or, the question whether the law of value still operates under oligopoly capitalism (and, if so, whether it has undergone modifications) is inextricably tied to the question of whether there is a tendential formation of an *international* rate of profit.

If the question is one of international, rather than national, production and distribution of value, the extension of the law of value to the international

Reprinted from Guglielmo Carchedi, *Frontiers of Political Economy* (London: Verso, 1991), 234–36, 261–73, with the permission of the author.

315

context requires that we shift the focus of our analysis to the *internationali-zation of capital*. This is the process through which capital crosses national boundaries, thus (a) acquiring foreign means of production, (b) incorporating foreign labor power, (c) moving (parts of) the production process abroad, and (d) selling its products in foreign markets.[1] But if production has become international, the national labor powers have entered the international production relations, have become part of the *international labor power*. This international labor power now produces *international value*—labor expended by the laborers of the different nations under capitalist production relations and producing material and mental use values—and is expropriated of international surplus value. It is this surplus value which is redistributed among the capitalists of the different nations through the formation of the international production price....

The question as to whether there is a tendential formation of an international rate of profit, in its turn, immediately raises another one: Among whom, or what, would the rates of profit have to be tendentially equalized in order for an international price of production to emerge? The answer is that it is capitals of different nations which compete within the same international branch (thus, if technological competition is sufficiently strong, bringing about an international modal production process in each branch) and between branches, by moving from one branch in a nation to another branch in another nation (thus, if mobility is sufficiently strong, bringing about an international production price). Therefore, a proper extension of the law of value to the international scene requires that national branches are replaced by *international branches*, that is, by branches made up of the several similar national branches and thus cutting across and encompassing different countries.

It follows that the hypothesis of the tendential equalization of the different capitals' rates of profit into an international average and of its realization by modal capitals could be empirically substantiated by time series of profit rates for each international branch, as represented by its modal capitals, showing a pattern in which the modal capitals of the different branches overtake each other in terms of profitability.[2] ...

If access to sound direct evidence is barred, we can turn to indirect evidence. Suppose we can observe that capitals compete internationally (1) by introducing new techniques, (2) by moving from one country to another within the same branch, and (3) by moving from one country to another across branches. The first two points would allow us to assume the formation of an international modal production process and thus of a modal rate of profit for each international branch. The third point would allow us to assume the tendential equalization of all rates of profit into an average. The three points taken together would allow us to assume the tendential realization of this average by the modal producers....

Different national real wages are often taken to be a measure of the superexploitation of the workers in the low-wage countries. But if we assume different national levels of technology in the production of wage goods, this is not necessarily the case. Actually, the contrary may well be true. The reason for this is that exploitation is the relation between surplus value and the wages of the productive laborers. It follows that exploitation is not only, and cannot be measured only by, the level of wages.

Consider a high-technology country, A, and a low technology country, B, both producing corn. In A laborers can produce 18 kg of corn per day, 6 kg of which are wages. The rate of exploitation here is 200 percent. In B total production is 6 kg, 3 kg of which are wages; the rate of exploitation is 100 percent. In this case, A has both higher wages and a higher rate of exploitation. If A and B do not belong to the same wage zone, A has higher wages and rate of exploitation than B (as above). If the two countries do belong to the same wage zone, A has higher (and B has lower) wages and rate of exploitation than a tendential average.

So far we have assumed that two countries produce the same wage good by using different technologies. But this is only part of reality. Given the transfer of technology inherent in the internationalization of production, "modern technology in some industries is such that relatively unskilled labour can be combined with fairly sophisticated equipment" so that capital (usually, oligopolies) can take high-productivity, modern technology (either entire production processes or parts of them) to low-wage, low-skill countries (Adam 1975, 91). Under these conditions, if both the length of the working day, the intensity of labor, and the technique used are the same, the level of wages is sufficient to indicate the level of exploitation: Lower wages also indicate higher exploitation. Or, other things being equal, the country (capitalist) which pays less than the other country or less than the average wage level forces its workers to produce more international surplus value. In this case B's workers are both poorer and more exploited than A's workers, if the two countries do not belong to the same wage zone. B's workers are more exploited, and A's workers are less exploited, than the average if they belong to the same wage zone.

In view both of the possibility of transferring technology and of the huge national wage differentials it is quite clear that such differences are a very important stimulus for the imperialist countries to invest in the dominated ones. Moreover, working conditions (length of the working day and intensity of labor) are often much worse in the low-wage (dominated) countries than in the high-wage (imperialist) ones. This greatly increases the rate of exploitation, sometimes reaching the limit of the physical reproduction of the working class (Frank 1981). Of course, other considerations (tax "holidays," export incentives, subsidized credits, duty-free imports of foreign goods for local assembly, environmental control in the imperialist countries, protectionist tariffs in the dominated countries, the "docility" of the local work force due to political repression, etc.) play a role as well, but wage differentials and conditions of work are the central and by far the most important item.[3] Unfortunately, examples abound. In the words of an Indian manufacturer-exporter of garments, due to cheap labor, "we can make garments so cheaply that foreign buyers['] . . . mark-up is four to five times on their bargains, giving them a huge profit" (Sharma 1988).

However, it is not only foreign capitalists who profit from low wages in the dominated countries. Local capitalists profit from them too, especially when they import advanced technology from the imperialist countries. Moreover, the higher rates of profit deriving from lower wages and comparable technology allow them to reduce their prices in order to undersell their competitors;[4] thus some capitalists in the dominated countries can become formidable competitors of capitalists in the imperialist countries. Some countries, the so-called newly industrialized countries, can even achieve high, even though temporary, surpluses in their balance of trade. This explains the imperialist countries' grumbling and their calling on the newly industrialized ones to pursue "policies that allow their currencies more fully to reflect underlying fundamentals" (*Financial Times*, June 11, 1987), that is, to increase their prices by appreciating their currencies.[5]

Of course, the capitalists' paradise is a combination of high levels of productivity (appropriation of value produced by other capitalists) and high levels of exploitation (appropriation of value produced by their own laborers). One example of what this "paradise" means will suffice. It pertains to the production of lap-top computers by the Japanese manufacturer Toshiba.

> A scarlet sign saying "4 Hours" hangs over the portable computer assembly line at Toshiba's Ome factory. . . . That means four hours a day of compulsory overtime for the full-time production workers, extending their working day from 8 am to 9 pm, with an hour's lunch break. . . . White collar engineering and administrative staff . . . work even longer hours, often from 7 am to 11 pm. (Cookson 1988)

The world capitalist system is divided into two blocs: . . . the imperialist and the dominated bloc. It is now time to specify the meaning which should be attached to these terms.

From a purely economic point of view, the relation which unites the imperialist bloc (of countries) to the dominated bloc is one of determination in the sense that capital accumulation in the dominated bloc is a condition for the extended reproduction of capital accumulation in the imperialist bloc. This is the economic meaning of imperialism, even though imperialism is far from being only an economic phenomenon.

In terms of distribution of value, this means that there is a built-in transfer of value from the dominated to the imperialist bloc. As seen above, transfer of value is inherent in exchange, through price formation, when the same commodity is produced by capitals with different levels of productivity and is sold for the same price. This, in turn, means that even when—as is nowadays usually the case—the dominated countries undergo a process of industrialization (which for a few of them can be considerable), there must be a self-reproducing process which prevents the dominated countries from achieving the same level of technological development as, or from competing technologically with, the imperialist countries. This does not preclude the emergence of new imperialist countries and the decline of old ones. But it does imply that the separation between the two blocs is a permanent feature of the capitalist system.

. . . [T]he notion of determination implies that the determined instances realize themselves (as conditions of either reproduction or supersession of the determinant one) in the process of their mutual interrelation and thus in the process of their mutual modification. The determined instances thus can (and do) assume a variety of forms. This means that the dominated countries can undergo different levels of industrialization and that this requires different forms of class structure taken in these countries. But the variety of forms taken by "underdevelopment" is what makes it clear that "underdevelopment" is not lack of development but another type, with different forms, of development; that is, that part of the global movement (process of accumulation) determined by accumulation in the imperialist countries. Having said this, only one aspect among the many relevant ones will be touched upon in this section. In what follows, the imperialist countries will be referred to as IC and the dominated countries as DOC.

As just mentioned, if only the IC are considered, the implicit assumption is (as it has been up to here) that there are no objective obstacles which prevent some countries from gaining access to the most advanced technologies and thus from engaging in technological competition. But once we consider the international economy, it is evident that there are countries, the DOC, which cannot engage in the technological race with the IC. What can they do, then, to increase their rate of profit? They can increase the rate of exploitation. By lengthening the working day or by increasing the intensity of labor, that is, by forcing the laborers to make more commodities with the same wage, they can raise their rate of profit. Or, *increased exploitation is the DOC's antidote against technological competition from the IC.* This is the capitalists' side. But, on the laborers' side, when a certain quantity of use values (say, twenty pairs of shoes) produced by a DOC is exchanged for another quantity of use values (say, one computer) on the international market and through the medium of international money (prices), much more sweat, tears, and blood are exchanged than when twenty pairs of shoes produced by an IC are exchanged for that computer.

The DOC's sometimes incredible conditions of exploitation and misery necessary to compete on the international markets can also be created through very high rates of inflation, that is, low real wages. The difference from the case above is that longer working hours and more intensive labor increase output and surplus value while real wages remain the same. Inflation, on the other hand, does not increase output and value but decreases real wages. Of course, whenever possible, the capitalists in the DOC will both increase the intensity of labor and the length of the working day on the one hand and on the other see to it that real wages fall due to inflation. The figures in table 1 below are telling.

This is fine as long as the capitalists of the DOC do not have to sell abroad. But if those goods have to be sold on the international market, the DOC's competitive position is worsened. The remedy is depreciation. Through depreciation, the capitalists in the DOC get less international money, or less international value. Therefore, *inflation is meaningful for the capitalists of the DOC only if accompanied by depreciation*. It is not by chance that whenever a DOC signs an agreement with the IMF it must inevitably combine savage cuts in welfare expenditure—as subsidies for subsistence items—with drastic depreciation.

This is an important aspect of the mechanism which explains both the extreme poverty of the working class in the DOC and the high rates of inflation in those countries.[6] But this is only of indirect concern to the capitalists. Through inflation they rob the laborers of a greater part of the new value produced, and through depreciation they can sell their booty at competitive prices (that is, transfer part of the new value they have appropriated from "their" laborers to capitalists in the IC, through unequal exchange). The greater the technological gap between the IC and the DOC, the greater the need to compete through high rates of inflation and depreciation, and the greater the misery of the local populations.

The effects on real wages are grave in the IC but disastrous in the DOC. The effects on the value of the national currencies are the opposite. A country which produces more by improving its productivity tendentially revalues its currency, but a country which produces more through increased exploitation (inflation) tendentially reduces the value of its currency.[7]

Between the two paradigmatic cases of the most technologically dynamic countries of the imperialist bloc (Japan and West Germany, whose currencies are revalued because they successfully compete basically through technological innovation) and the technologically backward countries of the dominated bloc (whose currencies are devalued because they compete basically through high rates of exploitation and inflation) there is a gamut of intermediate cases with specific features for which the theory submitted here can only serve as a framework within which those cases can be studied in

Table 1 Developing Countries: Changes in Consumer Prices, 1970–87 (% change from preceding year)

	Average 1970–79	1980	1981	1982	1983	1984	1985	1986	1987
Developing countries	18.1	27.3	25.9	25.4	33.0	38.6	38.9	29.8	40.0
Africa	12.7	16.2	21.2	13.1	18.9	20.4	13.2	15.3	15.8
Asia	9.5	13.1	10.5	6.4	6.6	7.3	7.1	7.8	8.8
Europe	12.3	31.8	23.6	33.1	22.8	25.4	25.4	24.8	30.3
Middle East	11.6	16.8	15.2	12.7	12.2	14.8	12.2	11.4	14.7
Western Hemisphere	34.8	58.3	60.7	66.8	108.6	131.8	143.5	88.3	131.2

Source: IMF 1988, 15

their specificity. For example, a country like Italy which has relied not only on improved technology but also, in order to break a very strong workers' movement in the 1970s and 1980s, on relatively high rates of inflation (compared to those of the other imperialist countries) shows a tendency to a moderate depreciation of the lira, starting from the second half of the 1970s.

Up to now I have dealt with nominal exchange rates. A few words are now in order on *real exchange rates*. These are nominal exchange rates corrected for inflation. Suppose that the DM is revalued vis-à-vis the dollar. More value is appropriated by West Germany (and less is appropriated by the United States when fewer DM are exchanged for one dollar. This transfer of value is reinforced if German prices rise (or if U.S. prices fall) and weakened (or reversed) in the opposite case. It follows that the real exchange rate can be conceptualized as the national currency price of a unit of foreign currency multiplied by the ratio of the foreign to the domestic price level.

If RER stands for real exchange rate, N for the quantity of national currency units, F for one unit of foreign currency, $CPI(n)$ for the national consumer price index (which is a measure of inflation) and $CPI(f)$ for the foreign consumer price index, then

$$RER = \frac{N}{F} \cdot \frac{CPI(f)}{CPI(n)}$$

In the case of, say, the real exchange rate between West Germany and the United States, this ratio decreases when West Germany appropriates more value, either because the DM is revalued or because prices in West Germany increase (or increase more than in the United States). Conversely, this ratio increases when West Germany appropriates less value, either because of a devaluation of the DM or because prices in the United States increase (or increase more than in West Germany).

What is the relevance of the RER for a theory of international prices? This rate isolates the effects of inflation on the transfer of value implied in the nominal exchange rate. However, this rate does not indicate the actual transfer of value associated with the process of price formation. In fact, different levels of productivity determine, in a contradictory way, different monetary, fiscal, budgetary, and other policies (including different levels of inflation) and these policies—as well as a host of other factors—determine capital movements. These latter, in their turn, determine the level of prices and thus also the exchange rate. This is the nominal exchange rate, the rate which emerges as a consequence of capital movements, and thus of the demand and supply of currencies, due not only to different levels of inflation but also to all other factors. If the level of inflation, or of taxation, or of interest rates were to change, capital movements would change too and the nominal exchange rate with them. It is this rate, then, which indicates the actual transfer of value associated with price formation; this, of course, in the case of flexible exchange rates. In the case of fixed rates, the rates of profit would tendentially be equalized on the basis of those fixed rates.

Since it is the nominal exchange rate, rather than the "real" one, which indicates the actual transfer of value inherent in the process of price formation and since these transfers show regular and predictable patterns (that is, an increase in productivity determines an international appropriation of value while the opposite holds for lack of competitivity), we can expect the nominal exchange rates to show regular and predictable patterns, or a trend toward revaluation when productivity increases consistently more than that of the competitors and a devaluation in the case of productivity lags. However, there is no reason to expect the same regular and predictable pattern if the nominal rate is corrected for differences in, say, interest rates. The same applies if the nominal rate is corrected for inflation differentials, that is, in the case of the "real" exchange rate. The theoretical basis of mainstream economics' search for regular and predictable patterns in real exchange rates is thus unclear.[8]

There is perhaps one exception to the point just made. In the imperialist countries (IC), the technological leaders' rate of inflation is usually lower than that of the other countries. In fact, inflation is basically a means to counter both the realization and the profitability crisis. The technological leaders (countries) contribute to a decreasing production of international surplus value but realize more surplus value (that is, the capitalists in those countries realize higher profits) at the expense of the other countries. The former type of countries need a lower rate of inflation than the other IC and certainly a much lower rate than most dominated countries (DOC). The appreciation of their real rates of exchange (i.e., a fall in RER as defined above) is basically due to productivity gains rather than to high rates of inflation. However, the movements in the RER of the other IC are much less predictable.

In the DOC, productivity lags cause depreciation of the nominal exchange rate. However, the course of the real exchange rate is unpredictable, given the wide range of fluctuation of the rate of inflation in these countries. If domestic inflation rises more than both foreign inflation and nominal depreciation, the national currency appreciates in "real" terms (i.e., the RER, as defined above, falls); but this latter case is quite different from the appreciation of the IC's currencies due to higher productivity. In such a case, an appreciation of the RER indicates relative economic backwardness rather than greater economic competitivity. . . .

What is submitted above is only a first step toward a theory of exchange rates based on Marxist value theory. The four results which have emerged are the following. First, the crucial exchange rate for the Marxist theory of international prices is the nominal one. Second, nominal exchange rates behave in a predictable way, that is, appreciation is the manifestation of sustained productivity growth and depreciation of a sustained lag in such a growth. Third, the tendency of the real rates is clearly predictable only for the leading IC (they tend to revalue relative to the other IC). Fourth, for the DOC, the movements of the real exchange rates are much narrower than the movements of the nominal exchange rates. This last point means for the DOC that, while inflation greatly increases the rate of exploitation, nominal devaluation counters the negative influence of price increases on the international markets so that the purchasing power of the IC's capitals in the DOC is not significantly dented. These are only provisional results which hopefully will be subjected to serious scrutiny by further research. However, the concepts developed in this chapter should provide a solid platform on which further attempts to develop a Marxist theory of exchange rates and international prices can stand.

Notes

1. This process is accompanied by the internationalization of the financial funds needed to start the production process (to purchase labor power and means of production): "The loans that finance any country's industry come from many countries (or the stateless international pool)" (Coakley and Harris 1983, 43).
2. This average rate of profit would be an unrealized tendency (an average, or a tendency of the third type). This is one of the reasons why attempts to find actually equalized prices of production per unit of output are bound to fail. For such an attempt, see Andrews 1980.
3. Besides the work by Fröbel, Heinrichs, and Kreye (1980), see also Frank 1980 and 1981. For Mandel too, wage differentials are the main reason for capital movements from the imperialist to the dominated countries (Mandel 1975, 68). Therefore whenever, for whatever reason, the importance of low wages is reduced, the flow of investments to the dominated countries decreases too. This seems to be the case for some transnational corporations (TNCs). The introduction of automated manufacturing has drastically cut the proportion of wage costs to total costs so that some TNCs in the developed capitalist countries reorient the location of their investments away from low-wage countries and toward the home market.
4. This is the "secret" of the newly industrialized countries.
5. This case is not the same as that of countries (capitals) with low levels of productivity which must compete through very high levels of exploitation.
6. Very high rates of inflation have led in the 1980s to the phenomenon of "dollarization," that is, to the substitution of the dollar (for local currencies in certain countries and for certain products) as a store of value, as a unit of account, and also as a means of payment. See Salama 1988.
7. This allows us to understand why people who have a low standard of living in

an IC can have, with the same money, a high standard of living in a DOC. It is of course trivially true that this is possible because of the depreciation of the DOC's currencies vis-à-vis those of the IC. The point, however, is why the IC tends to appreciate and the DOC tends to depreciate, so that not only the capitalists but also all those in possession of the IC's currency can benefit from this mechanism. It is then understandable why a tourist from an IC with modest financial means can have "a rich life" in a DOC.

8. For a review of the difficulties encountered in this enterprise, see Coughlin and Koedijk 1990.

References

Adam, G. 1975. "Multinational Corporations and Worldwide Sourcing." In H. Radice, ed., *International Firms and Modern Imperialism*. London: Penguin Books.

Andrews, S. M. 1980. "Unequal Exchange and the International Law of Value: An Empirical Note." *Economia Internazionale*. Maggio-Agosto.

Coakley, J., and L. Harris, 1983. *The City of Capital*. Oxford: Blackwell.

Cookson, C. 1988. "The Lap-Tops That Mean Business." *Financial Times*, Sept. 14.

Coughlin, C. C., and K. Koedijk. 1990. "What Do We Know about the Long-Run Real Exchange Rate?" Federal Reserve Bank of St. Louis *Review*, Jan–Feb., 36–48.

Financial Times. 1987. "Countries in Surplus Promise Action to Strengthen Domestic Demand." June 11.

Frank, A. G. 1980. *Crisis: In the World Economy*. London: Heinemann.

————. 1981. *Crisis: In the Third World*. London: Heinemann.

Fröbel, F., J. Heinrichs, and O. Kreye. 1980. *The New International Division of Labour*. Cambridge: Cambridge University Press.

IMF. 1988. *Annual Report*. Washington, D.C.

Mandel, E. 1975. *Late Capitalism*. London: New Left Books.

Salama, P. 1988. *La Dollarisation*. Paris: La Découverte.

Sharma, K. K. 1988. "India Fashion and Export Boom from Backstreet Tailors." *Financial Times*, June 22.

Marxism and Ecology

JUAN MARTINEZ-ALIER

IN THE MARXIST VIEW, capitalism is a passing historic system and the capitalist economy cannot be understood in isolation from social organization in conflicting classes, one of which is forced to sell its labor power since it lacks its own means of subsistence; the market value of production is appropriated by the capitalists, who have to pay the inputs used and the labor power; this last is paid according to the cost of its reproduction including a historically variable surplus above physical subsistence, though not including the cost of "free" domestic work usually supplied by women. The capitalists' profits go partly on luxury consumption and partly on investment or accumulation of capital which allows them to become even more wealthy. It may easily happen that the capitalists' activities have contradictory results, because accumulation of capital may be high and yet consumption by the exploited wage workers relatively low, which provokes crises and possibly wars for the domination of external markets. The workers may change from being a class in themselves to being a class for themselves, organized and aware of their historic goals; therefore capitalism, subject to periodic crises, may give way to socialism after a revolution. Then, eventually, the state, which is always an instrument of class domination, will fade away. Within this Marxist scheme, actions are explained by the class position of the participants.

Marx wrote sometimes that capitalism misused natural resources, but this did not seem to him to be a relevant fact in explaining capitalist dynamics. The concepts required were those of exploitation (based on the theory of

From Juan Martinez-Alier, "Marxism and Ecology," in *Ecological Economics* (Oxford: Basil Blackwell, 1987), 218–25, 232–33, with the permission of the author.

labor value), class struggle, crises of overinvestment or underconsumption (words are tricky—in any case, *not* precapitalist crises of subsistences). Crises were a sign that the relations of production were blocking the development of productive forces. Marxists tend to believe that the protests of the ecologists against capitalism are of the same order as the moral and aesthetic protests of Ruskin, Morris, and the "utopian" socialists. They may agree with them, but they find that they are of no use in *analyzing* the dynamics of the capitalist system. The social actors of that system are really motivated by the desire to accumulate capital and to increase production, so as to sell more and make more profits. They are also motivated by the desire to increase workers' exploitation (or to resist it).

Marx's starting proposition was that total production exceeded what was required to replace used means of production (such as seed, in an agricultural economy), and to sustain the producers (and their dependants) not only in the capitalist system, but also in feudalism, in slavery, and in fact whenever social differentiation exists. In capitalism, the surplus of work was not as obvious as in other types of relations of production; it adopted the form of surplus value, disguised by the sale of labor power in the market as a commodity.

Marx analyzed the capitalist system with theoretical instruments which were outside capitalist accounting, and outside the frame of mind of at least some of the social participants: labor value, exploitation, commodity fetishism, alienation. The very concept of "capital" did not refer to "produced means of production" (even less to financial capital), but to a social relation specific to the capitalist stage in human history. In contrast, Marx's discourse on "production" and on "productive forces" is historically unspecific.

Production and surplus production were concepts which did not belong specifically to the analysis of capitalism. One interesting line of discussion— which will not be pursued here, as it is irrelevant to the theme—is that suggested by Sahlins, that surplus production arises historically not so much because of the "development of productive forces" as because incipient political structures force an intensification of work. One line of discussion has been opened up by pointing out that Marx "imported" the concept of production and of surplus production into industrial capitalism without giving a place in analysis to the question of replacement of used-up means of production. The meaning of workers' maintenance was clear enough: physical subsistence, plus a cultural, historically variable element, not excluding gains obtained by class struggle. But there is nowhere in Marx, nor in later Marxists, an analysis of the replacement of used-up means of production in an economy based on exhaustible resources, that is, resources which cannot be replaced, at least in the sense that corn seed or a mule can be replaced.

To the extent that Marxist economics has preoccupied itself with natural

resources, the treatment has not been an ecological one (that is, consideration of availability of resources, of waste disposal and of intergenerational
allocations), but a Ricardian one, that is, how rent paid to the owners of
natural resources would alter the pattern of distribution of income, and of
savings and investment (Massarrat 1980).

The Marxist schemes of "simple" and "expanded" reproduction do not
take into account whether the availability of exhaustible resources would
put a limit even to "simple" reproduction. This merely reflects the metaphysical status that the concept of "production" has in Marxist economics,
no different from that of mainstream economics. This is also applicable to
Sraffa's schemes of "production of commodities by means of commodities"
whose intention was to show that the distribution of income cannot be
explained as a by-product of price formation in the market because prices
will be different if distribution is different. The question of exhaustible resources and intergenerational allocation could probably be fitted into Sraffa's
schemes, but it was not.

In conclusion, Marx believed that it was possible to talk about investment and about increased production not only in the language specific to
capitalists, or in a language appropriate only for the analysis of capitalism,
but in a language applicable to all economic systems, even to socialist economies (in his not-abundant writings on socialism and communism). The first
models of economic growth which were used for planning in the Soviet
Union, based on the division of the economy in sectors (for example, consumption, "light" industry, "heavy" industry, as in Feldman's model which
preceded Keynesian theories of growth) are truly of Marxist origin: A preoccupation with the intertemporal allocation of exhaustible resources is
generally absent from Marxist economics, and this is not because the "problem" did not "exist" before 1973.

Although Marxists would be in principle in a good position to mistrust
the market's perceptions, this does not mean that a "technologically determined" Marxism, or an even more restricted "energy-flow determined" Marxism,
could exist, because judgments on technology and on the availability of
energy cannot depend only on the "facts," they also depend on social structure and social interests. One relevant question is, whose perceptions are
substituted for the market's myopic and class-biased perceptions? How is
scientific and technological knowledge socially constructed and socially used?

It is recognized that it is easy to document Marx's and Engels's interest
for ecological questions. Marx knew the work of the so-called vulgar materialists, Moleschott (1822–93), Büchner (1824–1901), Vogt (1817–95). Although Marx did not quote him, Moleschott influenced Marx's use of the
expression "metabolism (Stoffwechsel) between man and earth." Marx was
opposed to the notion of decreasing returns, on the grounds that modern

British agriculture showed an increase in production and simultaneously a decrease in the number of workers employed: Malthusian conclusions were, thus, most inappropriate (*Das Kapital* 1:457). However, Marx mentioned that the concentration of population in the great cities damaged the natural conditions for the fertility of agriculture, and he quoted Liebig's notion of an agriculture of spoliation in contrast to an agriculture of restitution. In volume 3 (chapter 47), Marx showed himself in favor of Liebig's argument for small-scale agriculture in terms of its greater capacity to return fertilizing elements to the ground, as compared with large-scale agriculture producing for large and distant cities. Alfred Schmidt (1978, 86–89) was therefore right in pointing out that Marx's use of the expression "metabolism between man and earth" was not metaphorical: It referred specifically to the cycles of plant nutrients. However, this approach, which in any case did *not* also comprise the flow of energy, was not integrated into Marx's view of history, and this is why there has been no school of Marxist ecological historians or economists.

In Engels, some early references to the flow of energy can be found, perhaps the first one in a letter to Marx of 14 July 1858, from Manchester, where Engels mentioned Joule and the law of conservation of energy. Joule of course also lived in Manchester. Writing thirty years later to Nicolai Danielson (15 October 1888), Engels said that the nineteenth century would be remembered as the century of Darwin, Mayer, Joule, and Clausius; it had been not only the century of the theory of evolution but also of the theory of the transformation of energy.

The second law was mentioned by Engels in some notes written in 1875 which became, posthumously, famous passages of the *Dialectics of Nature*. Engels referred to Clausius' entropy law, found it contradictory to the law of conservation of energy, and expressed the hope that a way would be found to reuse the heat irradiated into space. Engels was understandably worried by the religious interpretations of the second law. In a letter to Marx of 21 March 1869, when he became aware of the second law, he complained about William Thomson's attempts to mix God and physics.

It is risky to judge anybody's views from private notes, and the significance of such passages by Engels on the second law, together with his comments on Podolinsky, have to be viewed rather in their reception. Thus, in a book published in 1925 on Engels as a "natural scientist," on the occasion of the publication of *Dialectics of Nature* and on the thirtieth anniversary of Engels's death, the Austrian Marxist Otto Jenssen printed Engels's letters to Marx on Podolinsky, and explained that in these letters Engels had anticipated a critique of Ostwald's social energetics before Ostwald himself appeared on the scene (Jenssen 1925, 13).[1]

Engels's reaction to Podolinsky's article was certainly a crucial missed chance in the dialogue between Marxism and ecology. Engels's position was that the energy productivity of human labor (which Podolinsky had calculated for an agriculture which did not make use of a large input of energy from fossil fuels) would depend "only on the degree of development of the means of production" (as he wrote on his letter to Marx of 19 December 1882). It could amount to 5,000 kilocalories, to 10,000 kilocalories, to 20,000 kilocalories, or to one million kilocalories per day. Of course such figures were not given by Engels as reasoned estimates. But it is fair to infer that (given the adequate relations of production) he saw no limits to the amount of energy which could be harnessed by the work of a man. Oil workers, or workers at nuclear power stations or hydroelectric works, would show extremely high ratios of energy output to direct human energy input. Such types of work did not exist in 1882, but coal mining certainly did, and Engels referred to it: He wrote to Marx that "Podolinsky has completely forgotten that a man who works does not only incorporate *present* solar heat, he is rather a great squanderer of *past* solar heat. How we squander energy reserves, coal, minerals, forests and so on, you know better than I do." It is certainly not true that Podolinsky had forgotten this, though he did not extend his energy accounts to industrial activities. Although Engels understood perfectly how a calculus of energy inputs and outputs could be established in hunting and in agricultural activities, even to the extent of remarking that the calculus would be difficult in agriculture because one should include the energetic value of fertilizers and other auxiliary means, he thought on the other hand that "the energetic value, according to their cost of production, of a hammer, a screw, a needle, is a quantity which cannot be calculated." Whatever the practical difficulties of such calculus, this is what is done in energy accounting.[2] Not only the energy analysis of industrial processes but that of agriculture also would be impossible if the energetic worth of machines, pesticides, fertilizers, etc., could not be calculated. But Engels was prejudiced against this: "In my view," he wrote, "the wish to express economic relations in physical terms is quite impossible." Podolinsky had only managed to show one fact already well known, that the industrial producers had to live from the products of agriculture: This "could be translated, if one so liked, into the language of physics, but little would be gained by it." This is how Engels ended his second letter to Marx on Podolinsky, and many economic historians would have agreed with him until recently. Agriculture feeds the towns, and greater agricultural productivity (because of "technical progress," "growth of productive capacity," "development of the means of production") will allow industrial expansion and greater incomes for those peasants and land workers still left behind. Each agricultural worker would be able to feed ten, twenty, fifty, or one hundred town dwellers. This was taught by economics (with the sociological corollary that small-scale or, rather, labor-intensive agriculture was a leftover from the past). But when the facts are translated into the language of physics (*ins Physikalische übersetzen*, as Engels wrote), what in economic language is called "greater productivity" should be called "smaller productivity."

Although Marxism is clearly interdisciplinary history, it has not encompassed "natural history" or the history of the natural sciences. The Marxist concept of *Produktivkräfte* may be translated as productive forces or productive powers (Wittfogel 1985), and it is not related to the meaning of *Kraft* as force or power or energy. G. A. Cohen has written (1978, 104–5) that Marx complained that Ricardo's views on diminishing returns and differential rent reckoned without the further development of fertilizers. This complaint shows that the Marxist explanation of economic processes must not abstract *on principle* from the physical processes underlying them. Cohen quotes Marx's letter to Engels of 13 February 1866, where he stated that Liebig's agricultural chemistry was more important for the discussion of diminishing returns than all that the economists had said. Even if it is agreed that the separation of economics from physics was not a matter of principle for Marx (nor for Engels, despite his polemical asides against Podolinsky), the question is whether the physical processes used to overcome diminishing returns in agriculture should qualify as productive forces. This point is symptomatically not discussed at all by Elster (1985). This writer, who deals with a peculiarly ahistorical, or perhaps posthistorical Marxism, feels no need to define "production," "productivity," or "productive forces."

Perhaps it could be said optimistically that Engels understood the principles of agricultural energetics though not of industrial energetics, also that he clearly understood the difference between spending the energy stock in coal and using the flow of solar energy, and that he was far in advance of many later economists, sociologists, and historians in his knowledge and interest in science. But it must be said that Marx and Engels had the opportunity of reading one of the first attempts at ecological Marxism, and that they did not use it profitably. Of course, it was very late in their lives. Marx, in 1880–82, was still quite active intellectually—his letter to Vera Zasulich on the role of the peasant commune in socialism was drafted in March 1881. A proper definition of increases in agricultural productivity would have been of the essence in order to analyze social differentiation in the countryside (as it nowadays appears so clearly in India and in China). Marx was to die in 1883. Engels died in 1895. It should have been left to later Marxists to modify Marxism in the light of the ecological critique of economics, but there have been epistemological obstacles (the use of categories of political economy) and ideological obstacles (the vision of a two-stage transition to communist equality) to such an undertaking.

The ideological obstacles can be sensed in the *Critique of the Gotha*

Programme, of 1875. The Marxist idea is that "production" would increase according to the "development of productive forces," which capitalism would in due course be unable to increase further, but which socialism would increase in such a way that, at the end, distribution according to need would be possible after a period of distribution according to the quantity and quality of work. Both Kropotkin (in *The Wage System*) and William Morris (in *The Policy of Abstention*) argued explicitly against distribution "according to work," on the grounds that while inequality in capitalism lacked legitimacy from the workers' point of view, the Marxists seemed bent upon giving a positive sanction to inequality after the revolution, for the sake of "revolutionary" principles. Though Kropotkin shared in the vision of future abundance he was simultaneously in favor of immediate equality. A Marxist discussion on *Kommunismus ohne Wachstum* ("communism without growth," Harich's expression introduced in 1975) is still pending. While Marx, writing in 1875, would adjourn communist distribution until the development of productive forces would have proceeded further, some of his followers, writing later, would even adjourn the first stage, socialism (in the sense of expropriation of the means of production), waiting for further growth in the productive forces.[3]

Also, Plekhanov lacked awareness of the flow of energy and materials in his writings of the 1880s and 1890s. His "monism" had nothing to do with Ostwald's and it was a "purposively clumsy" word used instead of "materialism" in order to deceive the censor. "Materialism" was not used by Plekhanov in an ecological sense, that is, it did not imply the study of the cycles of materials. Lenin's critique of Ostwald and of energy analysis in general in the context of his attack on Bogdanov and Mach in 1909 was a further step in the unauspicious start to the dialogue between Marxism and ecological economics. . . .

An ecological approach questions the definition of "productive forces," but it does not give a new theory of value; it destroys theories of value by asking the question of how the exhaustible resources which are susceptible of intergenerational allocation should be valued. There is nothing (in the East or the West) which forces scientifically to "commodity fetishism," and thus to establish equivalences between, for example, two days' less work "today" against an extra kilogram of coal used "today" and therefore a kilogram of coal less available for "tomorrow." The rates of exchange can be imposed only by the historic existence of the generalized market and the ethics of that market.

The "history of the future" of humanity cannot be reduced to blind confidence in the rationality of the market or to an economic planning exercise which imposes a false commensurability. The question of incommensurability posed by Neurath cannot be solved with an energetic theory of value either. An economic planner would be mistaken if his objective were to minimize the dissipation of energy or to maximize the flow of energy utilized; indeed, any objective expressed only in units of energy would be mistaken.

Planning "according to needs" is not immediately helpful either, even leaving aside the question of future demands. Apart from minimum biological needs, all other needs are cultural creations whose genesis requires explanation before they are taken as a point of reference for a plan. Studies by anthropologists of closed spheres of exchange (Barth 1970; Douglas 1970) show that the possibility of trade-offs (three kilograms less of beans in exchange for five more liters of ethanol) is also a cultural creation. Veblen produced the theory of ostentatious consumption, which may operate in reverse: When poor people know that they cannot consume certain products, they may decide that they do not need them. Elster (in Sen and Williams 1982, 219) called this *sour grapes*. Felt needs cannot be a starting point, because they depend on other people's levels of consumption.

A discussion of what alternative ends, present and future, should be served with the scarce resources available cannot, therefore, take as given the needs expressed in the market or the needs shown in opinion polls, influenced by the desire for imitation, by the hopelessness of the poor, by the economists' propaganda on consumer sovereignty and on the allocative virtues of the market.

What Hayek called "social engineering" and Karl Popper "utopian social engineering" is what Neurath called "construction of (many) scientific utopias"; which preferably would be called "ecological utopias." The discussion of achievable utopias and the study of ecological economics have been suppressed in secondary and university education. The construction of "ecological utopias" requires accounting *in natura*, an explicit discussion of moral principles, and an education in the history of science and technology, accepting, however, in the face of the irrationalist philosophies of science which have been in fashion, that there is progress in scientific knowledge (Newton-Smith 1982).

Notes

1. Russian I. K. Luppol (a "Deborinist," as opposed to a "mechanist" in the polemics of the 1920s, cf. Joravsky 1961) also mentioned Engels's letters in "Zur Frage des Verhältniss des Marxismus zur Naturwissenschaft," *Unter dem Banner des Marxismus* (1928), 197, but he did not discuss Podolinsky's article.
2. Max Weber understood how it should be done, when he compared the energy cost of a piece of cloth woven by hand and by machine (Weber 1909), although Weber also denied the relevance of energy accounting for economics.

3. This debate became familiar in a different context to the generation of 1968, because of the Cuban polemics on the management of the economy (between Guevara and Mandel on one side, and Bettelheim and the "old communists," on the neo-"Bernsteinian" side) and also because of the Maoist emphasis on moral incentives and communal agriculture and the subsequent reaction against it on the part of "intellectual workers" and party bureaucrats. Such debates on whether the relations of production could go beyond the limits set by the development of productive forces did *not* include a discussion of exhaustible resources.

References

Barth, Frederick, 1970. "Economic Spheres in Darfur." In Firth 1970.

Cohen, G. A. 1978. *Karl Marx's Theory of History: A Defence.* Oxford: Oxford University Press.

Douglas, Mary. 1970. "Primitive Rationing." In Firth 1970.

Elster, Jon. 1985. *Making Sense of Marx.* Cambridge: Cambridge University Press.

Firth, Raymond, ed. 1970. *Themes in Economic Anthropology.* London: Tavistock.

Jenssen, Otto, ed. 1925. *Marxismus und Naturwissenschaft: Gedenkschrifts zum 30. Todestage des Naturwissenschaftlers Friedrich Engels, mit Beiträgen von F. Engels, Gustav Eckstein, und Friedrich Adler.* Berlin: Verlagess. des Allgemeinen Deutschen Gewerkschaftsbundes.

Joravsky, David. 1961. *Soviet Marxism and Natural Science, 1917–1932.* London: Routledge and Kegan Paul.

Kropotkin, P. A. 1889. "The Wage System." In *The Conquest of Bread.* London: Allen Lane (1972 ed.).

Marx, Karl. 1867/1894. *Das Kapital,* vol. 1 (1867), vol. 3 (1894). Frankfurt, Vienna, and Berlin: Ullstein Verlag (1969).

Massarrat, Mohssen, 1980a. "The Energy Crisis: The Struggle for the Redistribution of Surplus Profit from Oil." In P. Nore and T. Turner, eds., *Oil and Class Struggle.* London: Zed.

———. 1980b. *Weltenergieproduktion und die Neueordnung der kapitalistichen Weltwirtschaft.* Frankfurt: Campus.

Morris, W. 1910–15. "The Policy of Abstention" (1887). In *The Collected Works.* London: Longman.

Newton-Smith, W. H. 1982. *The Rationality of Science.* London: Routledge and Kegan Paul.

Schmidt, Alfred. 1978. *Der Begriff der Natur in der Lehre von Marx.* 3d ed. Frankfurt and Cologne: EVA.

Sen. A. K., and B. Williams, eds. 1982. *Utilitarianism and Beyond.* Cambridge: Cambridge University Press.

Weber, Max. 1909. "Energetische Kulturtheorien," *Archiv für Sozialwissenschaft und Sozialpolitik,* 29, in Weber, *Gessammelte Aufsätze zur Wissenschaftslehre.* 3d ed. (1968). Tübingen: J. C. B. Mohr (Paul Siebeck).

Wittfogel, Karl. 1985. "Geopolitics, Geographical Materialism, and Marxism." Tr. G. L. Ulmen. *Antipode: A Radical Journal of Geography* 17, no. 1.

Racial Inequality and Capitalist Exploitation

GARY A. DYMSKI

1. INTRODUCTION

RACE HAS BEEN VIRTUALLY ignored in Marxian theorizing about exploitation. Race is assumed to enter in only at a level of abstraction lower than exploitation; and anyway, since minorities are disproportionately workers, racial inequality is simply a special case readily accounted for by a racially neutral exploitation theory.[1] But this theoretical inattention is inappropriate. Apart from class inequality, racial inequality includes bigotry, discrimination, and segregation. Each of these aspects of racial inequality leaves imprints in the form of economic injustice. If exploitation theory is to constitute a comprehensive moral indictment of economic relations, it should account for racial inequality in all its multifaceted complexity. This paper suggests how the gap between racial inequality and contemporary theories of exploitation might be closed.

2. MARXIAN EXPLOITATION THEORY TODAY

One task of a radical economic theory is to explain how people are unfairly used in production and exchange. In Marxian political economy, the theory of exploitation provides a way of categorizing economic behavior and describing injustice. The definition of exploitation then delimits the nature and causes of economic injustice. This has been a matter of continuing controversy.

A new article written specially for this volume and printed with the permission of the author.

Three approaches to exploitation occupy center stage in radical theory today. Until the 1980s, Marxian theorists uniformly adopted a "production relations" approach to exploitation, based on Marx's insight that "the essential difference between the various economic forms of society . . . lies only in the form in which . . . surplus labor is in each case extracted from the actual producer, the laborer" (quoted in Cohen 1978, 82). Here, the sine qua non of exploitation under capitalism is the transfer of surplus labor from labor to capital via wage labor. Exploitation occurs at the site of production and is a class relation. The size of this transfer increases if capitalist domination exists at the point of production, but domination is not strictly necessary.

Since the 1980s, Marxian economists have used the toolkit of mainstream economics to reconsider exploitation. One such effort of John Roemer (1982, 1994), has adapted exploitation to an equilibrium model with competitive markets. In this "rational choice" approach, an agent or coalition of agents S' exploits another agent or coalition S if "S' gains by virtue of the labor of S" (1994, 110), such that the member(s) of S would be better off (have more utility) if they withdrew from the S–S' economy with their proportionate share of S–S' productive assets. So exploitation does not require the extraction of surplus labor in production. Contrary to the production-relations approach, the unequal distribution of wealth lies behind the transfer of surplus labor; further, this transfer can occur if *either* a labor market *or* a credit market opens. By implication, economic injustice stems not from exploitation in production but from unequal wealth.

Roemer derives these conclusions from individual agents' utility-maximizing behavior. Specifically, given complete and competitive markets, rational agents pick one of three optimal strategies: sell their labor to others (or rent others' capital); buy the labor of others (or rent capital to others); work for themselves with their own assets. In consequence, class becomes a second-order concept: Agents' class positions are determined entirely by the endowment and preference structure, and most social conflict involves conflict over property.

In another contemporary reassessment of exploitation theory, Sam Bowles and Herb Gintis (1990) also build a theory based on the behavior of rational agents. In contrast to Roemer's general setting with complete information, Bowles and Gintis focus on a particular problem, conflict between capitalists and workers, which they interpret as a principal/agent problem under asymmetric information. In the labor market, the agents (workers) have an informational advantage over the principal (the employer), and they have an incentive to put forth less effort than the principal expects. But the principal abhors low agent effort, because it means low output. If agents fear unemployment, the principal can resolve this incentive problem favorably by monitoring agents' effort and disciplining agents who slack off.

How this comes out depends on capitalists' relative power over workers, which in turn depends on whether workers can exit from the workplace. The unemployment rate is just one determinant of this relative power; others include state welfare policies and household relations. So capitalists' profits depend on the extraction of labor from labor power in production, and this in turn depends on a broad set of social relations.

Bowles and Gintis agree with Roemer that the labor theory of value is superfluous or even misleading. But whereas all markets clear in Roemer's model, unemployment normally arises in Bowles and Gintis's labor market; and unlike Roemer's model, their model reserves a special role for the labor process in capitalist dynamics.

Bowles and Gintis have not explicitly linked their ideas to exploitation per se; but this is readily done. Let E_1 denote the level of exploitation that would occur given a market-clearing equilibrium in perfectly competitive markets with complete information. This E_1, as Roemer has pointed out, exists because of unequal wealth. But more exploitation than this may arise if information is incomplete (and asymmetric, as above) and the labor market does not clear. That is, workers must work harder than in Roemer's general equilibrium because they are subject to *domination*.

In any given social relationship, an agent is dominated when she is forced to submit to treatment to which she would not agree if she could instantaneously replace this relationship with another on identical ex ante terms. Class domination can arise for agents who are unable to withdraw from situations of economic disadvantage; for in this event, principals can offer worse contractual terms to agents (and/or require greater effort) than they otherwise could. In production, a worker can be dominated if she is not certain of finding an equally good job to replace her current one. Domination conveys an edge to capitalists, and leads to an additional quantum of exploitation E_2, beyond E_1. If the level of domination is D, then writing E_2 as $E_2(D)$, exploitation, E, is given by $E = E_1 + E_2(D)$. So whereas Roemer builds an exploitation model in which workers are both free to choose and (because of unequal wealth) "free to lose," this approach envisions more constraints on workers' choices.

This expanded view of exploitation has some novel implications. First, domination of *any* sort in any social venue may lead to extra exploitation. For example, female workers can be exploited more deeply when they are not free to make their own decisions about where and with whom they will live. Second, workers in any given setting may be exploitable to different degrees because they are subject to different forms and types of social domination. Indeed, since "multiple oppressions" can affect economic outcomes, Van Parijs suggests that class itself be redefined:

There should be as many class divides as there are factors systematically affecting the distribution of material advantages. . . . Which of these class divides is most relevant in a particular historical context simply depends on which factors most powerfully affect the distribution of income and power. (Wright 1989, 226)

3. SOME "STYLIZED FACTS" ABOUT RACIAL INEQUALITY

As a reference point for ensuing discussion, this section suggests some "stylized facts" about racial inequality. These describe the scope of racial inequality as it has developed in the institutional and historical development of the United States.[2]

Most obviously, race affects market outcomes because of the differential treatment of (racially "different") individuals in market interactions—that is, because of discrimination. This differential treatment takes any of three forms:

Price discrimination—lower wages for minority than for white workers, and/or higher loan rates for minority than for white borrowers

Application discrimination—a lower probability for minorities than for whites of approval in labor hiring, loan application, or house-bidding processes

Performance discrimination—a higher probability for minorities than for whites, once hired, of being fired, disciplined, or suspected of non-performance

Price and performance discrimination can arise because those hiring workers or making loans are personally bigoted—and will only hire (lend to) minorities if they can pay them less (charge them higher rates); they can also occur because minorities have fewer economic options, and hence less economic power. Application discrimination can arise because of bigotry (personal discrimination), or also because of "rational discrimination," wherein race or characteristics correlated with race are used to make statistical inferences about different racial groups' market prospects.

Two types of segregation have also arisen in recent U.S. experience:

Absolute segregation—the concentration of all members of a given minority, regardless of income and wealth levels, in common residential areas

Differentiated segregation—the concentration of most members of a given minority in common residential areas which are spatially separated on the basis of income and wealth levels

Over time, personal discrimination and differential racial power have cumulative effects; because of segregation, these cumulative effects affect resource levels in specific geographic areas. The dynamic trajectory of race leads to two kinds of gaps:

Individual racial deficits—differences in the average economic function-ing and success of white and minority individuals. This gap could include minorities' lower average income and wealth levels, lower average levels of training, less experience on average, and so on.

Community racial deficits—the difference in the average economic func-tioning and success of geographic communities whose residents are pri-marily white, on one hand, and primarily members of one or more minorities, on the other. The average individual in a minority community might have, ceteris paribus, access to lower-quality public services, lower-valued homes, and so on.

Taken together, these gaps embody "structural discrimination," racial differ-ences in the average economic capacity of any individual depending on her own racial identity and on the racial composition of the community in which she lives. When segregation is differentiated, and not absolute, then the racial amenity deficit is greater, the lower the class/wealth ranking of a given minority community (geographic area).

4. PRODUCTION-RELATIONS EXPLOITATION AND RACIAL INEQUALITY

The production-relations approach to exploitation views all social relations through the prism of production. The leads to an incomplete mapping, since many social relations and even many forms of exploitation occur outside the capitalist labor exchange. Production-relations theorists have used func-tionalist arguments to suggest how materialist forces may steer or influence social dynamics in nonproduction spheres.

The racial "stylized facts" expose the incompleteness of this approach. For one thing, the deproletarianization of Black male labor is problematic: The disappearance of this segment of the exploited labor force, albeit into prisons, the informal economy, and the armed services, puts it out of ex-planatory reach. But if disproportionately few Black men are employed in the capitalist workplace, does this mean that black men are less exploited than are other men? Similarly, the expanding numbers of (say) Latino and Asian women employed in noncapitalist production, and in nonproduction service jobs, cannot be incorporated within the strict logic of this capitalist exploitation theory.

Further, what is the link, if any, between residential segregation and the labor process? A functionalist argument that, say, segregation is a tool for dividing the working class and facilitating a higher rate of exploitation raises further questions: A tool of whom? Why does absolute segregation arise in the rural United States South, outside the orbit of capitalist production per se? And why does differentiated segregation persist in communities whose

residents have escaped the working class? Unless very thoroughgoing func-
tionalist relations are allowed, the production-relations approach is silent
on why racial separation and bigotry, which allow price discrimination, arise
and persist.

The two other contemporary approaches to exploitation have turned away
from functionalism. Instead they use another contentious method—the exploitation of social behavior as the result of individual agents' rational decisions—given differential wealth, in the one case, and differential social
power, in the other.

5. RATIONAL-CHOICE EXPLOITATION AND RACIAL INEQUALITY

Racial inequality is absent in the models developed by analytical Marxists,
including those of Roemer.[3] In Roemer's model, discrimination is ruled out
by the implicit assumption that all agents have racially neutral preferences.
Further, with complete markets, application and performance discrimination become irrelevant. A minority community is simply a location whose
residents have disproportionately small asset endowments; racial dynamics
are not among the fundamental forces exploiting inner-city residents. Racial gaps are outside the theory. Roemer makes several passing references to
racism as a form of false consciousness, a "public bad"; in his view, it will
eventually disappear once assets have been distributed equitably.[4]

The racial "stylized facts" summarized above, however, expose the fact
that there are more dimensions of wealth, and hence of asset inequality,
than Roemer has recognized—and some of these missing dimensions are
crucial in reproducing racial inequality. In consequence, the redistribution
of assets as Roemer envisions it will not suffice to make racist outcomes
transparently irrational.

Assets fall readily into two categories—those that are separable (alienable) from the agents who own them, and those that are not (that are
embodied). Rational-choice theorists recognize this distinction, and intend
any asset redistribution to encompass separable and embodied productive
assets. The problem is that the distribution of both types of assets is racially
nonneutral for reasons that rational-choice theorists overlook.

Separable assets are either portable or geographic (Dymski and Veitch
1996). Portable assets can be relocated at will; but geographic assets are
rooted in specific spaces. This rootedness matters if there are locational
spillovers; for then these assets' productivity depends on where other assets
are located. When the returns to geographic assets are subject to spillover
effects, the level of economic activity in any community is path dependent.
Path dependence makes it difficult to equalize wealth by redistributing

assets, for spillovers are notably hard to measure with any accuracy.

It seems unlikely that individual racial gaps (as per the racial "stylized facts") can be attributed entirely to differences in the distribution of separable assets. Some portion of these gaps is due independently to community racial gaps, which arise because of the differential levels of geographic assets. Redlining in the credit market, for example, can arise independently of individual discrimination precisely because of the path dependence associated with geographic assets (Dymski 1995).

The second distinction separates embodied (human capital) assets into those which are tangible, and those which are not. A professional degree or a training course conveys tangible skills to an agent, which affect her productivity—and presumably her wage level, and hence her level of exploitation. Agent earnings, however, may also vary because a portion of perceived differences in productivity do not derive from tangible embodied assets, but from intangibles such as synergy, teamwork, "pull," attitude, and so on. But the valuation of intangible assets is context dependent.

In the familiar case, the aggressiveness of a female manager, while prized in a male, threatens and discomfits (male) coworkers. Similarly, how any agent's intangible assets are perceived, and whether they can be used effectively to be more productive, depends on that agent's race. The problem is especially difficult because it is difficult to separate the ascriptive characteristics of a given agent, attributable to their gender, race, age, and so on, from the level of their intangible assets. Here, too, problems arise because markets are incomplete—every embodied asset is not separately rewarded or even independently perceived. Yet these factors explain much "real world" application and performance discrimination, and would generate racially unequal outcomes *even if* all tangible embodied-asset differentials were somehow eliminated.

If racial asset imbalances involve differential endowments of geographic and intangible embodied assets, and if these assets are either underpriced or lack markets, then whether a given agent's labor is exploited cannot be determined solely from her share of alienable and tangible asset endowments alone, as Roemer would have it. Minority workers would be more exploited than white workers, ceteris paribus, independent of the extent of unequal wealth. In sum, some of the basic concepts of the rational-choice approach must be rethought to fully account for racial inequality.

6. DOMINATION, EXPLOITATION, AND RACIAL INEQUALITY

As in the two previous sections, here too the treatment of racial inequality in the domination/exploitation approach requires some translation, due to prior theoretical inattention. Specifically, the definition of domination must adapted: A person is *racially dominated* when she must submit to treatment which would be ruled out if she were able to instantaneously change ethnicities. Racial domination differs from class domination per se: whereas class domination depends on any one individual's skills and assets, racial domination is ascriptive—it depends on one's given racial classification. The alternative-employment "test" for evaluating class domination is not relevant for racial domination, because people cannot costlessly change race.

This notion of racial domination resembles Roemer's asset-withdrawal approach to exploitation. But there is more to changing racial places than shifting balances in endowment accounts. The "withdrawal" involved in changing ethnicities includes not just a change of tangible and alienable assets, but also a transformation of the racially charged perceptions and ties that affect agents' trajectories in the economy.

Racial domination has two dimensions, structural and perceptual; each has distinct effects on the exploitation of the racially oppressed. Structural domination arises when minorities, either as individuals or as communities, have lower average levels of productive assets than do other groups. Individual and community racial gaps in assets lead to racial gaps in income and amenity flows: Minorities may face lower probabilities of success in market searches, earn lower wages, face a higher likelihood of being disciplined or fired, and be more likely to live in neighborhoods with lower levels of amenities, ceteris paribus. These various aspects of domination are summarized by the three forms of discrimination listed above.

Racism, however, is not only a structural phenomenon, but also a perceptual one: members of majority and minority have preformed ideas—prejudices—about the behavior, capability, and intentions of the "other." The ascriptive aspect of race, its immutability, creates a chasm of experience on which prejudice can readily feed. Perceptual domination occurs when employers perceive racially based behavioral differences among workers, and adopt practices or policies which disproportionately affect members of racial minorities, and which those affected are unable to overturn.

Perceptual domination exists when employers are less inclined to hire a minority worker than a nonminority worker, ceteris paribus, because of a belief that minorities are less capable or work less hard; are more inclined to believe that a minority worker is guilty if detected slacking by the monitoring technology, because of a prior belief that minorities are more likely to slack; are inclined to believe that minority workers, ceteris paribus, put out less effort than nonminority workers.

The existence of racial domination alters patterns of economic exploitation. Both forms of racial domination increase the exploitation of minority workers relative to white workers. If minority workers face application and performance discrimination, then their probability of unemployment exceeds that of whites. Suppose they can reduce performance discrimination by putt. forth greater effort, and suppose productivity varies with worker effort. The the level of worker effort will vary systematically by race, and minority workers will be more exploited than whites—their E_2 will exceed that of whites because they face greater structural domination.

At the same time, racial bigotry can distort employers' perceptions of minority workers' relative level of effort; and this distortion may lead employers to dismiss minority workers for lesser offenses, or to mete out harsher punishments for given offenses. Again, the minority worker's only recourse for perceptual domination is to work harder to offset this perceptual bias.

In sum, the domination approach, when appropriately interpreted, allows numerous structural and attitudinal aspects of racial inequality to be captured within the theory of exploitation. Intrafirm discrimination ($E_2 > 0$) may exist for minority workers even when it is absent for nonminority workers, as long as *either* labor-market prospects are worse for the former than for the latter, *or* perceptual bias puts minority workers more at risk. This suggests, contrary to the production-relations view, that the extent of any worker's exploitation depends not just on the social relations in production, but also on the social context of production. And contrary to the rational-choice view, racial domination is sufficient to generate exploitation even in the absence of racial differences in asset ownership.

7. A QUESTION OF PLACE: DOMINATION AND SEGREGATION

A defining aspect of racial inequality is not only unequal racial wealth, but racial housing and labor-market segregation. Because it amplifies the effects of racial domination, segregation may contribute independently to the magnitude of exploitation. Darity (1989) has investigated what happens in racially segmented labor markets, wherein minority workers cannot migrate into the white job market.

Darity uses a Marx-Sraffa production model with mobile financial capital to set up his occupational segregation case. Capital moves between economic sectors, firms, or geographic areas to keep profit rates approximately equal; but workers cannot move to equalize wage gaps or resource differentials. So in equilibrium, white workers use more modern machines and are more productive in some firms or areas, white Black workers using antiquated machines are less productive and are paid less. Darity observes that this equilibrium is stable not just because profit rates are equalized, but also because the relegation of minority labor to segregated labor-market segments reinforces the positional advantage of white labor.[5]

Darity's segmented markets are implicitly geographic. And apart from ɔor-market segmentation, the very fact of geographic separation may it-elf independently affect the level of exploitation. Section 6 argued that geographic assets may generate not just private returns to their owners, but also external returns (spillovers), making it difficult to eliminate unequal wealth. Externalities stemming from geographic assets have still more implications here. For one thing, they generate nonlinearities in production and consumption technologies. A linear technology with external effects is characterized by increasing returns to scale—that is, the more this technology is used (the higher is employment and output), the higher will be the total social return. For another thing, situations of geographic increasing returns generate a strategic interaction problem for the capitalists or others who control the flow of resources. The prospective return on any one capitalist's assets is indeterminate until the action of all other capitalists is known.

This has immediate implications for the level of exploitation inside and outside the segregated enclave (the "inner city"). The existence of structural racial domination means there are fewer assets (human and physical) to be deployed and exploited in the inner city, and thus more benefit from directing flows outside the inner city. This is the kind of pattern evident in the creation of technopoles outside city centers and in the abandonment of inner-city industrial bases. Further, the existence of perceptual racial domination suggests that it will be easy to rationalize this direction of resources and jobs away from the inner city; indeed it will be all too easy to use area racial composition, implicitly or explicitly, as a "signal" of a community's investment potential.

Roemer himself provides the key for interpreting this case in light of the theory of exploitation: He has observed (1986, 110) that in the case of increasing returns to scale, it is groups and not individuals that are exploited. The residents of the segregated inner city are subject to additional exploitation beyond what they would experience if they lived elsewhere, due to the underutilization of their productive capacities. This underutilization encompasses both their human capital and any geographic productive assets located in the inner city.

Historically, absolute segregation has given way to differentiated segregation; so the residents of inner-city, minority communities have relatively fewer human and nonhuman assets than before. Further, inner-city areas are increasingly being sought out by new socially isolated migrants desperate for work. This situation is a recipe for the "superexploitation" of low-skill workers in these communities. Not only is the pay kept low, but the consequences of losing a job are dire—unemployment in an unsafe, low-asset community or (in the case of migrants) return migration.

The increasing number of Black men who are out of the labor force may itself affect the level of exploitation in two ways. First, these deproletarianized and marginalized men, with their short life spans and high incidence prison terms, are a poignant demonstration effect for Black workers who d have jobs, whether they have "made it out of the ghetto" or not. The consequence of losing work, in the worst-case scenario of zero family resources, is a return to the inner city—or, for those already residing there, a return to life on the inner-city margin. This threat, independent of other racial endowment differences, will spur Black workers to greater effort, and hence a higher level of exploitation. Second, increasing press and academic coverage of the underclass, and in particular the putative link between Black (and Latino) men and socially pathological behavior, feeds perceptual racism in society generally, and increases the degree of perceptual racial domination, ceteris paribus.

In sum, segregation independently influences the character and level of exploitation. Segregation leads to community racial gaps, above and beyond individual racial gaps, and generates group exploitation. The evolution of segregation affects the level and degree of perceptual and structural racial domination. Further, the "underclass" should be brought into exploitation analysis: The very presence of deteriorating inner-city conditions and of permanent unemployment among residents there spurs others to find work, or to work harder, and changes the level of exploitation by transforming the social context within which that exploitation occurs.

8. CONCLUSION

This paper has suggested that the phenomenon of racial inequality in capitalist society challenges the adequacy of contemporary versions of Marxian exploitation theory. To put it baldly, capitalist society has a class dimension and a race dimension, and the one cannot be derived from the other. The race dimension is rooted in history, and has become embedded in perceptions and structural gaps. Eliminating all traces of racial inequality from any theory substantially compromises its "real world" relevance.

More broadly, deepening racial and economic polarization in contemporary society poses a challenge to social scientists of whatever persuasion. Only when the role of racial inequality in capitalist dynamics is understood more deeply, and not simply treated as an inconvenient special case, will it be possible to effectively challenge the thrust of current policy, which seeks to "lock up the most disruptive, cut welfare, and turn the remainder into a reserve army of labor desperate to work whatever the wages" (Katz 1989, 214–15). The question is whether the theory of Marxian exploitation can be used to illuminate ways to reduce the racial dimensions of injustice under capitalism.

Notes

1. Two outstanding exceptions to this rule are Cox 1948 and Boston 1988.
2. In a longer version of this paper, available from the author, some aspects of the history of U.S. racial inequality are also presented. This longer version also describes three nonexploitation explanations of these "stylized facts" of racial inequality.
3. The one exception, Carling 1992, examines how ethnic and racial groups come into existence, not ex post racial inequality. This leads him to emphasize the voluntary aspects of ethnic affiliation, not the coercive aspects of racial inequality.
4. Roemer writes: "The level of public bads in a democratic society is the outcome of a political struggle in which different classes fight for their interests. If interests change, then so, in general, will the equilibrium level of public bads. I think that, to some extent, racism and sexism are public bads of this kind" (1994, 326–27). Racist ideas (e.g.) may persist; but "the change in property relations would dissolve one powerful class interest in the maintenance of discrimination" (327).
5. Van Parijs also suggests that racial exploitation may arise independent of wealth inequality: "Equality skilled men and women and blacks and whites frequently get unequal rewards because of their sex or race, even though they would not in a perfectly competitive economy. In other words, there is specifically racial and sexual exploitation" (Wright 1989, 225–26). He does not explore, as does Darity, how this racial exploitation could arise. I extend Darity's model to the housing market in Dymski 1995.

References

Boston, Thomas D. 1988. *Race, Class, and Conservatism*. London: Unwin Hyman.

Bowles, Samuel, and Herbert Gintis. 1990. "Contested Exchange: New Microfoundations for the Political Economy of Capitalism." *Politics and Society*.

Carling, Alan. 1992. *Social Division*. London: Verso.

Cohen, G. A. 1978. *Karl Marx's Theory of History: A Defence*. Princeton: Princeton University Press.

Cox, Oliver C. 1948. *Caste, Class, and Race: A Study in Social Dynamics*. New York: Doubleday.

Darity, William, Jr. 1989. "What's Left of the Economic Theory of Discrimination?" In Steven Shulman and William Darity Jr., eds., *The Question of Discrimination: Racial Inequality in the U.S. Labor Market*. Middletown, CT: Wesleyan University Press.

Dymski, Gary A. 1995. "The Theory of Credit-Market Redlining and Discrimination: An Exploration." *Review of Black Political Economy*, Winter.

Dymski, Gary A., and John M. Veitch. 1996. "Financial Transformation and the Metropolis: Booms, Busts, and Banking in Los Angeles." *Environment and Planning* A.

Katz, Michael B. 1989. *The Undeserving Poor: From the War on Poverty to the War on Welfare*. New York: Pantheon.

Roemer, John. 1982. *A General Theory of Exploitation and Class*. Cambridge: Harvard University Press.

———. 1986. "New Directions in the Marxian Theory of Exploitation and Class."

In John Roemer, ed., *Analytical Marxism*. Cambridge: Cambridge Univer Press.

Roemer, John. 1994. *Egalitarian Perspectives: Essays in Philosophical Economics*. Cam bridge: Cambridge University Press.

Wright, Erik Olin, ed. 1989. *The Debate on Classes*. London: Verso.

BIBLIOGRAPHY

SOME RELEVANT COLLECTIONS

Caravale, G. A., ed. 1991. *Marx and Modern Economic Analysis*, vol. 1, *Values, Prices, and Exploitation*. Aldershot, UK: Edward Elgar.

Elson, Diane, ed. 1979. *Value: The Representation of Labour in Capitalism*. London: CSE Books; Atlantic Highlands, NJ: Humanities Press.

Fox, Bonnie, ed. 1980. *Hidden in the Household: Women's Domestic Labour under Capitalism*. Toronto: Women's Press.

Malos, Ellen, ed. 1980. *The Politics of Housework*. London: Allison and Busby.

O'Connor, Martin, ed. 1994. *Is Capitalism Sustainable? Political Economy and the Politics of Ecology*, chs. 1–8. New York: Guilford.

Reeve, Andrew, ed. 1987. *Modern Theories of Exploitation*. London: Sage.

Ware, Robert, and Kai Nielsen, eds. 1989. *Analyzing Marxism*, sec. 3, "Marxian Exploitation." Calgary: University of Calgary Press.

THE CONCEPT OF EXPLOITATION IN GENERAL

Carling, Alan. 1987. "Exploitation, Extortion, and Oppression." *Political Studies* 35: 173–88.

Elster, Jon. 1983. "Exploitation, Freedom, and Justice." In J. Roland Pennock and John W. Chapman, eds., *Marxism* (Nomos 26). New York: New York University Press.

Feinberg, Joel. 1990. "Exploitation with and without Harm," ch. 31 of *Harmless Wrongdoing*. Oxford: Oxford University Press.

Goodin, Robert E. 1987. "Exploiting a Situation and Exploiting a Person." In Andrew Reeve, ed., *Modern Theories of Exploitation*. London: Sage.

Ryan, Alan. 1987. "Exploitation." In David Miller et al., eds., *The Blackwell Encyclopedia of Political Thought*. Oxford: Basil Blackwell.

Schweickart, David. 1993. "A Democratic Theory of Economic Exploitation Dialectically Developed." In Roger Gottlieb, ed., *Radical Philosophy: Tradition, Counter-Tradition, Politics*. Philadelphia: Temple University Press.

Wertheimer, Alan. 1996. *Exploitation*. Princeton, NJ: Princeton University Press.

Wood, Allen W. 1995. "Exploitation." *Social Philosophy and Policy* 12, no. 2: 136–58.

MARXIAN EXPLOITATION AND THE LABOR THEORY OF VALUE

Arneson, Richard J. 1981. "What's Wrong with Exploitation?" *Ethics*, 91, no. 2: 202–27.

———. 1992. "Exploitation." *Encyclopedia of Ethics* 1:350–52. New York: Garland.

Arnold, N. Scott. 1990. *Marx's Radical Critique of Capitalist Society: A Reconstruction and Critical Evaluation*, chs. 3–5. New York: Oxford University Press.

Bryceson, Deborah Fahey. 1983. "Use Values, the Law of Value, and the Analysis of Non-Capitalist Production." *Capital and Class* 20 (Summer): 29–63.

Bibliography

Ellerman, David P. 1983. "Marxian Exploitation Theory: A Brief Exposition, Analy̶ and Critique." *Philosophical Forum* 14, no. 3–4: 315–33.

Holmstrom, Nancy. 1977. "Exploitation." *Canadian Journal of Philosophy.* 7, no. 2 353–69.

Howard, M. C., and J. E. King. 1992. *A History of Marxian Economics*, vol. 2, 1929–1990. Princeton: Princeton University Press.

Laibman, David. 1992. *Value, Technical Change, and Crisis: Explorations in Marxist Economic Theory*, part 1. Armonk, NY: M. E. Sharpe.

Lebowitz, Michael A. 1992. *Beyond Capital: Marx's Political Economy of the Working Class*. New York: St. Martin's.

Mandel, Ernest. 1976. Introduction to *Capital*, vol. 1, pp. 11–86. Harmondsworth: Penguin Books.

Özol, Cengiz. 1992. "The Dual Theory of Value and the Theory of Exploitation." *METU* [Middle East Technical University] *Studies in Development* 19, no. 4: 529–47.

Peffer, R. G. 1990. "Morality and Marxist Concept(s) of Exploitation." In *Marxism, Morality, and Social Justice* Princeton: Princeton University Press.

Rosdolsky, Roman. 1977. *The Making of Marx's "Capital."* London: Pluto.

Shaikh, Anwar. 1987. "Exploitation." In John Eatwell, Murray Milgate, and Peter Newman, eds., *The New Palgrave: A Dictionary of Economics* 2: 249–51. London: Macmillan.

Weeks, John. 1981. *Capital and Exploitation*. Princeton: Princeton University Press.

MARXIAN EXPLOITATION UNDER DEBATE

Anderson, W. H. Locke, and Frank W. Thompson. 1988. "Neoclassical Marxism." *Science and Society* 52, no. 2: 215–28.

Bertram, Christopher. 1988. "A Critique of John Roemer's General Theory of Exploitation." *Political Studies* 36:123–30.

Christie, Drew. 1989. "John Roemer's Economic Philosophy and the Perils of Formalism." In Robert Ware and Kai Nielsen, eds., *Analyzing Marxism*. Calgary: University of Calgary Press.

Cohen, G. A. 1979. "The Labour Theory of Value and the Concept of Exploitation." *Philosophy and Public Affairs* 8, no. 4: 338–60.

———. 1983. "More on Exploitation and the Labour Theory of Value." *Inquiry* 26: 287–307.

———. 1988. "The Labour Theory of Value and the Concept of Exploitation." In *History, Labour, and Freedom*. Oxford: Clarendon.

Devine, James, and Gary Dymski. 1989. "Roemer's Theory of Capitalist Exploitation: The Contradictions of Walrasian Marxism." *Review of Radical Political Economics* 21, no. 3:13–17.

———. 1991. "Roemer's 'General' Theory of Exploitation Is a Special Case." *Economics and Philosophy* 7:235–75.

———. 1992. "Walrasian Marxism Once Again." *Economics and Philosophy* 8:157–62.

———. Dymski, Gary, and John Elliott. 1988. "Roemer versus Marx: Alternative Perspectives on Exploitation." *Review of Radical Political Economics* 20, no. 2–3: 25–33.

———. 1989. "Should *Anyone* Be Interested in Exploitation?" In Robert Ware and Kai Nielsen, eds., *Analyzing Marxism*. Calgary: University of Calgary Press.

———. 1989. "The Taxonomy of Primary Exploitation." *Review of Social Economy* 47: no. 4: 338–76.

ter, Jon. 1985. *Making Sense of Marx*. Paris: Editions de la Maison des Sciences de l'Homme; Cambridge: Cambridge University Press.

Foley, Duncan. 1989. "Roemer on Marx on Exploitation." *Economics and Philosophy* 1:187–99.

Holmstrom, Nancy. 1983. "Marx and Cohen on Exploitation and the Labour Theory of Value." *Inquiry* 26:287–307.

Houston, David B. 1989. "Roemer on Exploitation and Class." *Review of Radical Political Economics*, 21, no. 1–2: 175–87.

Laycock, Henry. 1989. "Exploitation and Equality: Labour Power as a Non-Commodity." In Robert Ware and Kai Nielsen, eds., *Analyzing Marxism*. Calgary: University of Calgary Press.

Nadvi, Khalid. 1985. "Exploitation and Labour Theory of Value: A Critique of Roemer's General Theory of Exploitation and Class." *Economic and Political Weekly* (Bombay) 20, no. 35 (Aug. 31): 1479–84.

————. 1986. "Exploitation and Labour Theory of Value." *Economic and Political Weekly* (Bombay) 21, no. 20 (May 17): 891–92.

Reiman, Jeffrey. 1987. "Exploitation, Force, and the Moral Assessment of Capitalism: Thoughts on Roemer and Cohen." *Philosophy and Public Affairs* 16, no. 1: 3–41.

————. 1989. "An Alternative to 'Distributive' Marxism: Further Thoughts on Roemer, Cohen, and Exploitation." In Robert Ware and Kai Nielsen, eds., *Analyzing Marxism*. Calgary: University of Calgary Press.

————. 1990. "Why Worry about How Exploitation Is Defined? Reply to John Roemer." *Social Theory and Practice* 16:101–13.

Roemer, John, 1981. *Analytical Foundations of Marxian Economic Theory*. Cambridge: Cambridge University Press.

————. 1982. *A General Theory of Exploitation and Class*. Cambridge: Harvard University Press.

————. 1982. "New Directions in the Marxian Theory of Exploitation and Class." *Politics and Society* 11, no. 3: 253–87. With discussion articles by Adam Przeworski, Margaret Levi and Douglass C. North, Erik Olin Wright, Andrew Levine, and Jon Elster and a reply by Roemer.

————. 1985. "Should Marxists Be Interested in Exploitation?" *Philosophy and Public Affairs* 14, no. 1: 30–65.

————. 1986. "Exploitation and Labour Theory of Value." *Economic and Political Weekly* (Bombay) 21, no. 3 (Jan. 18): 138–39.

————. 1987. "Marxian Value Theory." In John Eatwell, Murray Milgate, and Peter Newman, eds., *The New Palgrave: A Dictionary of Economics* 3:383–87. London: Macmillan.

————. 1988. *Free to Lose: An Introduction to Marxist Economic Philosophy*. Cambridge: Harvard University Press.

————. 1989. "Marxism and Contemporary Social Science." *Review of Social Economy* 47, no. 4: 377–91.

————. 1989. "Second Thoughts on Property Rights and Exploitation." In Robert Ware and Kai Nielsen, eds., *Analyzing Marxism*. Calgary: University of Calgary Press.

————. 1989. "Visions of Capitalism and Socialism." *Socialist Review* 19, no. 3: 93–100.

————. 1989. "What is Exploitation? Reply to Reiman." *Philosophy and Public Affairs* 18, no. 1: 90–97.

————. 1992. "What Walrasian Marxism Can and Cannot Do." *Economics and Philosophy* 8:149–56.

———. 1994. *Egalitarian Perspectives: Essays in Philosophical Economics.* Cambri Cambridge University Press.

Schwartz, Justin. 1995a. "What's Wrong with Exploitation?" *Nous,* 29:158–88.

———. 1995b. "In Defence of Exploitation." *Economics and Philosophy* 11, no. 2. 275–307.

Schweickart, David. 1989. "On the Exportation of Cotton, Corn, and Labor." In Robert Ware and Kai Nielsen, eds., *Analyzing Marxism.* Calgary: University of Calgary Press.

Skillman, Gilbert. 1995. "*Ne Hic Saltaveris*: The Marxian Theory of Exploitation after Roemer." *Economics and Philosophy* 11, no. 2 (Oct.): 309–31.

———. Forthcoming. "Marxian Value Theory and the Labor/Labor-Power Distinction." *Science and Society.*

Warren, Paul. 1993. "Why Marxists Should Still Be Interested in Exploitation." In Milton Fisk, ed., *Justice.* Atlantic Highlands, NJ: Humanities Press.

Wolff, Robert Paul. 1984. *Understanding Marx: A Reconstruction and Critique of "Capital."* Princeton: Princeton University Press.

SOCIALISM AND EXPLOITATION

Arnold, N. Scott. 1992. "Equality and Exploitation in the Market Socialist Community." *Social Philosophy and Policy* 9, no. 1: 1–28.

———. 1994. *The Philosophy and Economics of Market Socialism: A Critical Study.* Oxford: Oxford University Press.

Miller, David. 1989. "Exploitation [in the market]." In *Market, State, and Community.* Oxford: Clarendon Press.

Roemer, John. 1983. "Are Socialist Economics Consistent with Efficiency?" *Philosophical Forum* 14, no. 3–4: 369–88.

van der Veen, Robert. 1987. "Can Socialism Be Non-Exploitative?" In Andrew Reeve, ed., *Modern Theories of Exploitation.* London: Sage.

Van Parijs, Philippe. 1987. "Exploitation and the Libertarian Challenge." In Andrew Reeve, ed., *Modern Theories of Exploitation.* London: Sage.

EXPLOITATION AND FEMINISM

Bartky, Sandra Lee. 1990. "Feeding Egos and Tending Wounds: Deference and Disaffection in Women's Emotional Labor." In *Femininity and Domination: Studies in the Phenomenology of Oppression.* New York and London: Routledge

Benston, Margaret. [1969] 1980. "The Political Economy of Women's Liberation." In Ellen Malos, ed., *The Politics of Housework.* London: Allison and Busby.

Datar, Chhaya. 1981. *Redefining Exploitation: Towards a Socialist Feminist Critique of Marxist Theory.* Bombay: ISRE.

Ferguson, Ann. 1991. "Sex and Work: Women as a New Revolutionary Class in the United States." In *Sexual Democracy: Women, Oppression, and Revolution.* Boulder, CO: Westview.

Folbre, Nancy R. 1982. "Exploitation Comes Home: A Critique of the Marxian Theory of Family Labour." *Cambridge Journal of Economics* 6:317–29.

———. 1987. "A Patriarchal Mode of Production." In Randy Albelda, Christopher Gunn, and William Waller, eds., *Alternatives to Economic Othodoxy: A Reader in Political Economy.* Armonk, NY: M. E. Sharpe.

ad, Harriet, Stephen Resnick, and Richard Wolff. 1989. "For Every Knight in Shining Armor, There's a Castle Waiting to Be Cleaned: A Marxist-Feminist Analysis of the Household." *Rethinking Marxism*, 2, no. 4: 10–69. Followed by comments by J. Matthaei, Z. Eisenstein, K. Scheppele, N. Folbre and H. Hartmann, and S. Coontz. Reprinted with the authors' reply and other materials in H. Fraad, S. Resnick, and R. Wolff, *Bringing It All Back Home: Class, Gender, and Power in the Modern Household*. London: Pluto, 1994.

Glazer, Nona Y. 1984. "Servants to Capital: Unpaid Domestic Labor and Paid Work." *Review of Radical Political Economics* 16, no. 1: 61–87.

Holmstrom, Nancy. 1981. "'Women's Work,' the Family and Capitalism," *Science and Society* 15, no. 2 (Summer): 186–211.

Kotz, David M. 1994. "Household Labor, Wage Labor, and the Transformation of the Family." *Review of Radical Political Economics* 26, no. 2: 24–56.

Lebowitz, Michael A. 1992. *Beyond "Capital": Marx's Political Economy of the Working Class*. New York: St. Martin's.

Mies, Maria. 1986. *Patriarchy and Accumulation on a World Scale: Women in the International Division of Labour*. London: Zed Books.

———, Veronica Bennholdt-Thomson, and Claudia von Werlhof. 1988. *Women: The Last Colony*. London: Zed Books.

Seccombe, Wally. 1974. "The Housewife and Her Labour under Capitalism." *New Left Review* 83:3–24. See also his "Domestic Labour—A Reply to Critics," *New Left Review* 94 (1975): 85–96, and articles in Bonnie Fox, ed., *Hidden in the Household*. Toronto: Women's Press.

Tormey, Judith Farr. 1976. "Exploitation, Oppression and Self-Sacrifice." In Carol C. Gould and Marx Wartofsky, eds., *Women and Philosophy: Toward a Theory of Liberation*. New York: G. P. Putnam's Sons.

Vogel, Lise. 1983. *Marxism and the Oppression of Women: Toward a Unitary Theory*. New Brunswick: Rutgers University Press.

Wertheimer, Alan. 1992. "Two Questions about Surrogacy and Exploitation." *Philosophy and Public Affairs* 21, no. 3: 211–39.

EXPLOITATION EXTENDED

Amin, Samir. 1990. *Maldevelopment: Anatomy of a Global Failure*. London: Zed Books; Tokyo: United Nations University Press.

Carchedi, Guglielmo. 1991. *Frontiers of Political Economy*. London: Verso.

———. 1991. "Technological Innovation, International Production, and Exchange Rates. *Cambridge Journal of Economics* 15:45–60.

Devine, James. 1993. "The Law of Value and Marxian Ecology." In Jesse Vorst, Ross Dobson, and Ron Fletcher, eds., *Green on Red: Evolving Ecological Socialism*. Winnipeg: Society for Socialist Studies; Halifax: Fernwood.

Drydyk, Jay. 1993. "Exploiting Nature." In Jesse Vorst, Ross Dobson, and Ron Fletcher, eds., *Green on Red: Evolving Ecological Socialism*. Winnipeg: Society for Socialist Studies; Halifax: Fernwood.

Dymski, Gary. 1992. "Towards a New Model of Exploitation: The Case of Racial Domination." *International Journal of Social Economics* 19, no. 7–9: 292–313.

Emmanuel, Arghiri. 1972. *Unequal Exchange: A Study of the Imperialism of Trade* (with comments by C. Bettelheim). New York: Monthly Review Press.

Martinez-Alier, Juan. 1992. "Ecological Economics and Socialist Economics." *Our Generation* 23, no. 1: 26–45.

Martinez-Alier, Juan, with Klaus Schlüpmann. 1990. *Ecological Economics: Energ*, *Environment, and Society.* Paperback ed. with new introduction. Oxford: Bas Blackwell.

Omvedt, Gail. 1992. "Capitalism, Nature, Peasants, and Women: Contemporary Problems of Marxism." *Frontier* (Calcutta) (Autumn).

Omvedt, Gail. 1994. "Review Essay: Agrarian Transformation, Agrarian Struggles, and Marxist Analyses of the Peasantry." *Bulletin of Concerned Asian Scholars* 26, no. 3: 47–60.

Parsons, Howard, ed. 1977. *Marx and Engels on Ecology.* Westport, CT: Greenwood Press.

Schweickart, David. 1991. "The Politics and Morality of Unequal Exchange: Emmanuel and Roemer, Analysis and Synthesis." *Economics and Philosophy* 7:13–36.

Shaikh, Anwar. 1979–80. "Foreign Trade and the Law of Value: Part 1." *Science and Society* 43:281–302.

———. 1980–81. "Foreign Trade and the Law of Value: Part 2." *Science and Society* 44:27–57.

Thanawala, Kishor. 1992. "Exploitation and International Development." *International Journal of Social Economics* 19, no. 10–12: 317–21.

INDEX

Accumulation: and capitalism, 45, 213; and DORSPA, 217–18; women's movement on, 295; primitive, 302; industrial, 312; and global development, 319

Accumulation theory: and capitalist expansion, 123–24; in the corn economy, 126–27; discussed, 127–29

Ackerman, Bruce: on inheritance, 148

Advantage-exploitation: and vulnerability, 7–8, 9, 10, 11, 15, 16

Africa: agricultural failure of, 305; independence, 306; and resources, 307

Agricultural revolution: in Europe, 311

Alienation: separation from labor, 123–24, 128; in corn economy, 126–27; discussed, 135–39; differential, 136; and disempowerment, 289

Amin, Samir: on capitalism, xvii, 297

Analytical Marxism: Roemer, 213

Arneson, Richard: on exploitation, xiii

Assets: separable, 340; embodied, 340, 341; portable, 340; geographic, 340, 341, 344

Autonomy: Marx on worker autonomy, 37; and expensive needs, 44

Bargaining power: of children, 255, 257; of women, 258–60; and transition to capitalism, 260

Bartky, Sandra: on disempowerment of women, xvi

Bauer, Peter: on moral character of capitalism, xiv

Benefit-exploitation, 7–8, 10, 11, 15

Bennholdt-Thomson, Veronica: on peasant labor, 301

Bentham, Jeremy 54

Biological determinism, 264, 265

Bowles, Sam: on exploitation, 336–37

Callicles (Gorgias): on natural justice, 4, 5, 6–7, 15, 20

Capital, 249, 250, 268, 269, 297, 327; constant, 78; variable, 78, 79, 96, 118n. 8; and labor, 233, 234, 238, 239, 241, 242; hegemony of, 243; inequality of access to, 255; Africa's land, 305; modal, 315, 316; movements, 322–23, 324n. 3

Capital accumulation, 216, 296–303, 326, 327; reproduction of, 318

Capital Market Island (CMI), 211–12, 220–22

Capitalism: and exploitation, xi, 20–21, 28, 72–74, 76–77, 81, 84, 110, 111, 113, 114, 123, 125, 128, 155, 157, 166, 190, 282, 283; moral character of, xiv–xv, 183–84; defences of, xv–xvi; oligopoly, xvii, xviii, 315; and wage labor, 18–19; coercion and freedom, 32, 80; and self-realization, 44; Marx on, 76, 77, 83, 86, 133, 197, 200, 202, 209, 210, 226; overthrowing, 97, 98; of all commodities, 127; and justice, 129, 156, 185–88n. 2, 345, and domination, 131, 135, 272, 336; compared to feudalism and slavery, 155, 157, 327; and force, 160, 164, 165, 180, 183, 188n. 2; increased productivity of labor, 166; and class relation, 172; worker control of labor power, 175–76, 177; as a form of slavery, 179, 180, 183–84, 194; and alienation, 186n. 20; Roemer on, 202, 211, 215; competition, 204; and production, 205, 296, 297–99, 300; and difference, 243; reproduction of labor power, 250; and families, 255, 273; and relations of production, 256, 258; and unequal exchange, 260; patriarchal, 276; hope for crisis of, 294; and social movements in India, 295; and peasant labor, 299–302; and Sahel, 307; and agroindustrial integration, 311; productive forces, 332

Capitalist patriarchal nuclear family (CPNF), 275–77

Caregiving, 285–88, 290; emotional labor, 284; risk of exploitation, 289

Central planning, 58

Chamberlain, Wilt, example, 40–41

Children: exploited by parents, 233, 234; and labor, 236, 249, 254; and value of production, 253, 260; bargaining power of, 255, 257, 260; motives for rearing, 256; and reproduction of the economy, 258, 273; reduction in benefits of, 259; child care, 276

Chinese commune, 312, 313

Chodorow, Nancy: on female identification with maternal caregiver, 285

Class: market exchange, 29, 153n. 41; compulsion to optimize, 30; oppression and patriarchy, 75, 258, 260; and exploitation, 148, 206n. 3; and force or domination, 180, 337, 342; class position, 195; exploitation based on social class, 206n. 3; class struggle, 239, 303; of institutionalized poor, 273–74; lowering of, 276; agrarian class structure, 294; and new social movements in India, 295; and world system, 312; inequality, 335

Class Exploitation Correspondence Principle, 132, 134, 141–44

Class-Wealth Correspondence Principle, 140–44

Coercion, 13–14, 28, 32–36, 201, 216, 217, 222, 269

Cohen, G.A.: and labor theory of value, xi, 186n. 7; on worker freedom, 33, 183; on Marx on theft, 38; Marxists on justice, 129; on expropriation theory, 146–47; on forced labor power in capitalism, 155, 175–76, 178, 180–82; on Tannenbaum's objection, 181; on slavery, 184; on "the value controversy," 298–99; on Marx on diminishing returns, 331

Collective laborer: Marx on, 309

Colonization: and African agriculture, 305–06; and superexploitation, 307–08

Commodity(ies): use-value in market transactions, 95, 99, 104; labor power as, 96, 128, 228n. 3, 248, 249, 327; Marx on, 100, 119n. 23; and strict doctrine, 101; value of, 103, 105, 110, 113, 116, 127, 157, 172, 186n. 5, 246; and the labor theory of value, 113, 115, 157; values and "fair trades," 131; and exchange relations, 212, 214, 218, 219, 220, 223, 227; and subsistence, 233; and need, 240; neoclassical analysis, 257; expanded production of, 258; product of labor, 260; and sex/affective production, 251; production of, 297, 298, 308, 319; labor within family, 313; Sraffa on, 328

Communism: lower phase, 37, 41, 42; higher phase, 37, 41, 42; necessary labor, 77; unpaid labor, 84–85

Communist Manifesto, The, 174

Community: egalitarian, 267

Competition: perfect competition in a capitalist economy, 203, 204

Confession: and disempowerment, 286–87

Consciousness: merging of, 284–85

Contractual Incompleteness, 215; and DORSPA, 216–17

Contribution principle: in Critique of the Gotha Program, 42

Corn economy, 125–27, 136–38, 144–45, 169–70

Costa, Maria Dalla, 248–49, 295

Darity, William, Jr., 343–44

Debt: Marxists on, 301

Democratic principle: of exploitation, 62, 67n. 30

Deng Xiaoping, 313

Depreciation: and inflation, 320

Development: questioned by environmental movement, 296

Dialectical argument, 50, 59, 62, 65
Dialectical contradiction, 54, 56, 60
Differential ownership of productive assets (DOPA), 197–98, 199, 201–6
Differential ownership of relatively scarce productive assets (DORSPA), 208, 210, 212, 214–18, 220
Dinnerstein, Dorothy: on female identification with maternal caregiver, 285
Discrimination, 338–40
Disempowerment, 282–89
Dominated bloc: and world capitalist system, 318–19
Domination: domination[1] (D^1) and domination[2] (D^2), 129–35, 200–205; Marxist discussion of, 148; male, 274, 275, 281; class, 326; capitalist, 336, 337; exploitation and racial inequality, 341–45
Domination theory, 123–24, 129–35; in the corn economy, 126–27
Dumont, Rene: on "false start in Africa," 306
Dworkin, Ronald; on inheritance, 148
Dymski, Gary: on Roemer, xi–xii; on exploitation and race, xiii

East-West Institute: International Value of Children survey, 258
Eastern Europe, 50
Economic Democracy, 63–64
Economy: trading, 309; reserve, 309; concessionary companies, 309; capitalist, 326
Education, 257–59
Elliott, John: on Roemer, xi–xii
Elster, Jon: rejects labor theory of value, xi; on distribution according to need, 120n. 37; on force, 206n. 2; sour grapes, 333
Energetics: Engels on, 329, 331; value of fertilizer, 330; theory of value, 332–33
Energy: flow of, 328, 329, 333
Engels, Friedrich: on capitalist exploitation, xiv, xviii; slavery within the family, 233, 234; on origins of patriarchy, 278n. 3; interest in ecology, 328–31

Equal welfare (principle of), 43
Equilibrium price(s): Marx and Ricardo on, 106–7; corn economy, 127; under perfect competition, 130
Ethics of care, 287, 290
Euler's Theorem, 55
Exchange, 209, 211, 308; of labor services, 212; and class relations, 223; unequal, 254, 260, 281, 282, 283, 289; between parents and children, 256, 257, 260; and sex/affective production, 275; value, 298; and transfer of value, 319; unfair use of people, 335
Exploitation: term discussed, ix–xi, xii–xiii; pejorative sense, x, xiii–xiv, 3, 5–7, 12, 14, 21; technical concept of, xi; of environment, xvii–xviii; and justice, 2, 5, 6, 12, 17–18, 19, 20; moralized account, 3–4, 5–6, 14, 15; innocent, 4, 12, 16, 24n. 25; as use, 7; structural, 29, 30; Marxian, 49, 55, 335; definition of, 50, 154; democratic theory of, 50–51, 62–64, 65; feudal, 51, 59; Lockean/Neo-Lockean, 51–53, 55; Smithian/Neoclassical theory of, 54–56, 57, 58; labor value theory of, 56–58, 59–60, 62, 64, 172–73; property relations theory of, 58–62, 64; capitalist, 59, 62, 125; socialist, 59; sex-gender, 65; rate of, 72, 82–83, 96, 97, 253, 254, 317, 319, 324; Marxists on, 155, 282, 283; Marx on, 167, 197, 202–5, 326–27; definitions in Roemer, 167–71, 173–74; distributive definition, 171–72, 189; property relations definition, 189–94, 195n. 11; unequal exchange definition, 189–93; basic, primary, and secondary, 203–4; and family, 247, 255; expropriation and surplus value, 248; reproduction of labor power, 252; burden of, 253; and unequal exchange, 260; and productive labor, 268; and hierarchization, 267; Ferguson on patriarchy and, 282; of peasant labor, 299–302, 308–10, 312, 313; movement against, 303–4; and

colonization, 306; conditions of, 320; and racial inequality, 339–43; group, 345; racial and sexual, 346–47n. 5

Exploitation-Domination Correspondence, 134

Expropriation theory, 124, 146–47

Externalities: from geographic assets, 344

Family: and labor theory of value, 247, 248, 252; Marx on family size, 250; objective function of, 251; reciprocity within, 253; unequal exchange in, 254, 260; size of, 256, 259; relative rates of surplus value, 257; and biological determinism, 265, 267; planning, 270; exploitation of women in, 274, 275; and patriarchal production, 274; sexual division of labor in, 275; class status, 279n. 4

Feasible socialism, 62

Feinberg, Joel: on vulnerability, 10; on exploitation, 12–13, 14, 16, 282, 283

Ferguson, Ann, xvi, 281, 282–83, 289

Fertility: decline in, 249–50, 256, 258; impact of economic exchange, 260; of soil, 299; of agriculture, 329

Feudalism, xiv; Marx's paradigm of exploitation, 111–12; and domination, 130–32; compared with capitalism and slavery, 155, 167, 327; and nonwage labor, 274; and peasantry, 300; capitalism's development from, 302

Folbre, Nancy, xvi, 234, 235, 244n. 15, 278n. 3

Force: structural, 154, 160–65, 176, 177, 180, 182, 188n. 25; invisible in capitalism, 160; Roemer on, 174–75; synchronic, 177–80, 182, 183; Elster on, 206n. 2; and capitalist production process, 269

Freedom: choice under capitalism, 32, 175–76; individual and collective, 33, 36; and necessary labor, 77–78, 80; of labor under capitalism, 79, 80; workers' collective unfreedom, 175–76, 183.

Fundamental Marxian Theorem (FMT), 56, 127

Fundamentalism: and segregation, 339–40

Gender, 74, 75, 276, 277, 278n. 2, 284, 286, 287, 295

Generalized Commodity Exploitation Theorem, 128

Gintis, Herb, 336–37

Gorr, Michael, 4, 12, 14–15

Green revolution, 310–11

Ground rent, 213; Marx on, 228n. 4

Harding, Sandra: on social relations, 237–38

Hierarchy: and relationship in society, 264; between men and women, 265, 284, 286, 287; of consumers and producers, 267; and sexual division of labor, 269, 270

Hirst, Paul: Marxism not a science, 187n. 21

Historical materialism: and forced production, 167

Holmstrom, Nancy, xi, 185n. 1, 188n. 26

Household: exploitation of producer in, 234; social relations within, 235, 238, 254; control within, 236; and production of worker, 240; influence of patriarchy on, 246, 277; Marx on household labor, 248; labor, 249–51, 254, 259, 260n. 1, 295, 297; and labor theory of value, 251, 260; and social relations, 257; cost of children to, 257; women's contribution to, 266; Ferguson on women in, 282–83

Housework: women's second-shift, 276; and wage work, 277, 297n. 5

IMF: Africa's agricultural failure, 306; and welfare expenditure, 320

Immiseration, 240, 244–45n. 33

Imperialism, x; and environment, 296, 317; view of Africa, 306; crisis in, 310; economic meaning of, 318; and technological development, 319

Imperialistic bloc, 318–19

Income: nonwage, 96

India, 294, 295, 300

Industrial reserve army, 204, 206n. 4

Inequality theory, 139–46; exploitation from inequality, 124; in the corn economy, 126–27; equality in ownership desirable, 148

Inflation, 320, 322, 324n. 6

Inheritance, 148

Inner city: segregated enclosure, 344

Interference: protection from exploitation, 18, 19, 25n. 31

Intimacy: exchange of, 283; and caregiving, 285; heterosexual, 286, 290

Involuntariness: exploitation and consent, 12–13

Isomorphism theorem, 132–34

Italy, 322

James, Selma, 248–49, 295

Japan, 318, 320

Justice: Marx's critique of, 37, 40, 41

Kant, Immanual, 24n. 24

Kemper, Theodore: on love relationships and status, 283–84

Kropotkin, Peter, 332

Kulaks: supported by Western aid, 306; exploitation of laborers, 308; and agrarian reforms, 311

Labor: social division of, 70, 71; necessary, 77–83; free, 77–78; and ownership, 158–59; and structural force, 161; forced labor, 167; alienated, 203, 205; exploitation of, 203; distinguished from labor power, 209, 214, 217, 227; "social," 233; domestic, 248–49, 250, 290, 297, 311; socially-necessary, 248, 254, 259; nonwage, 249, 252, 297, 301, 302; family, 248, 252; sexual division of, 264–67, 269–70, 274–76, 278n. 3, 281; productivity of, 268; women's, 290; emotional, 290; peasants', 294–302, 304, 307, 308, 310–13, 316; reproduction of labor force, 307; market, 336–37, 343; Black male, 339

Labor-theory of value, 49, 53–54, 56, 103; Marx on, xi, 85, 246; attacks on, 94, 111, 115–17, 124, 147;

defined as socially necessary labor time, 95–96, 99; ambiguities in, 97, two versions of, 107; creation of value, 108, 113, 116, 120n. 36; is false, 115; and variable capital, 118n. 8; George Stigler on, 149; and the family, 247; of reproduction of labor power, 250; and household production, 251, 260; and time, 298

Labor Market Island (LMI), 211–12

Labor power, 29, 240; selling of, 27, 73, 87, 178–83, 191, 206n. 2, 234, 254, 326; class membership, 30; coercion, 32, 33, 35, 36; Marx on property and theft, 38, 39; in orthodox economics, 74; exploited by capital, 78, 84–86; value of, 78–79, 82–83, 127, 188n. 26, 233, 248, 250–53; defined, 96; Marx on value of, 117n. 5, 118n. 8, 239–40; under Labor Market Capitalism, 132; worker control of under capitalism, 175–77, 183–84, 204; Roemer on, 200; production of by capitalists, 205; distinguished from labor, 209, 214, 217, 227; and surplus, 216, 220, 248; as a commodity, 219, 327; does not belong to producer, 232; and use value, 237; and lower fertility, 247; reproduction of, 247–52, 274, 297, 311; proletariat, 303; of African peasants', 313; incorporating foreign, 316; and production process, 324

Laissez faire, 51, 52, 55

Lancaster, Kevin: and the collective bargaining model, 31–32

Lerner, Gerda: on women as first slaves, 278n. 3

Life's prime want, as work, 41, 42

Locke, John, 51–52

Macpherson, C. B., 130

Mao Zedong, 313

Market socialism, 62, 67n. 26

Market(s): inequality and transactions, 18, 19; credit, 132, 133, 336, 341; labor, 132, 133, 336, 337, 343; external, 326; outcomes affected by race, 338

Marx: 49, 50, 53, 56–58, 66n. 15, 66n.

.8; capitalist exploitation, ix, xi, 12, 13, 20, 23n. 15, 49, 70–72, 76–80, 82, 131, 167, 197, 202–5, 216, 218, 222–27; worker control of social production, xiii; justice, 22n. 11, 36–38, 42, 97, 185–86; market exchange, 22n. 11; utilitarianism and exploitation, 28; structural exploitation 30, 31, 32; workers and freedom of choice, 33, 34; critique of ideals, 37; Critique of the Gotha Program, 36–37, 42, 84, 88, 331–32; The Civil War in France, 37; Economic and Philosophical Manuscripts, 37; Grundrisse, 37; property as theft, 38–40; necessary labor and freedom, 78; value and labor power, 83, 117n. 5, 118n. 10, 246–48, 251, 309; exploitation viewed as evil, 85–89; capitalism, 90n. 27, 133, 166, 180, 200, 202, 297, 327–28; strict and popular doctrines, 100, 104–5, 118n. 14; redefinition of value, 106; critique of Ricardo, 106–7; feudalism as paradigm of exploitation, 111; unpaid labor, 156; "special" and "general" labor theories of value, 157; labor time, 158, 186n. 5; on force in capitalism, 164, 165, 179; force-inclusive exploitation, 168; rich and poor, 172; The Communist Manifesto, 174; exploitation and social class, 206n. 3; subsumption of labor under capital, 208, 217, 219; Roemer and Marx, 209–11, 214; account of usury, 213; distinction of labor and labor power, 217; accumulation, 218, 302; usury and ground rent, 228n. 4; social relation within family, 233–35, 238; missing book on wage labor, 238; conception of workers, 240; impact of capital, 241–43; family size, 250; productive and nonwage labor, 268–69; construction of state, 296; nature, 298–99; destruction of capitalist agriculture, 299; peasant production of capitalism, 300–301; "putting-out" work, 308; misuse of natural resources, 326; interest in ecology, 328–29, 331; surplus labor, 336

Marxists: Marxian theory of exploitation, ix, 168, 247, 248, 253, 254; capitalist exploitation, xi, xvi, 29, 97, 107, 109–11, 114, 122–23, 155, 160, 168, 191, 282–83; socialism, xiii; free market transactions, 27; traditional ideals, 45; class oppression and patriarchy, 75; inefficient labor, 100–101; labor theory of value, 115–17, 157, 159; elimination of exploitation, 140; interest in exploitation theory, 147–48; surplus labor, 156; forced selling of labor power, 178, 183; family, 234, 251; socialist feminism, 246; household labor, 249, 256–57; theory of distribution, 254; different access to means of production, 255; sexual division of labor, 264; productive labor, 268–69; nature, 299; peasantry, 299–300; indebtedness, 301; capitalism, 302, 326; value and international prices, 324; ecologists' protests, 327; economics, 327–28; discrimination, 340

Metabolism: Marx's use of term, 328, 329

Methodological individualism, 206n. 3

Mies, Maria, xvii, 301

Mill, John Stuart, 54; on justice, 17, 20, 25n. 34; "wage slavery," 130; restriction of women's labor, 238

Miller, Richard: on competition, 24n. 25

Monopoly, 52–55

Morishima, Michio, 56

Morris, William: on distribution, 332

Natural resources: capitalism's misuse of, 326; and Marxist economics, 327–28

Nature: and biological determinism, 265–66; and capitalism, 297; creates use value, 298; Marx on, 298, 299; Marxists on, 299; social movements and, 304

Needs principle: in Critique of the Gotha Program, 42; and consumption tastes, 43

Index

Nietzsche, Friedrich, 4–5, 6, 15, 20
Nozick, Robert, 49, 52, 66n. 7, 66n. 8, 52–53, 90n. 21, 180
Nurturance, 282, 283, 290

Object relations theory: and female caregiving, 290
Obligation: to help the weak, 14–15, 17
O'Connor, James, 298
Oligopoly, viii, xvii, 315, 317
Omvedt, Gail, xvii
Optimizing: labor power, 30, 35

Pareto principle, 41
Patriarchy, xvi, 234–38, 246, 248, 255, 259, 273–75, 278n. 3, 282
Peasant(s): bound to agriculture, 294–95; labor, 300–302, 304, 307, 310–12; and theory of capitalism, 297; exploitation of labor, 299–302, 308, 313; Teodor Shanin on, 299; Marxists on, 299–300; Africa, 305–8; means of production, 309; superexploitation of, 310; surplus labor, 311
Perfect competition, 55
Periphery, 269–70, 313
Petit bourgeois: Cohen on a worker trying to become, 176, 181; Tannenbaum on, 181; workers trying to become, 183; position compared to worker, 192
Petite bourgeoisie, 274; workers trying to get into, 176, 182–83
Plain Marxian Argument, 98, 109–10; and the labor contract, 113, 114
Political parties: social movements' suspicion of, 296
Popper, Karl: utopian social engineering, 333
Popular doctrine: value as congealed labor, 99–100, 101; compared with strict doctrine, 101–3; basis for charge of exploitation, 103, 117; in Marx, 104–5; appearance of substance, 106; contradicts strict doctrine, 107
Prejudice, 342
Private property: and structural force, 161–62

Product Market Island (PMI), 211-221
Production: personal, xiv–xv; sex/affective, xvi, 272–75, 281; and subsumption of labor, 210; household, 250–54, 259; age as a determinant of, 253; and biological determinism, 265; women's role in production of like, 265–66; family, 273, 279n. 5; social relations of, 274; different modes of, 274; capitalist ownership of means of production compared to men's domination of household, 281; subsistence, 295; capitalist, 296, 297, 299–304, 308, 316; agricultural, 312; international, 315; foreign means of, 316; internationalization of, 317; and laborers' value, 318; Marx on concept of, 327–28; and productive forces, 331, 332; unfair use of people in, 335; labor power in, 337
Production relations: Marxian approach to exploitation, 336
Productive contribution, canon of, 54–58
Productive forces, 331; Marx on concept of, 327
Productivity, 319, 324, 331, 324n. 5
Profit(s), 79, 80, 82–83
Proletariat, 294, 301, 303, 311
Property, as theft, 38–40
Property income, 57, 64
Property rights, 51–52, 53, 62
Przeworski, Adam, 131
Putting-out system, 212, 214, 226, 308

Race, xviii, 74, 75, 274, 335, 338, 342, 345
Racial inequality, 338–39; exploitation and, 339–43
Rate(s) of profit: equalization of, 316; international, 315, 316; modal, 316; increased, 318, 319; fixed, 323
Rational-Choice Marxism: critics on, 215; Roemer on exploitation, 336; and racial inequality, 340–41
Rawls, John, 49, 61, 165
Real exchange rates (RER), 322–24
Reciprocation: and emotional

change, 284; and caregiving, 286, 90; and emotional sustenance, 287
recognition, 284, 285
redistribution, 18, 19, 20
Reich, Wilhelm, 242
Reiman, Jeffrey, xi, 12, 14, 109, 189, 191–94
Reproduction: social organization of, 249; of labor power, 247, 248, 249, 250, 251, 252, 274, 297, 311; women's role in reproduction of life, 265–66; children and reproduction of the economy, 273; of labor force, 306; of the working class, 317; of capital accumulation, 318; simple and expanded, 328
Ricardo, David, 53; G. Stigler on his use of the labor theory of value, 149
Roemer, John: account of exploitation, x–xii, 12, 23n. 15, 25n. 32, 336, 337, 342, 344; model of Marxian exploitation, 29, 30, 31, 45n. 10, 46n. 15, 49, 50, 56, 58–62, 67n. 26; Radical Egalitarianism Theorem, 61; on distributive definition of "exploitation," 155, 168–75; on liabilities of labor theory, 186n. 7; exploitation linked to DOPA, 197–200; two types of domination, 199; irrelevance of exploitation, 201–2; on Marx, 203, 208–9, 219; notion of competition, 204; different from Marx, 205; and methodological individualism, 206n. 3; Walrasian account of capitalist exploitation, 210–18; analysis of CMI, 221; exploitation and circuits of capital, 223; on DORSPA, 227; on discrimination, 340
Rothschild, Joyce, 67–68n. 30
Rubin, Gayle: on sex/gender systems, 274

Sahel: not doomed, 307
Schadenfreude, 288
Schmidt, Alfred: on Marx's use of "metabolism," 329
Schweickart, David: critique of capitalism, xvi
Segregation, 338, 339, 343–45

Sen, Amartya, xiv–xv, 136
Service Market Island (SMI), 212, 220–21, 226
Sex class, 273, 275, 279n. 4
Shaikh, Anwar, xi
Shamin, Teodor: on peasantry, 299
Shara, Joshi: on farmer's movement in India, 295–96; on peasant labor, 301
Skillman, Gilbert: defense of Roemer, xii
Slavery, xiv; exploitation of labor, 71, 80–81, 132, 135, 232–33; unpaid labor in a capitalist economy, 155, 166; and justice, 166; forced labor, 167; and inequality in ownership, 172, 180, 183–84, 194; within household, 234, 238; Marx on, 235; compared to other nonwage laborers, 269; and colonization of Africa, 306
Smith, Adam, 53, 55, 56, 66n. 9
Social control of investment, 63–64
Social formation, 273, 303
Social movements, 297, 301, 303
Social relations, 235, 237–38, 240, 255–58, 267, 274, 337, 339, 343
Socialism: necessary labor under, 77; Marx on principle of distribution, 84
Soviet economic model, 58, 328
State: peasants and, 295; political parties pursuit of state power, 296; capture of, 303; control of means of production, 309
Status, 283–84, 284, 286, 288
Stigler, George, 149
Strict doctrine: compared with popular doctrine, 101–3; and inefficient labor, 105; contradicts popular doctrine, 107; is false, 115
Subjectivity: female, 287, 289, 290
Sub-Saharan Africa, 309
Subsumption of labor: Marx on, 208, 228n. 4; and exploitation, 210; formal, 222–25; real, 222, 225–27
Superexploitation, 269, 306–10, 312, 317, 344
Supplier Marxian Argument, 98–99, 109
Surplus labor (unpaid labor), 269; Marxian exploitation, 27; Marx on, 28, 70, 73, 77, 80, 87, 156–57, 222;

and class societies, 71, 72, 74; and feudalism, 71, 81–83; and free labor, 78; and necessary labor, 79, 83; and slavery, 155; Roemer on, 168, 171; extraction of, 190, 216, 232; in definition of "exploitation," 190, 191, 198; Reiman on, 192; and exchange, 209; absolute, 222, 223–26; relative, 222, 225–27; appropriation of, 296; by women, 297; African peasants, 305, 309, 311

Surrogacy contracts, 2, 5–6, 10, 11, 19

Tannenbaum, Chaim: on class mobility, 180–82
Technology, 316–19; in Japan and West Germany, 320; in Italy, 322; technologically determined Marxism, 328
Tenderness: female, 283, 287, 289
Third World, 295, 301–4, 308, 310, 311
Traditional Marxian Argument, 97–98

United States: real exchange rates, 322; and racial inequality, 338; and segregation, 339–40
Unpaid labor. *See* Surplus labor
Usury: Marx on, 213, 224, 228n. 4
Utility: evaluation of people under capitalism, 28; function, 250, 251; household, 256; labor theory of, 78–79, 157, 326–27

Value: nature of, x; exchange, 78, 95, 104, 204, 298; use, 78, 95, 104, 237, 243n. 2, 268, 298, 299, 316, 319; created by labor, 102–8, 110, 112, 113–17; of labor power, 233, 249, 250–53; created within household, 252; and children, 253; law of, 315–16; distribution of, 315, 318–19; international, 316; and real exchange rates, 322; and price formation, 323; energetic theory of, 332
van der Veen, Robert J., xvi
Van Parijs, Phillipe, xvi
Vulnerability(ies), 8–20, 288

Wage labor: and capital, 18; selling of

labor power, 35, 56, 57, 59, 64; Marx on, 81, 224; Roemer on, 214; capital based on, 220; and capitalist exploitation, 221; and SMI, 226; wage laborer compared to slave, 233; entry of women into, 235, 258; wage laborer as slaveowner, 236; Marx's missing book on, 238; Irish workers' entry into, 239; and production of worker, 240, 241–42; value of product, 248; and household labor, 249, 295, 297; and family labor, 252; and productivity, 269; sexual division of, 275, 276; impact of CPNF on, 276; and immigration, 311
Wages: relationship to profits, 82–83; impact of women's unpaid labor, 249; and sustenance, 251; real, 317, 320
Wallerstein, Immanuel: on superexploitation and capitalism, xvii
Walrasian economics, 203, 206n. 3, 210–18
Wertheimer, Alan, 2, 12, 13
West Germany, 320, 322
Whitt, Allen, 67–68n. 30
Women: and education, 259; exploitation of, 264, 274, 276, 289; women's labor, 266, 269; and nature, 268; exploitation in family, 274, 275; recognition of nurturance, 284; status, 288. *See also* Bargaining power: of women; Household: labor
Wood, Allen, 76, 85–88, 127, 185
Work day: division of, 79
Worker(s): compared to feudal serfs, 111; and exploitation, 114, 115, 123, 155, 224, 281–82, 326; labor's creation of value, 116, 117; unpaid labor, 156; Roemer on the domination of, 174; forced to sell labor power, 175–78, 180, 183, 206, 254; efforts to become a petit bourgeois, 181–82; and choice, 184; alienation from ownership, 204; and coercion by capitalists, 217; and real subsumption, 225; as patriarchal wage laborer, 236; Irish and English,

39, 242–43, production of, 240;
dependence upon capital, 241, 242;
varying efficiency, 247; wage worker
and family, 248–49; and peasants,
310; collectives of, 313; movement
in Italy, 322; capitalists' relative

power over, 337; Black, 344–45
Workplace democracy, 63–64, 67n. 30
World Bank, 301, 306

Zeuthen-Nash-Harsanyi: theory of
bilateral monopoly, 31